Sefer
Kav HaYashar
ספר קב ישר

The Just Measure

Kabbalist Rabbi

Tzvi Hirsch
Kaidanover

There is no known book without mistakes. Therefore, I ask in every language of application if anyone has any questions, comments, clarifications, corrections, please send to: **simchatchaim@yahoo.com**

All material used in this section may not be used for commercial purposes, but only for study and teaching.

To get this book or books and information Email me at:

simchatchaim@yahoo.com

Copyright©All Rights Reserved to

www.simchatchaim.com

YB"S©All rights reserved to the Editor

First Edition 2023

Kav HaYashar

Author's Preface

Speaking for the honor of his Maker. And summoning his strength. Hashem, straighten Your way before me. Hashem, guide me in righteousness.

It is written in the name of Moshe our teacher, peace be upon him, "And I pleaded with Hashem" (Devarim 3:23). Our Sages of blessed memory have explained (Devarim Rabbah 11:10) that he prayed 515 prayers — the numerical value of the phrase, "And I pleaded" (Va'eschanan) — that he be allowed to enter the Holy Land

I too will emulate the elders and pour out my prayer before God who answers me on the day of my troubles, reciting 515 prayers, the numerical value of my mundane name, "Hirsh."

Hashem, guide me upon the straight path, for the word "straight" — yesharah — also has the same numerical value as the phrase, "And I pleaded." I am like a beggar uttering supplication before all who know law and judgment and are sitting now in judgment, pleading that the words of my mouth find favor, for this holy composition that contains no falsehood.

I have called this book Kav HaYashar — "The Straight Line" or ["The Just Measure"] — for two fitting and proper reasons: The first is that in it I have written and presented 102 chapters, the numerical value of the word kav (קב) and also of my name in the holy tongue, Tzvi (צבי). As for the word "straight" — hayashar, it is comprised of the same letters as the name "Hirsh" (הירש = הישר) although in a different order.

The second reason for the name Kav HaYashar is that it is "a clean kav" (a small volume measure), resembling flour that has been sifted in thirteen sifters. It "straightens" people's hearts — even the hearts of the perverse — enabling them to walk perfectly along Hashem's paths, upon which the righteous tread. The righteous will see it and rejoice, recognizing the great illumination and benefit contained therein. For on the surface it is filled with chastisement but under the surface it is filled with love. It incorporates both plain explanation as well as parable, words that sit well with the reader and draw his heart on. It contains clear demonstrations from the Zohar and teachings of the Sages, of blessed memory.

I did not compose this work for the sake of glory nor to acquire a crown for myself. My only intention, in the time of my poverty and affliction, was to soothe my soul by benefiting the public, may I be credited with their edification. Surely the eyes of the Hebrews will be opened and whoever looks with open eyes will exult and rejoice! Let this text never leave your mouths nor the mouths of your offspring.

This day Hashem has allowed my prayer to be fulfilled halfway, for I have brought half of the book, Part I, to the printer, as you can see. Therefore, I asked myself: How shall I prostrate myself before the God of Heaven? With what shall I find favor with Him? With thousands of rivers of oil for all the good things that He has bestowed upon me? For He has delivered me from darkness to light and from death to life. He saved me from the iron furnace when many rose up against me to swallow me up.

They came out against me shamelessly and without cause. My assailants attacked and surrounded me like the furrow around the vine. They struck me a hundred blows and wounded me. But You, Hashem, will hear my case and my judgment.

For they have removed from me my mantle, that which was precious to me, my silver, my gold and my hidden treasures. Like the owner of the ox they caused me to go out "clean" of my possessions. They bit me like snakes and vipers. I dwelt in tranquility until the horned-ones butted me out. Strongmen answering to no prince or ruler surrounded me.

I said that although my soul has been crushed down to the dust, Hashem's lovingkindness will assist me. Then I made a vow on my day of trouble, with shattered loins and with tears in my eyes, that I would fulfill the dictum: "If a person has bad fortune in one town let him move to a different one" (Baba Metzia 75b). Thus, it occurred to me to abandon the land of my birth and the inheritance of my fathers and to plant the tents of my mansion near the home of my father-in-law in the holy city of Frankfurt-am-Main. Thus, the King of the Universe brought me to his chambers, naked and destitute. There remained to me nothing other than the work that I had composed for the benefit of the public and which I was certain would find favor with everyone, like the dew and the rain.

I allowed myself no rest and no repose until I had brought it to the printer. My intention was to point out the straight and good path to people of my ilk or of lesser worth, to lead them to the source of the living waters, just as I had been shown them by my holy mentors and parents who are in the earth. They are: My illustrious father, our teacher Rabbi Aharon Shemuel Kaidenover, of blessed memory, as well as my other teachers among the great scholars of the earth, whom I served, pouring water upon their hands. It is their words that sustain me even today.

"Serving Torah scholars is greater than study" (Berachos 7b). Thus, I observed the goodly and straight paths of my principle mentor, the saintly and illustrious Rabbi Yosef son of our teacher Rabbi Yehudah Yudel, of blessed memory. He was president of the court and dean of the yeshiva in the environs of the holy community of Minsk. Then towards the end of his life he was called to the Heavenly yeshiva of the holy community of Dubna, may the Most High strengthen it, Amein.

I drank in his words thirstily, as I will mention in the second part of the book. In some passages I will merely speak his praises while in other chapters I will actually quote his words, although at times I will augment them with explanations of my own or abbreviate them. And in order to cause his lips to move in the grave, as well as to avoid taking for myself a crown that does not belong to me, I will give praise to my teacher and crafter in every instance.

I will also raise my eyes to give credit to my parents and teachers, in fulfillment of the Sages' dictum (Megillah 15a): Whoever repeats a matter in the name of the one who said it brings redemption to the world.

As for me, my prayer at every time of favor is that whoever has fear of Hashem in his heart will read this book of goodly sayings twice and even three times and fulfill my words. For in this book I issue admonishment and reminders concerning numerous commandments that are commonly trampled under heel, urging that you fulfill them with your entire heart and soul. For these mitzvos are literally lying in the corner while no one pays them any mind! Therefore I resolved that I would speak of the matter even before kings, and not be ashamed.

I have translated it into Yiddish so that the wise will understand and every person will have access to it and acquire understanding and insight. You will see this for yourself, in small measure in this part of the book and in total in the second part.

Heaven is my witness that when I began the printing of this work, I did not own a penny. But then Heaven came to my aid and I have completed Part One. Now my prayers are to the Living God that He grant me the lovingkindness of being able to complete Part Two as well. I place my hopes in Him that I will be able to finish it by this coming Chanukah.

Therefore, hurry and do not begrudge the small sum that it costs to purchase this part, for it will enlighten your eyes like the noonday sun. And may whoever fulfill the words of this book merit witnessing the rebuilding of Tzion and Yerushalayim.

These are the words of the supplicant,
writing with weakened hands and shattered loins,
the lowly Tzvi Hirsh
son of the illustrious scholar, our teacher, Rabbi Aharon Shemuel, zlh"h, Kaidenover
5465

Chapter 1

"Hashem in wisdom has founded the earth; He establishes the Heavens with understanding" (Mishlei 3:19). This verse informs us that wisdom and understanding achieve their principle glory when they give rise to something useful that can serve as a foundation and resource for further development. This is what a wise man should revel in and the understanding man take pride in — the accomplishment through wisdom and understanding of some great and beneficial goal on behalf of his soul. The human soul is carved out from beneath Hashem's Throne of Glory and instilled into a lowly human body in order that it be adorned with the beautiful ornaments of good deeds and upright ways. Afterwards, it returns to its place when the appointed time comes for it to reside among the souls of the righteous with strength and joy. Regarding such wisdom it was written, "And wisdom grants life to its possessor" (Koheles 7:12).

By contrast, when a person's intelligence gives rise to things that are of no benefit, to vanity and emptiness, while the body fades away and is lost and all its appetites and pleasures come to naught, of what good is such intelligence? It is superfluous to mention that if he uses his intellect to perpetrate deception, and evil and corrupt deeds that fly in the face of our holy Torah he thereby sullies his soul with stains and blemishes. Woe to such wisdom! Woe to such understanding! For they bring his soul only sorrow, causing it to undergo painful tribulations and afflictions in Gehinnom and to be banished in great shame and disgrace from the realm of holiness.

Therefore, the best strategy to be urged upon every person worthy of the name "Yisroel" is that he humble his hard heart and take time out for introspection in some secluded spot, so that great humility and awe of the Holy One Blessed is He may fall upon him. Let him reflect upon the days and years that have already gone by, vanished as if they had never been. Day by day his time grows shorter and the day of departure, that is, the day of death, grows nearer. Who knows when it will arrive? For it swoops down suddenly like an eagle. Then the agents of the Heavenly court hurry him in to make his reckoning for every word, deed and thought, without overlooking a single detail! Woe to us on the day of judgment! Woe to us on the day of rebuke!

The heart of every man knows the bitterness that is laid up in his soul. He knows how he rebelled and angered the Holy One Blessed is He in youth and in old age, openly and privately. For everything is as if revealed before the Holy One Blessed is He. At the moment of judgment all must stand and give testimony before Him regarding the exact day, the precise hour when the evil deed was performed, and exactly where it took place.

Come and see what I have found written in the text Osiyos deRabbi Akiva. There it is explained that a certain angel stands by the first firmament and examines a man's deeds, which he relates to another angel. This second angel then makes a declaration of them before the holy enclosure. Upon hearing this declaration of his sins, all the angels who sought to sing songs of praise distance themselves from the spot upon which they stood until it has been purified through immersions.

Woe to us! Let us consider the following: If the ministering angels distance themselves from the place upon which they merely hear the declaration of a sin until it has been purified, how much more defiled must be the place upon which the sin was committed! And how much more defiled still must be the offender himself!

Yet a man should not say, "My heart murmurs regretfully within me. Woe to me! What remedy can there be for me after I have committed so many sins against the Holy One Blessed is He!" On the contrary, let him consider that Hashem, the God of the universe, is a merciful King. His hands are outstretched to receive the penitent, especially those who are of His people and His inheritance. If a person will take the time to reflect in this way God will surely come to his aid to help him avoid sinning in the future. Moreover, from that moment on Hashem his God will be with him. For the Sages tell us that whoever makes an effort to purify himself, Heaven comes to his aid (Shabbos 104a). Nevertheless, he must still make the effort on his own to straighten his ways and mend whatever damage he has done. He must not go easy on himself, saying, "It was only a minor infraction, not important enough to feel regretful or to repent. I will ignore my minor misdeeds and concentrate on the serious ones." For one must know that the Holy

Kav HaYashar

One Blessed is He never overlooks anything, even a minor misspoken word.

Come and see what the saintly Rabbi Yosef Katz relates in his work Rechev Eliyahu regarding an incident that took place in his time. One day a group of women were sitting together discussing the accounting a person must give of his deeds. One of the women said in jest, "When I come before the Heavenly court on the day of judgment and they ask me, 'Why did you do such-and-such?' I will make myself as if dumb and unable to respond!" Not many days went by before the woman was indeed stricken dumb and remained so until the day of her death! From this episode we see that every word we speak ascends On High and makes an impression.

A man must not tell himself after sinning or engaging in frivolity that since he has the enjoyment of all the pleasures in the world as well as prosperity and good health, why should he be afraid? On the contrary, concerning him was it written, "There is wealth stored up for its owner to his detriment" (Koheles 5:12). For the Holy One Blessed is He waits until a person's measure of sin is filled and then all at once pours out his wrath upon him. Then he is beset by enemies, and harsh afflictions come upon without grace and without pity, Heaven spare us.

O mortal man! If only you knew how many demons from the Side of Evil lie in wait for the half cup of blood in a person's heart surely you would dedicate your body and soul to the blessed Creator!

It is written, "Renewed every morning; great is Your faithfulness!" (Eichah 3:23). Each and every morning when a person awakes from his slumber he is created anew. We know that the human being was created in order to uphold the Torah, and the statutes and commandments of Hashem. Therefore, the moment he awakens from his sleep let him reflect on the giving of the Torah at Mount Sinai. Let him reflect on the Bnei Yisroel purifying and sanctifying themselves before confronting the mountain in awe and fear, trembling and sweating. Let him imagine the mountain covered with smoke from the fire that crowned it as the Holy One Blessed is He descended upon it accompanied by myriad angels and the sound of the shofar. Let him picture Moshe Rabbeinu, peace be upon him, master of all the prophets, acting as intermediary between the Holy One Blessed is He and His people Yisroel. After thinking these thoughts let him be quick to speak some words of holiness. Thus the author of Seider HaYom writes that immediately upon awakening a man should say, "I acknowledge You, O living and enduring King, for mercifully returning my soul to me; great is Your faithfulness." Then let him cleanse his body and wash his hands and go swiftly to the synagogue to pray.

It is well known that the atmosphere of the world is filled with influences from the Side of Evil. It is especially rife with accusing angels created from the sins and transgressions of human beings hovering about the air of the world, as is mentioned repeatedly in the Zohar (1:190a; 3:196b). Therefore, a person must be wary lest they cling to him as he makes his way to the synagogue. He must bear in mind the Zohar's teaching (3:263b) that to the left of the doorway lurks the Side of Evil. Concerning this was it written, "Sin crouches at the opening" (Bereishis 4:7). The mezuzah, on the other hand, a reminder of the holy Shechinah, is affixed to right. The mnemonic for this is the verse, "The heart of the wise is to his right" (Koheles 10:2). For that is its place. The mezuzah also represents the Divine attribute known as "Rochel." Were it not for the name Shaddai (inscribed upon the back of the mezuzah) facing him as he exits it would be impossible for a Jew to go out of his house, for the Side of Evil stands to the left of the door. This is alluded to in the acronym of the verse, "Sin crouches at the opening" — L apesach CH atos R oveitz, which is the exact reverse of the name "R o c h e l." Therefore, the name Shaddai is needed to subdue it, as it is written, "And Shaddai (the Almighty) will be your fortress" (Iyov 22:25).

The main time a person needs protection is when he exits the door of his home, to prevent the Side of Evil from clinging to him and causing him to sin, Heaven forbid. Therefore, when one places his hand upon the mezuzah at the doorway of his home one should have in mind that the final letters of the expansion of the word yeitzer, the evil impulse, spell out the name Shaddai (yu D, tzad I, rei SH). In other words, the name Shaddai has the power to protect one from the evil impulse.

Then when a person leaves his house let him pray this short prayer: "Master of the Universe! Please have pity upon me and spare me from the evil impulse and all its minions, Amein." Or else let him recite the first paragraph of the Shema: "Hear, Yisroel, Hashem is our God, Hashem is one" until the verse "You shall write them upon the door posts of your house and upon your gates" (Devarim 6:4-9). Then he will be spared that day from all iniquity and guilt.

Chapter 2

King David, peace be upon him, said in Tehillim (119:37), "Avert my eyes from seeing vanity, cause me to live in Your ways." A person must know that many things depend on sight. Therefore it seems to me that if upon arising from sleep one's gaze falls upon the house, one should reflect that the Holy One Blessed is He gave us the mitzvah of affixing a mezuzah to the entryway and the mitzvah of erecting a ma'akeh (a parapet) around the roof, as it is written, "And you shall make a parapet for your roof" (Devarim 22:8). And if upon going out the doorway he encounters clean animals, fit to be offered as sacrifices, let him reflect that the Holy One Blessed is He commanded us to offer sacrifices. And if he encounters impure domesticated or wild animals let him reflect that it is forbidden to consume them. Similarly, if he meets a gentile let him reflect that it is forbidden to intermarry with them. In short, each person should engage in reflection according to his knowledge and learning. This is a very great matter, for in this way one clothes his eyes with sanctity regarding everything they behold.

The converse is also true. Just as one who gazes at holy matters creates a garment of sanctity for his faculty of sight, so too when a man allows himself to gaze at forbidden sights and strange women, he clothes himself in deep defilement, Heaven forbid. A solid proof that sight has the power to cause harm to the viewer himself as well as to others can be adduced from the bird called the bas haya'anah. This bird's eggs lie in front of the mother while she stares at them, piercing them with her gaze until a chick emerges from each one. In the chapters to come I will bring demonstrations of further insights into this matter.

For this reason, our Sages of blessed memory (Avodah Zarah 20a) erected a protective fence forbidding a man from gazing upon anything that is liable to bring him to sin. For instance, he is forbidden from gazing at women and girls lest he be guilty of wasting seed. This is what King David had in mind when he wrote, "Avert my eyes from seeing vanity, cause me to live in Your ways" (Tehillim 119:37). The numerical value of the word shav (שוא), "vanity," is 307, represented by the letters ש"ז (shin zayin), which is also the acronym for the term, sh ichvas z era, "semen." (Dovid prayed that his eyes should not behold anything that could lead to shichvas zera.) This is a bold hint. It seems to me further that because Lilis and her cohorts are called "pangs of vanity" (shav) and also "pangs of death," as is mentioned several times in the Zohar (1:12b; 2:33a), therefore David prayed, saying, "Cause me to live in Your ways." That is, he asked to be influenced by the side of life and not the side of death, Heaven forbid.

The authors of the ethical literature write of a wonderful strategy for avoiding this sin: Let a man envision to himself continually that Hashem's four-letter name is written before him in black ink upon parchment, in keeping with the verse, "I have placed Hashem (i.e., the four-letter name) before me continually" (Tehillim 16:8). This is the principle that King David alludes to in the verse, "My eyes are always directed towards Hashem, for He will free my feet from the net" (ibid. 25:15). The meaning should be obvious.

The Maggid — the angel that used to appear to the Beis Yosef of blessed memory— offered him another useful strategy for avoiding this sin: A man should envision the image of his father standing before him. As proof he cited the example of Yosef HaTzaddik who was on the verge of lying with Potifera's wife when the image of his father appeared before him. As a result, Yosef withheld himself from sinning (Sotah 36a). There is another hint to this strategy in our holy Torah. In Bereishis (1:12) it is written, "a meadow of herbs giving forth seed each to its kind" (Bereishis 1:12). "Meadow," d e she, is an acronym for "the image of his father," d iukno sh el a viv. Thus, it is the medicinal "herb" to ensure that a man only gives forth seed "to his kind," and that none is spilled in vain.

Come take a look at what is stated in the Zohar, Parashas Pikudei (263b). There it tells of an angel called Patos who seduces (mefateh) men to gaze at and examine that which is not necessary for them in an adulterous and wanton manner. After a man dies and is buried in the grave this angel then comes and restores to him his soul, after which he takes hold of him cruelly and breaks the sockets of his eyes and plucks out his eyes. Later on, the man is sentenced to terrible afflictions and then lowered into a pit filled with snakes and scorpions, which attack him and execute upon him terrible judgments, Heaven spare us! The saintly Ari, z"l, discusses a certain small bird mentioned in the Torah (Devarim 14:13) called the ra'ah (literally, "it saw"), which is able to see great distances. The Sages say that it was given this name because it sees from afar and uses its sight to engage in lewdness (Chullin 63b). Therefore, the Ari adds, the punishment of a man who gazes at women is that his soul is reincarnated in the form of this bird, measure for measure, which causes the soul great suffering.

You must know that every sin is brought about by an antecedent and a cause. In this case, too, there is an antecedent and a cause that bring a man to gaze at forbidden women. The first cause is the gazing upon impure things until the eye is sated. Although it is permitted to look at the strange creatures from foreign lands, for which the Sages even instituted a blessing, "Blessed is He who diversifies the creatures," nevertheless, one should not sate the eye with gazing at them but only cast upon them a passing glance. For the eye is comprised of four colors (the white, the dark rim around the iris, the color of the iris and the black of the pupil) corresponding to the four letters of the Divine name (Tikkunim 70, 128a). When a man casts his gaze upon impure creatures, he draws upon himself the unclean spirit that hovers over them. This later causes him to gaze upon worse things, which then bring him to sin. For this reason the Sages warned that a man should not even gaze at his own wife when she is a niddah (menstruating woman) because defilement hovers over a woman while she is having her menstrual flow and through his gaze he draws it to him, causing it to adhere to his eyes. The proof to this is that when a niddah stares at a new mirror her vision makes a stain upon the glass that can never be removed. For the same reason the Sages forbade gazing at the face of en evildoer. Instead a man should accustom himself to looking upon holy things. That way he draws holiness upon himself, imbuing the four colors of his eyes with great illumination.

It is also beneficial for a man to gaze at the Heavens in order to behold the works of Hashem, may He be blessed. It written in the holy Zohar (Introduction 1b): Rabbi Elazar the son of Rabbi Shimon bar Yochai said, One day I was by the shore of the sea when Eliyahu came and said to me, "Rabbi, do you know the meaning of what is written, 'Raise your eyes on high and see who created these' (Yeshayahu 40:26)?" I said to him, "These are the Heavens and their hosts, the works of the Holy One Blessed is He. For it is incumbent upon human beings to gaze upon them and bless Him, as it is written, 'When I see Your Heavens, the work of Your fingers, the moon and the stars that You estab- lished' (Tehillim 8:4). Following which it is written, 'Hashem, our Master, how mighty is Your name in all the earth' (ibid. 8:10)."

Indeed the meticulous make it a practice to gaze at the Heavens at nightfall, just as the stars begin to shine, and recite, "How manifold are Your works, Hashem, etc." (ibid. 104:24). One should be especially zealous to gaze at the Heavens when the sun begins to shine and to "go out in its strength" (Shoftim 5:31), for at that time the Side of Evil and impure beings and the forces of strict judgment are aroused by the sun's fierceness. The same applies when the moon begins to shine. This is because the Side of Evil cannot appear in the light of the moon; therefore, its minions, which float about the world in great force, take refuge in the moon's shadow. Concerning this was it written, "The sun will not strike you by day nor the moon by night" (ibid. 121:6). One should have this in mind when reciting the morning prayer, "Who forms light, etc., who illuminates the earth and its inhabitants in mercy." That is, He causes the luminaries to shine in mercy so that no Jew will come to harm on account of their light.

If follows from the above that a person must be very protective of his faculty of sight. This is even more critical with regard to speech, which is reckoned like deed. Therefore, on the way to shul one should try to keep casual speech with one's companions to a minimum, and even more so, unnecessary speech with strangers. This is a wonderful strategy for ensuring that Hashem in His mercy accepts one's prayers. We find in the writings of the Ari, z"l, (Emek HaMelech, Intro. III, Ch. 4, p. 11b) that he once instructed one of his pious disciples, Rabbi Yitzchak Kohein, z"l, that he should go to the village of Ein Zeisim to the grave of Rabbi Yehudah bar Ilai and pray, having in mind certain special intentions that the Ari taught him. There Rabbi Yehudah bar Ilai would reveal to him an explanation of a passage from the Zohar in Parashas Ha'azinu. The Ari ordered further that he was not to speak with anyone along the way. So, Rabbi Yitzchak went and prayed with all the required intentions and prostrated himself upon the grave. But there was no sound and he received no response. At length he returned home dejectedly to his master the Ari and told him, "Master, I went to the grave of the sage Rabbi Yehudah bar Ilai and did all that you instructed me, but I received no response from him. The Ari, z"l, replied, "Did I not see with my unique insight that you spoke with a certain Arab? And not only did he not greet you but you greeted him first! Did I not instruct you to speak with no one?" Then Rabbi Yitzchak Kohein recalled that this was indeed the case and confessed to it.

Here you have proof that speech and sight cause harm. Although in our dispersion we are required to greet everyone we meet, even before the morning prayers, nevertheless one should try to minimize his words as much as possible. This is a tried and true strategy. Examine my words well because I have abbreviated the matter and will elaborate upon it further in later chapters.

Chapter 3

King David began the book of Tehillim with the words, "Fortunate is the man who has not walked in the counsil of the wicked ... nor did he sit in a gathering of scoffers" (1:1). Similarly, our Rabbis have said in Pirkei Avos, "When two people sit together and there are no words of Torah between them, it is a 'gathering of scoffers'" (3:2). Since, on account of our many sins, this is a very common circumstance a person must pay careful heed to this warning. Whenever he sits with his companions, he must be certain that the discussion consists of words of Torah or character development or awe of Heaven. It goes without saying that he must avoid the company of scoffers and idlers who sit together engaging in frivolity. For in the course of their endless chatter they inevitably come to utter words of mockery and derogatory speech, thereby giving rise to harmful forces that inflict damage upon their souls. Therefore, whoever fears the word of Hashem will distance himself from such company.

You should know that there is a certain category of malignant spirits called kesilim ("wicked fools") that have been appointed to appear to a man walking along the road alone at night. Sometimes they appear as a group of men and seduce him into joining their company. Sometimes they appear in the form of an in or a hotel, shining forth a light to entice him to approach. He believes that he is on his way to a nearby hotel or inn but they draw him farther and farther from the way. It is common for them to lead him into marshes and other places of filth or into a forest or among the swamps where his life is imperiled. These same spirits are appointed over those who gather to relate frivolous tales that are of no benefit. They are also the destroying spirits called the "workers of iniquity," that record all words of mockery and forbidden speech in a book On High called the "Workers of Iniquity." When the time comes for these people to meet their end groups of these kesilim come out to meet them and strike at their souls. Then they take them out to the desert or a marsh and inflict terrible suffering upon their souls. Therefore, one must keep away from these gatherings. It need not be said that if one sees people quarreling one must flee from them, for that is a gathering place for malignant spirits that assemble wherever there is bickering and quarreling.

From all this one can deduce the harm that is done by speaking frivolity in the synagogue, a place of sanctity designed to reverberate with the sound of song and praise and supplication.

See what is written in the Zohar, Parashas Terumah (131b): "Woe to the one who converses in the synagogue! He has no portion in the God of Israel, for he detracts from faith in the King." (Examine the rest of what is written there because I have greatly abbreviated the matter.) We are His people and His flock. Each of us must erect his own protective fences to prevent him from speaking any mundane words in the synagogue at all. For on account of this seemingly small matter one loses his portion in the God of Israel, Heaven forbid! as it is written in the Zohar

A person should be especially careful not to utter words of mockery or tale-bearing in the synagogue, for the dwelling place of the Shechinah is in the synagogues and study halls. When people are not careful to refrain from jocularity, lightheadedness, tale-bearing and derogatory speech in the synagogue it causes the Shechinah to depart from Israel. In this connection the Zohar (Tikkun 6, 22b) ascribes to the Shechinah the verse, "And the dove found no resting place" (Bereishis 8:9). As a result of this sin numerous synagogues have been destroyed, to our chagrin, because people allowed the Side of Evil to mix into the camp of the Shechinah, which was to have been entirely holy. It is not good to bring foreign matters into places of holiness. Therefore, a person should be careful whenever he engages in holy matters not to cause malignant spirits to mix in, Heaven forbid.

You should be aware of what is written in the Zohar, Parashas Pekudei (263b). There we learn that there is one agent of the Side of Evil that looks out for and awaits anyone who allows a disgraceful utterance to leave his mouth, whether it be deceit, derogatory speech, tale-bearing, mockery or anything similar, and afterwards utters words of holiness. That agent, accompanied by other malignant spirits under its command, then goes and takes that holy utterance and defiles it so that the speaker receives no credit for it. For the malignant spirits take those words of holiness and derive and augment their own power with them. Woe to that person in this world! Woe to him in the next world! And the cause of all this was excessive speech, for in the course of speaking excessively it is impossible to avoid a mixture of good in the bad and bad in the good. Through this the Side of Evil gains power and strength, Heaven forbid.

Therefore, it is better for a person to accustom his mouth and tongue to uttering words of awe and admonishment and to speaking the Holy Tongue, which is a refined language that benefits the soul. Our rabbis explain that from the nature of a person's speech one can discern the source of his soul On High. If he is accustomed to speaking imprecations or words of contention it is clear that his soul derives from the Side of Evil, the source of the serpent and the viper. He is not from the holy stock but from the mixed multitude. And even if his father and mother are modest and pious, nevertheless his soul is a reincarnation of a soul from the mixed multitude. The same is true if his mouth utters frivolity or crudity, Heaven forbid. The Ari, z"l, explains that one who speaks crudity impairs the attribute represented by the moon, inverting the letters of the word l e v a n a h, "moon," and changing them to n e v a l a h, "crudity," Heaven forbid. The different kinds of harmful speech are too numerous to elaborate upon. Even ten chapters would not suffice to mention the magnitude of the punishments they evoke. Therefore I will simply issue this brief admonishment: A person must know that a mouth that is fenced in and guarded against uttering slander and imprecations and that does not engage in forbidden speech or mockery, is called a "holy mouth" and with it the Holy One Blessed is He may be praised. Moreover, if a person is immersed in Torah study, prayer, songs and praises, the Holy One Blessed is He takes his utterances and makes them into a crown for his head, provided that he prays with intention.

A man should select a fixed place in the synagogue to pray, next to a good neighbor, someone who is upright and honest. Conversely, let him distance himself from a bad neighbor so that he will not come to stumble through emulating his ways, Heaven forbid. If it is impossible to distance himself from a bad neighbor because no other seats are available, let him rebuke him daily. Perhaps he will find a favorable moment in which his rebuke will be accepted and perhaps in this way his colleague will benefit through him. But if he sees that the man is evil-natured and lawless and unbending in his wickedness, let him abandon his place and go in peace.

Chapter 4

The prophet Yeshayahu, peace be upon him, said, "For as the new Heaven and the new earth that I will make stand before Me, etc." (66:22). The Zohar explains in Parashas Bereishis (Introduction 5a) that when a person goes along the path of innocence and righteousness, serving Hashem with all his heart, with all his soul and with all his might, studying Torah with pure motives and revealing true insights according to his intellect, based upon true and clear premises, being extremely careful that there is no doubt or falsehood, Heaven forbid, in his insights. Then the Holy One Blessed is He rejoices greatly both in that man and in his Torah.

Each and every Torah insight that a person reveals ascends On High and stands before the Holy One Blessed is He. The Holy One Blessed is He kisses it and crowns it with several crowns, creating from it a new heaven and a new earth. These then stand before Him in order that His eyes may be upon them continually to watch over him personally by means of them. And in order that the ministering angels not be jealous of him, the Holy One Blessed is He covers over and conceals those insights until He has fashioned from them the new Heaven and the new earth. This is what is meant by the verse, "And with My hand I have covered you to plant heaven and to found the earth" (Yeshayahu 51:16). But this applies only if he does not become conceited over his learning and the novel insights he has revealed, Heaven forbid, as the Zohar teaches in Parashas Terumah (129a):

The moment Yisroel begin reciting the Kedushah of Uvo Letziyon it is announced On High: "Listen O lofty ones and lowly ones! Who is the one who is arrogant in matters of Torah? Who is the one whose words are only a means to lord over others through words of Torah?" For a human being must be humble in this world in matters of Torah, for there is no exaltation in Torah except in the World to Come! There is a reason why this announcement is made specifically when the congregation recites the Kedushah in the prayer of Uvo Letziyon. The Sages teach that the world is only sustained by this Kedushah (Sotah 49a). Yet this person through his pride is destroying the world because arrogance in Torah causes one to establish vain and false premises. He makes interpretations solely for the sake of glorying in his insight, even though it is not true.

Come see what is written in the Zohar, Parashas Bereishis (Introduction 5a) regarding one who creates insights from the Torah based upon false premises:

These are words of vanity. And when they come out into the atmosphere of the world the Samech Mem, who is called "a man of deceit" (Mishlei 16:28) and a "false tongue" (Mishlei 12:19), comes out to meet them. He summons his strength and goes out towards those words from the opening of the deep chasm and leaps towards them five hundred parsaos. He takes these words of falsehood and makes from them a firmament of vanity called "Chaos" and floats about that firmament, this "man of deceit," six thousand parsaos at a time. Once that firmament is established the wanton wife, the wicked Lilis, goes out to meet them. She, too, goes along increasing in strength in that firmament. Then thousands and myriads of destroyers join with her and enter into partnership with her. In that firmament they are able to traverse the entire world in a moment. These evil troops of destroyers dress up as the troops of the nations of the world and fall upon Yisroel committing great slaughter.

Included in the same category are those who put themselves forward as halachic authorities although they are not yet qualified to issue rulings. This also causes terrible decrees to befall the "enemies" of Yisroel (i.e., Yisroel themselves). Concerning this was it written, "For she has caused many to fall as corpses and tremendous are all those whom she has killed" (Mishlei 7:26). All this is brought about by one who issues rulings before he is qualified to do so or by one who reveals insights into the Torah based upon false premises and ideas that are not true. For this reason, Rabbi Shimon bar Yochai said to his disciples (Zohar, ibid.):

I beg of you, do not allow out of your mouths words of Torah that you did not learn and did not hear from a great "tree" (i.e., a great scholar) in order that you will not incite that sinful one (i.e., Lilis), who wishes to bring on [enemy] camps to slaughter the children of Israel.... Upon which the disciples all spoke up, saying, "May the Merciful One spare us! May the Merciful One spare us!"

In these generations this iniquity is very widespread, to our chagrin. Many preachers deliver public lectures based upon false premises and ideas that are not clear. They blind the eyes of the populace, receiving their praise and glory while exchanging the eternal world for this transitory life. Moreover, they bring on all the evil decrees mentioned above. Whoever fears the word of Hashem will reckon the great loss and damage that he causes against the reward he receives, whether it be honor or financial remuneration in this world, the world of transitory existence. All the honor he receives in this world in response to his lecture will be like a thorn or bramble pricking at his soul. One day a great and fearful darkness will suddenly fall upon him and no light will appear for him thereafter. Woe to him for the shame and disgrace he will experience on the day appointed for his end! These darshanim will certainly not merit hearing the Torah insights of the lecture that the Holy One Blessed is He will deliver in the future, as is related in the Midrash (Osiyos deRabbi Akiva, Version I, Letter 7; Yalkut Yeshayahu 429):

In the future the Holy One Blessed is He will sit in the Garden of Eden and interpret the Torah's secrets. And all the righteous will sit before Him while all the hosts of Heaven stand before Him to the right of the Holy One Blessed is He and the sun and the moon, the planets and constellations to His left. Then the Holy One Blessed is He will interpret for them the meanings behind the new Torah that He will one day deliver to them by the hand of the righteous Moshiach. After the lecture Zerubavel ben She'altiel will stand upon his feet and proclaim, Yisgadal veyiskadash shmei rabbah, etc. ("May His great name be magnified and sanctified, etc."). His voice will travel from one end of the universe to the other and all the inhabitants of the universe will answer Amein, yehei shmei rabba mevorach le'olam ule'olmei olmaya ("Amein, may His great name be blessed for ever and ever"). Even the wicked of Israel and the righteous of the nations of the world who remain in Gehinnom will answer, Amein, yehei shmei rabba. And they will be saved in the merit of their response of Amein, yehei shmei rabba.

Therefore, a person should be very careful only to say true Torah in his lectures and to establish true premises. Let Hashem's Torah be in his mouth and then he will merit hearing true Torah insights from the mouth of the Holy One Blessed is He. Amein, so may it be His will.

Chapter 5

It is written, "And you shall love your fellow as yourself" (Vayikra 19:18). The Sages have remarked that this verse is a fundamental principle of the Torah (Toras Kohanim, Parashas Kedoshim 4). And there is no greater display of love than the mandatory rebuking of one's Jewish brother if he sees in him some unseemly matter, that is, a sin or transgression. For the souls of all Israel are intimately connected to one another. But the guideline for this rebuke is that if one understands the tribulations, effects and punishments that the soul of a person is subjected to after it leaves the body, he must inform him. For perhaps through this his companion will also have the merit to abandon his evil path, and then he will see the fulfillment of the verse, "He will return and heal him" (Yeshayahu 6:10).

In this chapter I will describe briefly the punishment that is suffered in the next world by a soul that has been sullied in this world. You must know that the atmosphere of the world is filled with human souls that are not yet allowed to ascend to their place of rest, as one of the disciples of the Ari, z"l, relates in the name of his teacher (Emek HaMelech, Introduction 3, ch. 4). He relates further that one time when the Ari went to study in the field, he saw for himself that every tree was covered with countless souls, as was the field itself and even the water. The Ari asked these souls what they were doing there and they responded that they had been banished from the holy enclosure On High because not only did they fail to repent of their iniquities, they prevented their companions from repenting as well. Therefore they were condemned to wander about the earth and the air of the firmament, this one here and that one there. But now they had heard a Heavenly voice proclaiming throughout all the worlds that there was a certain righteous man — i.e., the Ari himself — who had the power to rectify banished souls. They had gathered there to request of him that he have mercy upon them and rectify them so that they might ascend to their resting place and be released from their great suffering. The saintly Ari promised that he would do whatever he could on their behalf. Afterwards the Ari related this conversation to his disciples because they had seen him speaking with someone but they did not know with whom he was speaking nor who was responding to him.

In his writings he explains that these souls could have ascended with the prayers of a righteous person. Because a perfectly righteous person prays with intention his prayer ascends beneath the Throne of Glory. At that time numerous souls are clothed in his prayer and accompany it On High. Thus, the Zohar explains in connection with the verse, "A prayer of a poor man when he is enwrapped [with affliction] and he pours out his thoughts before Hashem" (Tehillim 102:1):

Numerous souls enwrap themselves in, and cling to, the prayer of a poor man and there is no prayer that is more beloved to the Holy One Blessed is He than that of the poor and that of the righteous. They ascend in a great and terrible flame consuming everything around them. The Side of Evil fears to approach the prayer of the poor or the righteous and in this manner banished souls are able to ascend along with these prayers.

The exact same principle is at work when the soul of a righteous person, upon departing this world, passes through Gehinnom (Zohar 3:220b; Tikkunim 32, 76b). It does so in order that in its merit the lost souls can take hold of it as it passes by and ascend along with it.

Similarly, one of the disciples of the Ari z"l, the pious Rabbi Gedalyah z"l, told his companions that every Friday they would all go out of the city to greet the Shabbos. One time the Ari related to them what he had witnessed on numerous occasions while standing on a mountaintop outside of the city. From there he was able to observe the entire cemetery of the holy community of Tzefas, may it be rebuilt speedily in our days. From his vantage point he observed hosts of souls ascending from their graves towards the Garden of Eden on high. But he also noticed thousands of souls descending towards them. These were the extra souls that are bestowed upon the righteous every Shabbos. Because of the great confusion and the milling about of such a tremendous number of souls and hosts his eyes were nearly blinded and he was forced to close them. Yet even with his eyes closed he could still see them.

As one can see clearly from the words of the Ari's disciple, the prayers of the righteous are of tremendous benefit to the souls of the banished. There can be no greater act of lovingkindness than this. Obviously, we are not in the same league as the righteous of earlier generations. We would have reason enough to be thankful if our prayers were adequate to benefit ourselves and to atone for the sins and transgressions and the rebelliousness and deceit with which we have angered our Creator. Nevertheless, one should strive to be among those who benefit these banished souls with their prayers and then the Creator, may He be blessed, will exercise His abundant lovingkindness. Indeed, it is fitting for every Jew to strive to benefit others. One should pray especially on behalf of the wicked of the generation that they should repent. Thus, we learn in Berachos (10a) that Rabbi Meir's wife Beruryah said to him, "It is written, 'let sin come to an end' (Tehillim 104:35), not the sinners!" Therefore, I will set out here for the use of every man and woman a Yehi ratzon prayer to be added to the blessing, "Return us our Father to Your Torah and draw us near to Your service," the fifth blessing of the Amidah. The text of the prayer is as follows:

May it be Your will, Hashem, our God and God or our fathers, to open a tunnel beneath Your Throne of Glory for the repentance of So-and-so son of So-and-so (mother's name), and all those who transgress Your commandments. May their hearts be transformed to do Your will with a whole heart, for Your right hand is extended to accept the penitent. (Then continue with the blessing of the Amidah) …and cause us to turn back in complete repentance before You. Blessed are You, who desires repentance. After reciting this, a person will arouse himself as well to repent for his sins so that they will not chide him, "Adorn yourself and then adorn others!" If he will only recite this prayer with heartfelt intent surely the Merciful One, in His abundant lovingkindness and mercy, will accept his prayer. And even though this prayer should really be accompanied by esoteric meditations in which we are not fluent, nevertheless, let him pray briefly and think these requests in his heart. For it is proper for everyone to leave such requests to the meditations of the heart and not speak out everything with his lips. It is a tremendous matter that before standing in prayer one recites the meditation: Leshem yichud Kudsha brich hu uShechintei — "Let this serve to unite the Holy One Blessed is He and His Shechinah." For the heart corresponds to Hashem's four-letter name (represented in this meditation by the designation "the Holy One Blessed is He"), while the mouth corresponds to the name Hashem ("Lord"; represented here by the term Shechinah). The Zohar (1:169a) explains that this is what King David had in mind when he wrote, "Let the words of my mouth and the meditations of my heart be acceptable to You, Hashem, my Rock and my Redeemer," that is, the awesome unification of mouth and heart.

From this one can infer the terrible punishment owing to one who divorces his heart from his mouth by uttering prayers with his mouth without intention in the heart, or to one who speaks to his colleague something other than what is in his heart. This grievous iniquity causes a separation between the two Divine names mentioned above, as well as between the letter vav and the letter hei of the four-letter name. As we know, the vav of the Divine name represents the Written Torah, while the hei represents the Oral Torah (Tikkunim 18, 35a). Thus, he also separates between the two Torahs, preventing them from being united. Unfortunately, this failing is very common, may Heaven spare us from it. One must know that God will search the matter out and bring the offender to justice. This sin resembles that of the heretics and the Karaites who deny the words of the Sages of the Talmud.

This being so, let the foresighted reflect that if a person grows used to speaking with his mouth other than what is in his heart his children will undoubtedly stray and eventually deny the Torah, measure for measure. Moreover, he alienates himself from the holiness emanating from above and forfeits that distinction that is ascribed to Israel in the verse, "And as for you who cling to Hashem your God, you are all alive this day" (Devarim 4:4). To understand the significance of this verse, consider that when a man tightens his belt until it clings tightly to his waste, not even dust can penetrate between the belt and the garment. So too, when Israel cling to Hashem through their meritorious ways and deeds, no accuser can intervene between them and their Heavenly Father. Take a look at what the Zohar (Parashas Pekudei 225a) writes on this topic:

Rabbi Abba, Rabbi Acha and Rabbi Yose were walking along the road from Tiberius to Tzippori. While they were walking, they saw Rabbi Elazar coming towards them accompanied by Rabbi Chiya. Rabbi Abba said, "Surely by joining up with them along the way we will connect ourselves with the Shechinah." So, they waited until they caught up with them. Rabbi Abba said, "This is surely the case, for it is written, 'The eyes of Hashem are upon the righteous,' that is, to watch over them so that the Side of Evil does not approach them. Now Heaven's assistance will be here and all the supervision from above will be here and the Side of Evil will have no dominion....

Then Rabbi Elazar spoke up and said, "It is written, 'And the number of the children of Israel will be like the sand of the sea' (Hoshea 2:1). What is meant by the 'sand of the sea'? When the sea hurls up its waves in wrath and anger so that they threaten to inundate the earth, just as soon as they reach the sand of the sea and behold it, they immediately break and retreat, unable to flood the world or to have dominion over it.

"Israel is also like the sand of the sea. When the waves of the sea — that is, the harmful spirits and destroying accusers, agents of anger and strict judgment — wish to have dominion and to flood the world, as soon as they observe that the children of Israel are tied fast to the Holy One Blessed is He they break and retreat before them, unable to achieve dominion in the world."

Israel is likened to the sand of the sea; just as the sand of the sea is piled up forming bulwark encircling the sea, high as a mountain and dazzlingly white, so too Israel, through repentance and good deeds, whiten their sins and transgressions. Thus, it is written in Yeshayahu, "If your sins are like scarlet, they will become white as snow; if they are as red as crimson, they will become like wool" (1:18). This is because the mitzvos and good deeds that Israel perform in this world form a barrier encircling the judgments facing them so that these judgments are delivered into their hand. Moreover, they transform judgment into mercy and the accuser himself into a defender. This is not the case, however, when people speak benevolently with their mouths while in their hearts they are thinking otherwise. Then their deeds have no positive effect and they have no protective barrier against the waves of the sea. Then the "waves" mentioned earlier, the agents of strict judgment, overwhelm Israel. Strict judgment increases, Heaven spare us, and mercies are few. On the contrary, mercy itself is transformed into judgment.

Therefore awaken! Awaken! My brothers and friends. Let each one repent according to his ability and multiply his good deeds. Let him study with increased zeal and pray with intent and let him pray that his colleague will also repent. Then the pious and the righteous will increase until in their merit and righteousness they come to resemble a mountain. Then they will be like the sand holding back the waves of the sea. For these "waves" are the destructive accusers whose desire is to destroy the world. These are the agents of strict judgment. But the righteous weaken the power of these accusers. Then Israel enjoys a respite and deliverance, joy and happiness. Amein, so may it be His will.

Chapter 6
"One who comes to purify himself, Heaven helps him" (Shabbos 104a). The idea of this dictum is that whenever a person looks to perform a mitzvah or when he travels along the road engrossed in study, although he is alone, he is joined by numerous souls [of the righteous]. Thus the Zohar relates (Bereishis, Introduction 5a) :
Rabbi Elazar once went to visit his father-in-law Rabbi Yose ben Lakonya, accompanied by Rabbi Abba. Meanwhile another man loaded their donkeys and came after them. Rabbi Abba said, "Let us begin studying Torah, for it is time to prepare for the way." So they began exchanging Torah insights. Then the fellow leading the donkeys revealed to them a number of esoteric Torah insights and Rabbi Elazar and Rabbi Abba came and kissed him, saying, "Who are you that you walk around with all this wisdom in your hand while leading the donkeys after us?" He answered, "My masters, do not ask me who I am. Let us just go along engaging in study." And he continued revealing to them esoteric insights into the Torah. They said to him, "Who compelled you to come here and load donkeys?"...... Rabbi Elazar and Rabbi Abba rejoiced and wept, saying, "Go ride and we will lead the donkeys after you." Then they said to him, "See here, you have not even told us your name nor where you home is located!" He said to them, "My home is in a good place. It is in a certain tower in which the Holy One Blessed is He resides along with a certain poor man (an allusion to the Moshiach who is called "A poor man riding upon a donkey"). This is my home. But I went up from that place and now I am loading donkeys.
Rabbi Elazar and Rabbi Abba wept and kissed him and then went on, while he continued revealing to them additional insights. Rabbi Elazar and Rabbi Abba fell upon their faces and when they arose,

they no longer saw the man. They look in every direction but did not see him. They sat and wept and were unable to speak to one another for a long time. Finally, Rabbi Abba said, "Surely this is an illustration of what we learned, that whenever the righteous travel along the road speaking words of Torah, tzaddikim come to them from the upper world. Surely this was Rabbi Hamnuna the Elder who came to us from that world to reveal to us these things and afterwards he disappeared from our sight.

From here we have a proof that the souls of the righteous join with those involved in the performance of a mitzvah or in Torah study. It is worth remembering that every meritorious reflection or thought has the effect of eliciting holy illumination from On High. But meritorious speech, such as engaging in study while on the road, has an even great effect. It even brings benefit to banished souls. Some of these souls are banished to such an extent that they are reincarnated in the form of vegetation or the fruits of the earth and the trees. When a person recites a blessing over that fruit or engages in study, those souls are clothed in his meritorious words and in this way, they are released from the cycle of reincarnation.

Another principle to be derived from the passage from the Zohar is the importance of clinging to scholars and accompanying them along the way to listen to their words of Torah, for the Shechinah dwells among the upright while they are alive and even after their deaths. Thus we see that in earlier generations people were very concerned about the site in which they would be buried. Yaakov Avinu, for example, instructed, "And I will lie with my father and you shall bury me in their burial place" (Bereishis 47:30). The reason for this is that the souls of the dead hover over their graves and are taught each night esoteric insights from the Heavenly yeshiva. Seifer Chassidim (705) relates an incident involving a certain tzaddik who was buried among the wicked. Every night he would appear to his friends and relations, crying out to them in a tearful voice and begging to be moved from there. He explained that because he was buried among the wicked the Heavenly yeshiva refused to reveal to him any secrets of the Torah. As a result his soul was becoming increasingly desiccated until no moisture remained. He gave his relatives no rest until at last they were forced to exhume him from his grave and bury him elsewhere.

Kav HaYashar

This was why the pious of earlier generations in Eretz Yisroel were accustomed to purchase a plot in the cemetery during their lifetimes, in the vicinity of individuals whom they knew to be righteous. They would then come to that spot from time to time to pray and to recite a few words of Torah and make a pledge of charity. In this way they purified and sanctified the spot, preparing it to serve as their grave. The sanctity with which they imbued it also prevented the Sitra Achra from being able to approach them after their deaths. Another illustrative account in this same vein is that of the pious Rabbi Amram. * The following story is not in the original Kav HaYashar. It appears in the Yiddish version, and is cited in M'orei HaEish, a commentary on Kav HaYashar.

Rabbi Amram was originally from Maintz, a large city on the Rhine. At some point Rabbi Amram left Maintz to help strengthen the yeshiva of Cologne. When he was very old he instructed his students that after his death they should bury him in the cemetery of Maintz where his fathers were buried, next to the grave of Rabbi Yehudah HaChassid.

His students replied that such an undertaking would involve great danger and risk. Therefore, Rabbi Amram said to them, "Just purify me and place my body in a coffin along with a letter stating that the deceased was the great Rabbi Amram." Afterwards they were to place the coffin upon a small raft on the river and allow it to drift on its own.

Upon his death the students fulfilled their master's request, placing his body on a pram on the river. The boat immediately began drifting with the current until it came to the vicinity of the city of Maintz, whereupon it stopped still in the water. This sight astonished the townspeople, who informed the lord mayor. The lord mayor commanded some boatman to go out and fetch the pram and bring it in. But when the sailors reached the boat with the coffin it lurched backward so that they were unable to grab hold of it.

The lord mayor then told his servants that it appeared that the boat contained the body of a Jew wishing to be buried in their country, so he commanded that some Jews be summoned to fetch it. When the Jews reached the bank of the river the boat immediately began to draw nearer. They opened the coffin and found the letter that had been placed there by Rabbi Amram's students. However, in it they found written the following message:

My brothers and friends of the holy community of Maintz,

Know that I have come to you because I have passed from this world in the city of Cologne. I request of you that you bury me alongside my fathers in the city of Maintz. May all of you be blessed with life and peace. Thus says, Amram

When the Jews from the town saw this letter, they unloaded the coffin from the boat, intending to bury him in his family plot as per his instructions. However, the lord mayor instructed his servants not to allow the Jews to take the corpse to burial. Instead all the non-Jewish residents of the town gathered to take the body away from the Jewish community by force and they posted guards to prevent any Jews from coming near the coffin. Afterwards they built over it an edifice for their own false worship, which is called to this day, "the House of Rabbi Amram."

When the Jews saw this they were filled with sorrow and expended lavish sums in attempts to retrieve the coffin. But their efforts were in vain and at last they knew of no further avenues to try. Every night Rabbi Amram would appear to a number of his disciples and plead, "Take out me of here and bury me with my fathers!"

So the disciples took counsel together and went out of the city limits that night to the place where a thief had recently been hung. They took down his body and wrapped it in burial garments. Then they secreted out the body of the pious Rabbi Amram and replaced it with the body of the thief. Meanwhile Providence caused a deep sleep to fall upon the guards so that they did not notice a thing.

At last Rabbi Amram was buried with his fathers. Hashem was with them and nothing was known of the matter to the people of the town until this day. (Until here is taken from the Yiddish version.) If it is true that the place of a person's burial is so important after his death, as illustrated by the accounts above, consider how important it must be that a person situate himself among good company while he is alive. Thus, in former times it was the custom of the men of Jerusalem that they would refuse to sit either in a court or at a feast until they knew with whom they would be sitting (Sanhedrin 24a). For the celebrations of frivolous people lead to many evils such as tale-bearing and mockery, especially among the gluttonous and intoxicated.

A person should also recite this prayer: "May it be Your will to save me this day from an evil person, from evil happenstance and from an evil companion." This is in order that he will not join with the wicked or with sinners or with groups of the treacherous, who gather to engage in bickering and quarreling. Their mouths are sharp swords and their curses, insults and blasphemies are like hot coals. The fire of Gehinnom burns within them enflaming their quarrels and contentions. Their thoughts are entirely for evil, even when they are in shul. They are filled with deceit, inventing pretexts against the upright who adhere to Hashem's ways, in order to do them harm. Woe to them and woe to their souls! For the day will come suddenly when the wheel will turn against them and Heaven's judgements will overwhelm them, stripping them of all their possessions. They will become objects of contempt and disgrace but no one will have pity upon them because of Heaven's harsh decree. Let those who fear Hashem and who tremble at His word distance themselves from such people and from their gatherings and their tumult. Let the upright not heed their advice nor accompany them and certainly not join with them. Instead let them cling to love of Hashem and to the God-fearing and to those who tremble at His word. From such individuals they can learn the path of life. Concerning this was it written, "And as for you who cling to Hashem your God, you are all alive this day" (Devarim 4:4).

Chapter 7

"He caused me to be desolate and in misery all day long" (Eichoh 1:13). Our Rabbis teach that this verse is speaking in the name of the Shechinah, remonstrating against the arrogant who cause the exile of the Shechinah's to be prolonged. This is also alluded to in the verse, "And my splendor was transformed for me into destruction" (Daniel 10:8). That is, the arrogant transform הוד — "splendor" into דוה — "misery." In short, a person must reflect how much evil is caused by this attribute. Let him realize that it was not in vain that the Sages said that a haughty person is considered as if he worshipped idolatry (Sotah 4b). This is because he delivers his soul into the hands of powerful impure forces (chitzonim) so that it is only with great difficulty that he can escape them. Therefore, it is as if he is under the dominion of foreign gods, Heaven spare us. Therefore, let the wise see and take heed, appreciating the severity of both the iniquity and its punishment.

In any event, of what does a man have to be proud? If he is proud of his wealth, the Holy One Blessed is He has already declared, "Mine is silver and mine is gold says Hashem of Hosts" (Chaggai 2:10). Hashem can deprive a man of his wealth in an instant. In fact, we have already heard of several wealthy men who were murdered for their riches. Bandits set their eyes upon them, pursued them and struck them down, subjecting them to dreadful suffering before their souls departed. Some did not even merit burial, which is itself a terrible fate. We have observed that no adversary or mishap came upon the numerous others who traveled along the same road but only upon the wealthy man on account of his wealth. Let a man reflect that many people have labored and wearied themselves, eschewing sleep, enduring the heat of the day and icy cold at night. They travel in the dark, in the rain and in the snow to amass a nest egg of a hundred or a thousand or more. Then just at the moment when they can at last rejoice in their portions and indulge themselves with the fruits of their labors — suddenly death strikes and they are compelled to abandon it all. They depart for the next world leaving to others all the wealth they labored so hard to accumulate. They gather one penny after another by the sweat of their brow until it adds up to the desired sum. But then they must leave it all in the hands of another.

Sometimes a man's wife claims all of his wealth for her kesubah. Then after he dies she marries another man and gives him all her money, while the first husband's children go barefoot and in rags, deriving no benefit from their father's riches. They see their mother sitting and eating and drinking with another man, enjoying life with her second husband while they, the orphans from the first husband, sit between the oven and the stove (like mourners on Tisha B'Av)! They look on as their mother enjoys meat and wine and other

Kav HaYashar

delicacies while they would be happy just to receive her leftovers! They sigh as they recall to one another that all that wealth was once their father's and now they have no access to it.

Let a man remember that this can easily happen through the decree of the King of Kings the Holy One Blessed is He. For with my own eyes I have seen many children who were raised in luxury but their delight (עונג) was transformed into plague (נגע), sorrow and tribulations. After their father's demise they went to his grave and poured out their troubles but they received no reply because the dead are too preoccupied with the reckoning they must give for their sins and transgressions. Let a man take all this to heart and he will surely not fall into pride over his wealth.

And if he is clever and proud of his intellect, let him consider that numerous clever people have been ensnared by their own cleverness. More numerous than those who sought out wisdom were those who trapped themselves with a single misspoken word and were unable to recover. For example, many have sought to display their wit before kings and nobles but afterwards were ensnared by a misspoken word and met with misfortune for which there was no remedy. By contrast, those people who nullify themselves, saying things like, "I do not know," enter in peace and exit in peace.

This being so, what advantage does the clever person enjoy through his cleverness in worldly matters? No one is fed or earns his living through cleverness but only through whatever channel the Holy One Blessed is He has granted him to provide sustenance for his household, and obviously not through cheating his colleague. Therefore, a person should remind himself that a day will come suddenly when his cleverness will come to nothing — on the day that he falls upon his sickbed and his wits are addled by the intensity of his illness. At that time even a young child will outshine him. Nor can his cleverness save him from the angel of death. What benefit is there, then, in such cleverness? Therefore, let a person see to it that he does not take pride in his intellect.

Suppose that a man takes pride in his Torah study, in his fluency, his sharpness and his understanding in depth and breadth. Suppose he is persuaded that he has no equal in this generation and refuses to acknowledge that there are indeed other scholars on his level who can hold their own in a debate and apply themselves diligently to their studies. Even so, he should consider that compared with the tannaim and the amoraim, the scholars of the Talmud, he and the other scholars of the day are as nothing. Moreover, the greater those earlier scholars were the more humble they were. This is clear from a number of passages in the Talmud and midrashim describing their great humility. It was for this that they merited the crown of Torah. If a person takes pride in his study, Heaven forbid, he gives strength to the Sitra Achra, meanwhile the Sitra diKedusha — the side of holiness — eludes him.

In the seifer Giv'as HaMoreh the story is related of a certain pious man who was walking along the way when Eliyohu HaNavi joined up with him. At one point they came upon an animal carcass cast by the wayside. It gave off such a terrible stench that the pious man was obliged to place his hand over his nose. But Eliyohu went right up to the carcass without noticing a thing. Later on as they were walking they spied a man walking towards them at some distance. He was walking in a haughty manner, swaggering and strutting. While he was still quite far away Eliyohu placed his hand over his nose. The pious man said, "Why did my master not place his hand over his nose when we passed the carcass?" Eliyohu replied, "This fellow is much more foul than the carcass. For if one comes into contact with a carcass one becomes defiled for only a single day, but contact with such a fellow imparts much more serious forms of defilement.

The general rule, then, is this: Pride is a despicable trait. It increases strife, jealousy, hatred, lashon hara, anger, falsehood and mockery. When one considers the matter, he realizes that every sin in the Torah is included within it. The damage that pride causes is very great. Woe to whoever indulges in it on a regular basis. Fortunate is he who holds fast to the trait of humility and contrition, for this is a pleasing and praiseworthy trait that brings him into the World to Come and saves him from affliction in the grave. There is no other trait that purifies and whitens the physical human being like the trait of humility. Through it the very substance of one's body becomes spiritualized. Thus, if a person adheres to this trait his entire life even his body will shine in the grave like a bright light and receive illumination from the holiness of the upper realms.

Moreover, he will merit receiving esoteric insights into the Torah from the Heavenly yeshiva and body and soul shine as one. All of this is achieved through the trait of humility.

We know that it was commonplace for the tannaim, rabbanim and amoraim to experience miracles, visits from Eliyohu HaNavi and Divine inspiration. All this they earned in the merit of their humility. For a humble person admits the truth and accepts rebuke. He speaks in a calm, pleasing manner and is beloved On High and admired down below.

Therefore, a person must pray that he merit this trait. The pious author of the seifer Shalheves (i.e., the Shlah) writes that at the end of the Amidah, before reciting, "May the words of my mouth be acceptable, etc.," one should say this meditation: "Master of the Universe, allow me to merit the traits of humility and contrition so that I will be acceptable and desirable to the people." Afterwards let him recite, "May the words, etc." In truth, a person should pray fervently to the Holy One Blessed is He with tears and entreaties asking that He free him of arrogance and help him acquire humility. For as a rule arrogant people live out only half their years. The reason for this is that they are generally hated by others. This causes them to be removed from the world. And even if such a person achieves his desire to become head of the community or rabbi of his congregation, his pride causes him to think of those under him as nothing and to belittle their honor. This is another factor in the shortening of his life span, may Heaven spare us.

After that, one transgression leads to another. In every disagreement he wishes to be the victor rather than the defeated. In pursuing this end, he neglects to discern between good and bad and between straight and crooked, because his only concern is victory. This leads him to corrupt the law and pervert justice and as we know, tipping the scales of justice causes the judge's own verdict to be tipped suddenly from the side of life to the side of death. Arrogance also causes him to inveigh against the scholars who come to rebuke him for his improper words and conduct. This, to our chagrin, is very widespread. It is especially common for communal leaders to become increasingly bold until they join the ranks of the "oppressors of the scholars." Then suddenly they are singed by the "hot coals" of the scholar and they vanish from the world like fleeting shadows. They also become "oppressors of the scholars" when they rule over them by force.

Come let us reckon: Whoever causes a fellow creature anguish places himself in great danger. A person is punished even for causing anguish to beasts and birds. This is because every creature has its own spiritual guardian (mazal) who lodges a complaint on its behalf against the oppressor. How much greater, then, is the punishment of one who causes anguish to the scholars!

Come take a look at an incident cited in Seifer Chareidim involving a certain righteous man who once hosted the Ari, z"l in his home with great honor. Before resuming his journey the saintly Ari, z"l asked, "How can I repay you for the great affection you have shown me? I would also like to repay you for trouble you went to on my account."

The host replied that after his wife had given birth to a few sons she mysteriously stopped conceiving. He thought that perhaps the Ari, z"l might be able to offer some remedy for her. The Ari, z"l responded by first revealing to him the reason for his wife's barrenness. "You know," he said, "that there was once a small ladder in your house upon which the little chicks would ascend and descend to drink water from a nearby vessel. In this way they would drink and be quenched.

"Then one day your wife instructed the servant to remove the ladder. Clearly her intention was not to cause sorrow to the chicks but only to make the house more tidy. Nevertheless, from the moment the ladder was removed the chicks have been in great sorrow. Because they were still too small to fly, they endured great thirst and their chirping ascended before the Holy One Blessed is He, whose mercy is upon all His works. On this account it was decreed that your wife should become barren." Naturally the host restored the ladder to its place and Hashem allowed the wife to conceive and give birth as before. From this story it is evident that Hashem in His abundant mercy and lovingkindness watches over every creature, punishing those who oppress any of them. For every deed a man does he must give a reckoning. Clearly, then, one must be very careful not to oppress anyone in vain.

Come see what is written in the first chapter of Chagigah (5a):

What is meant by the verse, "For God will bring every deed to judgment, concerning every hidden matter, whether for good or for evil" (Koheles 12:14)? This refers to one who spits in the presence of his fellow causing him disgust.

Seifer Chassidim (44) relates an incident involving a certain pious man who used to cover up any spittle that came from his mouth as well as any other spittle that he knew came from the mouth of a Jew. His concern was that another person might come along and be disgusted and then fail to forgive the spitter!

We can see, then, how scrupulously the pious of earlier generations observed the injunction against causing sorrow to others. Yet many individuals are not careful in this matter, especially in this generation in which the ignorant, who know neither law nor judgement, have gained the upper hand. They conduct their affairs as a rule through force, refusing to heed the directives of the rabbinical court. What they fail to realize is that when there is no justice on earth, then there is justice in Heaven and that their day and their judgement will come suddenly.

For this reason, the Rosh in Orchos Chaim (Day Five, 90) advised: "Let not your friends seem to you too many but let even a single enemy seem too many." This is not the way of the multitude, however, for on account of some paltry sum in a business transaction or other matter they call down upon their colleagues the most severe curses, Heaven spare us. They do not consider that all mankind is like a single individual and that it is not fitting that the mouth of a descendant of Avraham should be accustomed to cursing. Instead it should be accustomed to uttering blessings and other good and gentle things that give pleasure to the Creator.

For the man who curses his fellow is hated by the Holy One Blessed is He, who promised Avraham, "I will curse those who curse you and those who bless you I will bless" (Bereishis 12:3). Thus, He put a hook into the mouth of the wicked Bila'am, who wished to curse Israel, transforming his curses into blessings.

Know that I have found it written that whenever someone curses his fellow in vain, for no real offense, the Creator spreads His wing over the innocent victim, shielding him from the effects of the curse.

Know further that there are those with an evil temperament, Heaven spare us, whose eyes, mouths and hearts are rooted in the Sitra Achra. The curses of such individuals are extremely dangerous. Rabbi Yehudah HaChassid writes that malignant spirits called chitzonim are prepared to actualize these curses by lodging accusations against the victim. If the Holy One Blessed is He did not shield him on account of His promise to Avraham, "And you will be a blessing" (Bereishis 12:2), the curses would take effect on that person, Heaven forbid.

One must also know that not only do undeserved curses not take effect, on the contrary, the victim is rewarded. Thus, it is written in the Jerusalem Talmud (Peah 8:6):

Rabbi Yose appointed over them leaders and charity collectors, but the appointees refused to accept (out of humility). So, he spoke up and said to them, "Ben Baba was appointed over the wicks (in the Beis HaMikdosh) and merited being numbered among the great leaders of the generation. Now you have been appointed over people's very lives, how much more so!"

Rabbi Elazar was appointed over the charity fund for a time. One time he entered his house and said to them, "What [manner of charity] have you done?" The people of his household replied, "A group of beggars came around and they ate and drank and prayed for you."

He said to them, "This is not a goodly reward." On another occasion he came and said to them, "What have you done?" They said to him, "A group of beggars came around and they ate and drank and cursed you." He said to them, "This is a goodly reward."

Note that Rabbi Elazar was happy over being cursed in vain!

The fact that cursing is so common among the masses is a great impediment to their repentance (see the list of things that impede repentance in Chapter 43). For this reason, we must admonish those who fear Hashem and are concerned for the honor of His name not to allow a single curse to escape their lips. This will make it easier for them to repent of their sins. For the Holy One Blessed is He issues a call to repentance every day, saying, "Return O straying sons!" (Yirmiyohu 3:14), for His hand is always open to accept the penitent.

Know that when this call is issued On High it is heard down here in this world. The sound of it arouses the trees of the forest until they are clothed in trembling, singing songs of praise in dread and awe. This is related in the Zohar, Parashas Bereishis (Introduction 5a-7a):

Rabbi Elazar and Rabbi Abba were walking along the way engaged in a Torah discussion when they were joined by Rav Hamnuna the Elder (who had already died). They came to a certain mountain just as the sun was about to set and the branches of the trees began banging against one another, singing songs of praise. While they were still walking, they heard a certain powerful voice saying, "Holy ones scattered among the living! Holy luminaries! Members of the yeshiva! Gather to your places to converse with the scholars!"

So Rabbi Elazar and Rabbi Abba sat down, remaining in their places in fear and dread. Then a voice was heard, saying, "Mighty boulders! Lofty hammers! (Alluding to the dead tzaddikim who came to hear the Torah of the living.) Come gather!" At that moment they heard a great sound coming from the branches of the trees, saying, "The voice of Hashem is powerful ... The voice of Hashem breaks the cedars...."

From all this one can learn the importance of refraining from cursing others and also of repenting for one's sins. Then all will be well with him, selah!

Chapter 8

It is taught in the Jerusalem Talmud (Brachos 1:1): "One who stands to pray must place his feet together. Two amoraim argued, Rabbi Levi and Rabbi Simon. One said, 'Like the angels,' and one said, 'Like the Kohanim.'" It seems to me that both views are the word of the Living God. Because prayer is in place of the sacrifices (Brachos 26b) one must conduct oneself as if one were a Kohein. Just as the service of a Kohein is disqualified by stray thoughts, so too one must be careful not to have any stray thoughts during prayer in order that one's sacrifice will not be disqualified. One should not think that only thoughts of sin are forbidden. Thoughts of business and the like are also forbidden because one must resemble the angels who have no mundane affairs.

It is written in Seifer HaChinuch: When a man thinks about matters of silver and gold and coins, he violates the negative injunction, "You shall not make gods of silver and gods of gold alongside of Me" (Shmos 20:20). It is worth examining the rest of the passage as well.

The Zohar relates in Parashas Pekudei (245a) that a certain appointed angel stands by the portal through which pass all the prayers of Israel that were prayed with concentration of the heart and without any mixture of stray thoughts. This angel then opens the Gateway of Prayer, allowing these prayers to enter the palace where all the prayers gather. From these prayers a crown is made for the head of the King of the Kings of Kings the Holy One Blessed is He. But if one prays without concentration or with a mixture of stray thoughts the angel pushes the prayer away from the entrance, whereupon it goes and floats about the air of the world until at last it comes to another appointed angel. This angel holds onto all the disqualified prayers that were denied entrance to the Gateway of Prayer because of stray thoughts. He stores them up until the man himself realizes how many prayers he has prayed without proper concentration, for which reason he received no response.

He then confesses and regrets his sin, because a prayer without concentration is like a body without a soul. He laments, "Woe to me! Woe to me! What have I done? I have detracted from the honor of our Lord, the great, mighty and awesome God, by speaking before Him without concentration of the heart!" He establishes fences for himself to ensure that he does not repeat his error and from then on prays with concentration of the heart. At that time the earlier prayers that remained in the care of the second appointed angel ascend along with the first one that he prayed with concentration. The same angel takes all the disqualified prayers and causes them to ascend until they come before the Holy One Blessed is He and are fashioned into a crown for his head along with all the acceptable prayers of Israel.

Here we see an example of Hashem's great lovingkindness, for He allows a single prayer to rectify all of them!

Who can refrain from taking these things to heart and doing kindness with one's own soul? Certainly, one should not take lightly the matter of omitting a prayer completely, Heaven forbid! For even if one wishes to immerse oneself in Torah study, nevertheless, the time for prayer is one thing and the time of study is another (Shabbos 10a). Let him not imagine that for the sake of his studies it is better in the eyes of the Holy One Blessed is He that he neglects one prayer service. Heaven forbid that a person should think this way!

Come see what is written in the seifer Holeich Tomim :

Rabbi Yeshayohu HaChassid related to me in the name of Rabbi Yehudah HaChassid that the Ramban in his day had a certain disciple with a tremendous thirst for Torah, so that he literally never slept. If he ate now and again to sustain his soul, a book would be open before him from which his eyes would never deviate. However, in his great love for Torah he never took the time to pray.

The Ramban warned him, "Eat at the time for eating, sleep at the time for sleeping and pray at the time for praying. Then you will enjoy the merit of the Torah and it will protect and sustain you. But do not transgress on the Torah's account, for prayer will demand redress from the Holy One Blessed is He for its disgrace and you will be punished, Heaven forbid. Therefore, be careful about prayer!"

But the disciple paid no heed to his words and did not take them to heart. Not long afterwards the disciple went to the market to make a purchase. When he returned home, he found a cavalryman violating his virgin daughter on the very table upon which he was accustomed to study. He mourned over this incident for many days. The Ramban told him, "I warned you to be careful about prayer! For our Sages enacted that a man recites every day the petition: "May it be Your will, Hashem our God and God of our fathers, that we be spared this day from an evil man and an evil mishap, etc." (Brachos 60b). Yet you refused to listen to me. That is why this has befallen your daughter!"

The disciple realized that this was an act of Divine Providence because of his neglect of prayer and from that time on he began praying properly. "Therefore," writes the author of Holeich Tomim, "go out and see the acts of God, who has issued a statute and a judgement against those who belittle prayer and are accustomed to reciting their prayers in an offhand manner. And let the rest of the nation hear and tremble!"

A person must be concerned, therefore, when he recalls the many days on which he prayed by rote without concentration of the heart. He must also seek mercy and ask that the Holy One Blessed is He remove the stumbling block of disturbances that hinder concentration in prayer. One should also try to pray with tears, for prayers that are accompanied by weeping are highly valued and readily accepted, as Chazal have told us (Zohar, Part II, 245b; Zohar Chodosh Rus 98a).

In fact, tearful prayers are so desirable that the gate through which they enter the Heavenly palace is opened not by an angel but by the Holy One Blessed is He Himself. For this reason, too, those gates are never locked but are always open. They are called the "Gates of Tears" (ibid. Part II, 165a). When such a prayer ascends On High it is met by an Ofan (a lofty class of angels) that is appointed over six hundred Heavenly Chayos (another class of angels). This Ofan personally causes the prayer along with the tears to ascend until it becomes connected to a very lofty place.

Come see with what concentration earlier generations prayed. It is related in the Jerusalem Talmud (Brachos 5:1) that when Rabbi Chanina ben Dosa stood in prayer and a snake came and bit him he did not interrupt his prayer. Afterwards they found the snake lying over its hole, dead. The students asked him, "Rabbi, did you not feel any pain when the snake bit you?" He replied, "Let that which I was concentrating upon during my prayer befall me if I felt it!"

Rashi explains (Brachos 33a) that when an arod (a poisonous reptile) or a snake bite a person, if the animal reaches water first, the person dies, and if the person reaches water first, the animal dies. Rabbi Yitzhak tells us that we may infer that the Holy One Blessed is He created a spring beneath Rabbi Chanina's feet, in fulfillment of the verse, "He performs the will of those who fear Him and hears their cry and saves them."

Today it is impossible for us to concentrate as those earlier generations did. There are two reasons for this: For one thing, our iniquities weigh too heavily upon us. And for another, we are too ignorant. Nevertheless, we must certainly not give up trying to concentrate.

Come see what is written in Seifer Chassidim (18 and 977). It is explained there that if a person is standing in prayer and notices a seifer fall to the ground he should not interrupt his prayer to pick up the seifer, for he is standing before the terrifying and awesome Creator, may He be blessed.

All of our prayers and songs of praise should be recited with a whole heart, especially when we recall the Creator's supervision over us in our exile, for we are all but oblivious to the many miracles and wonders that He performs for us.

Sometime it seems at first that some misfortune has befallen a person, but then Hashem transforms it for good. This is illustrated by a passage in the midrash (Yalkut Yeshayohu 417). It is related that two merchants decided to travel together by ship along with their merchandise. One of them boarded the ship but the other tripped over a rock along the way and fell, becoming temporarily crippled. As a result, he was forced to remain behind and his merchandise remained behind with him. He wept and fretted that his merchandise would now fail to reach its destination to be sold. A few days later, however, word was received that the ship had sunk along with all its passengers. Then the merchant began praising and thanking the Holy One Blessed is He, reciting, "I will acknowledge You, Hashem, because You were angry with me!" (Yeshayohu 12:1).

And so is it fitting for every individual who fears Hashem and trembles before Him to utter upon every occurrence the phrase, "This too is for the good." And even if in the meantime it does not appear to be for the good, let him rejoice in his heart and resolve in his mind that it is indeed for the good. For it is an atonement for the sins and transgressions of the past and an admonition and a warning for the future.

In most cases the occurrence itself will turn out to be an illustration of the principle that, "It was for his own good that his cow broke its leg" (Jerusalem Talmud, Horios 3:4). In fact, retroactively it will turn out to have been miraculous.

This is why Chazal instituted that we recite every day Chapter 100 of the book of Tehillim, "A psalm of thanksgiving." Because in truth we owe praise and thanks every single day for the miracles and wonders by which we continue to survive in this bitter exile. But we fulfill our obligation of thanksgiving through the recitation of this psalm since we are incapable of sensing the miraculousness of our survival every day.

Come and see what is written in the Zohar, Parashas Mikeitz (201b):

Rabbi Abba was sitting at the gate of the town of Lod when he saw a man approaching. The man sat down in a cleft in a mountain, exhausted from his travels, and fell asleep. While he slept [Rabbi Abba] saw a snake drawing near to the man. Then a piece of wood fell and killed the snake. When the man awoke, he saw the dead snake, whereupon he straightened up and a piece of the mountain fell to the valley below and was again spared. Rabbi Abba came to him and said, "Tell me what meritorious deeds have you done? For the Holy One Blessed is He has performed for you two miracles! Surely they were not for nothing." The man replied, "In my entire life no one ever wronged me without my making peace with him and forgiving him. Moreover, if I am unable to make peace with him I do not go to bed until I have pardoned him along with all those who have caused me distress.

From here we learn that the Holy One Blessed is He watches over those who conduct themselves with wholesomeness, behave uprightly, trust in Hashem and act with lovingkindness towards their fellow creatures. Such individuals can rest assured that the Holy One will bestow upon them a goodly reward.

You must know how great is the attribute of trust. For if a person trusts in Hashem, angels of lovingkindness surround him, protecting him from all mishap. Thus, it is written, "And the one who trusts in Hashem, lovingkindness will surround him" (Tehillim 32:10). It is only fitting that trust should earn a person great reward, for one who trusts in Hashem will surely conduct his affairs in good faith and refrain from pursuing ill gotten gains.

If a person does not have trust in Hashem, the moment his fortunes take a downturn he is afraid that he will never again enjoy light and goodness. Conversely, he believes that if he only had such-and-such a sum of money in his house no decree of Heaven could affect him nor could any misfortune befall him because his great wealth would protect him from every contingency. This is why money is so precious to him. Even theft, fraud and infringement seem permissible to him.

This is not the case, however, with those who trust wholeheartedly in the Holy One Blessed is He. Even if at times they suffer from poverty and deprivation, nevertheless they lift their eyes to Hashem's lovingkindness, confident that their time will arrive all of a sudden, their fortunes will change and they will enjoy salvation through permissible and fitting means. Who can list all the evils that derive from the lack of trust in Hashem? Those without trust are perpetually on the lookout for ways to deny debts and deposits. They are willing to swear falsely, make dishonest claims in court and bring false witnesses. As a result, the Holy One Blessed is He brings retribution upon them and their families (Shevuos 39a); Gehinnom comes to an end but their punishment does not.

But as for those who trust in Hashem the verse says, "And the one who trusts in Hashem, lovingkindness will surround him" (Tehillim 32:10). One who speaks fitting words (כשרון) is enwrapped in them like a suit of mail (כשריון). No injustice will befall the tzaddik when his time comes and he will enter the King's palace without shame, in the merit of his trust and faith.

Chapter 9

Why is it that the leaders of the Jewish people are called Nesi'im ("Elevated Ones")? It is to indicate that as long as a leader merits conducting himself with fear of Heaven, he is elevated higher and higher and in the next world his soul is bound up in the bonds of life in the highest sanctity.

But if he does not act properly, he is reckoned among the nesi'im veruach, the "clouds and wind" (Mishlei 25:14). Just as a cloud dissipates and the wind passes by never to return, so too, a communal leader who does not act as a Jewish leader should — by failing to bear the community's burden or behaving with arrogance — passes from this world abruptly and his descendants are forgotten.

Many communal leaders have fallen into this trap due to pride and arrogance. They intimidate the community unnecessarily and indulge and pamper themselves. They exempt themselves from communal taxes, making life easier for themselves but harder for others. They claim first pick of every honor and distinction. Their faces glow from plenty and they are strong and healthy through the satisfaction of their every desire. "They have no share in the toil of other men, nor are they afflicted along with other men" (Tehillim 73:5).

The result is that the congregation of Hashem, the seed of Avrahom, Yitzchok and Yaakov, are crushed and humbled and rendered naked, harried and barefoot by the levies that the tax collectors and other public officials impose upon them. They callously barge into their homes and grab whatever they find.

It is fitting in their eyes that the heads of households should be naked and penniless so they take even their clothing, even their tallis and kittel, selling them for a pittance. They leave the members of the household with nothing other than the straw on their beds, shivering from the cold and rain, all of them weeping — husband, wife and children — one in this corner and another in that. If only the leader would shoulder part of the tax burden himself it would weigh less heavily upon the middle class and the poor.

Yet there is another iniquity that is even worse than this: Many leaders eat and drink on the community's account, taking from its coffers for the dowries of their sons and daughters and for wedding gifts for their sons- and daughters-in-law! All of this from the hard-earned income of their Jewish brothers! Regarding them a Heavenly voice proclaims: "This one has consumed the blood and flesh of the holy people Israel, stealing from the poor, the orphaned and the widowed!" Then the voice heaps upon them curses. In addition, their prayers are not heard, may Heaven spare us their fate!

Therefore, let the man who has been appoint to a position of communal leadership behave with mercy and not with callousness, especially towards those "broken vessels," the poor and the destitute. For the Holy One Blessed is He desires their honor and the indictments against the community on their behalf in Heaven bring in their wake terrible decrees, Heaven forbid.

It is related in the writings of the Ari, z"l that one time he and his disciples were sitting in the field in which the prophet Hoshea be B'eiri was buried. The Ari, z"l delivered a lecture in the esoteric wisdom of the Torah.

Suddenly in the middle of the lecture the Ari, z"l said, "In the name of Hashem, quickly gather tzedakah from among yourselves that we may send the money to a certain poor man who lives nearby in such-and-such a place. His name is Rabbi Yaakov Altortz and he is sitting and weeping, complaining to Heaven about his poverty. His voice is ascending On High, piercing all the firmaments and entering into the innermost chambers.

"As a result, the Holy Blessed is He is filled with wrath against the entire city for not taking pity upon him. In fact, a proclamation has just been issued throughout all the firmaments that a massive plague of locusts is to descend upon all the environs of Tzfas. It will devour all the crops, that which is heaped into piles and that which still stands in the fields and even the olive orchards. Therefore, let us quickly send him tzedakah. Perhaps with God's help we can still annul the decree."

Immediately each one gave his donation, which the Ari, z"l then handed to his disciple Rabbi Yitzchok HaKohein, instructing him to go quickly to the home of Rabbi Yaakov. Rabbi Yitzchok did as he was told and when he arrived, he found Rabbi Yaakov weeping and pleading by the entrance to the house. Rabbi Yitzchok inquired, "Rabbi, why are you crying?"

Rabbi Yaakov answered that the water barrel had broken and he did have so much as a penny with which to replace it. In his great distress over his poverty and want he was at a loss what to do. Rabbi Yitzchok immediately delivered to him the funds, whereupon Rabbi Yaakov was filled with joy, showering upon him blessings.

When Rabbi Yitzchok returned to his master the Ari, z"l informed him, "The decree has been annulled and there is no more need for concern."

While they were still speaking a mighty wind began blowing, bearing with it a swarm of locusts of unfathomable proportions. The disciples were thrown into confusion but the Ari, z"l calmed them, "Do not be afraid, the decree has already been annulled." And so, it was. The entire swarm continued on until it reached the ocean where all of them drowned. Not a single locust remained in the entire country.

This should be a warning to all Israel to attend carefully to the needs of the poor and the indigent, who are known as "broken vessels." For the Holy One Blessed is He takes up lodgings with them, causing His Presence to dwell among them.

Our Rabbis have taught, "Whoever gives a coin to a poor man is blessed with six blessings and one who appeases with words is blessed with eleven blessings" (Baba Basra 9b). The heart of the poor man sighs continually over his inability to obtain his desires because he would also like to obtain his share of goodness, yet it remains beyond his grasp.

In the season of cold and chill the rich man sits like a prince in a well-built winter home. Meanwhile, not only is the poor man's home filled with holes, he does not even have the wherewithal to purchase firewood so that he is unable to warm himself properly. The bitter cold shatters his body and spirit, as well as those of his entire household. And when it rains, the drops fall upon his neck.

The poor man lives in distress day and night all the days of his life. He and his household sigh continually, yet they accept all their afflictions with love. When Shabbos and Yom Tov arrive and it is time to take delight in food and drink and clean coverings, the poor man lacks even bread. Nevertheless, he gives praise and thanks.

The rich mean marries his sons and daughters off to whoever he chooses. But the poor man, because of his lack of means, must accept whatever match he can find. Often, he must marry his daughter to an ignoramus utterly lacking in Torah and fear of Heaven, which is tantamount to binding her before a lion. Yet he is unable to save her from him. He simply looks on as his ignorant son-in-law abuses his daughter day after day, causing her great suffering.

Who can record all the bitterness and anguish endured by the poor man? But if a poor man accepts his poverty with love and affection the fires of Gehinnom have no dominion over him (Eiruvin 41b) and his reward is very great. For the one who is poor in this world is considered as if dead (Nedarim 64b).

I admonish you, therefore, that whoever gives money to a poor man in his hour of need should do so in a way that does not cause him shame, Heaven forbid. For his poverty causes him enough suffering, as we have already explained. Rather one must give to him privately. And if one does give a gift in public one must accompany it with words that will put his heart at ease.

Whenever one offers hospitality to a wayfarer one must do so with a pleasant countenance. Chazal tell us, "Welcoming guests is greater than greeting the Shechinah" (Shabbos 127a). It is a mitzvah of great importance, for whoever gives bread to a poor man weakens the power of 480 bands of destroying angels, as well as that of Lilis, mother of the sheidim, who is always on the look out for accusations to make against the Jewish people. (See Chapter Ten.)

To return to our topic, let leaders be warned that they must not impose excessive fear upon the community and they must contribute their share of the taxes like any other citizen. They must not be guilty of favoritism, lightening the burden of the rich and their kin while increasing that of the poor and needy. If they will do these things they will flourish, meriting offspring and length of days, amen.

Chapter 10

When one makes a seudas mitzvah, such as a bris, an engagement or a bar mitzvah, it is important to see that the poor and needy are among the invitees and that they are well taken care of. For if a person makes a simchah for his son or daughter but fails to invite the poor, the wicked Lilis and the Samech Mem bring indictments against him in the Heavenly court until he is beset by afflictions.

The midrash tells us, for example, that this is what happened to Avraham because he did not invite any poor people to the feast that he made upon Yitzchok's weaning. Commenting on the verse, "And after these matters" (Bereishis 22:1), the midrash explains that it was in response to the Satan's indictment that the Holy One Blessed is He subsequently commanded Avraham, "Take, now, your son, your only one, Yitzchok ... and offer him there for a burnt offering" (Bereishis 22:2).

Similarly, because Iyov made a feast for his children to which no poor people were invited the Satan was given permission to kill all his sons and daughters and to deprive him of his wealth and livestock as well. Yet even this was not sufficient to satisfy the Satan until he was allowed to afflict Iyov's person.

Therefore, whoever holds a feast should be sure to invite the poor so that the accuser will have nothing to say against him. Moreover, he will actually be transformed into an advocate! Thus Midrash Tanchuma (Ha'azinu 8) relates the following story.

A certain wealthy and learned man whose only daughter was as beautiful as she was modest and pleasant mannered. The father betrothed her three times to three different worthy suitors in succession. But in each case the groom was found dead the morning after the wedding night.

At last the widow proclaimed, "Let no more men die on my account. I will remain a lonely widow from now on until the Holy One Blessed is He has mercy upon me." And so, she remained single for many years.

Now it so happened that this wealthy man had a brother living in another country who was extremely poor. He had ten sons and every day he and the eldest son would bring back wood from the forest to sell in order to maintain his household. One day they were unable to sell the wood they had brought and consequently had no money with which to buy bread. That night they all went to bed hungry. The next morning, they went again to the forest to fetch wood for sale, but the father fainted along the way. The son's eyes brimmed with tears over his father's poverty and he raised his eyes to Heaven.

After considering the situation he asked his father for permission to go visit his uncle. Upon is arrival at his uncle's home the uncle and his wife and their widowed daughter all rejoiced to see him and inquired after the wellbeing of his parent's and siblings. He remained there seven days, at the end of which he said to his uncle, "I have a request to make and I beg of you not to turn me down." The uncle replied, "Please, my son, ask whatever you desire." The son said, "I will not ask for anything until you swear that you will not refuse me," and the uncle complied. The son then continued, "My request is that you give me your widowed daughter in marriage."

Upon hearing this request the uncle began to wail. "Please, my son," he begged, "do not make this request. For on account of our many sins whoever marries my daughter dies after the first night." But the son insisted, "It is with full knowledge of this that I am asking to marry her." The uncle told him, "If it is money you are after, do not marry her and I will heap upon you silver and gold. For you are a pleasant and wise young man and I do not wish for you to endanger your life." But the son was adamant, "You have already sworn to me."

When the uncle saw that the young man would not yield, he went to inform his daughter. Upon hearing the news, she, too, began weeping bitterly, crying out, "Master of the Universe! Take my life and do not kill this young man!"

But a short time later the two were betrothed. The father of the bride, who was also the groom's uncle, invited all the elders of the city to the wedding. They erected a canopy for the groom to sit in at the wedding and while he was sitting there Eliyohu HaNavi arrived in the guise of an elderly man.

He called the groom over to him and told him, "My son, I am going to give you some good advice and I warn you not to deviate from it. Today, while are sitting at your feast a poor man will come to you. He will appear to you the most wretched individual in the world. As soon as you see him you must rise from your place and seat him beside you. Give him to eat and drink and wait upon him with all your might and all your personal attention." When he finished speaking the old man turned and left.

Kav HaYashar

The night of the wedding the groom was sitting at the head of all his guests when a beggar entered. The moment the groom noticed him he stood up, seating the beggar in his own place and obeying all the instructions that Eliyohu had given him.

When the feast was over the groom entered his chamber and the beggar went in after him. "My son," he said, "I am a messenger from the Omnipresent and I have come to take your soul."

The groom replied, "Grant me a year or even half a year." "No," the beggar said, "I will not do as you ask." "Grant me thirty days!" The groom pleaded. "I will not," said the beggar, whom the groom now knew to be the Angel of Death. "Grant me until the end of the seven days of feasting." "No," said the Angel of Death, "I cannot do you the kindness of granting you a single day because your time has come."

The groom made one last request, "Allow me to take leave of my wife and my uncle who is my father-in-law." Then the Angel of Death said, "I will grant you this because you acted with kindness towards me. But return quickly."

So, the groom went to the chamber where the bride was sitting alone and crying and praying to the Holy One Blessed is He. When the groom came and called to her she arose and opened the door. She clasped his hand and kissed him and asked, "Why have you come to me alone?"

The groom answered, "I have come to take leave of you because my time has come to go the way of all the earth. The Angel of Death appeared to me and told me that he has come for my soul." The bride said, "Do not leave. Sit here while I will go and speak with him." So she went to the Angel of Death and said to him, "Are you the emissary that has come for my husband's soul?" "Yes," he acknowledged.

"But is it not written in the Torah, 'When a man takes a new wife, he shall not go out to the army nor shall he go out to any task. He shall be free for his household an entire year and cause the wife whom he has taken to rejoice' (Devarim 24:5)? The Holy One Blessed is He is a God of truth and His Torah is a Torah of truth, but if you take the soul of my husband now the Torah will appear false, Heaven forbid!

"If you heed my words, good and well. But if not, then I summon you to din Torah before the Heavenly court before the Holy One Himself!"

The angel listened and then said, "Because your husband acted with kindness towards me and honored me, I will grant your request and bring your case before the Holy One Blessed is He."

So the angel went before the Holy One and in the blink of an eye he returned rejoicing. "The Holy One has granted the groom his life!" he exclaimed. "In the merit of his kindness towards the beggar."

All night long the bride's father and mother wandered about outside of the bridal chamber listening to the voices of the bride and groom rejoicing. In the morning they entered the room and saw that they were both safe and sound and they all rejoiced together. Then they revealed the matter to the entire community and they all offered words of praise and thanks to the Holy One Blessed is He. This is the story as it is related in the midrash. And it was all because of the groom's display of lovingkindness towards the poor. Therefore, a person must be wary of ever showing a stern countenance towards the needy who come to his door. And one must be especially careful not to glower at those who come to partake of a seudas mitzvah. For by shaming the poor one brings on great misfortune.

And let the host not be concerned if he must add a little to the cost of the feast on their account because their presence is an atonement for him. Thus the illustrious Maharam HaBavli writes in his Ta'amei Mitzvos (Positive Mitzvah 40):

There is great benefit to the hosts of a feast in the eating of the poor that are invited to participate. This is completely analogous to the case of a sacrifice in which the Kohanim eat and the owner receives atonement. Moreover, let him be generous towards them so that to him may be applied the verse, "One with a generous eye, he will be blessed" (Mishlei 22:9).

Chapter 11

It is well known to anyone who has studied our holy Torah that there are two pillars that support the world and that sustain us in our exile. These are: the merit of the Torah and the merit of the Patriarchs. In the merit of these twin pillars, the pillar of Torah and the merit of the Patriarchs, Divine favor and mercy shine every morning upon the children of Israel. For they have been banished from their land to live among seventy nations, who hiss between their teeth to do them only evil, but the Holy One Blessed is He foils their schemes. And since He desires Israel's prayers it is proper for them to pray every morning that the merit of our holy Torah and the merit of the Patriarchs, Avraham, Yitzchak and Yaakov, should continue to stand by us.

The first blessing we recite in the morning is the blessing over the washing of the hands: "Blessed are You, Hashem our God, King of the Universe, who has sanctified us with His commandments and commanded us concerning the washing of the hands." This blessing begins with the letter beis (Baruch) and ends with the letter mem (yadayim). The numerical value of these two letters is 42, which is twice 21. This is an allusion to the two pillars mentioned above, the merit of the Torah and the Patriarchs. For the Torah's five books begin, respectively, with the letters: beis (Bereishis), vav (Ve'eileh shemos), vav (Vayikra), vav (Vaydaber … bemidbar), and alef (Eileh hadevarim). The sum of these five letters (beis, vav, vav, vav, alef) equals 21, corresponding to the Divine name E-h-ye-h ("I will be"), the numerical value of which is also 21.

Similarly, the initial letters of the names of the Patriarchs also total 21: alef (Avraham), yud (Yitchak) and yud (Yaakov). For this reason, the zealous have a custom of reciting immediately after the blessing over the washing of the hands the following prayer: "God, the God of all spirits, may it be Your will, Hashem my God and God of my fathers, that the merit of Avraham, Yitzchak and Yaakov will stand by us, saving us and our offspring from all transgression and iniquity, that we may fulfill the commandments of Your holy Torah without any alien thought. And purify our hearts to serve You in truth and innocence, Amein."

Kav HaYashar

Let this not seem a trivial matter in your eyes, for I have found this text written in a work dating from the time of Rashi, z"l. The scholars of those days possessed an oral tradition stating that from the time the Temple was destroyed and the sacrifices discontinued, prayer took the place of sacrifices as the means for arousing Heaven's mercy.

This is especially noteworthy in our time when we are so much in need of mercy on account of this bitter exile. Yet our minds are not clear enough to pray properly because of the burden of earning a living, for we literally earn our bread with our lives. Sometimes, one's craving for money causes him to commit deeds bordering upon fraud and theft, merely to sustain his life.

For this reason, our rabbis composed this prayer asking the Creator to save us from iniquity, transgression and sin. And since no other time of the day is as auspicious for prayer as the early morning, which is a time of Divine favor and mercy, it is praiseworthy to recite it immediately after the blessing for the washing of the hands. This is especially appropriate in light of the hint it contains to the merit of the Torah and Patriarchs as explained above.

But if a person shirks his prayers he may very well be stricken by the attribute of strict judgement before he has a chance to pray. Then Hashem's wrath will be poured out upon him suddenly at a moment of strict judgment. For the attribute of judgment is always prepared to strike.

O mortal man! If you will heed my advice you will arouse and gird yourself to seek the Creator's favor. For He is a great, mighty and awesome God. He simultaneously: slays and resuscitates, wounds and heals, impoverishes and enriches, humbles and exalts, starves and satiates, lowers into She'ol [the grave] and raises up again, drowns in mighty and deep waters and brings back up to the surface.

He responds to a man in his time of trouble and to a woman when she sits upon the birthing stool. He saves from the Sea of Reeds and travelers in the desert from wild beasts and venomous snakes. He heals the sick, hears the cry of the poor and needy and rescues the oppressed from his oppressor.

Sometimes, when Israel fails to repent, He elevates over them a man like Haman, whom He allows to promulgate evil decrees against them on the basis of libelous pretexts, placing Israel in great distress. At such times they lift their eyes to the Heavens in weeping, enduring great and numerous sorrows until salvation arrives in the blink of an eye.

But this occurs only in the merit of repentance, for their souls weep in their innermost chambers as they confess their sins and transgressions. They also recall the misdeeds of their youth and the harm that they caused when they refused to follow Hashem's ways, choosing instead to go after their heart's desire and to ignore their end.

But then they turn back, experiencing a change of heart and abandoning their evil path. Again, and again they tearfully confess, resolving to repent completely. In light of this the Creator heeds their cries and sends them deliverance in His mercy. Therefore, let a man not be remiss in his prayers to Hashem. Moreover, let him not rely upon his wisdom, saying, "Fear of Heaven is already so ingrained in me that my enemy (the evil inclination) cannot possibly induce me to veer from the straight path."

Come and see what is related in the Jerusalem Talmud (Shabbos 1:3). There the Sages tell us of a pious old man who used to say, "Do not trust yourself until you reach old age." (That is, he believed that having attained old age sin could no longer tempt him, in contradiction to the Sages' teaching that a person must not trust himself until the day of his death.) One day the Satan appeared to him in the guise of a beautiful woman, drawing closer and closer to him until he was overwhelmed with thoughts of sin. At that point the pious man actually began flirting with the Satan! Instantly he caught himself, however, and was filled with remorse, saying, "What have I done?" He then arose, crying, "Woe to me! To whom have I approached?" He was brimming with sorrow for the words that had escaped his mouth and that might very well have led to sin.

When the Satan saw how pained he was he said to him, "Rabbi, do not be distraught, for you did not speak with a woman but only with the Satan in the form of a woman. I have only come to admonish you not to tamper with the words of the Sages, who said, "Do not trust yourself until the day of your death," not "until old age." The pious old man resolved that from then on, he would recite the

Sages' dictum in its original form, in keeping with the Satan's admonishment.

We spoke earlier of the need to prayer with a broken heart. Now let us discuss another matter that is of benefit in causing one's prayers to be accepted. That is, cleanliness. A person's body must be free of stains and filth.

Consider the words of Ma'aseih Merkavah that were mentioned in the first chapter. According to this beraisa certain angels are sent into this world to make known that which has been decreed upon the world. After these angels have flown in the world, they are not permitted to sing songs of praise On High until they immerse themselves 365 times in the River of Fire and another seven times in "white fire."

All these immersions are required simply because they entered into the proximity of human beings. If these supernal beings must purify and sanctify themselves before they may sing songs of praise before the Holy One Blessed is He, it is certain that human beings must do likewise before they pray.

The primary form of purification that is required of a person is the washing of his hands immediately upon leaving the bathroom. But hand-washing is also required upon exiting the bathhouse, letting blood, cutting one's nails, taking a haircut or touching any part of the body that is normally covered, as explained in the works of the halachic authorities. Whoever is careful about washing his hands under all these circumstances will not swiftly come to sin.

But someone who is not careful about washing his hands will inevitably commit grievous sins. This is because one who is lenient in this matter becomes enveloped in the shells of impurity that linger in unclean places. Washing the hands compels these shells to distance themselves from him.

Come and see what is written in the Zohar (Introduction to Bereishis 10b):

Whoever enters a bathroom must not read from the Torah until he has washed his hands. Woe to those who pay no heed and know nothing of the honor due their Master and who do not they realize upon what the world stands. For there is a certain spirit dwelling in the outhouse that immediately settles upon the fingers of a man's hand.

This is a support for those who ensure that there should be a vessel near the bathroom with which to wash hands immediately upon exiting. I have also seen some people who wash their hands into a basin immediately upon awakening in the morning. Others keep a vessel of water nearby while they are studying in case, they happen to touch a part of the body that is normally covered. This is also very appropriate.

But one must be especially careful about washing one's hands before prayer, as it is written, "I will wash my hands in cleanliness, etc." (Tehillim 26:6). And it is also written (Tehillim 103:1): "My soul shall bless Hashem and all my inwards His Holy Name" (that is, one must be sure that one's intestines are clean as well).

Another practice that allows one's prayers to be more readily accepted is to avoid sitting beside evildoers, as I have already mentioned in Chapter Three. This is because the Side of Evil lurks in the vicinity of an evildoer. Moreover, the area of the sinner is prone to mishap, Heaven forbid.

The Sages warn that from every sin that a person commits — and does not erase through repentance, weeping and confession — a destroying angel is formed. This angel clothes itself in a piece of wood or a stone and then on some later occasion causes the sinner to trip and come to harm. The sinner believes that it is the wood or the stone that has injured him but this is an error. He does not realize that it is his own iniquity that has tripped him us and caused him harm. This is the meaning of the verse, "Return, O Israel, until Hashem your God, for you have stumbled over your iniquity!" (Hoshea 14:2).

I have heard a similar idea in the name of the saintly Rabbi Yehudah of Shidlovche, z"l. He spoke of those who betray their wives by traveling to distant lands where they hire themselves out as pedagogues. After a time, they begin engaging in business, amassing their fortunes little by little.

Inevitably, while they are abroad, they are guilty of wasting seed. Then as they make their way home, they are set upon by pirates and highwaymen who deprive them of everything they have accumulated. What they fail to realize is that from every droplet of seed a destructive angel is created, Heaven spare us, and it is these destructive agents in the guise of men who attack them, plundering their wealth.

The authors of Keli Chemdah and Megaleh Amukos write in a similar vein, that when a man chooses to sin with a certain object the angel appointed over it shouts, "Let not the foot of egoism overtake me, nor the hand of the wicked move me away!" (Tehillim 36:12). In short, the power of a transgression is that it summons the Sitrah Acharah and from that moment onward the scene of the crime becomes a place of danger.

Come and see what the Zohar relates in Shemos (49a):

Rabbi Chiya and Rabbi Yose were traveling along the road through the desert, engaging in study when they spied a certain man coming towards them bearing a burden. Rabbi Chiya said, "Let us not join up with him lest he turn out to be an idolater with whom it is forbidden to associate, or an ignoramus with whom it is inappropriate to associate."

Rabbi Yose replied, "Let us test him. Perhaps he is a Torah scholar or even a halachic authority."

Meanwhile, the man caught up with them. As he passed by he said, "Your company would be agreeable to me and I would like to join you. Indeed, I know of another road, different from the one you intend on taking, for although you are unaware of it, that one is very dangerous. Heaven forbid that I should withhold this information from you and thereby become accountable for your lives!"

Rabbi Yose said, "Blessed be the Merciful One who encouraged us to wait here and join up with this man."

The man added, "Listen, we must still travel some way along the dangerous road. Let us say nothing and walk swiftly until we have passed the place of danger."

After they set out, he said to them, "Blessed is the Omnipresent who has enabled us to leave this place of danger!" He then explained, "One time a certain scholarly Kohein was traveling in the company of an ignoramus. Along the way the ignoramus overpowered the Kohein and killed him. From that day forward whoever passes along the road that you wished to take, as soon as he comes to that spot he is injured. This is because from then on the site became a place of peril, where murderous bandits lie in wait. No one who passes there is spared from the bandits because the Holy One Blessed is He demands the blood of that scholarly Kohein, etc. It is worthwhile examining the rest of what is written there.

As is clear from this incident, sin causes the vicinity in which it was committed to become a place of danger. Therefore, a person should be particular about sitting beside a good neighbor in the synagogue rather than an evildoer. Then his prayers will surely be accepted and the Holy One Blessed is He will put it into his mind to purify his body and soul in this world through complete repentance, so that his soul will be received with joy before Hashem's Throne of Glory.

Chapter 12

How important it is for a person to pray tearfully to the Holy One Blessed is He that he will not be ashamed when he comes before the Throne of Glory for judgment upon the expiration of his soul. He must not imagine that on account of his many merits he has nothing to worry about and that there is therefore no need for him to pray. Come see what is related in the Tikkunei Zohar (Tikkun 29; 73a):

Rabbi Shimon ben Yochai was sitting engaged in Torah study when an old man (i.e., the prophet Eliyahu) stood behind the wall and called to him: "Rabbi! Rabbi! Holy light! Arise and kindle the lamp. That is, the mitzvah lamp of the holy Shechinah (i.e., draw down an outpouring of illumination to the Shechinah, which is called the "mitzvah lamp"). For concerning it was it written, 'Let a continual fire burn upon the altar, let it not be extinguished' (Vayikra 6:6). And it is also written, 'To kindle a continual lamp' (Shemos 27:20). The Shechinah is certainly called the "lamp of Hashem." It is the source of Adam HaRishon's light, that is, his soul. Arise and kindle it!" So, Rabbi Shimon ben Yochai stood on his feet (out of deference to the Shechinah) and then sat for a moment and said, "Master of All the Worlds, you are the ruler over kings and the revealer of secrets. Let it be Your will to arrange the words in my mouth in fulfillment of the verse, "And I will be with your mouth" (Shemos 4:12), so that I will not come before You in shame (after my death)."

If Rabbi Shimon ben Yochai, who is called the "holy lamp" and who brought into being numerous holy universes through the breath, found it necessary to pray that he would not be ashamed when he came before the Holy One, how much more must we do likewise. This is especially so in light of our involvement with the frivolities of this world. Therefore, we must pray and beseech our Creator that we will be neither ashamed nor mortified when we stand and give an accounting on the great and terrible Day of Judgment. Woe to us, for who knows what our circumstances will be like there?

Let a man reflect day in and day out, in the time that he sets aside for introspection, that he must take himself aside and rectify his sins and transgressions with all alacrity (see Chapter One). It is absolutely essential that a person introspect well, for then perhaps a spirit of wisdom, understanding, knowledge and fear of Heaven will come upon him from On High to guide him along the straight path and keep him from straying from the ways of our holy Torah. If only our deeds were pure enough to merit the understanding of earlier generations, then our comprehension would be complete and we would attain whatever we desired.

Come see what is written in the holy works of the pious Rabbi Chaim Vital, z"l (Sha'ar HaGilgulim, Introduction 38, 51a). He writes: I consulted with my soul regarding the comprehension that I sought and it answered me that I must fast in sackcloth and ashes for forty days straight. Afterwards I would have to fast every Monday and Thursday for two and a half years. Then at last I would achieve total comprehension without any interference from the Sitrah Acharah. My soul also said to me that after I had conducted myself with sackcloth and ashes and fasting for an entire month I would begin comprehending things, provided that no trace of frivolity ever escaped my lips, Heaven forbid. Moreover, I must conduct myself with the utmost humility and lowliness. Then after three days straight of fasting in sackcloth and ashes I would merit

Divine inspiration and after two and a half years I would attain tremendous comprehension.

The reason my soul insisted on two and a half years was that in my youth I had sat for two and half years with out applying myself diligently to the study of Torah, nor was I meticulous about my deeds. Therefore, it was necessary for me to spend two and a half years in repentance. It was also my custom to spend the Monday, Thursday and Monday fasts and the nights that followed in sackcloth and ashes and weeping. I would lie upon the earth or upon ashes dressed in sackcloth with a rock beneath my head. And I would contemplate the Divine name spelled out in expanded form so that together with the addition of one, corresponding to the name as a whole, the numerical value is equal to that of the word "rock" — אבן — even (= 53). Or else I would contemplate the Divine name in a different expansion so that it equaled the value of the word "rock" even without the additional one for the word as a whole.

The most important thing was to behave with great humility and to avoid anger and petulance. The Ari, z"l, warned me to observe scrupulously all that my soul had told me. For undoubtedly in the course of the specified period I would encounter hindrances to distract me from the course of repentance outlined above. I would also find it difficult to bear the yoke of my self-imposed afflictions. However, the choice was mine and I would have to see that I overcame these obstacles with Heaven's help. A few days later on a Thursday the Ari said to me that I would experience with my own eyes that very week the embrace of a certain spirit of holiness and purity. This would be a sign that Heaven was assisting me by dispatching this spirit of holiness to keep me from slackening from the course of repentance and to imbue me with strength and courage to attain a high level of comprehension. He also informed me that I would attain Divine inspiration, as indeed was the case. My teacher the Ari, z"l, told me that I had merited this because I possessed such a great longing for new insights into the Torah. It was because of this that my soul assisted me. The Ari then assured me that another soul, one of the souls of the righteous, would soon be engendered within me through the principle called "conception." This soul would aid me in increasing my awe.

The main way to merit comprehension of Hashem's Torah was through the two attributes of humility and awe, as expressed through restriction of one's speech to the absolutely necessary. Thus we find regarding the pious man who appeared to his wife in a dream after his death. When she saw that all the hairs of his head and beard were glowing like a great torch she inquired, "Through what did you merit such tremendous illumination?" He replied, "Although I was pious, I would not have merited such great illumination were in not for my practice of restricting all speech unrelated to Torah and awe to a minimum. The Holy One Blessed is He took note of this and rewarded me for restraining my speech. For the Holy One Himself watches over those who minimize their discussion of mundane matters and who desire nothing other than to cling to the awe of Hashem."

It is a sign on behalf of all who pursue the way of awe that through this they receive special protection from the Creator to keep them from stumbling in iniquity, Heaven forbid. Thus, it is written, "No wrong will befall the righteous" (Mishlei 12:21). Even when he sleeps the Holy One Blessed is, He protects him from all mishap.

This is illustrated by another incident involving a pious man. One time one of the cohorts of Lilis appeared to him in a dream in the guise of his wife in order to lure him into wasting seed. But just as the vision was beginning, he heard the sound of a fist pounding on his window as if someone had come along and was banging upon it forcefully. This continued until he awoke. Then the pious man recognized the lovingkindness of the Creator, may He be blessed, who had not ceased bestowing His kindness upon him. For He had saved him from the sin of wasting seed.

From this excerpt one can see that the Holy One Blessed is He desires the qualities of holiness and purity. Therefore, it is advisable for every Jew to arouse himself to repent even in a small way. Afterwards the dictum will apply which states that "One who comes to purify himself, Heaven helps him" (Shabbos 104a). Then he will be able to gird himself like a warrior to repent in a major way. And let him develop the habit of washing his hands so that he may pray and study in a state of purity. Through this he will merit what the Sages have promised, "Purity brings a man to holiness" (Avodah Zarah 20b). And since a person's hands are the primary focus of purification, I will now present a brief chapter dealing with this subject on its own.

Chapter 13

It is written in the Tur, Orach Chayim, that a person must wash his face and hands in the morning to remove the evil spirit that attaches itself to a person when he sleeps. For this reason, a person must also wash his face and hands when he sleeps during the day, and most certainly when sleeping at night.

I have noticed that most people are not meticulous about this matter. When they sleep in the daytime, they do not wash at all and even if they do, they use only a small amount of water. Even in the morning when hand-washing is certainly obligatory they use only a small amount of water that is insufficient for a single hand, yet with this they wash both their hands and face. These people believe that they are purifying themselves by washing in this manner, but in fact they are only adding to the impurity of their hands and face. For the Sages have taught in numerous places in the Gemara (Sotah 4b; Yadayim 2:3) that water itself is very susceptible to defilement. Therefore, when one washes in the morning and also after sleeping in the daytime, one must first pour three times one According to most authorities only the washing of the hands is to remove the malignant spirit resting upon them. Concerning many points in this chapter opinions vary and guidance should be sought as to how to conduct oneself. on the right hand to remove the impurity that settled upon it during sleep, then a fourth time to remove the defiled water remaining on the hand. Afterwards one must pour three times on the left hand to remove the spirit of impurity resting upon that hand and a fourth time to remove the remaining water. Finally, one must wash one's face and rinse one's mouth in whatever way one chooses.

I have noticed, however, that many ignorant people wash the first hand only once and then immediately wash the other one while the spirit of defilement is still upon it. In this manner they only increase the defilement of their hands. Then they wash their faces, defiling them as well. Finally, they take some water and wipe out their mouths, defiling their mouths, too, by contact with their hands. Then after they have added defilement to defilement, they recite the blessing over the washing of the hands, thereby reciting a blessing in vain. And for the rest of the day they go about with the spirit of impurity still resting upon them.

Therefore, anyone for whom the fear of Heaven is close to his heart should conduct himself as the Sages have ordained. Let him pick up the vessel in his right hand and pass it with the water into his left hand. Then let him pour with his left hand upon his right three times to begin with, each time a volume of a revi'is. 2 Opinions range from 86 to 150 cc. Then let him pour a fourth time to rinse the defiled water from his right hand. Next, he should pass the vessel into his right hand and pour with his right hand upon his left hand four times. Only after he has done this should he wash his face and mouth. Let him conduct himself in this manner after sleeping in the daytime as well so that the spirit of purity settles upon him.

As for the hand washing prior to eating, one must first wash the left hand and then the right. There is a great esoteric principle behind this, as is explained in the writings of the Ari, z"l. 3 This view is not found in our editions of the Ari's writings but it is mentioned in other works.

Along the way I would like to bring to the attention of the public some important points regarding the hand-washing after the meal. I have observed that the general populace has become lax about this mitzvah, by which they incur mortal guilt for transgressing the words of our Sages. For the importance of this mitzvah is indicated clearly in a passage in [the Gemara] Eruvin (17b): Abaye said: All who go out to fight in an obligatory war, as well as those engaged in the performance of a mitzvah are exempt from washing the hands. Concerning what was this said? Concerning the first waters (i.e., the hand-washing preceding the meal), but the last waters (the hand-washing following the meal) is obligatory.

If even those engaged in battle or in the performance of mitzvos, who are exempt from other mitzvos, are obligated in the hand-washing after the meal, those who are not thus engaged are certainly obligated. According to the Zohar and other Kabbalistic works there is a deep esoteric reason why the hand-washing after the meal is more obligatory than the one before the meal, as will be explained in a later chapter (Ch. 27).

We find in a passage in Shabbos (62b) that Rav Ashi said, "I washed with my hands full of water and I was granted my hands full of goodness." In other words, because Rav Ashi used to pour a full vessel of water over his hands whenever he washed, both before and after the meal, the Holy One Blessed is He repaid him by filling his house with the goodness of wealth, for Rav Ashi was a very wealthy man. This is because when a man dines at home with his family numerous harmful spirits would also like to partake of the meal. This is why, for example, earlier generations were careful not to drink even numbers of cups, lest they be endangered by a certain category of harmful spirit. Similarly, the Sages instituted the washing after the meal to remove the foulness from one's hands [so that these spirits, which love filth, will not settle upon them].

Our teacher Rabbi Yeshayahu Segal (the Shlah) writes that when one washes after the meal one must wash specifically into a basin and not upon the ground. This is because the water from this washing is the portion of the Sitrah Acharah and should therefore be presented to it in a dignified manner. Through this the harmful spirits will be prevented from causing him any harm.

One must also be sure to wash and purify one's hands when going to the synagogue. This also requires a revi'is of water. Whoever is meticulous about the various hand-washings mentioned here will attain purity and holiness. And as the Sages tell us, holiness leads to Divine inspiration (Avodah Zarah 20b), and Divine inspiration leads to the coming of the prophet Eliyahu and the revival of the dead, Amein.

Chapter 14

It is written, "Do not turn towards the obstinacy of this people and its wickedness and its sinfulness" (Devarim 9:27). This is explained in the Zohar in Parashas Kedoshim (83b): Come and see.

Kav HaYashar

When a man performs a mitzvah, it ascends and stands before the Holy One Blessed is He and proclaims, "So-and-so made me." And the Holy One Blessed is He appoints it to remain before Him so that He will lay His eyes upon it the entire day and bestow goodness upon that person on account of it. And if a person transgresses the Torah that transgression ascends before the Holy One Blessed is He and says, "So-and-so made me." And the Holy One Blessed is He appoints it to remain before Him so that He will lay His eyes upon it and remove the person from the world. This is the meaning of the verse, "And Hashem saw and reviled" (Devarim 32:19). "And He saw" — the transgression standing before Him. If the person repented it is written concerning him, "Hashem has also removed your sin; you will not die" (II Shmuel:12:13). That is, He removes the transgression from before Him so that He will no longer look upon it. This is the meaning of the verse, "Do not turn towards the obstinacy of this people and its wickedness and its sinfulness."

Sometimes a person sits at home in peace and tranquility, feeling secure, happy and lighthearted. Meanwhile, he is totally unaware of the effect that his transgression is having On High. It stands there in Heaven declaring, "I am the product of So-and-so!" provoking against him a sudden outpouring of a bitter judgment and a harsh decree, may Heaven spare us. Eventually he regrets his deed but by then it is too late since the decree has already been issued. This is especially the case with regard to interpersonal crimes, such as theft, fraud and the like, because the guardian angel of the victim protests on his behalf in the Heavenly court.

Come and see what is written in the Zohar (ibid. 85a) regarding one who withholds the wages of a worker and does not pay him. His punishment is particularly great because a worker puts his very soul into his labor and his craft, therefore when his employer withholds his wages it is as if he is holding captive the soul of the worker as well as the souls of his entire household. Every breath that comes out of the worker's mouth as he engages in his craft — for it is usual for a worker to breathe heavily while he works — ascends before the Holy One Blessed is He. That night the souls of the worker and the members of his household, who are dependent upon those breaths, ascend before the Holy One Blessed is He. Hashem then sees that those breaths were not remunerated for their efforts. In consequence, even if much blessing and success had been decreed for the employer, it is all taken away from him. Moreover, his own soul is no longer allowed to ascend On High each night, all because he withheld from his worker his wages. This iniquity also causes the employer's life to be shortened, Heaven spare us.

For this reason, Rav Hamnuna the Elder was accustomed to pay his workers their wages the moment they finished their tasks, saying to them, "Take back your soul that you deposited with me." Even if the worker said to him, "Let it remain in your safekeeping," he would refuse, saying, "It is not fitting that you should deposit even your body in my care, let alone your soul. This deposit should only be left in the care of the Holy One Blessed is He, as it is written, 'Into Your hand I commit my spirit' (Tehillim 31:6)."

This should serve as a stern warning to people. If one hears one's worker weeping over his labors, even if he is not Jewish — if he goes after his employer seeking the wages of his toil but the latter closes his ears, refusing to listen and telling him to come back another time — there can be no greater desecration of the name of Heaven than this. His punishment will be swift in coming and his property will be irretrievably lost. Even if currently he enjoys a generous income, prosperity and success, it will not remain with him. Ultimately, he will undoubtedly be impoverished and no one will take pity upon him. Many other afflictions are also brought about by this sin. Therefore, one must be extremely careful not to stumble in the sin of withholding a worker's wages.

Let us now return to the subject with which we began. Whenever a person performs a mitzvah an angel is formed from it which pleads continually on his behalf. Thus, the Sages teach in Midrash Rabbah, Parshas Vayikra (32:6), "If a person did a single mitzvah, he is granted a single angel to protect him. If he did two mitzvos he is granted two angels. As it is written, 'For He will appoint His angels on your behalf' (Tehillim 91:11)." The expression "he is granted" indicates that from the mitzvos that the person performed these angels are fashioned to protect him from harm. Come and see an incident illustrating this principle. A certain pious man lived in a small village in which there were no books to be found with the exception of a single volume of the tractate Chagigah. All his life the pious man poured over this text. He lived to a ripe old age and then just before his death the tractate Chagigah appeared to him in the form of a woman. After his death this form went before him and brought him into Gan Eden.

The converse is also true, Heaven forbid. If a person commits a single transgression one accuser is created. If he commits two transgressions two accusers are created. Then, after he dies, those transgressions take on the form of a woman and lead him to Gehinnom. Thus, the Torah tells us that Yosef refused to listen to Potiphar's wife "to lie with her, to be with her" (Bereishis 39:8-10). The Sages explain, "'To lie with her' — in this world; 'to be with her' — in the World to Come" (Sotah 3b).

I once read an explanation of this: When a man commits adultery, a malignant spirit is created in the form of the woman with whom he strayed. Then, when his time comes to leave this world, she wraps herself around him and drags him down to Gehinnom. It seems to me that this is what the Sages were alluding to when they said (Sanhedrin 100a), "In the future the Holy One Blessed is He will bestow upon every righteous person three hundred and ten worlds. As it is written, 'To cause those who love Me to inherit substance (yeish, the numerical value of which is 310)' (Mishlei 8:21)." I have heard this passage explained as follows: As we have already mentioned, when a man does a single mitzvah a single angel is created. The Sages tell us (Chullin 91b) that each angel is two thousand parsaos across (1 parsah = 2.80 mile.), as it is written, "And its body was like [the Sea of] Tarsus" (Daniel 10:6). According to tradition this sea was two thousand parsaos wide. Now altogether there are 613 Torah precepts and seven rabbinical enactments, totaling 620, the numerical value of the word keser — "crown." Therefore, when the Jewish people keep the entire Torah, including the rabbinical injunctions, they acquire 620 angels.

Now, in this world Israel has the legal status of an almanah — a "widow." Thus, the verse in Eichah (1:1) reads, "O how does she sit in solitude! The city that was teeming with people has become like an almanah." This word is derived from a denomination of currency called a manah (= 100 zuz), which is the amount that is guaranteed to a widow in her marriage contract when she remarries. In the future, however, Israel will again have the status of a virgin bride, as it is written, "Arise O virgin of Israel" (Amos 5:2). A virgin bride is guaranteed a base sum of 200 zuz, but Israel will receive on top of this an addition of a third (reckoned from the "outside," so that the addition comprises a third of the total). Now, the Sages tell us in Midrash Bereishis Rabbah (68:12) that three angels comprise an entire "world," since each angel is 2000 parsaos wide and a "world" is only 6000 parsaos in diameter. Therefore 600 angels equal 200 worlds. The additional 20 angels comprise another six and two-thirds worlds. If one adds a third (from the "outside") to the 200 it comes to 300. Then if one adds a third to the 6 worlds it comes to 9. Finally, if one adds a third to the remaining two-thirds it comes to a single world, for a total of 310 worlds. May it be Hashem's will that we merit this speedily in our days, Amein.

Chapter 15

Peace is such a valuable commodity that the Sages comment in Midrash Bamidbar Rabbah (11:7) that no vessel is more capable of holding blessing than peace. They note that for this reason the priestly blessing ends with the words, "And He will grant you peace" (Bamidbar 6:26). Similarly, we are told that the Holy One Himself, "makes peace On High" (Iyov 25:2), that is, among the angels. And if peace is needed among the angels, who have no evil inclination and who are free of jealousy and hatred, how much more is it needed between man and his neighbor, between the minority and majority, whom the Satan is perpetually goading into discord and quarreling.

The cause of all this is baseless hatred, which the Sages have said outweighs the sins of idolatry, sexual immorality and bloodshed (Yoma 9b). Baseless hatred is aroused by the voice and by the words that come from a person's mouth, in particular from a mouth that is accustomed to curse people. Then even a minor disagreement with a colleague will immediately fill him with wrath and indignation and cause his curses to burn like coals. What he does not realize is that he is in fact endangering his own soul and the souls of his family members and bringing great evil upon himself. For it is stated explicitly in the Zohar (Parashas Kedoshim 85a) that every curse that leaves a person's mouth goes and floats about the world until it links up with an evil spirit, Heaven spare us. Then it descends into the great chasm where the destructive spirits dwell, always prepared to bring suffering upon someone. They stand there watching for an opportune moment when the astrological fortune of the habitual imprecator takes a turn for the worse. Then they immediately call down upon him evil decrees, Heaven spare us, causing injury to his property or his person or to the members of his household. We have already mentioned in the third chapter that if a person is accustomed to uttering curses it is a sign that his soul does not derive from a holy source but from the primordial snake, which is the source of the Sitrah Acharah. Such a person has cause, therefore, to be concerned lest he be beset by many afflictions. On the other hand, if a person guards his mouth, not allowing it to utter curses but accustoming himself to uttering blessings instead, he can be certain that his soul emanates from a very holy source and that he is worthy of the World to Come.

Similarly, if a person's mouth is accustomed to bearing evil tidings, Heaven forbid, and he enjoys speaking derogatorily of others, it is a very deplorable trait. Moreover, his prayers go unheard, being unable to pass through the holy partition. But if he is accustomed to bearing good tidings [and relating good news he is referred to as a "holy mouth." This is especially true of one who has the merit of delivering good news] to a Torah scholar. For this he is immediately granted a goodly portion in Gan Eden. The proof to this is the case of Serach bas Asher who informed Yaakov that Yosef was still alive, on account of which she merited entering Gan Eden while she was alive (Derech Eretz Zuta, Ch. 1).

The most effective way to avoid developing the habit of cursing others is to recall that there are times when a curse reverts back upon the one who utters it, may Heaven spare us. And when a person causes himself to be cursed through cursing his fellow undeservedly, so that what he decreed upon his fellow was decreed upon him instead, there is no remedy for it. For it is as if he issued the decree upon himself. The main cause of all this is the habit of quarreling and fighting, as a result of which even minor disagreements turn into major altercations. Thus, the Sages have said, "A quarrel is like a river flooding its banks, once a breach opens up it will open further" (Sanhedrin 7a).

Therefore, a person should distance himself from quarrels and strife, which will save him from cursing as well. And let him honor his fellows, especially those who are greater than him. In particular let him honor his Torah mentor. An epistle sent by the holy community of Eretz Yisroel to the holy community of Babylon and the Diaspora illustrates well how a person should conduct himself: Listen, we would like to inform your holy community of a praiseworthy custom among our holy community in Eretz Yisroel, namely that you will not find in our community any fighting or quarreling. And even if there should arise on occasion a disagreement that might lead to a quarrel, there are among us saintly individuals who immediately arouse themselves regarding every matter of holiness and intervene to prevent the quarrel from spreading. Even if it is a minor issue, they immediately make peace between the two sides, who then return to a spirit of brotherhood and friendship so that peace and tranquility are restored to our camp as before. Afterwards the parties embrace one another and each man forgives his fellow. If one party is younger than the other, the younger party asks forgiveness and his fellow immediately embraces and kisses and forgives him. And if someone detracts from the honor of his Torah mentor, Heaven forbid, he accepts upon himself a ban of excommunication, casting himself forcefully to the ground and removing his shoes and sitting upon the earth. Then when his rabbis behold his remorse and his weeping he does not allow him to remaining seated on the earth for longer than the time it takes to roast an egg. After which he gives him permission to get up from the ground, saying, "Rise!" And when the disciple has risen, he falls at his master's feet and asks for release from the ban and for forgiveness. His master then pronounces three times, "You are released," and adds, "There is no longer any interdiction or ban of excommunication; your iniquity has passed and your sin is atoned for."

Let me describe for you the great humility that reigns among us. The illustrious Rabbi Menachem son of the illustrious Rabbi Avraham Galanti, z"l, related to me this incident: It happened one time that his father was carrying a sack of flour on his shoulder from the market when he was approached from behind by our great teacher the illustrious Rabbi Shlomo Sagig, z"l. The latter grabbed the sack from the shoulder of Rabbi Avraham Galanti and swore by his life that no one would carry this sack to the house of Rabbi Avraham other than himself, explaining that he, Rabbi Shlomo, was younger and stronger than Rabbi Avraham. Rabbi Avraham pleaded with him not to do this, for Rabbi Shlomo was greater than he was in Torah and wealth. But Rabbi Shlomo would not listen. Instead he bore the sack himself all the way to the home of the elderly Rabbi Avraham.

On another occasion our teacher the pious Rabbi Avraham Galanti was on his way back from the village of Ein Zeisim where he had purchased a jug and filled it with water from a particularly famous well nearby. Along the way he encountered the pious Rabbi Masud, who said to him, "Rabbi, give me some water for I am thirsty." But when Rabbi Avraham lowered his shoulder to pour him a drink Rabbi Masud immediately took the jug from his shoulder and swore that he would carry it to Rabbi Avraham's house. He also made an oath that he would not give in to pleading. So, too, when any of the other members of the community would see Rabbi Avraham from a distance of thirty cubits they would stand up for him. Then when he approached them they would kiss his hands, saying, "If only we could be a spread beneath your feet in the World to Come!" For he was tremendously pious and humble, admonishing us continually to be sure that peace, friendship and brotherly love reigned among us. May his merit stand by us and by all Israel, Amein.

Chapter 16

It is written in Sodei HaRazim (by the author of the Roke'ach): Regarding all the transgressions in the Torah, if a person commits them in private, the prophet Eliyahu will not reveal them. But if someone violates a ban (cheirem) then he does announce it and reveal it. For it is written, "I am going to send you Eliyahu the prophet, etc." (Malachi 3:23). And it is written immediately afterwards, "And I will strike the land [with] a ban."

The idea is this: Although everything that happens is open and evident to Hashem, may He be blessed, nevertheless, a violation is not made public until Eliyahu comes along and proclaims it in the midst of a gathering of Israel. Then the violator's shame and disgrace will be very great, for violating a ban is akin to violating the five books of the Torah and the prophets as well (Tanchuma, Vayeishev 2). For this reason, the numerical value of the concluding words of the Torah is equal to the word cherem [חרם].
4 Bereishis ends with the word beMitzrayim, which begins with the letter beis and ends with the letter mem for a total of 42. Shemos ends with the word mas'eihem, which also begins and ends with a mem for a total of 80. Vayikra ends with the word Sinai, which begins with a samech and ends with a yud for a total of 70. Bamidbar ends with the word Yereicho, which begins with a yud and ends with a vav for a total of 16. Devarim ends with the world Yisroel, which begins with a yud and ends with a lamed for a total of 40. 42 + 80 + 70 + 16 + 40 = 248 = cherem. Moreover, the Prophets also conclude with this word (see the final verse of Malachi cited above). Clearly, then, whoever violates a ban will not escape punishment and terrible afflictions. The sentence that is pronounced upon him will befall him with wrath and cruelty and the house in which the violation occurred will ultimately be destroyed and left desolate, Heaven spare us.

The main factor leading to this sin is the prior violation of the prohibition against coveting another's wealth or property. Then one transgression leads to another. Coveting leads to actually taking his money or belongings and violating the prohibition against theft. Afterwards the culprit violates the ban as well, finding rationalizations for not returning the stolen goods in his possession. But all these excuses are merely thorns and brambles causing him to stumble. Therefore, the wise person with eyes in his head will avoid causing harm to himself, Heaven forbid. For when the evil has already befallen him, he will surely regret his deeds but by then it will be too late.

See what is written in the Zohar (Zohar Chadash 17a): Rabbi Aba said: How important it is for a person to introspect and examine his deeds every day. Rabbi Yitzchak taught: Four winds blow every day from the four directions of the world: The East Wind — This wind generally holds sway and blows from the morning until midday, bringing with it a storehouse of desire, for there is a storehouse above the gates of the East that is called "desire." It has three thousand and seventy-five winds of healing for the world. Rabbi Yochanan ben Zakkai said: A certain angel named Micha'el is appointed over the wind that comes from the east from the morning until midday. Micha'el is appointed over the eastern side along with his flag. Rabbi Yochanan ben Zakkai also said: This is Micha'el, as it is written, "Behold My angel will go before you, etc." (Shemos 32:34). The word for "My angel" (מלאכי) is comprised of the same letters as the name "Micha'el" (מיכאל). It was taught: When the eastern wind is stirred up to go forth over the world if a person traveling along the road will concentrate on our saying that Micha'el is the prince of lovingkindness, the Holy One Blessed is He will arouse him and all the blessings uttered by the person's mouth at that moment will be fulfilled. Moreover, he will be happy the entire day.

The West Wind — This wind blows for most of the year from midday until nightfall. It brings with it a storehouse with four hundred and sixty-five winds that cause the herbs, the trees and the harvest to prosper. It was taught: A certain angel named Refa'el is appointed over the western side. Rabbi Yose ben Pazi said: If this is so it raises a difficulty. For we have learned: "The angel appointed over healing is named Refa'el." Yet you say that healing comes from the East and Micha'el is the angel appointed over the East, as mentioned above! Come and hear: Rabbi Yochanan said, All that the Holy One Blessed is He does to thwart human beings is intended to instill in them awe and trembling for the fear and service of Hashem. Thus, He wounds and heals, strikes dead and revives so that they will not direct their hearts towards any angel or prince. For the same reason He varies the seasons, so that people will not say, "Angel So-and-so did this for me." It is to demonstrate that everything is in His hands. For this reason, too, He varies the winds, until a person is prompted to pray to the Holy One Blessed is, He and to repent completely. Then the Holy One Blessed is He commands healing to settle upon him and the angel appointed over healing does what he has been commanded by the will of his Master.

The South Wind — This wind generally blows from the beginning of the night until midnight, bringing with it from the storehouse of the sun two hundred and seventy-five winds to fertilize and warm the earth so that the cold will not dominate. The angel appointed over it is named Uri'el. He is appointed over his watch on the southern side, over that wind. That wind is very hard on people with severe illnesses. It was taught: That is the primary time of judgment when the wicked in Gehinnom are judged with fire, while all the world lie in sleep and there is no one to pray for them.

The North Wind — This wind blows from midnight until the morning. It was taught: Three hundred thousand storm and tempest winds come with it. It interferes with everything. Yet for the infirm it is good, for these winds are cool and the feverish find relief in this coolness. It was taught: Rabbi Shimon ben Yochai said: At that time the Holy One Blessed is He leaves the many worlds to delight with the righteous in Gan Eden. And a herald's voice proclaims, "Awake, O North, and come, O South" (Shir HaShirim 4:16) and cause the spices of Gan Eden to waft. For it is taught: At the time that the north wind blows at midnight and the Holy One Blessed is He enters Gan Eden, all the spices and all the trees of Gan Eden give forth their fragrance and sing before Him, as it is written, "Then the trees of the forest will exult before Hashem" (I Divrei HaYamim 16:33). And all the angels of Heaven and all the firmaments and the Holy Creatures and the Ofanim shudder and open their mouths in exultation and praise to the One who spoke and the world came into being. Until the Holy One Blessed is He enters Gan Eden together with the righteous, which takes place at midnight.

Rav Yehudah said in the name of Rav: Whoever has a holy soul hears the sound of the rooster crowing at midnight. For then a spark of fire goes out from between the wheels of the Creatures over the entire world, reaching beneath the rooster's wings so that at that moment the rooster beats his wings together in fear and proclaims, "It is midnight!" Then, whoever has good sense and awakens and arises from his sleep to engage in Torah study — his voice goes forth and is heard in Gan Eden and the Holy One listens together

Kav HaYashar

with the righteous. The righteous ask, "Who is this man?" And the Master of the Universe answers, "This is So-and-so son of So-and-so studying Torah with his holy soul. Listen, all of you, for this sound is more pleasant to me than all the songs and praises that are recited On High!"

O mortal man! See and reflect and seek out every possibility for increasing your Torah and good deeds to bring pleasure to the Holy One Blessed is He, for to this end where you created. And recall that we, His people Israel, are His treasured congregation. Hashem chose us from among the seventy nations to draw us close to Him. At each and every moment He watches over us, taking note of all of one's deeds to see whether they are bad or good and then summoning corresponding benevolent and malignant forces. The benevolent forces are the holy angels. They receive a person's soul with love and joy and show him the entrances of Gan Eden. The malignant forces are the cruel and destructive injurious spirits, which snatch a person's soul and subject it to terrible and bitter afflictions, as is related in Midrash HaNe'elam, Parshas Noach (Zohar Chadash 27a):

Rabbi Yehudah said: There are seven categories of ministering angels at the gates that are called "the Gates of Righteousness." It was over these that Dovid HaMelech claimed, "Open for me the Gates of Righteousness! I will enter them and give thanks to God. This is the Gate of Hashem; the righteous shall enter it" (Tehillim 118:19-21). And there are seven gates through which the souls of the righteous enter into Gan Eden until they reach a place that is commensurate with their station. At every gate there are guards. Through the first gate the soul enters into the Cave of Machpelah (the Tomb of the Patriarchs), which is near Gan Eden. Adam HaRishon stands guard over it. If the soul merits, Adam HaRishon proclaims, "Make way for the pious one! Come in peace!" Then the soul exits the first gate and enters the second gate of Gan Eden. There the cherubim and the flame of the revolving sword stand guard.

If the soul is not entirely meritorious it receives punishment there to refine it and remove its dross and impurities through the judgments it is subjected to by the flame of the revolving sword. If it merits exiting this gate in peace it is given a note indicating that it may enter Gan Eden. When it reaches Gan Eden, there is a pillar comprised of cloud and light mixed together, surrounded by smoke. And there is an embedded pillar extending from down below upwards until the Gate of the Heavenly Jerusalem, which is aligned with the earthly Jerusalem. If the soul merits, and it is sufficient that it be granted a dwelling place here in which to receive its reward and not ascend further, then it remains there delighting in the goodness that is poured down to it from above. This Gan Eden radiates with light from above, for Rabbi Yose has said: I have seen Gan Eden and it is aligned with the curtain of the Holy of Holies. There you will find the awesome Heavenly Ice. Here the soul delights in the splendor of the Divine Presence but does not derive nourishment from it. If the soul merits ascending further, it ascends by that pillar until it arrives at and enters the third entrance. This is the one called Zevul ("Dwelling-place"). It is watched over by many guards. They open it and the soul enters the gate and praises the Holy One Blessed is He in the Heavenly Beis HaMikdash. Then the great prince Micha'el, High Priest of God the Highest, offers the soul as a sacrifice.

Rabbi Chiya said: This offering is not like others. Rather it is like a man offering a present to the king. Micha'el elevates the soul until the fourth, fifth and sixth entrances, proclaiming, "Master of the Universe! Fortunate are Your children, the children of Your beloved ones, Avraham, Yitzchak and Yaakov and fortunate is the soul that merits this!" Afterwards the soul is elevated to the seventh gate, the one known as Aravos, where the secrets of life are found. Every soul that merits entering the seventh gate is immediately transformed into a ministering angel. But if a person violates a ban his soul does not merit entering even the third gate, even after it has been subjected to afflictions and punishments. For the Sages have said (Tana Devei Eliyahu Rabbah, Ch. 29): If a person is under a ban down below [in this world] for a single day, On High he is under a ban for thirty days. And if he is under a ban down below for thirty days, On High he is under a ban for a year. And if he is under a ban down below for a year, On High he is under a ban forever and there is no cure for his wound. I have observed that when common people are placed under a ban by the court or if they are summoned to court to comply with a directive or to give testimony on pain of a ban, they take the matter lightly as if excommunication were a laughing matter. They do not realize that violating a ban is more serious than swearing in vain or even falsely. Heaven's wrath will be stored up against them forever and the prophet Eliyahu will make their shame known in public!

Therefore, let a person not take lightly any ban made by the community or even by ten laymen, and certainly let him be wary of violating a ban proclaimed by Torah scholars. Then all will be well with him.

Chapter 17

There are eleven sources of defilement:
1. contact with the dead;
2. contact with the carcasses of certain small creatures;
3. contact with the carcasses of larger animals;
4. contact with semen;
5. contact with the purification water used after contact with the dead;
6. involvement in the preparation of the ashes of the red cow;
7. tumas zav (a certain abnormal emission in a male);
8. tumas zavah (a certain abnormal flow of blood in a woman);
9. menstruation;
10. childbirth;
11. tzara'as (a certain spiritually-induced skin disease). These eleven sources of defilement hint at the various worlds of defilement inhabited by the chitzonim (a type of malignant spirit), who derive their sustenance from the eleven emanations (sefiros) of defilement. Corresponding to the eleven emanations are the eleven ingredients of the incense used in the Temple service, the function of which was to weaken the power of the emanations of defilement. It follows that if a person takes precautions to avoid these forms of defilement, he distances himself from the influence of the chitzonim at the same time. But if he is drawn towards these sources of defilement, he envelops himself with and roots himself in the sources of impurity.

Kav HaYashar

One must appreciate the great power of menstrual defilement. There are one thousand four hundred and five types of chitzonim that dwell on the portion of a woman's fingernail that grows during the time of menstruation! That is why the Holy One Blessed is He commanded that she cut her fingernails at the time of her purification. And let her be careful not to cast them in a place where people walk, for the one who treads upon them, even with shoes on, may come to harm, Heaven forbid. Sorcerers use these nails in their sorcery and female sorcerers try to conduct their craft specifically during menstruation because that is when their spells have the best chance of succeeding. Therefore, a man should avoid interacting with his menstruating wife to the greatest extent possible, even through speech and certainly through sight. Let him restrict himself to the absolutely necessary and adopt every precaution to avoid eating together with her from the same bowl. Other members of the household should also avoid eating with the menstruating woman, for traces of her saliva may remain on the spoon and then be introduced into the bowl, thereby exposing them to danger.

It once happened that a certain fellow saw in his dream that his feet were soiled with excrement. When he awoke the following morning, he was very disturbed, for he knew that he had not experienced this dream in vain. So he went and related the dream to the Ari, z"l, who responded, "Your bed is too close to that of your menstruating wife. In the course of the night while you were asleep your uppermost blanket came into contact with your wife's bed." Upon hearing this the man immediately went home and corrected the matter, separating the two beds properly. Afterwards the Ari then mentioned to his disciples that as a rule dreams are sent as warning of the transgressions that a person is guilty of.

Therefore, let a man adopt every precautionary measure to distance himself from his wife while she is menstruating. And let him also instruct his sons from early childhood to avoid coming into contact with a menstruating woman. If a man is careful to avoid contact with his wife until she is purified, he should know that during that time the Shechinah itself becomes his partner, as is related in the Zohar (Bereishis 50a). After his wife is purified let him join with her modestly, as the Zohar admonishes in Parashas Vayishlach

(165b): "Let him behave with modesty in marital relations out of deference to the two angels on his right and on his left, the good inclination and the evil inclination." Elsewhere it is written in the Zohar (ibid. 176a): "Wherever marital relations [are performed for the sake] of a mitzvah are to be found, the Shechinah dwells there," provided that he sanctifies himself at that time. And let him reflect that Hashem created the eighteen vertebrae of the spine, through which seed passes from the brain to the site of the covenant. Corresponding to these eighteen vertebrae our Rabbis instituted the eighteen blessings that we recite three times a day in our prayers. And in every blessing, we mention the Divine name.

Correspondingly, he should contemplate the holiness of the Divine name at that time, as is mentioned in Ra'ya Meheimna (Parashas Kedoshim 126b): Fortunate are the limbs that are sanctified at the time of marital relations, for they are like the logs of a burnt offering, to which the holy fire attaches itself, and then the name of Hashem adheres to them. For this reason, it is written: "With pyres shall you honor Hashem" (Yeshayahu 24:15). Similarly, it is written elsewhere in the Zohar (Parashas Metzora 56a): At the time of marital relations a man should reflect upon the will of his Creator in order that he bring holy children into the world. And in Parashas Kedoshim (84a): When Rabbi Shimon ben Yochai was walking through town with his disciples following after him and he spotted a woman, he would lower his eyes and say to his colleagues, "Do not turn to look, for whoever looks upon a woman in the daytime will have forbidden thoughts at night. And if a man has relations with his wife while engaging in forbidden thoughts it is said of the children thus conceived, 'Do not make for yourself molten gods' (Shemos 34:17). As rule from these come the apostates.

There are several kinds of conduct on the part of the parents that result in epileptic offspring, Heaven spare us. I will mention here just a few of them so that a person will affix them in his heart and then pass on to his children so that they will also observe them: First: It is explicit in the Gemara (Pesachim 112b) and in the Zohar (Introduction to Bereishis 14b) that one who has relations by the light of a lamp will bear epileptic children, Heaven forbid, and even more so by the light of the moon. Second: If a man sees the image of a woman in a dream, even if it is the image of his wife or an unmarried woman, and awakens filled with passion and desire he must not have relations with his wife in the heat of that desire. For if he does so, the child thus conceived will be subject to epileptic attacks whenever the moon is full, Heaven forbid, with no possibility of a cure his entire life. For the image that appeared to him was the female demon known as Na'amah. Thus, the Zohar (Part III 77a) writes: "since it was out of desire for her (i.e., Na'amah) that he had relations, the child will be born from her side ... and so he will be affected at each and every moon." Third: The Zohar warns in Parashas Vayikra (19a) that a woman must be very careful not to nurse her infant for a full hour after marital relations. And even if he cries, let her make every effort to pacify him until at least half an hour has passed. In any event she must not nurse during the first half an hour, Heaven forbid. The reason for this is explained there. Fourth: It is taught in Pesachim (112b) that they must not have relations on a bed upon which a child is lying, for this poses a danger to the fetus thus conceived. The Zohar has amazing things to say about this.

The general rule is that they must conduct themselves with modesty and confine their relations to the time that is designated for this, that is, after midnight when all the members of the household are asleep. And let them be careful not to have relations in the presence of any living creature. Thus, the Gemara relates that Abaye used to chase away the mosquitoes and Rova used to chase away the flies. In Zohar Chadash (15a) it is taught in the name of Rav Huna: "A person must sanctify himself to the name of Heaven at the time of relations, as it is written, 'If Hashem does not build a house, its builders have toiled in vain' (Tehillim 127a)." The idea is this: If their intentions are not for the sake of Heaven, to produce God-fearing and scholarly children, but for the sake of their own pleasure, then their toil is "in vain" because their intentions are for pure vanity. That is, to satisfy the evil inclination and fulfill their alien thoughts of pleasure.

The Zohar continues: Rabbi Yose ben Pazi said: One time I was walking along the road when I came upon the mountain that is near the village of Kardo. There I found people who were happy with their lot and dealt with one another in good faith. And there was neither jealousy nor hatred among them. I arrived on Shabbos eve and saw my host standing to one side praying while his wife stood to another side praying. I asked them, "What is this prayer that you are saying at this hour?" They told me, "Our time for marital relations is every Shabbos night, so we pray to the Holy One Blessed is He that we will be granted a child who will toil in Torah and fear sin….. " I said to them, "May it be Heaven's will that your request be fulfilled, for your deeds are for the sake of Heaven."

Rabbi Yose said: May I behold the Shechinah (a form of oath to the truth his testimony), I came to the same village several years later and saw the child that was born to them. He was now seven years old. I wanted to speak to him but he refused! His father told him, "Go to the man, for he is of great stature." But the child said, "I am afraid to speak with him or even to approach him since I do not know whether he possesses a holy soul or not. For my teacher taught me just today that it is forbidden to speak with or approach anyone who does not have a holy soul." His father said to him, "Heaven forbid! He is a man of great stature and one of the greatest scholars of the generation!" So, the child approached me. But before he had a chance to say anything else to me he said, "I see that you possess a new soul that has only recently entered and was not imbued in you at the time that you entered the world." I replied in astonishment, "That is indeed the case! For when I was a young student toiling in Torah I was imbued with a new soul." Then I asked, "Who is your teacher?" He replied, "Rabbi Alexandrus." "And what did you study today?" He said to me, "This verse, 'The beginning of wisdom is the fear of Hashem; they have good understanding all those who do the commandments' (Tehillim 111:10). Our Rabbis have interpreted: 'Those who do for the sake of Heaven.'" And his teacher revealed to him amazing insights. I said to him, "What is your name?" He answered, "Ahavah" (i.e., "Love"). I said to him, "Master Ahavah, 'I have loved you with an eternal love' (Yirmeyahu 31:2)." I also had the merit of meeting his son, Rabbi Ada the son of Rabbi Ahavah, and related to him all the above.

Therefore, a person must sanctify himself at the time of marital relations so that he will merit sons who are Torah scholars. And let him pray throughout the first forty days: "May it be the will of the Master of the Universe that we merit God-fearing and flawless sons who tremble at the word of Hashem. And may we observe in them the sanctity of the Sages of the Mishnah and Talmud. Amein." In Chapter Eighteen I will explain that all of a person's deeds should be for the sake of Heaven.

Chapter 18

"How many are Your works, Hashem, all of them You have fashioned with wisdom, etc." (Tehillim 104:24). As we mentioned in an earlier chapter (Ch. 8), our Sages instituted that one recites Tehillim Chapter 100 ("A psalm of thanksgiving") every day. This is because a person should really thank Hashem every day and offer up a thanksgiving sacrifice, for the beneficiary of a miracle is often not even aware of what the Holy One Blessed is He has done for him. Therefore, when a person recites this psalm let him have in mind that it should be reckoned as if he offered a thanksgiving offering. For it was the custom of earlier generations that for every event that befell them they would offer praise and thanks, acknowledging immediately that the matter was from Hashem. Thus, he would affix it in his heart so that he would never forget Hashem's providence.

In this vein we find the following episode recorded in the Zohar (Parashas Emor 106b): Rabbi Shimon ben Yochai was walking along the road accompanied by Rabbi Aba and Rabbi Yose when they came upon a water channel. Rabbi Yose tripped and fell into the water channel, soiling his clothing, whereupon he said, "If only this water channel had not been created!" Rabbi Shimon said to him, "It is forbidden to speak in this manner, for it is of service to the world and it is forbidden to speak disparagingly of the servants of the Holy One Blessed is He. For it is written, 'And God saw all that He had made and behold it was very good' (Bereishis 1:31). This includes even snakes, scorpions and mosquitoes, all of which are called 'servants of the King' and 'servants of the world,' although human beings are unaware of it."

While they were still walking, they saw a snake dancing before them. Rabbi Shimon said, "This snake is surely going to perform some miracle. The snake ran on ahead and entangled itself with a certain viper. The nature of the viper is such that if it gazes at a human being or a human being gazes at it, the person immediately dies from the poison of its gaze, Heaven spare us. After the snake entangled itself with the viper, they began striking each another until they both died. When they arrive at that spot and saw the two of them lying dead upon the road Rabbi Shimon recited the verse, "No evil shall befall you, and no plague shall come near your tent" (Tehillim 91:10). He continued, "The Holy One Blessed is He has created every creature to perform an errand. Thus, we must not disparage anything that He has made, for it was created for the sake of its mission. Concerning this was it written, 'Hashem is good to all and His mercies are upon all His works' (Tehillim 145:9)."

It seems to me that this is also the meaning of the verse, "How many are Your works, Hashem, all of them You made them all with wisdom, the earth is filled with Your possessions" (Tehillim 104:24). And it is also written, "All Your works will thank You, Hashem" (Tehillim 145:10). Suppose, then, that Hashem in His mercy and lovingkindness has granted someone a particularly amazing deliverance — from bandits, for instance, or from fire or water or the like, or if he was severely ill and recovered. Surely, he has an obligation to institute some beneficial matter that will serve manifestly in the place of a thanksgiving offering in Hashem's honor.

Come and see what the pious rabbi, our teacher Rabbi Avraham, author of SRibbolei HaLekket testifies about himself in the introduction to his work. He writes: I will retell here the wonders that the Holy One Blessed is He performed for me when I suffered tribulations at the time of my illness. As I lay upon my sickbed, rendered desolate by the tremendous pain, may you be spared, I declared, "I am bereft of my remaining years! My sorrows have increased until my relatives avoid me, for I have become a burden to my household and before my fathers. My innards churn and my heart trembles within me as I recall the length of the journey that lies before me and the meagerness of my provisions."

Those who stood by me to await the expiration of my soul — for they saw that my limbs and flesh had gone cold and that I was in the throes of death — those who stood by me hastened my wife and children and other family members from the room. For they saw upon me the indications of approaching death — as is usual when the soul departs from the body — and my features had already become altered. But Hashem in His mercy, although He afflicted me He did not deliver me to death. This was not in my own merit but in the merit of my holy ancestors. With my own eyes I beheld in a vision a miniature man standing before me holding in his hand a lamp that was on the verge of extinction. But then, before my eyes, it was swiftly rekindled. "Tell me, master," I pleaded, "what are you doing before me with this lamp?" The man replied, "This lamp symbolizes your soul, for the days of your life were already completed. I hinted this to you in this way because the human soul is likened to a lamp. But just as the lamp was swiftly rekindled, so will you swiftly recover. This is what I was showing you with my hints.

"Know also," the man went on, "that at your trial there were accusers and defenders and that your merits were weighed upon a scale. I have come to inform you that the merciful God added to your days, telling the Angel of Death, 'Loosen your hand! For he is still capable of benefiting the multitude.' I have decreed concerning you that on the third day you will get up from this illness." This incident took place three days before the festival of Shavuos and just as the man had predicted, so did it fall out. On the first day of Shavuos I went to the synagogue and became literally like a new man. Immediately I girded my loins like a warrior and arose to my post and began composing a commentary upon the Torah, the Prophets and the Writings. I called my work, Shibbolei HaLekket as a remembrance.

Thus, should every person do. For there is no one for whom miracles have not been performed, especially in these generations in which our troubles increase daily — horrendous wars, the sword, famine, siege, hardship and terrible illnesses. Whenever the Holy One Blessed is He shines a thread of lovingkindness upon someone and saves him from these afflictions, that individual must recall Hashem's kindnesses forever lest he be guilty of ingratitude. Moreover, whenever the Holy One Blessed is He bestows upon someone an outpouring of blessing enabling him to sit at home in peace and tranquility enjoying a reliable income, he must give praise and thanks to the Omnipresent.

Seifer Chareidim admonishes sternly that this is included in the commandment, "And I will relate this day to Hashem your God that I have come to the goodly land, etc." (Devarim 26:3). This, he explains, is a strong warning to anyone who has received goodness and bounty from Hashem, that he must give praise and thanks. And certainly, he must not complain like the misers who cry and complain to the world all day long, no matter how much food and sustenance Hashem grants them, that they lack bread to eat, when in fact their hands are filled with all manner of goodness. Their real goal is simply to keep the poor and needy at bay. Concerning this was it written, "This poor man cried out and Hashem heard" (Tehillim 34:7). The poor man's prayer does not move from its place until a cup of punishment is poured out upon these people and they themselves are rendered destitute. Of course, it is also praiseworthy to fulfill the Sages' teaching (Ta'anis 10b) that one should not display one's wealth ostentatiously before the nations of the world. Thus, Yaakov said to his sons, "Why should you show yourselves?" (Bereishis 42a). This is especially important in these times when, on account of our many sins, the nations have their eyes on Jewish wealth. Therefore, it is a very good idea to conceal one's wealth from them. Nevertheless, showing a pleasant countenance and demeanor of love and good will towards the poor, the destitute and the needy brings pleasure to the Creator. This is especially so of those who bring the honorable poor and needy into their homes and grant them lodgings. Through this they merit many blessings and many a barren woman has been granted children in the merit of feeding and supporting worthy poor and needy people for the sake of Heaven.

The story is also related of a certain elderly gentleman named Rabbi Yechiel, who lived at the time of the expulsion from Spain. At the time of all the edicts and oppressions in that country many Jews fled to Italy, where Rabbi Yechiel resided in a town by the ocean, while they awaited the opportunity to move on to Turkey. The elderly Rabbi Yechiel was an upright and honest man who received everyone, poor or rich, with a pleasant countenance. He would supply them with water and food and escort them along their way. He also made sure that they also had provisions for the journey ahead, spending liberal sums upon the needs of his guests. One day there arrived at his house four elders from among the exiles, all of them great Torah scholars. When they saw Rabbi Yechiel's wealth and splendor and his pure and generous heart and the kindnesses that he performed for the exiles, rich and poor alike, they asked, "What request would you like to make of the Creator?" He answered, "My request is that I merit sons," for he was childless. The four elders said to him, "Rest assured that within the year you will father a son who will be a great scholar. And you shall call him "Avraham," as a remembrance of the kindnesses you performed for the seed of Avraham." As they promised, so was it fulfilled. The son that was born to him grew to become the illustrious Rabbi Avraham of Piza, who reached great heights in Torah and composed many works.

We hear of many similar incidents. This is to inform you that every good and proper deed is engraved and inscribed before the Holy One Blessed is He, to be accredited to the doer's account in this world and the next, provided that he does them for the sake of Heaven. For everything that a person does, whether by deed or word, should be for the sake of Heaven and with heartfelt concentration, especially the utterance of prayers and blessings. Seifer Chassidim (46) relates the story of a man who died a number years before his time. Twelve months after he passed away he appeared to one of his relatives in a dream. The relative inquired, "How do you spend your time in the world that you are in?" He answered, "Every day I am judged for not reciting the blessings over bread and fruit and the Grace After Meals with heartfelt concentration. Meanwhile those appointed over me say to me, 'You ate only for your own enjoyment!'" The relative inquired further, "Have we not been taught that the wicked are punished in Gehinnom for twelve months? More than twelve months have passed since your death, so why are they punishing you further?" The dead man replied, "They are not subjecting me to severe punishment in Gehinnom but to lesser punishment outside of Gehinnom. The appointed ones tell me that it is all for my good so that I will merit entering Gan Eden and enjoying my portion to the fullest."

The general rule is that everything one does is recorded On High and for every deed there is either reward or punishment. Fortunate are those who are declared meritorious by the Heavenly Court!

Chapter 19

"The Torah of Hashem is flawless, restoring the soul" (Tehillim 19:8). Hashem has given permission for every Jew to interpret the holy Scriptures according to his own understanding, "as a hammer shatters rock" (Yirmeyahu 23:29). Therefore, we may interpret the verse as follows: Hashem's Torah is flawless in that it is lacking no "limb" of the six hundred and thirteen commandments. It is incumbent upon a human being to fulfill all six hundred and thirteen, for they correspond to the limbs of his body. Thus it is absolutely essential that he do all those that can be done, not neglecting any of them. As for the rest, he must study the Torah, the statutes and laws pertaining to them. For they are all derived from the benevolent hand of Hashem. In this way one completes the "Torah of Hashem," which is "flawless." But if a person passes from this world without completing his "limbs" through the performance and study of the commandments, then it "restores the soul." That is, the soul must return to earth to be reincarnated in another body that it may fulfill its task and make good its deficiency.

This being so, a person should reflect that it is only fitting and proper that he not be lax in the study of Torah and the fulfillment of those commandments that can be fulfilled. For who knows what the future will bring? While a person is yet on this earth the announcement of his imminent demise is made On High, but he does not hear it and therefore cannot make preparations for himself. Once the announcement has been made in Heaven, the day that his soul must take leave of his body approaches. Then all of a sudden he is made cognizant of the decree through the bodily afflictions and pains that overwhelm him. But what advantage does he have at that point if he has not prepared himself through good works ahead of time?

Kav HaYashar

The Zohar writes (Parashas Vayechi 217b): When the time approaches for a person to depart from this world, it [the time of his departure] is announced, thirty days beforehand, in Gan Eden. It was taught: During these thirty days his soul departs every night and sees its place in the other world, although the person himself is unaware of this. Moreover, during these thirty days he no longer has dominion over his soul as he did previously, as it is written, "A man cannot rule over the spirit, etc." (Koheles 8:8). Rabbi Yehudah said: Once these thirty days begin a man's visage darkens and his form can no longer be seen on earth.

Rabbi Yitzchak was sitting beside Rabbi Yehudah's doorway one day, filled with sadness. Rabbi Yehudah came out and found him sitting there filled with sadness and asked, "Why is this day different from other days?" He replied, "I came to you to request three things: First, that when you speak words of Torah and mention things that I have said, say them in my name in order that my name will be mentioned. Second, see to it that my son Yosef merits Torah. And third, go to my grave every day during the seven days of mourning and pray for me." Rabbi Yehudah said to him, "How do you know [that your time is approaching]?" He answered, "My soul departs from me every night and no longer enlightens me with dreams as formerly. Moreover, when I pray and arrive at the blessing, 'Who hears prayer,' I contemplate my form but I can no longer see it. Therefore, I said to myself that since my image has departed from me so that I can no longer see it, it is clear that the announcement has already been made. For thus is it written, 'Yet in his image a man walks' (Tehillim 39:7). [That is, as long as a man's image is perceivable] his spirit is maintained on account of it. But once it has departed and is no longer seen, [it is proof that his passing is imminent]."

Rabbi Yehudah said to him, "All these things that you have requested, I will do. But I have a request from you, too — that I should not be separated from you and that you will choose a spot for me next to you in the other world, just as I was near to you in this world." Then Rabbi Yehudah wept and said, "Please, let me not be separated from you during these thirty days!" Then they went together to Rabbi Shimon ben Yochai and found him engrossed in Torah study. Rabbi Shimon ben Yochai raised his eyes and saw the Angel of Death leaping and running before Rabbi Yitzchak. Rabbi Shimon ben Yochai stood up, grabbed Rabbi Yitzchak's hand and declared, "I decree that whoever is accustomed to come into my room may enter but whoever is not accustomed to come into my room may not enter." Whereupon Rabbi Yehudah and Rabbi Yitzchak entered but the Angel of Death remained bound outside.

Rabbi Shimon ben Yochai looked and saw that Rabbi Yitzchak's time had not yet come, for his time was not until the eighth hour. Rabbi Shimon ben Yochai sat Rabbi Yitzchak before him and began studying with him. Rabbi Shimon said to his son Rabbi Elazar, "Sit at the entrance and do not speak to anyone that you see. And if someone wishes to come in, pronounce an oath that he may not enter. Rabbi Shimon said to Rabbi Yitzchak, "Have you seen the image of your father today? For we have learned that when a person departs from this world his father and relatives are present with him and he beholds and recognizes them. Then all those who will dwell with him on the same level in the other world gather around and join him. Afterwards they accompany his soul to the place where it is to dwell." Rabbi Yitzchak said to him, "I have not yet seen him."

In the meantime, Rabbi Shimon arose and said, "Master of the Universe, Rabbi Yitzchak is known to us, for he is one of the seven 'eyes' (i.e., one of Rabbi Shimon's seven principle disciples). See that I am holding onto him; grant him to me!" Then a Heavenly voice proclaimed, "The Throne of the Master is upon the wings of Rabbi Shimon. Behold he is granted to you. You shall bring him with you when you come to rest in your place." Rabbi Shimon replied, "So shall it be." In the meantime, Rabbi Elazar saw that the Angel of Death had departed. He said, "The decrees of Heaven do not stand in the place of Rabbi Shimon ben Yochai."

Rabbi Shimon said to his son Rabbi Elazar, "Come and hold Rabbi Yitzchak, for I see that he is afraid. So, Rabbi Elazar entered and held onto Rabbi Yitzchak while Rabbi Shimon turned his face aside and immersed himself in Torah. Rabbi Yitzchak dozed off and beheld his father, who said to him, "Fortunate are you, my son! Happy is your lot in this world and the next. For from among the leaves of the Tree of Life in Gan Eden has come a great tree that is strong in both worlds, that is, Rabbi Shimon ben Yochai, and it holds you in its branches. Happy is your lot, my son!" Rabbi Yitzchak said to him, "What is my status there?"

His father answered, "For three days they were feverishly preparing your bedroom. They opened windows on your behalf so that you would have illumination from all four directions. When I saw your place I rejoiced, saying, "Fortunate is your lot … Up until a moment ago the souls of twelve righteous scholars were preparing to come to you. But while they were setting out a voice went out throughout all the worlds, saying, 'Who are these scholars standing here preparing to meet the soul of Rabbi Yitzchak and to escort it to Gan Eden? Depart and return to your places! For Rabbi Shimon ben Yochai has made a request and it was granted to him." Not only in this was the power of Rabbi Shimon great. Because the granted to him "seventy" — for the seventy adorned places that are mentioned here are his. And each place leads to seventy worlds, and each world leads to seventy messengers (of God), and each messenger leads to seventy lofty crowns. From there, the paths lead to the obscure Ancient One, so that they could view the lofty sweetness, the One who illuminates and delights all beings. As it says, "To behold the pleasantness of Hashem, and to meditate in His Sanctuary." What is the meaning of "to meditate in His Sanctuary"? This is what is written: "In my entire House he is trusted."

Rabbi Yitzchak inquired, "Father, how much more time has been granted to me in this world?" He said, "My son, I do not have permission to reveal that to any man, but at the rejoicing of Rabbi Shimon ben Yochai (i.e., at his departure) you will be the one to set his table …."

In the meantime, Rabbi Yitzchak awoke. He was smiling and his countenance was shining. Rabbi Shimon noticed and looked into Rabbi Yitzchak's face. He asked, "Have you heard anything new?" He said to him, "Most certainly," and he related to him all that he had seen. Then Rabbi Yitzchak prostrated himself before Rabbi Shimon and refused to leave him, but toiled continually in Torah. From that day forward Rabbi Shimon never separated from Rabbi Yitzchak. When Rabbi Yitzchak would enter Rabbi Shimon's presence he would call out, "Hashem, steal me away and be my

Kav HaYashar

guarantor!" (Yeshayahu 38:14). [This was the prayer of King Chizkiyahu at the time of his illness, but Rabbi Yitzchak said it as an expression of praise and thanks to the Holy One Blessed is He, who stole him away from the Angel of Death and delivered him.] The outcome of all this is that when a person's time comes, he must pray that Hashem take him "from peace to peace." (This prayer is mentioned in the Ma'amados for the second day of the week.) Let him have in mind that he should be granted the death of the righteous. For when a righteous man dies, he is met by many other righteous souls that come to escort him to Gan Eden and he wishes them peace. Afterwards as they are escorting his soul three classes of angels also arrive, declaring, "Peace! Peace be upon his resting place!" This is the meaning of the prayer, "Take me from peace to peace."

Chapter 20

It is related in Berachos (26b) that the Patriarchs established the three fixed prayers. The Sages elaborate: Avraham established the morning prayer, and corresponding to this Men of the Great Assembly instituted the blessing Magen Avraham, "shield of Avraham." Yitzchak established the afternoon prayer and corresponding to this the blessing Mechayeh HaMeisim, "Who revives the dead" was instituted. Yaakov established the evening prayer and corresponding to this the blessing HaE-l HaKadosh, "the holy God" was instituted. Thus, all the blessings were called after the names of the Patriarchs since they established them. It follows that every person should be careful to pray at least the Shemoneh Esrei with concentration. Yet on account of the burden of the exile and the pressure that our brothers find themselves in not everyone is learned in the deeper meanings of the prayers. Nevertheless, a person should at least enwrap himself in trembling and awe when he says the words, "God of Avraham, God of Yitzchak and God of Yaakov," for the merit of the Patriarchs is very great. It is their prayers that continue to sustain us in this bitter exile.

It is related in the Zohar (Parashas Vayechi 225b): Rabbi Yehudah said: How thickheaded are the people of the world, for they do not understand matters of the world. For instance, the Holy One Blessed is He stands over them every day at all times yet no one notices! Three times a day a wind enters the Cave of Machpeilah (the Tomb of the Patriarchs) and blows upon the graves of the Patriarchs, compelling their bones to arise ... Then the dew falls and the Patriarchs awaken. It was taught: That wind descends via specific levels, one after the other, until it arrives at the lower Gan Eden. Wafting with the spices of Gan Eden it enters the mouth of the cave, whereupon the Patriarchs and Matriarchs awaken and pray for their children. It is the prophet Eliyahu who washes their hands before they pray. Three times every day they pray for Israel and before each prayer Eliyahu washes their hands.

From this one can see the holiness of the hand-washing before prayer, for it is the task of the prophet Eliyahu to wash the hands of the Patriarchs. Likewise, every individual should see that his hands are washed by upright Jew and not by an evildoer, before he goes to pray.

Now let us return to the topic with which we began, which was the merit of the Patriarchs in his prayers with concentration — his prayers will be cherished by the Holy One Blessed is He. In times of trouble, he should proclaim with heartfelt intent, "Master of the Universe! Remember the covenant of the Patriarchs and Matriarchs and the Tribes!" This presumes, of course, that he himself has not abrogated the covenant of the Patriarchs who walked wholeheartedly before the Holy One Blessed is He. This prayer is very effective when recited by the righteous and wholehearted, but not by a person who has taken the twisted path and did not conduct himself as our holy Patriarchs; but rather conducts himself with arrogance, and jealousy, while seeking ill-gotten gains and immoral pleasures, Heaven forbid! Such a person is worthy of suffering shame and disgrace upon the expiration of his soul.

Our forebears used to pray: "May it be the will of Hashem our God and God of our fathers that we be prevented from sinning so that we will neither be ashamed nor disgraced before our ancestors." Such shame makes it impossible for a person to enter the King's presence, for his soul is naked without any raiment. Thus the Zohar relates (ibid. 226b): Come and see. Woe to those who see but do not understand, nor do they realize upon what the world stands ... For out of every commandment that a person fulfills, a garment of honor is fashioned for him to wear in the World to Come and he will be in need of them all. Furthermore, each day that he performed good deeds, garments are also fashioned. Rabbi Yehudah the Elder became anxious one day (regarding his portion in the World to Come). He was shown in a dream a vision of his radiance, which shone to the four directions. "What is this?" he inquired. "This is the garment you will wear when you come to reside in this world," came the reply. From that day on he was joyful. Rabbi Yehudah said: Every day the spirits of the righteous sit by rows in Gan Eden dressed in their garments, praising the Holy One Blessed is He with highest honor. This is the meaning of the verse, "Surely the righteous will give thanks to Your Name; the upright will dwell in Your Presence" (Tehillim 140:14). This is the way of the righteous — to live in constant trembling and fear lest they be disgraced in the World to Come on account of their deeds in this world. All the good deeds that they do are in their eyes like a drop in the ocean against their wicked deeds.

It is also the way of the righteous to be zealous for Hashem whenever they see a desecration of His Name or the evil deeds of the wicked. And although it may cause them to face persecution and even death, they refuse to show the wicked a smiling countenance but only one of displeasure, so that they will understand on their own that their actions find no favor in their eyes. It pains them that the wicked incite Hashem's anger. In their hearts they pray that the hearts of the wicked will be transformed and inclined towards the way of awe. Thus, it is the duty of all who are faithful in their service of Hashem to admonish the wicked and to be pained whenever they witness or hear of the deeds of the wicked. This is explained in the Zohar (ibid. 238b-240b): Rabbi Yehudah and Rabbi Yitzchak were traveling together along the road. Rabbi Yehudah said: "It is written, 'She will not be afraid for her household on account of the snow, for her entire household is dressed in crimson' (Mishlei 31:21). Our colleague Rabbi Chizkyahu has explained this as follows: The punishment of the wicked in Gehinnom lasts for twelve months. During half of them he is punished with heat, while during the other half he is punished with snow. When they enter the fire they say, "This is surely Gehinnom!" But when they enter the snow they say, "This is the cool of winter!" And they rejoice, saying, "We are content, for after the judgment in fire we have come to cool off in a cold place." What they do not realize is that the snow is a continuation of their judgment. There they suffer terrible and bitter punishments. But lest it should occur to someone that Israel will also endure punishment in the snow, for this reason it is written, "She will not be afraid for her household on account of the snow, for her entire household is dressed in crimson." Do not read, "dressed in crimson (shanim)" but in "two" (shnayim ; that is, they perform the commandments in pairs) — circumcision and pri'ah (the tearing of the membrane underlying the foreskin), tzitzis and tefillin, mezuzah and the Chanukah lamp ....

While they were still walking, they encountered a child guiding a donkey upon which an elderly man was riding. The old man said, "My child, cite me your verse." The child responded, "One verse? I do not have only one verse! Either you should alight or you should let me ride with you and I will tell you." "I do not wish to equate myself with you," the old man said, "for I am an elder and you are but a child." The child said, "If so, why did you ask me to cite you a verse?" "In order that we may travel together," he answered. "May this old man be filled with despair!" said the child. "He rides although he knows nothing and then he says that he does not wish to equate himself with me!" So, he parted company with the old man and set out alone.

When Rabbi Yehudah and Rabbi Yitzchak arrived, he approached them and related to them what had happened. Rabbi Yehudah told him, "You did the right thing. Come with us and we will sit and listen to what you have to say." The child said, "I am tired, for I have not eaten anything today." They took out some food and gave it to him. A miracle occurred for them and they found a spring under a tree and drank from it. Then the child began, "It is written, 'For Dovid, do not grieve over the [success of] evildoers; do not be jealous of the iniquitous' (Tehillim 37:1). That is, do not turn to observe the deeds of the wicked, for perhaps you will not be jealous on behalf of Hashem of Hosts and you will be punished on this account. For whoever sees the deeds of the wicked and is not jealous for the honor of the Holy One Blessed is He transgresses three injunctions: 1. 'Do not have any other gods before me' (Shemos 20:3). 2. 'Do not make for yourself an image nor shall you bow to them' (ibid. 4-5). 3. 'Do not serve them' (ibid. 5). "Therefore, a person must separate from them and direct his path away from them. For this reason, I separated from the old man and directed my path away from him. And now that I have found you, I will explain another verse." So, he began, "And He called (ויקרא) to Moshe" (Vayikra 1:1) — "The alef (at the of the word vayikra) is written small because this 'calling' was not complete. Why not? Because it took place outside the land of Israel. For completion exists only within the land."

He then proceeded to reveal to them additional insights of great depth, whereupon Rabbi Yehudah and Rabbi Yitzchak came and kissed him on the head and said, "Blessed is the Merciful One who allowed us to hear these things. And blessed is the Merciful One for not allowing these things to be wasted on that old man." Then they arose and began walking. They spied a grapevine growing in a certain garden and the child began, "He will bind his donkey-foal to the vine and the son of the donkey-mare to the vine-branch" (Bereishis 49:11) — "The idea is this: The 'foal' and the 'mare' are two potent shells of impurity. In order to weaken their power so that they will not confuse the world the Holy One Blessed is He formed the world with the name Ya-h, as it is written, 'For with Ya-h Hashem formed the worlds' (Yeshayahu 26:4). "This is what is hinted at here, that the Holy One Blessed is He took the name Ya-h (י-ה) and included it within the word for 'his foal.' For the verse should have said simply 'foal' (עיר), but it said 'his foal' (עירה) instead, to include the letter heh of the name Y-h within it. "Similarly, the word 'branch' should have been written soreik (שורק) but instead it is written with an extra heh at the end, soreikah (שורקה), while the word 'son' is written with an extra yud — b'ni (בני) instead of ben (בן)." The child then went on to reveal to them other esoteric insights.

Rabbi Yehudah said, "If we had traveled this way for nothing other than to hear these things it would have been sufficient for us." Rabbi Yehudah then said, "It would have been better for the child if he did not know so much, for I am afraid that he will not be allowed to remain in the world on this account." Rabbi Yitchak asked, "Why not?" "Because he may glimpse at what is not permitted," he replied. "I am afraid on his behalf that before he grows up and reaches maturity he will contemplate and glimpse at what he should not and be punished." The child overheard him and said, "I am not afraid of punishment at all, for when my father departed this world, he blessed me and prayed for me. And I know that my father's merit will protect me." "Who was your father?" they asked. "I am the son of Rav Hamnuna the Elder," he answered, whereupon they took him and carried him upon their shoulders for three miles. After this they continued walking together for a time and then blessed him and went on their way. When they came to Rabbi Shimon ben Yochai, they related what had transpired. Rabbi Shimon said to them, "Surely the Torah comes to him by inheritance!"

From this passage we can see that one should join up with Torah scholars along the road and avoid the company of the ignorant, just as the child did. Secondly, from this incident we learn of the great humility of Rabbi Yehudah and Rabbi Yitzchak. For they were leaders of the generation, yet when they heard that the child was the son of Rav Hamnuna the Elder they carried him upon their shoulders in order to listen to his Torah. Nor were they too proud to hear Torah even from the mouth of a child. For a man who renders himself like the dust upon which all trample is called, "Beloved above and valued below." Moreover, he is called one of the "lovers of Hashem," concerning whom it is written, "And the lovers of His Name will dwell in it [in Tzion]" (Tehillim 69:37).

Chapter 21

It is written in the book of Tehillim, "Be a guarantor for Your servant for the good; do not allow the arrogant to oppress me" (119:122). This verse can be understood by an analogy of a man burdened with many debts, but with enough silver and other valuables to satisfy all his creditors. However, since the creditors are unaware that he has enough for each of them all they are intent on confiscating whatever they can find. For each one is afraid that the debtor will pay the others and have nothing left for him. The only solution is for the debtor to find a guarantor who will keep the creditors at bay while he sells his merchandise. Then when he has the money in hand, he can pay each of them what he owes him. In this way he will be saved from the injury, loss of reputation and other misfortunes that result from the hounding of creditors. It seems to me that this is what Dovid HaMelech meant when he wrote, "Be a guarantor for Your servant for good" (Tehillim 119:122). That is, he wished for the Holy One Blessed is He to serve as his guarantor against his accusers and pursuers to prevent them from falling upon him on the pretext of some misdeed on his part. For he also possessed many merits to counterbalance the debits of his transgressions. Therefore, he adds, "Do not allow the arrogant to oppress me" (Ibid.), which indicates that his accusers were waiting for the day when this "sinner" (i.e., Dovid) would fall into their hands. For they wished to "collect" what he owed in the form of sins and transgressions by carrying out the sentence of the Heavenly court after he was found guilty.

A person must possess much merit to be found innocent, for the reckoning is thorough and exact. See what is written in the Midrash on Mishlei (10:3): Rabbi Yishmael said: Woe for that shame! Woe for that disgrace! Along will come one who has mastered Scripture but not Mishnah and the Holy One Blessed is He will turn His face away from him and allow the agents of Gehinnom to overwhelm him like wolves of the evening. They will take him and cast him into Gehinnom. Along will come one who mastered two sections of the Mishnah and the Holy One Blessed is He will ask him, "My son, why did you not master the law?" If the Holy One says, "Leave him be," fine. But if not, they will treat him as they did the first one. Along will come one who mastered the law and they will ask him, "My son, why did you not master Toras Kohanim [the halachic Midrash on Vayikra]? For it contains the laws of defilement by small creatures and the form of purification from them, the defilement and purification from skin plagues, the defilement and purification of houses, males with a flow, women after childbirth, menstruating women, the order of the confession on Yom Kippur, the laws of pledges, the comprehensive summary of Torah law contained in Parashas Kedoshim, the laws of sacrifices, and the laws of the Sabbatical and Jubilee years.

If the Holy One Blessed is He says, "Leave him be," that is fine. But if not, they will treat him as they did the first one. Along will come one who mastered Toras Kohanim and they will ask him, "Why did you not master all five books of the Torah?" For they contain the Shema and many other commandments, such as tefillin, mezuzah, etc. Along will come one who mastered all these and they will ask him, "Why did you not study and master the Aggadah? For when a Torah scholar sits and interprets (these texts), Hashem grants atonement for Israel's sins. Moreover, when the listeners respond, Amein, yehei shemei rabba (at the end of the lesson in Aggadah), even if a decree has been written and sealed against them Hashem will forgive them and grant atonement for their sins."

Along will come one who mastered the Aggadah and the Holy One Blessed is He will ask him, "Why did you not master the Gemara, which is called the "Sea of the Talmud"? Concerning this was it written, "All streams flow to the sea but the sea is not full" (Koheles 1:7) — this alludes to Gemara.

Along will come one who mastered Gemara and the Holy One Blessed is He will ask him, "My son, since you toiled in Gemara, did you contemplate the Throne? For the only time I have pleasure from My world is when Torah scholars sit engaged in study and glimpse, peer, behold and contemplate from their Talmud studies how the Throne of Glory stands. How the first leg stands and what it is used for; then the second leg and the third and the fourth. "How Chashmal is situated and to how many directions it turns every hour. Which wind is used by the lightening and which by the cherub. How the cherubim and the ministering angels stand and minister. And most important of all, how the Throne of Glory is situated; is it circular, and fashioned like a frame, established like a bridge. How many bridges does it contain and over which one do I pass. Upon which bridge the Ofanim pass. Upon which bridge do the wheels of the Throne pass, etc. "Is this not My glory, my magnificence, the splendor of My beauty — when My children appreciate My glory?" Concerning this Dovid HaMelech said, "How many are your works, Hashem!" (Tehillim 104:24).

Who can possibly stand up to such inquiries? This is what prompted our Sages to declare (Bereishis Rabbah 23:11), "Woe to us for the Day of Judgment! Woe to us for the Day of Rebuke!" Nevertheless, one must neither slacken nor become depressed, for the Holy One Blessed is He examines the heart and searches out the kidneys. He sees that a person intended to cling to the good, that his soul wished to pursue Torah and good deeds and that it was only the vicissitudes of the times that caused him to fall short. Concerning this the Sages said (Berachos 5b), "It does not matter whether one did much or little as long as his intentions were for the sake of Heaven."

A person must always rejoice when he has the opportunity to become involved in the fulfillment of any of the commandments. For whoever performs them joyously is beloved and precious to the Holy One Blessed is He. Thus, it is related in Zohar Chadash (20b) that it is a very beloved matter to the Holy One Blessed is He when He sees a father rejoicing when his son becomes obligated to fulfill the commandments, upon reaching the age of thirteen. For this reason, there is a great obligation to make a feast on that day, for this brings pleasure to the Holy One Blessed is He. Thus, the Zohar relates: Rabbi Yitzchak said: From the age of thirteen and upwards [one is obligated to fulfill the commandments] and on that day it is the duty of the righteous to celebrate as if it were a wedding day. In this merit the Holy One Blessed is He will one day arouse them and dispatch a herald ahead of them, proclaiming joyfully, "Go out and see the daughters of Tzion...."

Rabbi Elazar said: From the age of thirteen and up, if a person wishes to be a tzaddik he is granted a holy soul from On High, carved out from beneath the King's Throne of Glory. Rabbi Shimon ben Yochai invited penitents and masters of Mishnah to partake in the great bar mitzvah feast that he made for his son Rabbi Elazar. He covered his entire house with precious vessels and seated the scholars on either side, and the rejoicing was indeed great. The scholars said to him, "Why is our teacher's joy greater on this day than on other days?" Rabbi Shimon answered, "For on this day a holy soul is descending from On High upon the four wings of the Chayos to my son Rabbi Elazar. At this feast my joy is complete." He seated his son Rabbi Elazar beside him, saying,

"Sit, my son, for today the Holy One Blessed is He is sanctifying you with the lot of the holy ones." After Rabbi Shimon ben Yochai had said one word the house was surrounded with fire. The scholars went out and saw the smoke rising from the house all that day. Along came Rabbi Yose ben Lakonya and found them standing in the marketplace staring in amazement. He said to them, "The smoke that is rising from the house of Rabbi Shimon ben Yochai is there because on this day his son Rabbi Elazar is being crowned with a holy crown." The scholars watched as the pillar of fire descended and Rabbi Yose remained there [until the fire had departed]. Then they all rejoiced, saying, "Let this rejoicing be complete!" They all blessed Rabbi Shimon's son Rabbi Elazar and sat there sharing in their happiness and engaging in study.

Fortunate, then, is the person who fulfills the commandments, causing one holy soul to cling to another, and he is crowned with a holy crown. But this is only true if he sets aside fixed times for study and engages in acts of lovingkindness and good deeds. But if he goes after his heart's desire, pursuing gluttony and drunkenness, spending all his days in business and wasting all his time on the needs of the body rather than those of his soul, then his holy soul abandons him, since his nature is that of a beast. Concerning this was it written in Zohar Chadash (21b): Rabbi Yehudah said: Woe to the wicked who do not wish to cling to the partner of the Holy One Blessed is He. And who is this? Rabbi Yitzchak has said, "This is the soul that the Holy One Blessed is He has instilled in him." But instead he clings to the behavior of the beasts. This is the meaning of the verse, "But man does not endure in his splendor; he is likened to the silenced animals" (Tehillim 49:13). (See also what I will write on this matter in Ch. 61).

Why do people not consider that the Holy One Blessed is He has only created them for His honor and not to fulfill their appetites? If only a person would take to heart how they curse him On High for his lack of concern over his Creator's honor. And how fitting it is that a person should run to see his Creator's deeds. Thus the Zohar relates (ibid. 23a): Rabbi Elazar the son of Rabbi Shimon ben Yochai said: When the sun inclines its wings to go forth by the might of its wheels, trampling with their hooves upon the leaves of the trees of Gan Eden, then all the holy Beings, the King's Throne of Glory, the spices of Gan Eden and the trees, Heaven and earth and their hosts — all of them tremble and give praise and acknowledgement to their Master. They arise and see the explicit holy Name engraved upon the sun in its journeys and they give praise to the Master of the Universe. Then a voice is heard, proclaiming, "Woe to the creatures who do not contemplate the glory of the King!" As it is written, "And all the hosts of Heaven bow to You, etc.," (Nechemyah 9:6). It is also taught (ibid.): When the Holy One Blessed is He enters Gan Eden after midnight together with the righteous then all the gates of Heaven are opened and it is a favorable time to engage in study. At that time bands of ministering angels and all the spices of Gan Eden burst out in exultation and song along with the righteous before the Holy One Blessed is He.

This is what is meant by the verse, "Surely the righteous will acknowledge Your Name; the upright will dwell in Your Presence" (Tehillim 140:14). When will the righteous give thanks to Your Name? When the upright dwell in Your Presence. That is, when they sit before You in Gan Eden at midnight. Afterwards the three bands of ministering angels that are appointed over the watches of the night sing songs of praise until dawn. Then at dawn it is Israel's duty to rise and with strength offer songs and praises before the King of the Universe. Why is this? Because they must take over serving after the ministering angels have finished. Moreover, at that time the Holy One Blessed is He is found nearer to earth. This is the meaning of the verse, "And those who seek Me will find Me" (Mishlei 8:17). (The word for "those who seek Me" — meshacharai — contains the word for "dawn" — shachar.) Rabbi Yehudah added: Provided that they do not leave off until it is time to pray as the sun rises.

Rabbi Yochanan said in the name of Rav: When the Holy One Blessed is He exits those worlds that He desires and enters Gan Eden together with the righteous, He pauses to see whether He hears the sound of Torah study. For it was taught: That sound is more pleasing to Him than all the songs and praises that are recited by the ministering angels On High, as it is written, "I descended into the Nut Garden to see, etc." (Shir HaShirim 6:11). What is meant by "to see"? To observe those engaged in study. Rabbi

Yitzchak asked, "Is Gan Eden then called the 'Nut Garden'?" Rabbi Yochanan replied, "Yes, certainly Gan Eden is called the 'Nut Garden.' Just as a nut is sealed up from every side and is surrounded by many shells, so is Eden sealed up on every side and surrounded by numerous defenses so that it cannot be seen by any angel, saraf. Chashmal and beheld by the prophets. Thus, it is written, "No eye has seen it except for You, O God" (Yeshayahu 64:3). Rabbi Shimon ben Yochai said: One time I was standing before Rabbi Beroka and he said to me, "So shall I merit the level of the Nut Garden together with the pious of Israel." But I did not understand what he meant until I heard from Rabbi Yochanan ben Zakkai that the Holy One Blessed is He refers to Gan Eden as the Nut Garden. Just as a nut is surrounded by many shells while the fruit is situated in the middle, so too Gan Eden — the garden is on the outside while Eden is on the inside.

Fortunate is he who walks innocently and toils in Torah and whose ways are all for the sake of Heaven. For then his soul is prepared to enter Eden, which is called the "Nut Garden," that is, the World to Come.

Chapter 22

In the second chapter we commented on the terrible punishment awaiting the man who wastes his seed. Concerning this Dovid HaMelech wrote, "Avert my eyes from seeing vanity, cause me to live in Your ways" (Tehillim 119: 37). It seems to me that this verse was a prayer that he be saved from gazing at forbidden sights, such as women, so that he would not defile himself at night, for the word "vanity" — שוא — has the same numerical value as the acronym for seed, זו. Dovid HaMelech pleaded that the cohorts of the demon Lilis, who are known as Keri, not appear to him, for they cause a man to waste his seed at night. Since a child can be conceived from every droplet, wasting seed is considered akin to murdering those droplets with one's own hands. Thus, one who wastes seed is under the sway of the Sitrah deMosah, the Side of Death. This is why Dovid requested, "Cause me to live in Your ways." That is, he prayed to be under the sway of the Sitrah DeChayei, the Side of Life, and thereby to be saved from wasting seed. It is mentioned in the Zohar (Part II, 263) that there is an angel appointed over those who waste seed. It has in its charge thousands upon thousands of accusers and demons and destructive angels, all of whom cause a person to be defiled. Then they take the droplet that the man wasted and bring it on High, causing the mark of the covenant on his body to become enslaved to the Aspect of Impurity. Woe to the man who causes holiness to become enslaved to impurity!

There is a tradition passed down by the Ari's disciples that is important to know. The Ari z"l explained that the 613 limbs and arteries of the body are the sparks of the animal soul (nefesh). There are corresponding sparks of the spirit (ruach) and the soul (neshamah) as well, each of which is dependent upon one of the 613 commandments. The Ari z"l had the power to discern which commandment a person was lacking. He could also detect the sparks brought about by transgressions. Using this information, he would then give each person a set of instructions (tikkun) for returning each spark to its proper place. He was able to discover all this from the letters impressed upon a person's skin, which are particularly apparent in the region of the face and hair. He was also able to interpret the patterns of lines and follicles on a person's hands and face.

One day one of the great scholars of that generation, Rabbi Chaim Vital, came before him. The Ari told him, "I see that that all twenty-two of the letters on your forehead are illuminated with the exception of the letter gimmel, which is backwards." Upon hearing this Rabbi Chaim Vital was filled with trembling. He asked the Ari z"l to reveal to him why this was so, for it was surely not in vain! The Ari answered that Rabbi Chaim had not performed sufficient acts of kindness towards his father. "Although you do perform acts of kindness towards him, they are not complete and for this reason the gimmel is backward." The Ari revealed further that whenever a person performs one of the commandments it is recorded upon his forehead with one of the twenty-two letters of the alphabet. If he then performs the same commandment a second time the letter begins to shine. For the first time he performs it the letter remains sunken into the skin, but the second time it stands out and sparkles. This is true of all the commandments with the exception of charity, which is not sunken into his skin like the others but shines forth immediately upon his forehead as is hinted at in the verse, "And his charity enures forever" (Tehillim 111:3).

The same applies to transgressions. They, too, are indicated on a person's forehead in black fire. However, if he regrets his deed and toils to rectify it through repentance, he can remove the darkness and the black fire that the iniquity impressed upon his forehead. And on Shabbos after midday, when a Jew receives his extra soul, the iniquity is covered over completely with the exception of the defilement caused by wasting seed. For in that case even after he has rectified the deed the mark does not disappear until he immerses in a mikveh [ritual bath].

The basic principle is that a human being is called a miniature world. Therefore, just as when anything is decreed upon the world, for good or for bad, Heaven forbid, it is manifest in the fixed stars of Heaven, so too everything pertaining to the individual appears in the lines of his forehead.

Come see what is written in the Zohar (Parashas Acharei 75b): Rabbi Aba was on his way to Cappadocia accompanied by Rabbi Yose. While they were walking, they saw a man coming towards them with a mark on his face. Rabbi Aba said, "Let us turn aside from this road, for this man's face attests that he has violated the Torah's laws of sexual morality." Rabbi Yose asked, "Suppose that he has had this mark since childhood, what immorality could he have been guilty of then?" Rabbi Aba insisted, "Nevertheless, I see in his face that he has violated the Torah's laws of morality." Rabbi Aba called to the man and asked, "Tell me something, what is this mark on your face?" The man replied, "I beg of you, do not punish this man (meaning himself) any further! For his sins caused that mark." Rabbi Aba asked, "In what way?"

He explained, "One day my sister and I were traveling. We came to an inn and became intoxicated on wine. All night long I held onto my sister. Then when I arose in the morning, I heard the innkeeper quarreling with someone. I interposed myself between them intending to make peace but they both struck me, this one from this side and the other one from the other side, and this mark entered all the way into my brain. A physician named Rabbi Simlai managed to save me." Rabbi Aba inquired, "What was his treatment?" He answered, "It was a treatment for the soul, for from that day onward I have engaged in penance. Every day I weep over my iniquity before the Holy One Blessed is He; then I wash my face with my tears." Rabbi Aba declared, "And your iniquity has departed and your sin will be atoned for" (Yeshayahu 6:7), whereupon the mark vanished from his face. The man said, "I vow that from this day forward I will engage in Torah study day and night." Rabbi Aba asked, "What is your name?" "Elazar," he replied. Rabbi Aba observed, "Surely it was your name that caused God to help you ("Elazar" means "God helped"). May he continue to help you." Then Rabbi Aba sent him off with a blessing.

On another occasion Rabbi Aba was on his way to see Rabbi Shimon ben Yochai when he came to the town of that fellow Elazar. He found him sitting and expounding the verse, "A empty-headed man cannot know, nor does a fool cannot this" (Tehillim 92:7): "How foolish are the people of the world that neither take to heart nor know nor contemplate the ways of the Holy One Blessed is He to learn why it is that they are upon this earth! What is preventing them from discovering the ways of the Holy One Blessed is He? It is the foolishness of their hearts that prevents them from studying Torah. For if they would only study in order to learn the ways of the Holy One Blessed Is He, they would know. "This is the meaning of the words, 'A empty-headed man cannot know.' That is, he does not know to engage in study. 'Nor does a fool understand this.' That is, he cannot understand the ways of the Shechinah, which is called 'this' (zos), as it is written, 'With this [zos] Aharon shall enter the sacred precinct' (Vayikra 16:3)."

It is the practice of the Shechinah to afflict the righteous in this world so that they may inherit the World to Come. Conversely, the wicked are rewarded here for their few good deeds in order to deprive them of the World to Come. The "fool" does not understand "this," that is, the ways of the Shechinah. Therefore, expresses bewilderment and doubt, Heaven forbid. He says, "See how this righteous and upright individual suffers while we evildoers enjoy tranquility, inexplicably increasing in dominion and prospering in all that we do!" But the wise man has his eyes in his head. He realizes that the inexplicable success of the wicked is merely an instance of what is described in the verse: "When the wicked bloom like grass and the evildoers blossom" (Tehillim 92:8). The verse concludes, "It is only that they may be destroyed forever," that is, in the World to Come, the world of eternal life. For they will become ashes beneath the feet of the righteous, as it is written, "And you shall tread upon the wicked, for they shall be ashes under the soles of your feet" (Malachi 3:21).

That same person also expounded the verse, "And my leanness (or, my treachery) will rise up against me and bear witness to my face (or, upon my face)" (Iyov 16:8). The meaning of this verse is this: If a person sins and follows his heart's desire, ignoring the fact that he must one day die and be made to reckon before the Creator of the Universe, when he is summoned to judgment all his iniquities are engraved upon his face. Then when all the higher and lower angels see that mark upon which all his sins are recorded, they curse him, saying, "Woe! Woe! When your day comes you will fall into the hands of the cruel, who will pour out upon you harsh and bitter punishments! All of a sudden, your fortunes will take a turn for the worse. No one will have mercy upon you and no defender will speak on your behalf." Holiness will distance itself from him and his defilement will increase until it overwhelms his entire body and clings to him. As long as that the mark caused by his iniquity is still upon his forehead, any child that his wife conceives will be brazen, violent and an informer, and he will refuse to heed rebuke. The Zohar says of such children that they are the wicked of the generation whose will the Master of the World fulfills in this world in order to destroy them in the World to Come. Concerning this Iyov said, "And my treachery will rise up against me and bear witness upon my face."

But regarding the righteous of the generation, upright in their deeds, pursuing charity and lovingkindness, strong in their faith, remorseful over their misdeeds, who prepare for judgment every day that they may come before the Throne in holiness and purity — all their good deeds are engraved upon their foreheads. When the higher and lower angels behold them, they bless them, saying, "This is a holy child of the Holy One Blessed is He. He is a beloved child who brings joy to his Heavenly Father!" The Sitrah Acharah flies away from him and holiness clings to him, increasing day by day. Fortunate is he and fortunate is his lot! The Zohar continues: The man's listeners inquired, "Rabbi, how do you know that what you have said is true?" He replied that such a mark had been made upon his own face as the result of a sin and a certain tzaddik (Rabbi Aba) caused it to vanish. Rabbi Aba asked, "What is your name?" "Elazar," he replied. Rabbi Aba said, "Blessed be the Merciful One who has allowed me to behold you and to see you thus! Fortunate is your lot in this world and fortunate is your lot in the World to Come!" Rabbi Aba added, "I am the one you met along the road," whereupon the fellow prostrated himself before him. Afterwards he brought Rabbi Aba into his home and served him bread and a tender calf. When Rabbi Aba saw that the man was perfect in his learning as well as in his piety, he recited upon him the verse, "Peace to you and peace to your house and peace to all that you have!" (I Shmuel 25:6) — "Peace to you in this world and peace to you in the World to Come!"

Chapter 23

It is related in the Baraisa of Rabbi Yishmael Kohein Gadol (Pirkei Heichalos): Metat, 5 This is an abbreviation because according to the Ari, z"l, it is forbidden to refer to an angel by its full name.' Minister of the Interior, said to me: When the Holy One Blessed is He sought to elevate me to Heaven He dispatched a certain angelic prince who took me from the generation of Enosh before the eyes of all. He seated me with great honor upon a chariot of fire with horses of fire. Then He brought me, in the company of Heavenly ministers until the place of the Shechinah to serve On High. Once I arrived on High I was taken to the place of the holy Beings and the Ofanim, the Serafim, the cherubim and the Galgalim of the Throne, where there were servants made of fire-consuming fire. They sniffed my presence from a distance of five thousand three hundred and sixty myriad parsaos and complained, "Master of the Universe, what is one born of woman doing among us? For he is but a putrid droplet! Shall he ascend to the highest Heavens to serve us, who are carved out of flame?"

The Holy One Blessed is He responded, "My servants, My hosts, My cherubim, My Serafim, My Galgalim, My Ofanim! Let your hearts not be disturbed by this, for all mankind has repudiated Me and My magnificent kingship to go after their heart's desire. They have worshipped idols and banished My Holy Presence from among them. "But this man withstood the test and believed in the glory of My magnificence." Then the Holy One Blessed is He took me and opened before me six hundred thousand gates of lovingkindness, three hundred thousand gates of understanding, three hundred thousand gates of life, three hundred thousand gates of love, three hundred thousand gates of might, three hundred thousand gates of Torah, three hundred thousand gates of livelihood and three hundred thousand gates of fear of sin. From that moment on the Holy One Blessed is He steadily increased my wisdom, my understanding, my knowledge, my mercy, my might, my power, my strength, my splendor, my beauty, my Torah, my love, my loving- kindness, my belovedness, my humility, my visage and my majesty. I was honored and glorified with all those goodly and praiseworthy attributes above all other human beings.

After all these attributes had been bestowed upon me the Holy One Blessed is He placed His hand upon me and blessed me with five hundred thousand six hundred and sixty blessings and I was exalted and elevated the length and breadth of the world. I was granted seventy-two wings, thirty-six on one side and thirty-six on the other. Each wing was the dimension of the entire world. Five hundred thousand three hundred and sixty eyes were affixed in me, each one of which was as luminous as the great light. There was no radiant or splendorous thing among all the supernal lights that was not affixed in me. This passage makes clear how many distinct windows the Holy One Blessed is He put in his charge, windows of wisdom, livelihood, etc. Everything a human being requires was put in his charge, including Torah, awe, wisdom and livelihood. Thus, whenever someone prays to the Holy One Blessed Is He his prayer comes before this angel, whether for small matters or great, and he then brings it before the King of the Kings of Kings, the Holy One Blessed is He, who listens to Israel's prayers in mercy.

Blessed is He and blessed is His name. For everything is dependent upon His will, not only matters of the body but matters of the soul as well. For example, suppose that a person knows that he has a bad attribute such as a grudging heart or any other despicable trait to which he has become habituated, yet in the inner recesses of his soul he cries over this before Hashem. Hashem has the power to incline that person's heart to fear Him. He can help him transform a perverse heart or any other undesirable trait.

Moreover, the Holy One Blessed is He grants the person who prays to Him wholeheartedly the ability to benefit others. For instance, if someone observes that others, especially his own relatives and children, are headed in a bad direction, let him first pray that they leave off their sinning and repent. Only afterwards, if he sees that his prayer did not help, let him rebuke them. Perhaps he will find a moment of favor when Hashem will agree to put it into the hearts of the rebellious to repent. Then the one who prayed will also feel a sense of contentment that the Holy One Blessed is He accepted his prayer to incline the heart of the evildoer to repent.

Thus, it is related (Emek HaMelech, Sha'ar I, Ch. 4, 4a) that the Ramban had a disciple named Rabbi Avner who strayed and became an apostate. Because of his vast knowledge Avner reached great heights among the gentiles. One Yom Kippur he sent word to the Ramban to come to him. Then in the Ramban's presence the apostate took a pig, butchered it and then cooked it and ate it. Afterwards he asked, "Rabbi, how many penalties of excision have I incurred today?" The Ramban answered, "Four." The disciple replied, "Did I not transgress five prohibitions?" He then engaged his former mentor in a complex Torah discussion until the Ramban was compelled to admit that he had indeed incurred five penalties of excision. The Ramban then asked him, "Tell me, what brought you to deny the Torah of Moshe?"

The apostate explained, "I once heard in one of your sermons that all the commandments are contained in Parashas Ha'azinu and that all the events of history are hinted there as well. However, one requires the help of Heaven to understand all those allusions and secrets." Since the disciple considered all this to be impossible, he became persuaded that what the Ramban was saying was not true, whereupon he went out and cast off the yoke of Torah and became a different person. The Ramban replied, "I still insist that what I said was correct. Everything is hinted at clearly in Parashas Ha'azinu. If you do not believe me, ask me for an example and I will answer you." The apostate was taken aback and said, "If what you say is true, show me where my name, Avner, is alluded to there!" So, the Ramban prayed with all his heart and soul until there came to him the verse: "I said I would scatter them to the corners, I would make the remembrance of them to cease from among men" (Devarim 32:26). In this verse taking the third letter of each word spells out the name "R. Avner," as follows: Amarti (אמ ר תי) afeihem (אפ א יהם) asbisah (אש ב יתה) mei'enosh (מא נ וש) zichram (זכ ר ם).

When the disciple heard this, he was filled with trembling and fell upon his face. He asked his mentor whether there could be any remedy for him if he repented. The Ramban answered, "You have heard the words of the verse stating that this individual's remembrance would cease from among men, indicating that no remedy would help!" So, the disciple immediately went out and obtained a ship without a captain, a rope or a sailor, and allowed it to drift wherever it would take him, while he cried out bitterly to Hashem. No one heard what became of him. Afterwards the Ramban prayed profusely that the man be granted some degree of atonement. A long time afterwards he appeared to the Ramban in a dream and thanked him because his prayers had enabled him to enter Gehinnom where he would be punished severely for twelve months, after which he would be healed. For until then he had been allowed to enter neither Gan Eden nor Gehinnom but had remained in the "slingshot" [in which souls are punished after death]. As you can see, everything depends on prayer, even the partial atonement that was granted to the Ramban's disciple.

Prayer is especially effective in the synagogue, the place that is designated for prayer. The synagogue helps purify a person's thoughts. Thus, the Sages comment on the verse, "Like the winding brooks, etc." (Bamidbar 24:6): Why are synagogues likened to brooks? To teach you that just as a brook can raise a person from defilement to purity, so do the synagogues purify, etc." (Yalkut Shimoni 771). Therefore, a person should engage in introspection in the synagogue and speak with his whole heart before the One who knows thoughts. And let him weep and groan brokenheartedly at the thought of his sins, even those of his youth. For a man's heart knows how much damage he brought about through the sins of his youth, all of which are inscribed and kept on record. But if he repents completely his iniquities are erased from the record and the stains and blemishes that he caused are purified and whitened. In place of judgment and punishment he will find salvation and deliverance when he comes before the Throne of Hashem to make his reckoning, when he is called to the judgement that was decreed upon him by the Holy One, blessed is He. Therefore, let a man engage in prayer, for the Day of Judgment will come suddenly like an eagle swooping down. But Hashem in His mercy will receive his soul when his time comes, and he will go from peace to peace. What comes out of all this is that one should not treat prayer lightly, for the great minister Metat is appointed over receiving prayers. And when a person recalls that this angel was transformed from flesh into fire on account of his righteousness, let him also strive to conduct himself with innocence before Hashem his God. Then his righteousness will stand before him.

Chapter 24

The Kabbalists warn that one must not travel alone without contemplating thoughts of Torah or fear of Heaven lest the Sitrah Acharah cling to him. The Zohar states clearly (Parashas Vayishlach 169b) that even in town if a person is out alone at an hour that people are not usually found on the street the Sitrah Acharah will cling to him and he will not escape without committing some iniquity that very day. Therefore he must conduct himself in the following manner: If he plans on going out alone to tend to his affairs very early or very late in the day when few people are around, let him recite in front of the mezuzah the verse, "Cast your burden upon Hashem and He will provide for you" (Tehillim 55:23). And when he comes to the Divine name let him envision it with the vowels of the word yehavcha ("He will provide for you"), that is, with a sheva beneath the yud, a kamatz beneath the first hei, a sheva beneath the vav and a kamatz beneath the second hei. Since a sheva resembles two yudim, one on top of the other, and a kamatz resembles a reclining vav with a yud beneath it, the numerical value of this vocalization is equal to six yudim and two vavim, or seventy-two. This is the same as the numerical value of the word chessed — "lovingkindness."

I have also found it written in the name of a certain great rabbi of Ashkenaz that if a person intends on rising early to travel alone to another city he should recite the verse, "Commit your way to Hashem and trust in Him and He will do" (Tehillim 37:5). When he comes to the Divine name let him picture it with the vocalization of the word darchecha ("your way"), that is, with a pasach (which resembles a reclining vav) beneath the yud, a sheva beneath the first hei, a segol (which resembles three yudim arranged in a triangle) beneath the vav and a kamatz beneath the final hei, again for a total of seventy-two, the value of "lovingkindness." If he will do this, he will be protected so that the Sitrah Acharah will not cling to him. Nevertheless, in both these cases it is necessary that he also contemplate words of Torah or fear of Heaven while he is on the road. Only then will he be protected from the Sitrah Acharah. When he first sets out he is especially in need of protection, so let him be sure to recite the traveler's prayer as well.

A person must also resolve not to be too miserly, for although the Holy One Blessed is He can incline a person's heart at will towards generosity or miserliness, it is better that the individual motivate himself in this regard rather than praying that Hashem change his heart. Nevertheless, he must also not be to too liberal and give beyond his means lest he himself be in need of charity later on.

Now let us return to our original topic. It is preferable to recite the traveler's prayer at home before setting out, 6 As with all matters of practical halachah, the reader should seek guidance how to conduct himself. as is taught in the Zohar in Parashas Beshalach. Rabbi Abba began and said: It is most proper to recite the Traveler's Prayer at home before setting out. It is also good to recite the portion of the Binding of Yitzchak. Here is what the Zohar has to say on the matter in Parashas Vayishlach (178a): Rabbi Elazar and Rabbi Yitzchak were walking along the road when the time for the morning Shema arrived. Rabbi Elazar stood still and prayed and

recited the Shema along with the morning prayers. Rabbi Yitzchak asked, "Did we not learn that before a man sets out on a journey, he must seek the leave of his Master and pray?" Rabbi Elazar replied, "When I set out upon the road neither the time for the Shema nor the time for prayer had yet arrived, therefore now that the sun has arisen, I prayed. Nevertheless, before setting out I did make request of the Holy One Blessed is He and seek His leave...."
They walked until they came to a field. They sat down and and saw a mountain towering over them, upon which were strange creatures. Rabbi Yitzchak became frightened. "Why are you afraid?" asked Rabbi Elazar. Rabbi Yitzchak replied, "I see that this mountain is very rugged and I see that the creatures upon it are strange and I am afraid lest they begin a quarrel with us." Rabbi Elazar said back to him, "If a person is afraid, it is only because of his sins that he is afraid.

He then cited, "These are the sons of Tziv'on, Ayah and Anah — the same Anah who found the mules (yeimim) in the desert." "The word yeimim is written missing a yud (ימם)." The concept here is that there is a certain kind of destructive spirit, Heaven spare us, that focuses in particular upon those guilty of immoral acts from which mamzeirim are produced (i.e., adulterous or incestuous relations bearing the penalty of excision). These spirits are called yeimim. It is written without a yud to indicate that they were created on the eve of the first Shabbos just at dusk (relating yeimim to yom — day; it is plural but missing the plural yud to indicate that it is doubtful to which day this creature belongs). The proper place of these destructive spirits is upon the high mountains, where no seed or tree can be planted. That barren region is their proper place and these are the strange creatures that Rabbi Yitzchak saw. Anah, mentioned in the verse above, once visited that mountain where these creatures adhered to him. Therefore, as the Sages tell us in Pesachim (54a), he himself gave birth to mamzeirim and that he also was the first one to graft different species and produce the mule (a hybrid of a horse and a donkey). The Zohar mentions in the continuation of that passage that all desolate mountains are their dwelling place, however, concerning those who engage in study while they travel it is written, "Hashem your shelter is at your right hand" (Tehillim 121:5). Nevertheless, a person should avoid places where there is no human habitation.

According to a reliable tradition received from the pious scholars of earlier generations no Jew should take up residence in any house that has stood unoccupied for seven consecutive years. It is even perilous to build a new house on the site of such a structure, because it has already become a dwelling place for damaging and destructive spirits.

As for why the house was destroyed in the first place, there are three reasons: The first is that it contained a beam, board or stone that was stolen or purchased with ill-gotten money. This resembles plague of the house, which later spreads to the entire structure. The second reason is that the one who built it was violent and unjust towards his neighbors and misappropriated land that did not belong to him. The third reason is that even if no injustice was involved in the construction of the house, the builder had in mind only his physical welfare and enjoyment and did not intend that his actions be for the sake of Heaven. He did not consider, for example, which corner of the house would be designated for his fixed times for study and which for prayer. Moreover, thought alone is not sufficient, for one must actually make these designations verbally, as is clear from the following passage from the Zohar (Parashas Tazria 50a): When a person builds a house just as soon as he begins work he must mention that he is building it to serve the Holy One Blessed is He. Then Heaven's assistance will settle upon it and the Holy One Blessed is He will imbue it with sanctity and pronounce over it, "Peace!" Thus, it is written, "And you shall know that in your tent there is peace and you shall instruct your dwelling place and not sin" (Iyov 5:24). That is, you must give instruction verbally when you build it; then you will "not sin."

If a person fails to do this, the Sitrah Acharah awaits the opportunity to settle upon the house. This is especially the case if the builder's intention was to defile himself there. (For example, if one builds a house or designates a room in one's house for the uncircumcised to come and drink and engage in frivolity and immorality. This error has become common in Poland and Lithuania, and no one protests!) In such a case the spirit of defilement will certainly settle upon the house and the one who built it will not leave this world until he is punished through that very house. Whoever lives in such a house is also liable to come to harm, for the spirit of defilement resting upon it causes harm to all who are found there. And if you should ask, "How can one know [that the spirit of difilement is in the house]?" The answer is that if the builder or any of the members of his household have suffered harm from the house, whether physical or financial, the cause is the sins mentioned above. Therefore, if a person becomes aware that this is the case, he should transfer his lodgings elsewhere and not remain there. This is the idea behind the plagues that struck the houses that the Israelites found standing when they entered the Holy Land. Because of Hashem's great love and affection for Israel He decreed that any house that had previously been designated for immorality would be stricken with a plague so that it would have to be torn down and the wood and earth cast out of the city and replaced. The purpose of this was so that the Israelites themselves would not come to harm.

The Zohar relates further: One day Rabbi Yose came to a certain house. When he reached the threshold and entered, he heard a voice saying, "Come and gather round, for one of our opponents has arrived. Gather round and let us harm him before he leaves!" Then he heard another voice saying, "We cannot do so unless he dwells here for a time. But since he has only entered temporarily, we may not harm him."

Then Rabbi Yose went out and observed, "Surely whoever transgresses the words of his colleagues is worthy of death!" Rabbi Chiya asked, "But we see that gentiles frequently rebuild houses that have been abandoned for more than seven years, yet they are unaffected!" He replied, "Those people derive from the same source as the damaging spirits themselves. Therefore, they are not harmed because they form a single company, for they, too, engage in immorality. Thus, they are as if derived from the same shell. By contrast, one who fears sin may very well come to harm, Heaven forbid."

So, no matter what a person undertakes to do, let him begin with the Creator's service. For example, when he builds a house let him consider first where he will place his books and where he will study. Similarly, if he sets about fashioning clothing for himself or his wife let him have in mind when he first begins working and also at the time of the sewing that it should be for the sake of Heaven. For the Holy One Blessed is He has indicated to us in His holy Torah that a human being must be clothed, as it is written, "Hashem made tunics of skin for Adam and his wife and clothed them" (Bereishis 3:21).

The general principle is, "In all your ways, know Him" (Mishlei 3:6). In all your affairs recall and do not forget that everything is a gift from Hashem, for, "bread is not to the wise" (Koheles 9:11). You can see for yourself that many intelligent people go without food or sustenance, spending all their days in deprivation and suffering. Meanwhile there are foolish and lowly individuals who enjoy abundance and wealth. This demonstrates that everything is dependent upon the will of the Holy One Blessed is He.

For this reason, too, one must see that all his business affairs are conducted in a way that is pleasing to the Holy One Blessed is He, for the benefit of the soul, and not just the body. But if his heart is as hard as iron towards the poor, if all his toil is for his stomach, if he is absorbed with the pursuit of dainties and delights, for him was it written, "This is an evil matter that has been given to mortals" (ibid. 1:13).

Therefore, let every man pray to the King of Mercy that he be granted a heart of flesh, a heart that hears the pleas of the needy and the cries of the indigent, a heart that is inclined to do kindness towards poor Torah scholars. For even if a person supports the poor the Zohar (1:171a) admonishes that he must be sure to support the scholars. And even if they are not related to him they take precedence over his relatives. For if a person fails to support poor scholars, he gives succor and power to the primordial snake and its cohorts, on account of our many sins. Hashem in His mercy caused the snake to crawl on its belly and deprived it of legs, otherwise the holy Israelite nation would be unable to survive, Heaven forbid. But as a result of the failure to support the scholars, who are called the "needy" (evyonim), legs are given to the snake so that it increases in power, bringing on evil decrees, Heaven forbid.

Therefore, a person must pray to the Holy One Blessed is He that He incline his heart towards a level of generosity appropriate to his means, neither miserly nor spendthrift. He must not be too liberal lest he himself become dependent upon others, Heaven forbid, yet despite this concern he must not become overly tightfisted.

Come see what is written in the Zohar in Parashas Beshalach (65a): Rabbi Aba began with the verse: "There is a sickly evil that I have seen beneath the sun" (Koheles 5:12). How dense are people's hearts because they do not toil in Torah! Is there such a thing as a sickness that is not evil? Rather the concept is this: There is a certain category of destructive agents, Heaven spare us, which sometimes arise from the Female Aspect, from the Great Chasm [Minukba DeTehoma Rabbah]. They come and settle upon a man, subjugating him to them so that no longer has control over his own money. Not only is he unable to give charity to the poor, he does not even have enough control over his wealth to purchase food or clothing befitting his means for himself, his wife and the members of his household. His appearance is lowly and emaciated and he is hungry and thirsty. He is beset by afflictions and dressed in rags. And even though his house is filled with all manner of goodness he derives no pleasure from it, for it has been announced in Heaven that all this goodness is prepared for another. Thus, the verse states, "The wicked prepare and the righteous wear" (Iyov 27:17).

The category of destructive agents mentioned above are called "Evil." Concerning them it states, "No Evil shall befall you" (Tehillim 91:10). Their victim resembles a sick person who has before him every delicacy in the world, yet he is unable to enjoy any of it because of his sickness. Thus, the miser derives no benefit from his deeds in this world or the next, other than the shrouds in which he is buried. This is the meaning of the verse in Koheles (6:2), "As for the man upon whom God bestows wealth, property and honor, but God does not give him dominion over it, this too is a sickly evil." Therefore, let a man be sure to do what is upright in the eyes of God and men. For, "a good name is better than fine oil" (Koheles 7:1). Then all will be well with him while he is here, he will pass from the world with a good name and he will also enjoy good fortune in the World to Come.

Chapter 25

It is written, "Hashem will bless you and protect you" (Bamidbar 6:24). The Sages comment (Midrash Bamidbar Rabbah 11:5): "'Hashem will bless you' — with wealth; 'and protect you' — from harmful destructive spirits." This Midrash requires explanation. It seems to me that it can be understood in light of a passage in Chullin (105b): Some porters were carrying a barrel of wine. Wishing to stop for a rest, they placed the barrel under a drainpipe, whereupon the barrel was broken [by a destructive spirit dwelling there]. The porters came before Mar bar Rav Ashi, who took out a shofar and proclaimed a ban (cherem) on that destructive spirit, compelling the spirit to appear before him. Mar bar Rav Ashi asked him, "Why did you do it?" The spirit replied, "What was I supposed to do when they placed the barrel upon my ears?" Mar bar Rav Ashi said, "What were you doing in a place that is frequented by people? You are the one who deviated from the norm. Go and pay." The spirit answered, "Specify a date and I will pay them." So, Mar bar Rav Ashi specified a date. When the date arrived the spirit procrastinated and failed to show up on time. When he finally appeared Mar bar Rav Ashi inquired, "Why did you not come on time?" He answered, "We are not permitted to take any object that is bound and sealed or measured or counted. Therefore, I was delayed until I found something that was neither bound nor counted nor measured."

The Tosafos (Ta'anis 8b) note that according to this passage damaging spirits have dominion over that which has not been counted, yet in Ta'anis (ibid..) it is taught that blessing is only found in that which has not been counted! The Sages derive this from the verse, "Hashem will command that there be a blessing for you in your storehouses (asamecha)" (Devarim 28:8). The Sages interpret: "In that which is hidden (samui) from the eye." How are these two passages to be resolved? The Tosafos answer that while blessing is only found in that which is "hidden from the eye," meaning that it has not been measured or counted, these spirits have dominion over the excess deriving from this blessing. Accordly, we can understand the meaning of the Midrash above. It was stated: "'Hashem will bless you' — with wealth." Clearly this must refer to wealth that is "hidden from the eye" since, as we have seen, only there is blessing to be found. But if this is so, one might protest that the damaging spirits will have dominion over it! Therefore, the Midrash continues: "'And protect you' — from destructive spirits." That is, Hashem will grant special protection to prevent the spirits from having dominion over the excess wealth that comes of the blessing.

Alternatively, the Midrash can be understood in light of a story I once heard of a man who was blessed with fabulous wealth, possessing treasure houses filled with gold and silver and precious stones. That man also happened to be a tremendous miser. whose like was not to be found anywhere in the world. He refused to attend synagogue even on Monday and Thursday lest he be obliged to give a penny to charity! This man had only one mitzvah to his credit and it was that one mitzvah that stood by him and saved him on his day of judgment. On account of this mitzvah he also merited becoming extremely generous later on. For this man was a mohel. 7 One who performs circumcision. Moreover, when there was an infant in need of circumcision, he would travel to perform it even if the baby was many miles from his house. Nor would he take any remuneration, neither from the rich nor from the poor.

One day a destructive spirit appeared to him in the form of a human being. It said to him, "My wife has given birth to a son and the circumcision is due to take place on such-and-such a day. I would like you to come and circumcise my son." The mohel immediately went home to collect his circumcision knife and entered the carriage to go with the man to circumcise his son. He believed that this was indeed a human being and did not realize that it was a destructive spirit. The two of them traveled with the carriage until they came to a forest. Then the spirit led him through territory never before traversed by mortals. It was an arid mountainous region. They traveled for two days straight and on the third day they came to the man's house, which was situated in what appeared to be a small village comprised of about twenty houses. The houses were all very beautiful.

When they entered the spirit's house the mohel saw that his host was very wealthy, for the house was filled with delicacies, including meat and large fish. The host gave his horse to his servant to be fed in the usual manner and there was nothing to cause the mohel to suspect that his host might actually be a demon and a destructive spirit. While the host turned to his other affairs the mohel went to the room of the new mother. When the woman saw the mohel she was overjoyed and wished him well. Then she said, "Come over to me, sir, and I will reveal to you a great secret." She continued, "You must know that my husband is a demon and a destructive spirit while I am of human stock. When I was small, I was kidnapped by demons." "Now, as for me, I am already lost, for all their deeds are vanity and emptiness. But I warn you to save yourself. Be careful not to consume any food or drink while you are here and do not accept any gift from my husband or from anyone else." Upon hearing these words, the mohel's heart was filled with trembling and he became very frightened.

That evening numerous guests, male and female, arrived from the surrounding villages. They arrived by horse and carriage, all in the form of human beings although all were harmful and destructive spirits. The time came for the pre- circumcision feast and the host pleaded with the mohel to wash hands and join them for the mitzvah meal, but he refused to eat or drink anything, claiming that he was too exhausted. All that night (known in Yiddish as the vein nacht or the vach nacht) he neither ate nor drank. When morning came, they went to the synagogue to pray and the mohel was obliged to pray with them and to sing out loud, "And He made with him a covenant," as is the custom of the mohelim. When the service was completed the baby was brought in and the mohel performed the circumcision in accordance with Jewish custom. Afterwards the sandek 8 The one on whose lap the baby is held during the circumcision. invited the congregation to a glass of schnapps and some cake, as is the custom. The mohel was also obliged to go over to the sandek, but he still refused to eat or drink, claiming that he was observing a fast day on account of a bad dream. When half the day had passed the host declared that since the mohel had gone to the trouble of traveling more than forty miles to perform the circumcision, the feast would be postponed until the evening, after the completion of his fast. The host's only purpose in this was to compel the mohel to partake of his food and derive benefit from him so that he would take control of him. He was unaware that his wife had revealed to the man that he was a demon and a harmful spirit.

When evening came the feast was held but still the mohel refused to eat, claiming that his head and limbs felt heavy. Meanwhile the guests enjoyed all the best delicacies in the world. When they were in good spirits because of the wine the host said to the mohel, "Come with me to another room." The mohel was now very frightened and thought to himself that his final moment had come. But he followed his host to the other room where the host showed him all sorts of silver vessels. Then he took him to a different room and showed him vessels of gold. "Take something for a keepsake," he urged. But the mohel answered, "I already have golden and silver vessels and all the good things in the world. I also possess precious ornaments, pearls, rings, bracelets and necklaces." Nevertheless, the host insisted, "Take a ring or whatever precious item meets your fancy." But the mohel did not wish to take anything, so he replied that he had an abundance of precious stones and pearls.

Afterwards he led him to room that was filled with keys hanging on nails along the walls. The mohel was astonished, for it appeared to him that one bundle of keys was exactly like the one he had at home with the keys to all his rooms and strongboxes. The host saw his expression and observed, "Sir, I have shown you much silver and gold and treasure houses filled with precious stones, yet you showed no surprise. And now over this storage room you show astonishment although it is filled with mere metal!" For the keys were all made of metal. The mohel responded, "I am perplexed by this particular bundle of keys. All these keys resemble those to my own houses and treasuries and storage rooms, yet here they are hanging upon nails!" The host explained, "Since you have done me a kindness and come more than forty miles to circumcise my son, and since I have noted that Hashem has been with you preventing you from eating or drinking or taking anything from me, I will reveal to you the truth. I am the appointed head of the demons assigned over the miserly. "All their keys are given into our hands so that they will have neither the power nor the authority to perform any act of charity of lovingkindness with their property. They are unable even to indulge themselves by purchasing some dainty or delicacy. But because you performed this great act of lovingkindness I allow you to take this bundle of keys. Do not be afraid; I swear as Hashem lives that you will suffer no harm."

So, the mohel took the bundle of keys and returned home joyfully. Thereafter he was transformed into an entirely different person. He immediately constructed a large and beautiful stone synagogue. He began distributing charity to support the poor and clothe the naked. And so did he continue conducting himself in an exemplary manner until the day of his death, leaving the world with a good name.

In light of this episode I believe that we can understand the meaning of the Midrash with which we began. The Midrash stated: "'Hashem will bless you' — with wealth." This means that you will posses great wealth including storehouses of silver and gold. But you may ask, "Of what benefit to me are storehouses of silver and golden vessels if the keys are given over to demons and harmful spirits?" For this reason, the Midrash continues: "'And protect you' — from destructive spirits." That is, the keys will not be given over to them. Instead you will have dominion over the work of your hands so that with all the goodness with which you have been blessed you will be able to perform charity and lovingkindness. From all of the above it is clear that a person who is exceedingly miserly is in the hands of the Sitrah Acharah and under the dominion of the spirits that dwell upon his wealth. The generous, by contrast, are under the sway of the Sitrah DeKedushah, the Aspect of Holiness. Therefore a man should strive not to be overly miserly in order to connect himself with the realm of holiness so that he may also merit the World to Come. Amein.

Chapter 26

It states, "Do not eat the bread of one with a miserly eye … for it is like poison in his soul" (Mishlei 23:6-7). Most people understand this: "Do not eat the bread of one with a miserly eye, for it is like poison in the soul of the host." That is, he tries never to give of his bread to others because giving anything away is like poison to him.

The Zohar (3:3a), however, gives a different explanation: "Do not eat the bread of one with a miserly eye, for it is like poison in the soul of the guest." That is, the food that one's receives from a miser is like poison to the receiver. Moreover, not many days will pass before he actually takes ill, sometimes dangerously so. This is why Rabbeinu HaKadosh (Rabbi Yehudah HaNasi) did not wish to accept food from anyone (Chullin 7b), for he was afraid for his life lest he benefit from a miser and then inevitably take ill. It turns out, then, that the miser causes evil both to himself and to others.

It sometimes happens that when the guest eventually dies the miser is held responsible and must repent over it. Thus, the Sages comment (Shabbos 32a): "A meritorious act is brought about through the meritorious and a blameworthy act through the blameworthy." Sometimes a miserly and begrudging individual even forfeits his life because of some small matter. For example, on a number of occasions I have seen people refuse to give soldiers [sugar] cubes or tobacco, and because of this trivial matter the soldiers murdered them. Sometimes the lives of Jewish prisoners can be saved in exchange for a small bribe, whereas later on when anti-Jewish feeling is running higher it is impossible to save them even for a house full of money. Woe to such individuals! Concerning them did Shlomo HaMelech write, "There is wealth that is stored up for its owner to his detriment" (Koheles 5:12).

Come see what is related in Ta'anis (21a) regarding Nachum Ish Gam Zu. One time a beggar approached him, saying, "Rabbi, feed me!" So, he immediately went to unload some food from his donkey, but by the time he returned the beggar had died. The righteous Nachum then proclaimed, "May the eyes that had no pity upon him become blind; may the hands that did not give to him right away be cut off; and may my entire body that had no pity upon him be afflicted with suffering." Whereupon all that he had decreed upon himself was fulfilled. Afterwards when his disciples saw his suffering they began to weep. But he said to them, "Why are you weeping? I brought this upon myself! For I was not satisfied until I said that my entire body should be covered with boils." They said to him, "Woe to us that we have seen you like this!" He replied, "Woe to me if you had not seen me like this!"

Therefore, when a person has guests in his home let him be sure to serve them a generous portion or let him not invite them at all, lest he be punished as above, Heaven forbid. For it is likely that the host will be required to repent over the matter. In this light we can understand the meaning of the verse, "A righteous person eats to the satiation of his soul but the belly of the wicked is lacking" (Mishlei 13:25). For whoever partakes of the food of someone with a generous eye eats to the satiation of his soul, even if the quantity of what he eats is small. But one who partakes of food from the "belly of the wicked" will feel a lack, for even if the quantity of what he eats is great it will not satiate him. The principle is that a miserly individual cannot even satiate his own soul, let alone give of the blessings Hashem has bestowed upon him to others. Thus we find that Naval (I Shmuel 21:11) was unwilling to send a portion of what he had slaughtered to Dovid HaMelech. Through this he brought evil upon himself, for he was stricken down by plague on this account (ibid. 38). Therefore, a person must distance himself from this trait and then he will enjoy goodness, selah.

Chapter 27

"How good and how pleasant it is, when brothers dwell together in unity" (Tehillim 133:1). This verse refers to the man who fears Hashem and involves himself in Torah study for pure motives and also in the pillar of Divine service, that is, prayer. For these two pillars go ahead of a man's casket when he goes to the next world. Their voice precedes him like a herald, proclaiming, "Throughout this man's life he walked with us in a single company, therefore even now we will not abandon him until we have brought him to his palace, which speaks entirely of his honor. Then they address the holy Torah, "How much honor and glory has this man earned on your account because he always adhered to the Torah of truth! Such is not the case, however, with one who pursues vanity and emptiness, studying Torah in a way that is blemished and false. This earns him only sorrow on top of sorrow.

A proof to this can be found in the Zohar (Parashas Balak 185b), where it is related that when a man dies, before he is brought in for judgment a voice is heard proclaiming, "Let all the members of the academy gather to examine his case!" Then they all gather and his soul is brought in by two officials. Once it enters, it is made to stand beside a certain pillar, next to a burning flame. Then a record of all the insights of Torah that he propounded in his lifetime is brought in for their examination. If the insights are clear and true, that is, based upon true premises, each member of the Heavenly academy places a crown upon his head, which sparkles and shines with a clear light. But if there are false statements among them, then each of the members of the academy declares, "This is false! He only asserted that premise in order to glory in a false insight!" Then woe to him for the humiliation to which the members of the academy subject him!

Immediately thereafter an agent of Gehinnom comes and apprehends him in accordance with the ruling of the academy that delivered him into his hands. He is then catapulted from there straight to the depths of Gehinnom where he is made to suffer terrible and bitter punishments, as it related in the Zohar in Parashas Yisro (87a): Whoever propounds Torah insights that he does not know to be true and that he did not receive from his mentor, concerning him was it written, "Do not fashion for yourself an idol or any image" (Shemos 20:4). And in the future the Holy One Blessed is He will exact payment from him in the World to Come. For when his soul wishes to enter its place it will be pushed outside, away from the place that is bound up in the bond of life along with the rest of the souls. From this passage one can see the seriousness of the sin and the severity of the punishment.

Now let us discuss prayer. It is well known that Dovid HaMelech was known as the "singer of pleasant songs" and that he was a master of prayer. Therefore, as the Zohar teaches in Parashas Balak (195a), we must derive the proper order and content of our prayers from him. We find that Dovid sometimes counts himself among the "servants," as it is written, "Look, as the eyes of servants look towards the hand of their master, etc." (Tehillim 123:2). Sometimes among the poor, as it is written, "Hashem, incline Your ear and answer me, for I am poor and needy" (Tehillim 86:1). Sometimes among the pious, as it is written, "Of Dovid, guard my soul for I am pious" (ibid. 2). And sometimes he identifies himself with the holy ones who sacrifice their lives for the sanctification of

Hashem's name, as it is written, "Of Dovid; to You, Hashem, I lift up my soul, etc." (Tehillim 25:1).

The rule is as follows: When it comes to reciting songs and praises a person should make himself into a servant of Hashem, setting forth the praises of his master and owner. Then when he comes to the unification of Hashem's name with the recitation of the verse, "Hear, O Israel, Hashem is our God, Hashem is one," let him include himself among those who sacrifice their lives for the sanctification of the Name of Heaven. When he reaches the Shmoneh Esrei let him include himself among the poor, for the prayers of the poor are more readily accepted by the Holy One Blessed is He than all others. For when a poor man prays all the windows of Heaven are opened. His prayers envelop all the other prayers of Israel, because no other prayers are allowed to enter until his have entered, at which point the Holy One Blessed is He proclaims, "Let all the other prayers be enwrapped in that of the poor man."

Moreover, when all other prayers enter, the judges of the Heavenly court deliberate over them before the Holy One Blessed is He to determine whether they are fitting or not. This is not the case, however, with the prayers of the poor man. He stands in prayer, setting forth all his troubles and the needs of his household and his sons and daughters who are dependent upon him, and his lowly situation that causes his days to be wasted in sorrow and suffering. He sets all these things before the Holy One Blessed is He with eyes streaming with tears. This is the prayer that envelops all the others. And with what is the Holy One Blessed is He engaged at that moment? They say that His only desire is for His broken vessels — the needy and downtrodden of His people. These are His "broken vessels." No one appreciates what is done with the prayers of the poor man, pouring out his words with tears, for they enwrap all the other prayers in the world. This is the meaning of the verse (Tehillim 102:1), "The prayer of the poor man when he is enwrapped [with affliction]. That is, when it becomes a cloak, surrounding all the other prayers in the world, which may not enter until the poor man's prayer has come before the Holy One Blessed is He. For the Holy One Blessed is He proclaims, "Let all the other prayers be enwrapped in this one and then let them come before

Me." This is why Dovid reckoned himself among the poor, referring to himself as "the poor man."

From this we can deduce that if a person wishes he may count himself among the poor on a continual basis so that his prayer joins up with those of the poor to ascend with them. The entire company then ascends and is accepted with favor before the holy King. When one reaches the blessing, "Hear our prayer," one must include himself among the pious by making a confession of his sins. Through confession he is called "pious" (chassid) because he acknowledges his transgressions and sins, regrets them and resolves never again to be drawn after ways of depravity deriving from the Left Aspect. Instead he will cling to the lofty Right Aspect, that is lovingkindness (chessed).

The ideal way of making confession is by specifying each sin that he committed. A person's heart knows the bitterness of his own soul and he knows the damage that he did in his youth, in his middle age and in his old age. Therefore, each individual should make his own confession specifying his sins. This causes the Heavenly accuser to leave him alone, since he himself has already acknowledged his sins. And even if he has forgotten some of his sins and therefore fails to mention them, he should not be concerned. Since his neglect was merely due to forgetfulness, those sins will be included with the ones that he did confess and he will receive atonement for them all. However, while one is specifying his sins at length in the blessing, "Hear our prayer," he may miss out on responding to the Kedushah along with the rest of the congregation. For this reason, the authors of the masters of pious admonition recommended reciting this abbreviated confession instead: Master of the Worlds! I have done that which is evil in Your sight. Please act on my behalf for the sake of Your great name and let Your abundant mercy make good all the blemishes I have caused in Your Holy Names from my youth until this day. Pardon me. Forgive me. Grant me atonement. He should then continue, "For you hear the prayers, etc." The Holy One Blessed is He knows the intentions of the heart and will surely grant him atonement for his iniquities. The passage from the Zohar cited above concludes: We have learned: When a man sets forth all four of these orders of prayer with concenetration of the heart he gives great satisfaction to the Holy One Blessed is He, who then spreads His right hand over him, proclaiming, "You are My servant, Israel in whom I glory" (Yeshayahu 49:3).

However, one must know of another practice that facilitates the acceptance of one's prayers, namely, praying with the congregation. Thus, the continuation of that same passage of the Zohar (ibid. 196a) discusses a passage from Berachos (6b). The Gemara reads: Whoever is accustomed to come to the synagogue to prayer with the congregation every day and then fails to come one time, the Holy One Blessed is He asks after him, "Who is there among you that fears Hashem ... that went into darkness and has no illumination?" (Yeshayahu 50:10). If he went for the sake of a mitzvah — then he has illumination; but if he went for something discretionary — then he has no illumination. It is not clear from this passage why the Holy One Blessed is He uses the expression, "that went into darkness and has no illumination." But the explanation, according to the Zohar, is as follows: As long as we remain in this bitter exile, on account of our sins, shells of impurity separate between us and Heaven. Even though the windows of Heaven are open, nevertheless these shells intervene and create a barrier. However, three times daily they fly off to the Mountains of Darkness to their meeting place to hold a gathering of the forces of impurity including all types of abominable beings. At those times because they do not darken and intervene and the light is able to shine and sparkle through the windows.

For this reason, the early scholars of blessed memory, instituted that we should pray at those times three fixed prayers every day, the Morning Prayer, the Afternoon Prayer and the Evening Prayer. For at those three times the atmosphere is free of the shells of impurity, which have already left to go to a place of defilement as we have already mentioned. Then the holy nation of Israel enters the synagogues to pray. The light-giving windows are opened and their radiance shines forth and settles upon the synagogues and upon the heads of those praying there. This light then spreads out over their heads. It is then that the Holy One Blessed is He asks about the fellow who is absent, commenting, "It is a shame about So- and-so who is regularly here but now is absent. He has no portion in the light that is shining upon the heads of those who are praying. 'He has no illumination' as do the others. How much goodness has he forfeited!" The verse ends off, "Let him trust in the name of Hashem." According to the Sages this is addressed to the one who went to tend to a discretionary matter — that is, his business affairs — at the time designated for public prayer. He was afraid that the opportunity that arose at the time of the public prayer would slip away from him, but in this he was mistaken. He should have trusted that Hashem would provide him with profit from some other source.

His error was clearly due to a lack of trust in the Holy One Blessed is He, who sustains all creatures from the greatest to the smallest and grants special supervision to one who goes to fulfill a mitzvah. Thus, the Jerusalem Talmud (Peah 3:7) relates the story of an individual who left a grain-filled silo and went to fulfill the commandment to make a pilgrimage to Jerusalem during the festival, leaving no one to guard his grain. Upon his return he found the silo surrounded by lions!

In that same passage another incident is related regarding a man who went to make the pilgrimage and in the confusion of setting out, left his house completely open. When he returned, he found snakes coiled around the doorway in a manner that prevented anyone from entering.

And Rabbi Pinchas relates an incident involving two brothers from Ashkelon who had wicked non-Jewish neighbors. Their neighbors had said to one another, "Soon these Jews will make the pilgrimage to Jerusalem and then we will take all that they possess!" But when the brothers set out on the pilgrimage the Holy One Blessed is, He arranged for angels in human form to go in and out of the house. When the neighbors saw the brothers returning from Jerusalem, they went out to greet them and to ask after their welfare. Then they inquired, "Who did you leave to look after your houses?" "No one," the brothers replied. The neighbors then proclaimed, "Blessed is the Merciful One, God of the Jews, who has never abandoned them and will never abandon them!"

From these incidents one can see the tremendous care with which Hashem watches over those who trust in His loving-kindness and do not desist from performing any of the commandments out of concern for their livelihood. For the Holy One Blessed is He will grant them a goodly reward. Blessed is He and blessed is His name, who provides sustenance and a livelihood for His people Israel.

Chapter 28

Many errors come about through the failure to trust in the Holy One Blessed is He. Therefore, we will set forth here a number of admonishments regarding this matter: The first error is a common one among those who must earn their livelihood. When a person sees that his income has decreased, he should accept the Heaven's decree with love, recognizing it as an atonement for his sins and acknowledge that everything that happens is from Hashem. But instead, many try pitting their cleverness against Providence, seeking to affect their lot through sorcery. Woe to them! For this is a terrible iniquity, as we will explain with the help of Hashem.

We know that Balak ben Tzippor tried to use sorcery against Israel by means of a certain bird called a yado'a. This is why he was called "ben Tzippor" (a tzippor is a bird in Hebrew). He dispatched this bird to the place that is the source of the impure force of sorcery to inquire what strategy he should use against them. But as the bird was on its way back, he saw a tongue of flame overtake it and burn its wings. This filled him with great fear and trepidation, so he sent for Bilaam ben Be'or, who was firmly ensconced in the impure forces of sorcery.

The chief sources of sorcery are the angels Uza and Aza'el, who protested the creation of human beings and were subsequently cast down to earth by Hashem. They then became entangled with the filth of the primordial serpent, after which they laid their eyes on the daughters of the earth and turned to immorality. When the Holy One Blessed is He saw that they had begun leading people astray, He bound them in iron chains upon the Mountains of Darkness, where they remain.

Uza angered the Holy One Blessed is He as He was binding him with chains, so He cast him into the depths of the mountain up to his neck, covering his face with darkness. Aza'el, who did not anger Hashem as he was being bound was seated next to Uza but with his face uncovered, enjoying light in the midst of the darkness. For this reason, Uza, whom the Holy One cast into darkness, was called "the One Who Falls," while Aza'el, who enjoyed light amidst the darkness, was called "the One with Open Eyes." These Mountains of Darkness are called "the Mountains of Ancient Time," because darkness preceded light, that is, before the creation of light there was darkness.

Each day the wicked Bilaam would come to them to learn the impure names and other forms of sorcery. This is the meaning of the verse, "Balak summoned me from Aram, from the Mountains of the Ancient Time (Bamidbar 23:7), and the verse, "Thus says the man who perceives the vision of the Almighty, the One Who Falls and the One with Open Eyes" (ibid. 3-4). Before Bilaam was able to study sorcery, he was first obliged to defile himself through all sorts of impure acts such as having a carnal relationship with his donkey, for such is the custom of the students of sorcery. They must defile themselves and lie with an animal. That is why the Torah places side by side the injunctions, "Whoever lies [carnally] with an animal shall die," and, "You shall not allow a sorceress to live" (Shemos 22:17-18). For the power of sorcery emanates entirely from the great sources of impurity, Heaven spare us. To begin with, whoever wishes to go to the Mountains of Darkness must prepare incense to offer before Uza and Aza'el so that he may accept them as divinities. At the same time, he must abandon the service of Hashem and relinquish all portion in holiness. He must subjugate and indenture himself entirely to the Sitrah Acharah. These are the things that he must accept upon himself when he offers the incense.

How is this incense made? First, he must split open the head of a snake and extract the tongue. Then he must combine it with certain known herbs and burn them. This is one form of incense. Afterwards he must divide the head of the snake into four portions, from which he must concoct a second form of incense. With these two forms of incense in hand he travels to the Mountains of Darkness. As soon as he reaches the summit, he is spotted by Aza'el, the One with Open Eyes, who immediately calls to Uza. They then give a shout to summon large burning snakes that come and coil themselves around them. Afterwards they dispatch a small cat-like creature with the head of a snake, two tails and tiny hands and feet, in the direction of the visitor. Whoever sees this creature must cover his face and offer up a third form of incense not mentioned above, which is made by taking and burning a white chicken. Through this offering he demonstrates his submission to this demon, whose head is like that of a snake and whose body resembles that of a cat. This creature accompanies him until he reaches the end of an iron chain, which is imbedded in the ground, descending to the depths. In those depths is a pillar imbedded in the lower depths and it is to this pillar that the end of the chain is fastened.

When a human being arrives there, he must knock on it three times. Then they call him and he kneels and bows to the ground. He must keep his eyes closed until he reaches them, whereupon they seat him before them within a circle surrounded by snakes. When he opens his eyes and beholds them he is filled with trembling, falling upon his face and bowing down before them. He then offers the incense mentioned above and accepts them upon him as divinities, simultaneously relinquishing the service of Hashem. Thus he begins worshipping the "other gods" of the Sitrah Acharah.

Afterwards they teach him sorcery, divination and the interpretation of omens. He remains with them for fifty days and when the time comes for him to leave, the same cat-like demon, along with all the snakes, goes before him until he has left the Mountains of Darkness. All forms of the impure art of sorcery derive from the depth of the chasm. For this reason, sorcerers also work in the shadows. Thus, it is related in the Zohar (Parashas Tazria 43a) that they stand in the shadow of a candle or the moon and address the shadow, saying, "We are indentured!" In this way they place themselves under the dominion of the Sitrah Acharah, that is, Uza and Aza'el. Then using various spells and signs they bind the shadow with oaths based upon impure names until bodiless, naked spirits appear floating in the air. Two of these spirits then clothe themselves in the shadow. The sorcerer looks down at the two spirits dressed in the shadow and they inform him of what they have heard announced in the world, for everything that befalls mortals is announced in advance.

So, you see that the impure art of sorcery is intimately tied up with the impure institution of idolatry. It follows that whoever pursues and engages in sorcery cannot possibly be a servant of the Holy One Blessed is He. Rather, he is a servant of the Sitrah Acharah. Woe to him and woe to his soul! The crime is no less severe if he does not engage in the sorcery himself but asks another to do so on his behalf. For the sorcerer must approach the Sitrah Acharah and the demons appointed over magic and say to them, "So-and-so sent me to you to act as his agent, who is the same as himself. I stand in his place and offer his submission to you, placing him under your dominion to be your slave. He accepts and agrees to whatever you do, as long as you agree to do him this favor — for his livelihood or some other matter has taken a turn for the worse and he requests that you inform him of the cause and the remedy." Sometimes the sorcerer must make a feast including the blood of a black raven and the liver and heart of a raven, a cruel source of food. To this feast he invites the impure forces and the chief of the demons gather there. At that time, he must stand before them and request on behalf of the one that sought his services whatever deed the person wished for. Concerning this it is written in the Zohar (Parashas Balak 192a): "And Balak sent messengers to Bilaam ben Be'or to Pesor" (Bamidbar 22:5). This means that [those who come to inquire of the impure forces] must set a table before them (pesora — "to Pesor" — can also mean "table" in Aramaic) and offer up to them a kind of incense. Then all the destructive spirits come and inform them of what they wish to know.

When an individual who sought out the aid of sorcery dies, these spirits along with all the forces of the Sitrah Acharah come to receive his soul, declaring, "This fellow is one of our kind!" As the Zohar says in Parashas Tazria (43a): "That person goes out from the domain of his Master and his deposit (i.e., his soul) is given over to the impure Sitrah Acharah, may the Merciful One spare us, etc."

Therefore, I admonish those men and women who have strayed after this iniquity to desist and to remove this stumbling block. Let them regret the past and as for the future, let them cry out to the King of Kings, the Holy One Blessed is He asking that He extricate them from the hands of these accursed destroying spirits, into whose power he has fallen on account of this sin. A person must weep bitterly over this sin and through the power of those tears he can shatter the might of the destructive spirits. Their strength will be weakened by his tears a little each day until no trace of the sin remains. Behave with simplicity towards Hashem your God in all your affairs. And no matter what the misfortune, Heaven forbid, raise your eyes On High to arouse Heaven's mercy and lovingkindness through repentance, prayer and charity. And let your heart not be swayed when you see the multitude pursuing sorcery and succeeding. Woe to them for that success! And woe to them for the benefit that comes through sorcery! For it will vanish swiftly like smoke while the iniquity remains engraved and inscribed to exact from them terrible and bitter punishments on its account.

The Zohar writes in Parashas Tazria (51a): Rabbi Yitzchak was on his way to his father's house when he saw a man walking along and then veering from the road. He was bearing a load of sticks. "For what are these sticks on your shoulders?" he inquired. But the man did not answer him. He followed him until he saw him enter a cave. He went in after him and saw a column of smoke rising from beneath the earth. Then the man went and climbed into a small crack and disappeared from view.

Rabbi Yitzchak became apprehensive and exited the cave. While he was still sitting their Rabbi Yehudah and Rabbi Chizkiyah happened along. When he saw them, he went over and related what had happened. Rabbi Yehudah said, "Blessed is the Merciful One who saved you! In this cave dwell all the metzora'im (individuals with skin plagues) of the town of Saronya, all of whose residents are accomplished sorcerers. They go into the desert and trap black snakes that are at least ten years old and use them for their sorcery. They do not take any precautions against the snakes but hold them in their bare hands. It is through this that they become metzora'im. In this cave they store all sorts of appurtenances of sorcery."

They continued walking until they came across a man walking towards them leading a donkey to which his ailing son was bound. "Who are you?" they asked. "I am a Jew," the man replied, "and this is my son that is bound to the donkey." They asked, "Why is he bound?" He answered, "I live in a town populated by Romans.

My son used to study Torah every day and then he would return home and teach me what he had learned. I lived in that house for three years and saw nothing unusual. Then one day my son came home to review with me the Torah he had received from his teacher and a spirit passed in front of him and injured him so that his mouth, eyes and hands all became deformed and he was unable to speak. I am going to that cave to see if they can teach me some remedy." Rabbi Yehudah said to him, "Do you know whether anyone else was ever injured in that house previously?" "I know that some time earlier a man suffered harm," he said. "Some said that it was due to an illness while others said that a spirit living in the house injured him. But later on, a number of others lived in the house and suffered no harm." The rabbis said, "Let us go with the man and see what happens."

But Rabbi Yitzchak objected, "It is forbidden for us to go. If he were going to see a person of great stature and a fearer of sin the way that Na'aman went to Elisha, then we could go with him. But since he is not, it is forbidden for us to appear before them. Blessed is the Merciful One who has saved us from them. Furthermore, it is forbidden for him to go as well!" Rabbi Yehudah asked, "Did we not learn that one may be healed through anything other than idolatry or the wood of an asheirah (a tree designated for idol worship)" Rabbi Yitzchak responded, "Sorcery is clearly a form of idolatry. Moreover, it is written, "Let there not found among you anyone who passes his son or daughter through the fire...." So, they continued along their way while the man went to the cave, bringing his son with him. He left his son in the cave while he went to tie up the donkey. In the meantime, a column of smoke came out and struck his son on his head and killed him. When the father returned, he found his son dead, so he took him with his donkey and left.

A day later he met up with Rabbi Yitzchak and Rabbi Chizkiyah. He was walking along weeping before them and he related to them what had transpired. Rabbi Yitzchak said, "Did I not tell you repeatedly that it is forbidden to go there? Blessed is the Merciful One, all of whose deeds are truth and whose ways are just. Fortunate are the righteous, for they adhere to the way of truth in this world and in the World to Come. "As for those who pursue foolishness and sorcery, surely the end of their life will be very bitter and even more so after their deaths. Their souls will be banished so that they do not merit witnessing the light of the World to Come. To their bodies, also, terrible things will be done. It is worthwhile reading that source in the original, for I have abbreviated it.

Therefore, a person must be careful that no sorcery is performed on his behalf, even for the sake of healing. For the sin of sorcery is reckoned on a par with idolatry. Let every God-fearing individual distance himself from it and then all will be well with him.

Chapter 29

You should know that when the wicked Bilaam saw that he could not harm Israel through his sorcery, as it is written, "How can I curse whom God has not cursed?" (Bamidbar 23:8), he advised Balak to order the Maobite daughters into immorality in order to cause the Israelite men to stumble. Then, when the Israelites did indeed stumble and twenty-four thousand Israelite men fell, Bilaam came to collect his reward from Balak. Later on, when Israel waged war against Midyan, Pinchas saw Bilaam flying through the air and he shouted to his soldiers (see the Zohar, 3:194a) and asked, "Is there anyone who knows how to fly after that wicked one?" For he saw that Bilaam was flying like a bird. One man by the name of Tzalyah from the tribe of Dan responded instantly. He knew how to subjugate the forces of impurity and to fly after him. But when that wicked one saw him coming, he cut his way through five levels of the atmosphere and continued flying hidden from the eye. At that moment Tzalyah found himself in peril and suffered great anguish because he did not know what to do.

But right away Pinchas raised his voice and spoke to the shadow by means of which Bilaam had cloaked himself in the five levels of the atmosphere and commanded that it become transparent once more and cease to conceal that evildoer. So, the atmosphere became transparent once more and Tzalyah flew towards him. He succeeded in overpowering the wicked Bilaam and constrained him, forcing him to come before Pinchas. How did he constrain him? Tzalyah knew how to constrain the male as well as the female aspect of the chief impure forces of sorcery, both of which are called "Shefi." Bilaam, on the other hand, knew only how to overpower the male aspect. Therefore, regarding Bilaam it is written, "And he went [through the power of] Shefi" (Bamidbar 23:3). Whereas regarding the tribe of Dan it is written, "And Dan was a snake along the road, Shefifon along the path" (Bereishis 49:17). The "path" referred to is the path through the atmosphere in which the wicked one cloaked himself.

Similarly, in the future the vengeance against Hashem's enemies will also be executed by Serayah of the tribe of Dan. Thus, when Dan arises one should be on the lookout for Israel's redemption, as it is written, "I have awaited Your salvation, Hashem" (Bereishis 49:18). When Bilaam came before Pinchas the latter said to him, "Wicked one! How many evil tribulations have you brought upon the holy people!" Then Pinchas addressed Tzalyah, "Go ahead and execute him. But not with a holy Divine name lest his request be fulfilled in which he asked, "Let my soul die the death of the upright" (Bamidbar 23:10). Several types of gruesome deaths were executed upon him on the spot, but he did not die until Tzalyah took a sword upon which was a snake was engraved on both sides. Pinchas said to Bilaam, "Through the very defilement with which you were engaged shall you die." Whereupon he killed him and Bilaam was judged with that defilement in the other world. Meanwhile in this world all of his bones disintegrated and his flesh and body turned into snakes, evil snakes. Even the worms that consumed his flesh were transformed into snakes and from his bones were also fashioned great snakes.

This is the fate all sorcerers — their bodies are turned into snakes and scorpions while their souls become male and female demons. May the spirits and souls of all sorcerers be filled with sorrow! All those men and women who turn to sorcery deserve to be cursed before the Holy One Blessed is He, and to have their influence diminished in whatever way possible. And if certain women are known to harm Jewish children through their sorcery it is fitting that they be pointed out by name and that a severe ban be proclaimed against them, accompanied with shofar blowing and the extinguishing of candles and in the presence of seven Torah scrolls. They should then be ostracized so that they have no contact with the holy community of Israel.

You should know further that the wicked Bilaam gathered all types of herbs for use in his sorcery and then put them in a pot, which he buried deep in the earth, fifteen hundred cubits underground. Years later when Dovid HaMelech was excavating holes on the site of the Temple to bring up ground water for use in the libations on the altar, holes that were also fifteen hundred cubits deep, he came across the pot that Bilaam had buried. He then removed it and diluted it with water that was fit for the libations. Concerning this was it written, "Moav is my wash basin" (Tehillim 108:10), for he "washed" it and removed the power of sorcery that was in Moav's pot. Therefore, whenever there is suspicion of harm due to sorcery it is a good strategy to neutralize it by reciting the fifteen "Songs of Ascent" (Tehillim 120-135), which Dovid composed at the time that he excavated those holes to bring up the groundwater (Sukkah 53a). Afterwards let them pray to Hashem to remove from Israel all the harm caused by sorcery. It is also advisable for every Jewish man and woman to stay as far away from sorcery as possible. Let them avoid all acts of sorcery, augury and divination and let them avoid hearing the recitation of any incantation. For the Holy One Blessed is He takes pride in His people that, "There is no augury among Yaakov and no divination among Yisroel" (Bamidbar 23:23). Whoever stays far from sorcery will be allowed to enter a partition in the World to Come within which even the ministering angels cannot stand (Nedarim 32a).

Chapter 30

It is written, "And your charity shall go before you; the honor of Hashem will gather you in" (Yeshayahu 55:8). And it is taught in Berachos (58a): One who sees a large gathering of Jews should recite, "Blessed is the One who is wise in secret knowledge," for their minds are diverse. In the same vein, I will tell you that people have different mindsets regarding the giving of charity and the doing of lovingkindness:

The first group consists of the misers. They find it impossible to give charity or do kindness. They do not even have enough control over their wealth to provide for their own food, drink and clothing. Such individuals are surely under the dominion of demons, as I have already discussed in Chapters 24 and 25. They have no share in the realm of holiness, for the Sitrah Acharah has complete dominion over them.

The second group consists of those who are begrudging to- wards others and lack the heart to give charity beyond a pittance to satisfy their pride. Yet when it comes to their own enjoyment they eat and drink freely and indulge themselves lightheartedly, making themselves as plump and robust as fatted calves. Concerning this group, the Zohar comments (2:245a): These are the people who derive from the side of the snake. The mnemonic for them is the verse, "Whatever moves on its belly" (alluding to the snake; Vayikra 11:42). In other words, whoever has a large, fat belly emanates from the side of the one who was cursed with the words, "You shall move around on your belly" (Bereishis 3:14). Nevertheless, the members of this group have a little merit, even if they only give to satisfy their pride.

The third group consists of the rich, whom Hashem has blessed with wealth and who indeed use it for charity and acts of kindness. However, they do not give to the extent that is expected of them because they still possess a measure of miserliness. For this reason, they are unable to compel their inclinations to give while they are alive. Instead, when are upon their deathbeds they issue instructions that after their death's charity should given for the construction of synagogues or study halls or to support scholars to study in their merit for a number of years. This is the attitude of the average individual.

The fourth group comprises those whom Hashem has blessed with wealth and who in fact give charity while they are alive to a degree that is commensurate with their means, while also engaging in lovingkindness and the support of Torah. And not only to they support the students, they also give generously to the teachers so that they will teach the children of the poor. Concerning them was it written, "And your charity shall go before you; the honor of Hashem will gather you in" (Yeshayahu 55:8).

Let me explain this with an analogy: Suppose that a king is on his way to battle together with his army. If the army goes before him, the king will be in no danger if they should happen to meet the enemy. But if the king goes on alone ahead of the army then if, Heaven forbid, they come across the cavalry and knights of the enemy they will seize him and take him into captivity. And even if the king is a valiant warrior and knows how to fight, nevertheless, his courage will fail him when he realizes that his troops are far behind him.

The point of this analogy is this: If a person gives charity while he is alive it is said of him, "And your charity shall go before you." Then he has nothing to fear from the "enemy," for "the honor of Hashem will gather him in" without any opposition from any accuser. But if he does not give until after his death, who knows whether he will even receive credit for it since the dead are exempt from the commandments? Concerning the first group it is written, "And they leave their wealth to others" (Tehillim 49:11). And even if their own sons inherit their wealth, nevertheless they themselves may have no satisfaction from it even after death. For I have seen new attitudes afoot and the masses have become very casual towards the honor of deceased parents. They make for themselves black mourning garments of the finest quality, all in the latest gentile fashion, and then indulge themselves in feasting. Meanwhile they treat with disdain the honor of the parent whom they are meant to be eulogizing and mourning. This is entirely the father's own fault, for when one casts a stick into the air it comes back down on one's head (Midrash Bereishis Rabbah 53:15). Therefore, there is no greater foolishness than this and no more need be said about the matter.

Therefore, the best advice is for a person to give generously while he is alive and to engage in acts of lovingkindness as well. For who knows when his time will be up and whether his instructions will be fulfilled or not? The Sages' principle in all such circumstances is that one does not set aside the definite for the doubtful (Pesachim 9a). The best kind of charity is that which a person gives during his lifetime. And let him be sure that the recipients are worthy, as is explained in the Shulchan Aruch (Yoreh De'ah 251). Then all will be well with him.

Chapter 31

"Hashem, you hear my voice in the morning" (Tehillim 5:4). On the surface this verse is difficult to understand. Does Hashem hear only the voice of supplicants in the morning? Does He not hear our voices and listen to our prayers whenever we call out to Him? The explanation is as follows: When people pray at other times, their petitions are scrutinized first to see whether they are worthy of acceptance in light of their deeds. This is not the case, however, if one prays in the morning. Thus, the Zohar relates in Parashas Balak (204a) that Rabbi Elazar, Rabbi Aba and the rest of the company were traveling along the road when Rabbi Elazar began a discourse with the verse, "Hashem, You hear my voice in the morning."

Rabbi Elazar explained that every morning the influence of Avraham's lovingkindness is reawakened, as it is written, "And Avraham arose early in the morning" (Bereishis 22:3). For this reason, it is a very favorable hour, so much so that even the bedridden find relief in the morning through the agency of the angel Refael who reveals himself every morning. When the angels appointed to bring infirmity and sickness upon people behold the angel Refael, they take fright and flee. Then Refael extends healing to the invalid. And just as there is a favorable time to pray for physical healing, so is there a favorable time to pray for the sicknesses of the spirit and soul, that is, one's sins, transgressions and iniquities. The time for this is also in the morning. And since it is a time of favor, even if in light of his deeds the supplicant is not worthy of being answered, nevertheless the Holy One Blessed is He regards him as a penitent and instructs the court not to open an inquest. For lovingkindness and grace are the prerogatives of the Holy One Blessed is He, and the morning is the time that Avraham's lovingkindness is recalled. Therefore, the Holy One Blessed is He accepts prayers of the morning in a spirit of lovingkindness.

The Zohar continues: Rabbi Aba and the rest of the company responded, "If we did not set out upon a journey for any reason other than to hear this, it would have been sufficient for us." While they were walking, a lone dove came to Rabbi Elazar and began chirping to him. Rabbi Elazar said to the dove, "You have always conducted yourself properly in all your missions, as it is written, 'And Noach sent out the dove' (Bereishis 8:8). Go tell Rabbi Yose, 'Look, the companions are coming to see you, myself included. Do not be afraid, for in another three days a miracle will occur. Therefore, let him not be overcome with anxiety, for we are coming to him in joy.'" So, the dove went on ahead to Rabbi Yose ben Lakonya, Rabbi Elazar's father-in-law, to fulfill its mission. Then it returned to Rabbi Elazar with the message that Rabbi Yose ben Lakonya was grief-stricken on account of Rabbi Yose ben Peki'in who was on his deathbed. (For at first Rabbi Yose ben Lakonya was ill but afterwards he recovered and Rabbi Yose ben Peki'in became ill in his stead.)

While they were still traveling, a raven came along and informed Rabbi Elazar that Rabbi Yose ben Peki'in had passed away. Rabbi Aba and the companions were astounded by this but Rabbi Elazar merely told the raven, "Be on your way, for I already know this." He then addressed the companions, "Let us go and do lovingkindness with this 'pomegranate' called 'Rabbi Yose,' who was filled with everything. For he has passed from this world and there is no one fitting to tend to him, whereas he was our associate." So, they turned off the road they were on and headed there. As soon as the citizenry spied them coming, they all turned out to greet them. Then all the companions entered the house of Rabbi Yose of Peki'in.

Rabbi Yose of Peki'in left a young son who would not allow anyone else to approach his father's bed after his death but stood by it himself, weeping over his father. Then the boy began speaking and said, "Master of the Universe! It is written in the Torah, 'When you happen upon a bird's nest by the road ... you shall surely send away the mother and then take the offspring for yourself' (Devarim 22:6-7). Master of the Universe, why did you not fulfill this commandment of the Torah? For my father and mother had two children, myself and my younger sister. You should have taken us instead of them in compliance with the Torah's command! "And should You argue, Master of the Universe, that it is written 'mother' and not 'father,' in this case my mother has already died and You have already taken her from her offspring. But now you have taken my father, who was out protector, away from his offspring as well. What has become of the law of Your Torah?" When Rabbi Elazar, Rabbi Aba and the companions heard the boy's words they began weeping. Rabbi Elazar recited the verse, "The height of the Heavens and the depth of the earth and the hearts of kings are unfathomable" (Mishlei 25:3).

While Rabbi Elazar was reciting this verse a pillar of fire came and intervened between them; meanwhile the boy's mouth clung to his father's mouth and they could not be parted. Rabbi Elazar said, "Either the Holy One Blessed is He wishes to perform a miracle or he does not wish for anyone else to tend to him." While they were sitting there, they heard a voice, saying, "Fortunate are you Rabbi Yose, for the words and tears of that young kid have ascended to the Throne of the holy King and argued your case before Him. Then the Holy One Blessed is He gave over to the Angel of Death thirteen others in place of you and extended your life by twenty-two years, that is, until you have taught Torah to that flawless young kid whom the Holy One Blessed is He loves."

Rabbi Elazar and the companions stood up and would not allow anyone to enter. Then the pillar of fire departed and they saw that Rabbi Yose had opened his eyes. Meanwhile the boy's mouth still clung to his. Rabbi Elazar commented, "Fortunate is our lot that we have witnessed the revival of the dead with our own eyes."

When they approached Rabbi Yose, they discovered that the boy was asleep and seemed as if he had left this world. They remarked, "Fortunate is your lot, Rabbi Yose, and blessed is the Merciful One who has performed for you a miracle on account of your son's words. For he pushed aside the gates of Heaven with his comely words and on account of his copious tears they extended your life by twenty-two years." Then they took the boy and kissed him and cried with him tears of joy, carrying him to another room until his mind was settled and his soul returned to him as before. They rejoiced with Rabbi Yose for three days, propounding numerous novel Torah insights. Rabbi Yose said to them, "Companions, I do not have permission to reveal to you what I saw in the other world until twelve years have passed. But the holy King made a reckoning of the three hundred and seventy tears that my son shed. And I swear to you, my companions, that the moment my son began reciting the verse, 'When you happen upon a bird's nest,' and the other words mentioned above, all the benches in the Heavenly academy shook and everyone stood before the holy King and sought mercy on my behalf. "Then the Holy One Blessed is He was filled with mercy for me because my son's words and self-sacrifice on my behalf pleased him. One of the appointed angels argued, 'Master of the Universe! Look, it is written. Out of the mouths of babes and sucklings You have founded strength because of Your tormentors, to silence the enemy and the avenger (Tehillim 8:3). May it be Your will that in the merit of the Torah and of this child, who offered his own life for his father's. You will have pity on him and spare him.' "Then the Holy One Blessed is He summoned the Angel of Death and gave him thirteen other individuals as a security for me for another twenty-two years."

Now hear the truth of this matter, for Rabbi Yose explained further: What is the meaning of the verse, "Hashem strikes dead and gives life, etc." (1 Shmuel 2:6)? Does the Holy One Blessed is He really cause death? Rather the explanation is that before the soul departs the Satan wishes to cling to the body, which would cause the soul to become sullied as well, Heaven forbid. Therefore, when the time approaches for an upright individual to die, since it is not fitting that the Sitrah Acharah be allowed to cling to his pure soul, the holy Shechinah reveals itself. This weakens the Satan, compelling him to abandon that individual. In the eyes of the Satan the fact that he is not granted any dominion over the souls of the righteous is just as if he [the Satan] died. As for the soul, when it leaves the body it immediately cleaves to the holy Shechinah and is bound up in a holy place known as the "bundle of life." It is this that we refer to when we pray that the soul of the deceased be "bound up in the bundle of life." This is the meaning of the verse, "Hashem strikes dead." That is, He strikes the Sitrah Acharah dead, banishing and weakening it. Meanwhile He "gives life" to the soul of a righteous individual, bringing it into the "bundle of life." In light of this we can also understand the rest of the verse, "He lowers into She'ol and raises up." That is, the soul of a righteous person must descend into Gehinnom for a brief moment, which is like immersion in a mikveh [ritual bath], because, "There is no righteous person on earth who does only good and never sins" (Koheles 7:20). Therefore, in any event it requires immersion to remove the trace of filth with which it was sullied. But then immediately it is "raised up" and elevated to the place that is fitting for it in Gan Eden.

Rabbi Yose said to the other companions, "Know that when I left this world, I also underwent this immersion in Gehinnom and immediately thereafter ascended to my place in Gan Eden. And when my son began his petition, offering his life for mine, his soul also left his body, this is why he seemed to be asleep, for his soul "went out as he spoke" (Shir HaShirim 5:6).

"As soon as my son's soul went out, it encountered my soul ascending from the immersion mentioned earlier. It was then that the decision was made to grant me another twenty-two years of life on account of my son's tears and words. Now that I have been purified and my soul is pure and unsullied, it is essential that during these twenty-two years I engage only in matters pertaining to the World to Come. For I have already experienced the judgment of death and immersion in Gehin- nom. Now I must see to it that I will not be ashamed in the World to Come. "This is what Dovid HaMelech meant when he said, 'God has severely afflicted me, but He did not deliver me unto death' (Tehillim 118:18). That is, Dovid said, 'I see that the Holy One Blessed is He has subjected me to many painful afflictions. But this was only to cleanse me of sin. And now that I have been purified through the "immersion" of afflictions, I must be certain not to sully my soul again from this time forth, Heaven forbid. Rather, Open for me the Gates of Righteousness (ibid. 19), so that I may toil only in Torah and awe of Heaven in order that I will not be ashamed in the World to Come.'"

We may draw a lesson from this incident to the situation of every individual who has experienced the "arrows" of Hashem's judgments and suffered afflictions. Let him reflect that this was only to purify him of his iniquities. Therefore, from that time forth let him be wary of drawing near to the Sitrah Acharah and sullying himself with sin. For then he will need further afflictions to remove the filth.

One might ask, "What do afflictions have to do with the filth of the Sitrah Acharah?" But you must know that the filth of the Sitrah Acharah is a tangible substance. The proof to this is that when a menstruating woman gazes at a mirror a number of stains cling to it, clouding the image so that it becomes spotted with white and black marks, as I have already mentioned in Chapter Two. So, you see that a person can cause an impression even with a defiled look. One can understand, then, that the filth of the Sitrah Acharah is a tangible substance clinging to a person's body, from which it is impossible to be cleansed without afflictions. These cleanses because all afflictions are accompanied by a warming of the body. Therefore, just as the stains on the mirror can only be removed with hot coals, after which it returns to its original appearance, so too a person can only achieve atonement through scorching, which is achieved through the heating of the body caused by afflictions. When one accepts Hashem's afflictions with love and affection, he diminishes the power of the filth from the Sitrah Acharah to spread. Therefore, Heaven forbid that a person remonstrates against his afflictions! Rather let him accept them with love and affection, whether they strike his body or his money. For some individuals become very worked up and excited if they suffer any financial harm. Then with hearts filled brimming with ire then enter into conflicts and quarrels with others. This is the way of those who remonstrate against afflictions. Instead let a person enter humbly and exit humbly, with a broken and contrite heart and with submissiveness. And let him say on every occasion, "Hashem gave and Hashem has taken, may Hashem's name be blessed" (Iyov 1:21). In this way he will arouse Heaven's mercy, for the Holy One Blessed is He will take note of his submission.

I have received a tradition from earlier generations that on certain days of the year Hashem's emissaries are especially liable to bring afflictions upon a person, in particular upon those who remonstrate against them, for which reason whoever is concerned for his soul will stay away from them. These special days will be the subject of the next chapter.

Chapter 32

The author of Turei Zahav mentions in Yoreh De'ah (116:6) a number of days on which blood letting is especially dangerous, and therefore forbidden, because these are days of strict judgment. The reader is advised to examine that source. 9 The days mentioned there are: The first day of Rosh Chodesh of the months Iyar, Elul and Teves when they fall on a Monday or Wednesday. Here is something else that he should read and remember. For I have found it written in the name of a certain great and pious rabbi that the following days are also designated for affliction and are therefore forbidden for bloodletting: the 17th of Marcheshvan, the 5th of Shevat, the 20th of Adar, the 25th of Nisan, the 29th of Iyar, the 16th of Sivan, the 24th of Tammuz, the 26th of Tammuz, the 20th of Av, the 27th of Av and the 12th of Elul.

On all of these days one should be very careful not to allow one's children to walk alone, even in the street. There are many spirits out and about in the world on these days and they have permission to enter into a little boy or girl, Heaven forbid. For these are the designated times for the emissaries of Heaven's judgment to carry out their duties. How many fates and misadventures come upon those who are worthy of punishment! How many benevolent spirits there are, bringing goodly blessings upon the world! And how many malignant spirits there are, bringing noxious fumes and virulent and tenacious illnesses, Heaven forbid! Concerning all these things a person must awaken Heaven's mercy and pray to the Master of the Universe to save him, along with all His people Israel, from all these terrible circumstances.

On the days mentioned above the begrudging have the authority to inject the power of the evil eye into another person's children or wealth. Therefore, one should conceal his children when taking them through the street on those days, just as the Holy One Blessed is He did to Israel to protect them from the wicked Bilaam (Zohar 3:211b). For when Bilaam saw that he was unable to do them any harm he tried gazing at them with his evil eye, because whatever he set his gaze upon was cursed. This is the meaning of the verse, "Bilaam looked up and saw Israel dwelling according to his tribes and the spirit of God came upon him (meaning Israel!)." Explains the Zohar, "Like one who spreads a garment over the head of a child, to prevent the evil eye of the wicked Bilaam from harming them."

Know further that according to a tradition I have received from earlier generations, the eleven verses in Scripture that begin with the letter nun and end with the letter nun are efficacious in warding off sorcery and the evil eye. Therefore, after one recites these verses in the Ma'amados of Sunday it is good to recite this short prayer:

Master of the Universe! Save Your people the House of Israel from all forms of sorcery and from all manifestations of the evil eye. And just as You spread Your wings over our ancestors in the desert so that Bilaam's evil eye would have no dominion over them, so too spread Your wings over us in Your abundant mercy that we should be concealed with a covering and shield of Your holy names from every manifestation of the evil eye. Then recite the verse, "You are my shelter, from distress You preserve me; with glad song of rescue Your envelope me, selah" (Tehillim 32:7). And when a pregnant woman recites these eleven verses, she can rest assured that no evil eye will have dominion over the fetus. Therefore, a person should be certain to recite these eleven verses and he will be spared from the evil eye. Amein, so may it be His will.

Chapter 33

Our Sages instituted that we recite three times a day the verse, "And He, the merciful One atones iniquity, and does not destroy; He frequently withdraws His anger, and does not arouse all His rage" (Tehillim 78:38). It is said once in the prayer "Acknowledge Hashem, call upon His name," once in "And a redeemer will come to Tzion," and once at the beginning of the evening service. The reason for this is as follows: In this verse there are thirteen words, corresponding to the thirteen Divine attributes of mercy and three times thirteen is thirty-nine. Now, each day the evil impulse overwhelms a person so that it is only with the greatest difficulty that he is able to avoid committing sins carrying the penalty of thirty-nine lashes. Thus, the recitation of this verse is a way of requesting the Holy One Blessed is He to grant atonement for the person's sin as if he had actually received the lashes, in order that he will not be destroyed on account of it. For iniquity provokes the destructive forces called "anger" and "wrath." It was these that brought indictments against Israel continually while they were in Egypt so that the Holy One Blessed is He, through His graciousness and compassion only revealed Himself to save them in the merit of the three Patriarchs. When He did reveal Himself, it was in the form of the three Divine names: E-H-Y-H ("I will be"), Y-H-V-H (Tetragrammaton) and A-D-N-Y ("Lord"). The sum of the numerical values of these names is 112, which is equal to that of the acronym YB"K, the initial letters of the words, Ya'aneinu be'yom kareinu — "He will answer us on the day that we call out" (Tikkunei Zohar Chadash 130a). For this reason, after we recite the verse, "And He is merciful, etc.," we then recite the verse, "Hashem will save; the King will answer us on the day that we call out" (Tehillim 20:10).

Lashes are of tremendous benefit and can save a person from the thirty-nine curses with which the primordial snake was cursed (the acronym for 39 is lot, which means "curse"). In fact, they transform these curses in to the "dew" (tal) of blessing (tal is comprised of the same letters as lot in reverse). This dew drips down at specific times upon the heads of those who desire to cling to the awe of Hashem, awakening them to the ways of awe. It is identical with the "dew" with which the Holy One Blessed is He will one day revive the dead. Its special power is that it pulls the souls of the dead towards holiness.

Therefore, one should not neglect submitting to lashes at least once a month. This is what our forefather Avraham was alluding to when he said to Hashem, "Perhaps there will be found there forty [righteous men]" (Bereishis 18:29). As the Zohar (1:104b) clarifies the meaning: "Perhaps there will be found their individuals who submit themselves to the forty lashes," to which Hashem responded, "I will not destroy, etc."

In the same way that a person must submit to lashes in this world in order that he will not be subjected to them in the next world, so, too, are there many transgressions on account of which the Sages say that one is put under a ban (niddui). What this actually means is that he is worthy of being placed under a ban and if he is not placed under one by the earthly court then he will be placed under one by the Heavenly court. It is a very serious matter for a person to be placed under a ban On High, for all the while that he is under the ban his prayers are not heard and his soul is compelled to wander back and forth outside of the Holy Partition. He also forfeits the protection of the Guardian of Israel. Then when he is on the road or in any other place of danger he may easily come to harm, for he resembles completely a discarded object over which Heaven has removed its supervision. And if his wife conceives while he is under the ban the child will fall into the category of "those who willfully transgress and rebel" against the laws of our God (Yechezkeyl 20:38).

Therefore, whoever is very wise and perceptive will consider that it is imperative that he rectify this situation with all haste and without delay. For who knows what the day will bring? Perhaps he will die suddenly and his soul will be unable to return to the place from which it was excavated but will be given over to cruel destructive and damaging spirits.

Therefore, I will write the following plan of rectification found among the writings of the Ari, z"l (Or Tzaddikim, 35:14). First, he must select a day on which to set aside all other affairs and conduct himself in this manner: Let him choose a suitable place in his house and sit there as one under a ban and recite: I am hereby sitting here in order to accept upon myself a rebuke and a ban because I have been condemned by the Heavenly court for my sins, iniquities and transgressions, by which I have sinned, acted iniquitously and transgressed. I am a despised form. I have incurred much guilt on account of Your Torah. I have behaved treacherously with regard to Your awe. I have blemished Your emanations. I have brought defect to Your holy things. I have diverted the waters flowing from the House of Hashem towards the outhouse, a place of filth, a woman of harlotry. I have destroyed Your altar; I have defiled Your covenant by drawing a foreskin over the holy mark of the covenant. I have blemished the twenty-seven (the numerical value of zach — "pure") holy letters. I have strengthened the malignant spirits called chitzonim. And if I have incurred a ban from the court of righteousness or from the Holy One Blessed is He and His Shechinah, look, I have sat alone and accepted upon myself the decree. I am filled with remorse and weeping over my iniquities. I have sinned and done iniquitously, but I will return to those ways no more. Therefore, Fashioner of Creation, release me! Mighty One of Yaakov, pardon me! For You are a benevolent and forgiving King. Help me to be among those who return to You every day with a whole heart and do not recall my sin any longer. Amein, selah.

I would really like to present here a great and awesome formula for unifying the Divine name. However, since not all minds are on the same level, especially since our understanding has declined, I am concerned less the reader invert the order of things and cause further harm rather than rectification. Therefore, I will present a brief prayer instead, and may the One who examines hearts accept it with favor: Master of the Universe! It is openly known to You that my soul greatly longs to recite the verses of unification with the intention of bringing about a great and awesome unification of Your holy names with love. However, our iniquities have overwhelmed us and they weigh upon us like a heavy burden. For this reason physicality has come to dominate us to the degree that we are unable to have the proper intentions. Therefore, we are concerned lest we cause harm rather than rectification, on account of our iniquities. How, then, can we possibly draw near and approach the holy place? How can we enter the gates of the King of the Kings of Kings, the Holy One Blessed is He, while we are dressed in sackcloth? Therefore, Master of the Universe, please have pity and compassion upon us, Master of Forgiveness. And let our prayers be sweet to you, exalted and lofty God. And let all the blemishes be rectified and the stains cleansed through this prayer that I am reciting with a broken heart and a lowly spirit, just as if I had carried out the proper rectification. For, "a broken and contrite heart, O God, you will not despise" (Tehillim 51:19).

Afterwards let him rise from the floor and spend the rest of the day engrossed in prayer and Torah study. Then Heaven will have mercy upon him and remove from him the punishment of the ban imposed upon him by the Heavenly court, provided that he was not subjected to a ban by the earthly court as well. If he conducts himself as I have outlined let him feel confident and assured that, "He will return and heal him" (Yeshayahu 6:10).

Now I will dedicate a chapter especially to the question of which transgressions are subject to a ban (cherem or niddui).

Chapter 34

These are the offenses for which the court is obliged to impose a ban (niddui):

1. For using crude speech, Heaven forbid.
2. For holding one's reproductive organ and wasting seed.
3. For neglecting rabbinical ordinances such as the washing of the hands, the laws of muktzeh, etc.
4. For denigrating Torah scholars, whether in their presence or not in their presence.
5. For desecrating the Name of Heaven by [antagonizing a gentile into] cursing the Jewish people.
6. For refusing to obey the directives of the court, if one is powerful and stubborn, causing the plaintiff the aggravation of being unable to extract his due or of having to spend large sums to enforce the settlement.
7. For reciting the songs and praises from "Blessed is He Who spoke" until "Let His name be praised" hurriedly and without expressing the words fully and clearly.
8. For mocking an upright person.
9. For speaking excessively with a woman other than one's wife, in order to gaze at her beauty when it is possible speak more briefly but one's intention is to satisfy the evil inclination.
10. For affirming the deeds of an evildoer, causing his power to increase, either by supporting his faction in a quarrel or through flattery.

For these offenses the earthly court is obliged to impose a ban and if they fail to do so, one is automatically imposed from On High, requiring him to utilize the plan of rectification outlined in the previous chapter.

The most serious of all these offenses are: the use of crude speech, speaking irreverently about Torah scholars and behaving forcefully and uncooperatively in matters of litigation. But there is another form of conduct for which the Heavenly court also imposes a ban that is more serious than any of these. That is, speaking to others brazenly and without any shame at all. For this offence the ban discussed above is not sufficient, therefore his soul is reincarnated as a dog. This is the meaning of the expression, "And the brazen-souled dogs" (Yeshayahu 56:11). And if you suppose that being reincarnated as a dog is a minor punishment, consider that the same punishment is meted out to one who has relations with a married woman, Heaven spare us.

You should be aware of an incident cited in the writings of the Ari, z"l. In his day there was a certain pious man named Rabbi Avraham ibn Puah, z"l. He was very wealthy and his hand was always open to the poor and needy. Nearby there lived another Jew who was involved in commerce with Rabbi Avraham's wife, who was a clever business woman. One day the neighbor suddenly took ill and was bedridden for many days. Eventually his flesh began to rot away, including that of his reproductive organ. He spent enormous sums on medical expenses but found no remedy for his illness, and he finally died after intense and bitter suffering. Several years later a dog appeared and began lingering around the home of Rabbi Avraham ibn Puah. It was a black and very ugly dog. Those who saw it were very afraid, for its face was that of a malignant spirit. Again, and again they chased the dog away from Rabbi Avraham's house with sticks, but it kept coming back. Whenever he would arise to go to the synagogue, he would find the black dog standing by the door waiting for him to open it, whereupon it would try to force its way inside. Rabbi Avraham would chase the dog away and then instruct that the door be latched behind him. Nevertheless, the dog would return and wait for the door to be opened once more. One morning when Rabbi Avraham left the house, he forgot to latch the doors both to the main entrance as well as to the winter quarters therein. Immediately the dog sprang forward, running from room to room until he found the chamber where Rabbi Avraham's wife still lay asleep in bed. The dog leaped upon the bed and began biting her again and again causing many wounds and bruises. Afterwards it fled the house. The woman let out such a great cry that her voice was heard even in the house of the Ari.

Then her husband Rabbi Avraham, accompanied by other men of the community, went to the Ari to inquire about the reason for this incident. He replied that on account of our many sins this woman had committed adultery with her neighbor who had now died, and that this black dog was the reincarnation of his soul. She had seduced the man with words and with money to sleep with her, on account of which the dog had now come to take revenge.

Upon hearing this they made the woman take an oath to tell the truth and she admitted that her neighbor indeed used to sleep with her in the storehouse. It was because of this that his flesh, including that of his reproductive organ, had rotted away. Afterwards the woman sought to repent and died in the course of her penance. But the pious Rabbi Avraham sent her away from his house immediately.

So, you see that the punishment for brazenness, reincarnation in the form of a dog, is the same as that of an adulterer. Therefore, one must always behave with a sense of shame and let fear of Hashem be upon his face at all times. Then all will be well with him, selah.

Chapter 35

The custom of fasting on the anniversary of the death of a parent — known as the yarhtzeit — has spread throughout the Jewish world for reasons that are well known. Thus the author of Nishmas Chaim (Essay II, Ch. 28) explains that is because the son's own fortune (mazzal) is weak on that day. Alternatively, it is because the parent undergoes some aspect of judgment every year on this date and the reciting of Kaddish and fasting by his offspring give him some protection from this judgment. However, these actions are still not enough. Therefore, the son should also engage in good deeds on this day, and if he is a scholar, he should try to propound novel Torah insights, for this is of great benefit to the parent. At other times of the year, too, whenever the son propounds new insights for pure motives, he brings gratification to his parents and they are adorned with many crowns. And if the deceased merited marrying off his daughter to a scholar, whenever his son-in-law propounds a true insight the father and mother-in-law are also adorned with crowns.

This concept is already mentioned in the Zohar (Parashas Naso 144a). Thus, it is recorded that Rabbi Shimon ben Yochai selected a certain holy place where he sat with his disciples, propounding novel insights and revealing secrets of the Torah. Then they heard a Heavenly voice saying, "Fortunate are you, Rabbi Shimon ben Yochai and your disciples, for what has been revealed to has not been revealed to all the hosts of Heaven; these insights that have never been revealed since the time that Moshe Rabbeinu stood upon Mount Sinai!" Then several groups of ministering angels gathered round to hear those Torah secrets and that day became known On High as the "Rejoicing (Hilula) of Rabbi Shimon ben Yochai."

Rabbi Shimon ben Yochai said, "I am surprised at that one who is girded at the waist (i.e., Eliyahu the prophet). Why was he not here in our threshing floor when these holy matters were being revealed?" While he was speaking, Eliyahu arrived with sparks of light upon his face. Rabbi Shimon said to him, "Why was the master not present for numerous delicacies that we arranged before the Holy One Blessed is He on the Day of Rejoicing?" Eliyahu responded, "By your life, Rabbi, I wished to be present but was unable, because on that day the Holy One Blessed is He sent me to perform miracles on behalf of Rav Hamnuna the Elder and his companions who had been delivered to the king's palace. So I uprooted the palace and overturned it, and a miracle occurred in which two hundred and forty-five of nobles who had leveled accusations against Rav Hamnuna were all killed.

"I extricated Rav Hamnuna and his companions and stood them up at a distance in the Valley of Ono and they were spared. Then I prepared sustenance for them there — bread and water — for they had not eaten for three days. I did not part from them that entire day. "When I returned, I heard the sound of voices and rejoicing On High. 'What is the cause of this rejoicing?' I inquired. And they informed me, 'This is the Day of Rejoicing of Rabbi Shimon ben Yochai!' Fortunate are you Rabbi Shimon ben Yochai. Fortunate is your lot and fortunate are your companions sitting before you! How many paths have been prepared to bring you illumination from the rivers of pure balsam? Come and see that on this day fifty crowns were bestowed upon your father-in-law Rabbi Pinchas ben Yair..."

It is clear from this passage how valued are Torah insights that are propounded for pure motives. Similarly, all good deeds bring pleasure to Hashem when they are done for pure motives. But the opposite is also true, Heaven forbid, when these deeds are done for ulterior motives, as we find in another passage from the Zohar (1:190a): When Rabbi Chiyya emigrated to the Land of Israel he read from the Torah until his face shone like the sun. Then when those engaged in Torah study stood before him, he was able to say, "This one studied for pure motives and this one for ulterior motives." He would pray on behalf of those who study for ulterior motives that they learn to study for pure motives so that they may earn [a portion in] the World to Come.

One day a certain student was engaged in study when his face blanched. Rabbi Chiyya observed, "Surely he was contemplating a sin!" So, he took hold of him and led him into a difficult Torah discussion until his spirit settled. From that day forward he resolved never again to pursue wicked thoughts but to engage in study for pure motives.

The general rule is that whenever a person has the opportunity to do perform deed, he must reflect well whether or not it will bring pleasure to our Heavenly Father. And if it involves any trace of transgression, Heaven forbid, he can be certain that it will not find favor before the Holy One Blessed is He. The Zohar continues: A person must examine his iniquities every day, for when he arises from his bed, two witnesses stand before him to accompany him throughout the day. When he wishes to rise, the two witnesses say to him as he opens his eyes, "Let your eyes look straight ahead" (Mishlei 4:25) ...When he stands up and prepares to walk, they say, "Make straight the path of your foot" (ibid. 26) ... Therefore, as a man goes about, he must guard himself against iniquity the entire day. And every day when evening comes, he must reflect and examine everything he did that day in order to repent of whatever was improper. He must contemplate them continually in order that he will repent.

But suppose that he does not take to heart the obligation to reflect and examine his deeds to see of what they consisted, what they were like and whether or not they were upright. Suppose that instead he simply goes out and acts, engaging in numerous deeds and treading many paths without making any reckoning of whether his deeds are bad or good. Through this he joins the company of those who walk in darkness and never see the light. Heaven will bestow upon him no benevolence and nor will the Heavenly court bless him with peace. Our pious predecessors were careful not greet a person with "peace" in this world either until they examined his deeds well. Thus, it is related in the Zohar (Parashas Mikeitz 204b): Rabbi Chiyya and Rabbi Yose were walking along the way. Meanwhile they saw someone coming towards them wrapped in tzitzis and with his weapons tied beneath his clothes.

Rabbi Chiyya observed, "One of two possibilities is true regarding this fellow. Either he is totally righteous or else he is intent on deceiving the world." Rabbi Yose said to him, "Did not our lofty pious predecessors say that we should judge every person favorably? We have learned that when one sets out on a trip, one should have three strategies in mind: gifts, war and prayer. These are derived from the way Yaakov acted [when confronted with Eisov]. "Now since this fellow is traveling along the road, he has wrapped himself in preparation for prayer, while simultaneously bearing a weapon in case of war. And since it is evident that he has prepared two of the three strategies, we do not need to pursue the third." As he approached them, they greeted him with, "Peace!" but he did not respond. Rabbi Chiyya remarked, "The one strategy we did not see in him, he lacks. It seems that he has prepared no gifts for offering a greeting of 'peace' is included in the category of gifts." Rabbi Yose replied, "Perhaps he is immersed in prayer or perhaps he is reviewing his studies so that he will not forget them." The three of them continued walking together but the man still would not speak with them. After a time, Rabbi Chiyya and Rabbi Yose slipped away in order to engage in study. Then the man approached them and greeted them with, "Peace," inquiring, "My teachers, what did you suspect about me when you greeted me with 'peace' but I did not respond to you?" They said, "Perhaps you were saying prayers or reviewing your studies." He said to them, "Because you judged me favorably, may the Omnipresent judge you favorably. But I will tell you the truth. One day I was walking along the road when I encountered a man and greeted him with 'peace.' That man turned out to be a bandit, and he then attacked me, causing me anguish. And if I had not succeeded in overpowering him, I would have been sorry.

"From that day forward, I vowed that I would never offer a greeting of 'peace' to anyone until I examined whether or not he is righteous. For it is forbidden to offer 'peace' to an evildoer, as it is written, 'There is no peace, said Hashem, for the wicked' (Yeshayahu 48:22). "When I first saw you and you greeted me with 'peace' and I did not respond I was suspicious of you because I did not see any upon you any visible sign of a mitzvah. This is one reason. Another reason is that I was indeed reviewing my studies at that moment and did not wish to interrupt the words of Torah." It is clear from here that it is forbidden to greet an evildoer. It is even more certain that they do not wish "peace" upon an evildoer in On High, for in Heaven there is no flattery of the wicked as there is in this world. That world is the World of Truth in which there is no flattery or showing of favor. Everything is judged there according to measures, scales and line- measures that are precise.

The fact that nowadays we greet everyone with the word "peace" is also explained in the Zohar (2:23b). There it is related that if the evildoer may otherwise cause him harm, he is allowed to extend him a greeting of "peace" in order to escape. Perhaps this is also the reason that Rabbi Yochanan used to be the first to offer "peace" to everyone he met, even to a gentile in the market (Berachos 17a). My meaning should be clear. Therefore, a human being, sated with anxiety and carved out of clay, should contemplate that it is not fitting for him to be arrogant or avaricious. Rather let him speak gently; let all his deeds be thought out and measured; and let him make a reckoning every day before Hashem. Then through his own introspection he will refrain from sinning and then he will succeed in all that he does. Amein.

Kav HaYashar

Chapter 36

It is related in Ta'anis (25a) that Rabbi Elazar ben Pedas once underwent a bloodletting operation when he was in dire financial straits, but after the procedure he had nothing with which to strengthen himself. All he could find was clove of garlic, so he cast it into his mouth. This caused his heart to become faint and he fell into a deep slumber. When the rabbis came to inquire after his welfare, they saw him crying and then smiling, after which a spark emitted from his forehead. When he awoke, the rabbis inquired, "Why did the master cry and then smile and why did a spark then come out of his forehead?" He replied, "I beheld Hashem's Shechinah and He wished me 'peace.'" "Master of the Universe," I said, "for how long will I remain in such sorrow and deprivation?" He said to me, "Elazar, My son, would you like Me to destroy the world and create it anew on the chance that you will be born at a time ordained for a more generous livelihood?" I said, "Master of the Universe, which are more numerous, the years that I have already lived or those that I have yet to live?" The Shechinah said, "Those that you have already lived." "In that case I do not wish for You to do so," I said. They then showed me thirteen rivers flowing with balsam. I inquired, "Who are these for?" Hashem said to me, "They are for you." "Is that all?" I asked. To which the Shechinah replied, "What will be left for your colleagues?" ["Am I requesting of someone who lacks for anything?" I asked], whereupon He struck me with His finger upon the forehead, [after which a spark emitted from my forhead].

This passage is explained more fully in the Zohar on Bereishis (Tikkunim 69, 100a). There it is taught that a person's offspring, life span and livelihood are all dependent upon his astrological sign (mazzal), not his merit. If a person was born under a sign indicating poverty, merit cannot change it. The best that merit can accomplish is to cause the Holy One Blessed is He to take his soul out and instill it into a different body. Through this change in location he may be granted a more generous income. But even then, it is only a possibility.

This is what the Holy One Blessed is He meant when He asked Rabbi Elazar, "Would you like Me to destroy the world?" For it is well known that a human being is called a miniature "world." Thus, He was offering to destroy his current body by taking his soul from him and then to go back and create a new body into which to introduce his soul, opening up the possibility that he will merit a more generous income. This is why Rabbi Elazar responded, "I do not wish for You to do so." We can learn from this passage that a person should not try to change his circumstances forcibly. Rather, let him trust that Hashem does not withhold the just reward of any creature. If he did not merit a life of comfort in this world he should not be concerned, for undoubtedly his reward will be many times greater in the next world.

Every God-fearing person should rejoice over the lot that Hashem has granted him, whether bountiful or meager. He should not be at all concerned if he must live frugally and he should certainly not harbor any ill thoughts about the ways of the Holy One Blessed is He, Heaven forbid! Let him show no sign of anger or irritation when speaking of the matter with others, either, for that would be as if he were rebelling against Hashem. Instead let him reflect that his deprivation and poverty are atonements and tokens of forgiveness for his sins and iniquities. As the Sages warn, "Whoever forces time, [and extends himself in an effort to succeed more quickly] the time will force him [so that he will encounter setbacks and not succeed]" (Eiruvin 13b). Whenever the Holy One Blessed is He requites a person for his transgressions in this world it is in fact an act of lovingkindness. Thus, the wicked cry out in Gehinnom, "If only we had been poor and downtrodden in this world! If only we had suffered afflictions in this world to atone for our sins!" They say further, "The abundance of goodness and the financial power that we enjoyed was to our detriment. For now, we are caught in the terrible trap of Gehinnom.

Therefore, let a person reflect on these things every day. And although all moments are not equal, let him be accustomed to say, "Whatever the Merciful One does is for the good." And if Hashem has granted him wealth and bounty it is especially important that he conduct himself with justice, integrity and mercy. Let his hands be open to share his blessings with the poor and needy. Let every God-fearing individual bear in mind that whenever the opportunity to perform a mitzvah arises it is a sure sign that some evil decree has been issued against him, Heaven forbid, and it is only through this mitzvah that he can save himself from it. This is an essential principle leading to zeal in the performance of the commandments. Thus, the Zohar relates (Parashas Behar 110b): Rabbi Chiyya and Rabbi Yose were traveling along the road when they came to a certain mountain. There they noticed two people walking along. Meanwhile another person approached them, saying, "Please give me some bread! For I have been fasting for two days. I have been traveling through the desert and have eaten nothing." One of the two men immediately went and took out the provisions he had brought along for the way, and gave them to him following which he ate and drank. Then his companion said to him, "Now what will you do? For now, you have nothing to eat, since you have given everything to that beggar! Do not rely on mine because I have with me only meager rations." He replied, "What claim do I have on you? Of course, I will not ask you to give me anything. I will simply go without eating." Then the beggar came and sat down beside him and continued eating until there remained only a little bread. This, too, the man gave him for the way, and the beggar moved on. Upon seeing this Rabbi Chiyya was distressed that he had not been granted the mitzvah of sustaining the poor man. But Rabbi Yose said to him, "Do not be distressed. For it is not in vain that the Holy One Blessed is He presented this man with the mitzvah. Perhaps an evil decree had been issued against him and the Holy One Blessed is He offered him the mitzvah that he might be spared in its merit." Rabbi Chiyya responded, "Look, we have provisions. Let us give them to him to eat." "We must not give him anything," said Rabbi Yose, "because with the bread that we gave him we would deprive him of his merit. Let us simply go and see what transpires, for certainly a death sentence was hanging over him, from which he was saved in the merit of the sustenance that he granted the beggar."

In the meantime, the man had sat down and dozed off under a tree while his companion took leave of him to travel by a different route. Rabbi Yose said to Rabbi Chiyya, "Now let us sit at a distance and watch what happens because it is clear that the Holy One Blessed Is He intends to perform a miracle on his behalf." Meanwhile they saw a figure resembling flaming coal standing before him. Rabbi Chiyya declared, "Woe to him, for now he is about to die." But Rabbi Yose said, "How deserving he must be, for the Holy One Blessed is He is about to do a miracle on his behalf." While they were speaking a snake came down from the tree bent on killing the man. But the flame arose and trampled the head of the snake, killing it and then disappeared. Rabbi Yose said, "Did I not tell you that the Holy One Blessed is He wished to do a miracle for him and that you should not deprive him of his merit?" Soon the man awoke and stood up to continue along his way. But Rabbi Chiyya and Rabbi Yose caught up with him and gave him to eat. Afterwards they informed him of the miracle that the Holy One Blessed is He had done for him. Rabbi Yose then cited the verse, "And charity saves from death" (Mishlei 11:4). He explained, "There is a Tree of Life and a Tree of Death. Whoever does good deeds takes hold of the Tree of Life. Whoever does bad ones takes hold of the Tree of Death. This fellow who performed charity and gave sustenance to the poor was saved thereby from the snake and he thus weakened the power of the Tree of Death."

Therefore, let a person see clearly that this world is one of vanity and heartbreak, and that one's only goal should be to inherit the World to Come. To this end let him occupy himself with charity, Torah and acts of lovingkindness that we may all merit swiftly a [portion in] the World to Come, Amein.

Chapter 37

It is taught in the first chapter of Berachos (3a) that the night is divided into three "watches." During each watch the Holy One Blessed is He sits roaring like a lion, saying, "Woe to Me that I have destroyed My House, burned My Temple and exiled My children among the nations of the world!"

These three watches are explained more fully in the Zohar in Parashas Vayakhel (195b): One-night Rabbi Elazar and Rabbi Yose were engaged in study just before midnight. In the meantime, the rooster crowed, so they recited the blessing, "Who grants the rooster insight to discern between day and night." Rabbi Elazar said, "This is the time that the Holy One Blessed is He enters Gan Eden to delight with the righteous." Rabbi Yose inquired, "Why does the Holy One Blessed is He take delight in them?" Rabbi Elazar wept and said, "Come and see. Before this time the Holy One Blessed is He shook three hundred firmaments and struck them, wailing over the destruction of the Temple. Then He shed two tears into the ocean, recalling His children in the midst of His weeping.

The night is divided into three parts and each watch is four hours long. And when the night is shorter than twelve hours the day makes up for it. During the first watch the angels stand reciting the Psalm (24), "To Hashem belongs the earth and the fullness thereof ... Who may ascend the mountain of Hashem and who may stand in the place of His holiness?" During the first four hours of the night, which is a time for weeping, human souls ascend On High. Those righteous souls that merit ascending On High every night come first to the Temple Mount where they assemble to ascend en masse with great joy to the Heavenly Sanctuary, where they behold the countenance of the Shechinah and receive illumination. For this reason, the angels recite, "Who may ascend the Mountain of Hashem," referring to the Temple Mount, and "who may stand in His Holy Place," referring to the Heavenly Sanctuary.

The Psalm continues: "Those with clean hands" — that is, their hands must be clean of theft and other forms of injustice. "And a pure heart" — that is, their hearts must be pure of sinful musings and evil thoughts. They must be filled with mercy upon hearing the cry of the poor and needy and they must be as pliant as a reed when it comes to accepting rebuke and correction. Moreover, they must not rebel against parents and teachers when they guide them and urge them along the path of righteousness. Their hearts must be merciful and not cruel. These are the ones whose souls merit ascending every night to the Mountain of Hashem and to Hashem's Holy Place and they are the ones who will "bear a blessing from Hashem."

The second watch also consists of four hours, but it is divided into two parts. During the two hours preceding midnight the ministering angels weep bitterly over the destruction of the Temple, reciting the Psalm (137), "By the rivers of Babylon, there we sat and we also wept (when we remembered Zion). How shall we sing the song of Hashem song on alien soil..." At that time the Holy One Blessed is He weeps with them and the angels that the Holy One Blessed is He commanded to accompany Israel into the Babylonian and Edomite exiles also weep, as stated in the verse, "For they have cried for their altar in the street — emissaries of peace weep bitterly" (Yeshayahu 33:7). This is the meaning of the verse, "By the rivers of Babylon, there we sat down and also wept as we remembered Tzion." That is, we, Israel, also wept along with the angels who wept there over the destruction of the Temple and slaughter of the righteous.

As long as we remain in this bitter exile we must mourn in every generation for our brethren, the House of Israel, who are slaughtered, strangled, burned and stoned in sanctification of Hashem's name, suffering terrible and bitter tortures. For the nations of the world attack them with libelous charges and then the holy martyrs give over their souls and bodies to the sanctification of the Name, suffering terrible tortures while accepting the decrees of the King of the Kings of Kings with love and affection. At that moment the Holy One Blessed is He is stirred, giving the firmament a kick that sends a shudder through twelve thousand worlds. Then He roars with weeping over His Abode and from His Holy Place in Heaven He causes His voice to be heard crying over Israel who are held captive in this bitter exile and subjected to afflictions by Amalek and Yishmael and the other nations. Immediately He sheds two tears into the ocean. Then a great and awesome flame arises from the north. And a great light crashes against it, causing the flame to spread throughout the world. A single spark spreads beneath the wings of the rooster searing it until it begins flapping its wings as if to cool itself off from a fire. Then it begins to crow, disclosing and revealing amazing secrets with its cry. All this is only intended to awaken awe of Hashem in mortals. Meanwhile the moment the rooster crows that first time all the hosts of Heaven are filled with anguish over the destruction of the Temple as well as Israel's exile. Then when midnight comes the Holy One Blessed Is He enters Gan Eden to delight with the souls of the righteous, as is related in a number of places in the Zohar (1:77a and 82b). This is alluded to in the book of Esther when

Esther says to the king, "For I and my people have been sold to be destroyed and killed," to which the king responds, "Who is this and which one is he…?" Then it is related that, "The king arose in his wrath and went out to his garden pavilion" (7:4-7). The "king" referred to is the Holy One Blessed is He. "Arising in His wrath" means that He arises in anguish over Israel's exile and the destruction of the Temple. "His garden pavilion" refers to Gan Eden, which is also called by this name. When the Holy One Blessed is He enters Gan Eden to delight with the souls of the righteous, all the trees of the garden along with all the souls of the righteous open their mouths in holiness and purity, with song and exultation, saying, "Let the gates lift up their heads and let the entrances of the world be lifted up that the King of Glory may enter … Hashem of Hosts, He is the King of Glory, selah " (Tehillim 24:7-10).

After this, during the last four hours of the night, the angels of the third watch begin reciting songs of praise. At that time the righteous of this world awaken to Hashem's service and the angels recite, "Behold, bless Hashem, all you servants of Ha- shem who stand in the House of Hashem at night" (Ibid., 134:1). When dawn arrives, the stars and constellations begin singing in trepidation and awe, in keeping with the verse, "When the stars of the morning sang together and all the sons of God exulted" (Iyov 38:7). Afterwards, the sun appears, singing sweetly, "Acknowledge Hashem, call upon His name, tell of His deeds among the peoples" (Tehillim 105:1). At that time Israel go to the synagogue to pray and to accept upon themselves the yoke of Heaven, making their great and awesome declaration of Hashem's unity with the words, "Hear, O Israel, Hashem is our God, Hashem is one!" (Devorim 6:4). Then the name of the Holy One Blessed is He is sanctified and unified by all the hosts of Heaven and earth, granting Him satisfaction.

But the foolish, whose hearts are stopped up and who are drawn after worldly pleasure, give no thought to all these lofty and holy events transpiring every night and every morning. They have no longing to be among those righteous souls that give satisfaction to the Holy One Blessed is He. Their only goal is to fill their gullets with their appetites and to follow their heart's desire. When they arise in the morning they go outside to the boulevards and plazas to speak of vulgar and crude matters, or to discuss business. Or else they go to their chambers to pursue their occupations. If they go to the synagogue they do so perfunctorily, placing their tefillin upon their arms and head as mere tributes and praying without reflecting ahead of time on the sanctity of the place to which they are going. For the Shechinah dwells continually in every synagogue in this bitter exile, yet they go there in a state of confusion and with alien thoughts. And even when they pray, they utter the words with their mouths while their minds are occupied with other concerns. They view prayer as a yoke and a burden, fleeing from the synagogue quickly afterwards to follow their heart's desire and pursue worldly pleasures. They give no consideration at all to what good deed they will be able to take with them when they come before their Creator. But when evening comes and they are asleep upon their beds, their souls leave their bodies to testify concerning their deeds of that day. And when they come before the Throne of Glory, a soul that is sullied with sin and failed to serve Hashem in a complete manner is pushed out of the Holy Partition and delivered into the hands of the Sitrah acharah, Heaven forbid. He is given no chance to repent because "in the way that a person chooses to go, that is how he is led" (Makkos 10b). But this is not the case if a person shuns the confusion of this world and accustoms himself to rising early to Hashem's service.

If he is capable of engaging in study, there is no greater measure than that. And he is not capable of studying Torah, let him arise to pray with all his heart and mourn over the Temple and the exile. Then the Holy One Blessed is He will open for him the Gates of Repentance "and he will go back and be healed" (Yeshayahu 6:10).

Chapter 38

Our Sages instituted (Berachos 4b) that before beginning the Shemoneh Esrei one must say the verse, "Hashem, open my lips and my mouth will tell of Your praise" (Tehillim 51:17). This is a plea that the Holy One Blessed is He accept our prayers with favor and not say, as He does to the wicked, "What business do you have relating My statutes and bearing My covenant upon your mouth?" (Tehillim 50:16). The Creator, may He be blessed, is disgusted with the prayers of a person whose deeds are despicable. What, then, is the purpose of his life? He would be better off dead than alive. Therefore, when a person stands up to pray let him do so in fear and trembling and let his heart and mouth be in accord as the declare the unity of Hashem's great name with complete intention during the Shemoneh Esreh. Then the Holy One Blessed is He will call him by the name, "Peace," and for the rest of his life this will be his name On High throughout all the firmaments. Thus, the Zohar teaches (2:200b), "When he leaves this world his soul ascends, passing through all those firmaments and encountering no protest. Then the Holy One Blessed is He and all His hosts call him 'Peace,' as they open before him twelve gates of pure balsam."

To illustrate the loftiness of Israel's prayers we will cite here the continuation of the passage from the Zohar. To begin with you must know that there are certain angels assigned over all the entrances, gates and windows of every firmament by day and by night. The appointed ministers of the day are called, "the rulers of the day," while the appointed ministers of the night are called, "the rulers of the night" (Bereishis 1:16). At every entrance, gate and window there is one appointed minister, under whom are thousands of ministers and governors. Who can count or even conceive of all the ministers of these ministers and all the hosts and bands that are under them? Every day at nightfall and again at daybreak an announcement is made throughout all the firmaments instructing the appointed ministers to take up their positions, whereupon each one goes to its station. Then the Holy One Blessed is He descends and all Israel go to their synagogues to give praise to their Master with songs and prayers. If a person approaches Hashem's service with awe and trembling and prays with full concentration, so that his mouth and heart are as one as they declare the unity of the holy Name, then the Holy One Blessed is He is gratified and joyful with his prayer. Then each word he utters ascends On High to be received joyfully by the appointed angels until it reaches the highest heights where it is fashioned into a crown upon the head of the King of the Kings of Kings, the Holy One Blessed is He.

The process of its ascent is as follows: In each of the four directions of the world there are officers and ministers stationed On High. To begin with, the prayer comes before one of these appointed ministers, in front of whom are nine entrances, beside which are four other officers and ministers. All of these are overseen by a single angel named ABULYEL. This angel goes out to greet the prayer, accompanied by all the other angels. Then they take this prayer and kiss it, elevating it to the second firmament and bringing it to an awesome place where there are twelve entrances. Over each of these entrances are assigned many appointed ministers and hosts. Beside the twelfth gate is a single minister named ANEL who is appointed over all twelve gates. When Israel's prayer comes before him, he proclaims with a loud voice, "Open the gates and allow a righteous nation to enter, who keep the faith" (Yeshayahu 26:2). Then the gates are opened and the prayer ascends through all those entrances. Then another minister name AZRYEL is aroused, who is appointed over sixty myriad camps of angels. These all take hold of that prayer, proclaiming, "The eyes of Hashem are upon the righteous and His ears are towards their cry; the face of Hashem is upon the doers of evil to cut off their memory from the earth" (Tehillim 34:16-17).

Afterwards the prayer is elevated to the third firmament where it is brought before another appointed minister named GAVRY. This one also has at his command numerous bands of angels. In that firmament there is a certain hard rock. Upon this rock is a great light and under the rock are three hundred and seventy-five windows. The idea behind this is that at Mount Sinai these three hundred and seventy-five camps of angels joined together to protest against the bringing of the Torah down to earth. For this the Holy One Blessed is He punished them by placing them beneath that rock where they have remained since the Torah was given to Israel. Three times every day these angels are allowed out from under the rock. When a Jew utters a prayer with complete concentration it ascends to that place and it is displayed before those angels. Then the three hundred and seventy-five camps all come out to greet it with great honor, singing, "Hashem our Master, how mighty is Your name over all the earth, that You have set Your glory upon the heavens" (Tehillim 8:2).

Kav HaYashar

They shower it with numerous crowns and accompany it as it ascends still higher to the awesome and tremendous fourth firmament where another appointed minister named TAMSHAEL takes it and crowns it with wreaths made from the spices of Gan Eden. From there it ascends along with all the camps until the fifth great and awesome firmament and it is brought before the minister named GARDYEL who does battle with the guardian angels of the other nations, with the approval of the Holy One Blessed is He. When the prayer reaches that place, the appointed minister together with all his hosts and camps shudder and come out to greet it, bowing down before it. It then ascends to the awesome and tremendous sixth firmament where there are seventy ministers with a minister appointed over them named ANFYEL. This minister takes the prayer and bestows upon it seventy crowns, after which he brings it up to the seventh firmament. There it is delivered into the care of the great minister SANDLOFON who possesses the keys to all his Master's gates. The great minister ushers the prayer into seven mansions that are known as the "Holy Palaces." Although much more could be said on the subject, let this be sufficient, for I am in favor of brevity.

In light of these things, let everyone who fears God and trembles before Him take to heart the sublimity and glory of prayer and the importance of praying with concentration. Fortunate is he who honors his Creator with his voice, with love and with concentration of the heart, and who ascribes to the Holy One Blessed is He — unity, sanctity and blessing. Concerning this was it written, "You shall surely give to him from your flock, from your threshing floor and from your winepress" (Devarim 15:14). The phrase, "from your flock," alludes to the reciting the passages of the sacrifices before the morning service. One should have mind the verse, "And let us pay for [the offerings of] bullocks with [the prayers of] our lips" (Hoshea 14:3), as one recites them. The next phrase, "from your threshing floor (garnecha)," alludes to the prayers, praises and songs that one offers up with one's throat (garon). Finally, in the phrase, "from your winepress (mi y i kv echa)," the middle letters form an acronym for the words: "unification" (y ichud), "blessing" (b erachah) and "holiness" (k edushah), as is mentioned in Tikkunei Zohart (Zohar Chadash 130a).

Therefore, let a person ensure that his hands are clean of theft, fraud and infringement, and that his heart is pure through always dealing in good faith. And let him pray with concentration, according to his level of understanding. Then the words of his mouth and the meditations of his heart will be acceptable, as it is written, "Lift up your hands in holiness and bless Hashem!" (Tehillim 134:2). Amein.

Chapter 39

The verse states, "And Avraham was old, advanced in days [years]" (Bereishis 24:1). This is interpreted in Midrash Rabbah (Parashas Chayyei Sarah 59:6) by Rabbi Abba: "There are people who are 'old' but not 'with days' and there are others who are 'with days' but not 'old.' But in Avraham's case his old age corresponded with his days and his days with his old age."

I believe that the plain meaning of this Midrash is as that the term "old age" refers to length of years while "days" refer specifically to beneficial days. Some people merit "old age" — that is, length of years — but they do not merit beneficial days because the years of their lives are consumed by sorrow, poverty, destitution and troubles. Other people merit "days" — that is, days of wealth and comfort in which they enjoy all good things — but they do not enjoy length of years, never reaching old age.

Our forefather Avraham, on the other hand, merited both old age as well as beneficial days. Thus, the plain meaning of the Midrash is that Avraham enjoyed a desirable lot even in this world. In fact, the Sages tell us in Baba Basra (16b) that there were three people to whom the Holy One Blessed is He gave a taste of the World to Come while they were yet in this world. They were: Avraham, Yitzchak and Yaakov. As it is written, "With everything" (Bereishis 24:1), "From everything" (ibid. 27:33), "Everything" (ibid. 33:11). However, I have heard a deeper explanation of the Midrash in the name of my illustrious mentor, Rabbi Yudel, ztz"l, president of the court and dean of the yeshiva of the holy community of Kauli. It is based upon a passage in the Zohar

(Parashas Vayechi 221b) commenting on the verse, "And the days approached for Yisrael to die" (Bereishis 47:29). The Zohar asks: "On how many days does a person die (i.e. why is "days" in the plural)? Does the soul not exit in a single moment?" Explains the Zohar: When a person passes from this world all his days come for a reckoning before the Holy One Blessed Is He. Not one is omitted. If a person behaved righteously and feared Hashem continually, if he clung to Him lovingly every day and was whole in his commitment to Torah, fear of Heaven, mitzvos and good deeds, then all his days will be crowned and garbed with splendor and majesty.

Such days are fit to approach the King of the Kings of Kings, the Holy One Blessed is He so that the virtues of one who never deviated from Torah, mitzvos and good deeds his entire life may be put on display. This is the meaning of the verse, "And the days approached for Israel to die." That is, every one of Yaakov's days came before the Holy One Blessed is He. But this is not the case with the wicked. They give no thought to Hashem's service. Instead they fritter away their days in the pursuit of vanity, following their heart's desire and engaging in injustice, corruption and deceit. Because they gave no thought to improving their ways, upon their deaths their days hide and are ashamed to appear before the Holy One Blessed is He. Then they are punished severely for the days that are missing out of their tally of years. This is what the Midrash above is referring to as well. Those who have only "old age" are the elderly among the wicked. They may live for many years but they do not "come with their days." They spend their entire lives in sin and transgression and then afterwards their days hide and run away to avoid being brought before the Holy One Blessed is He.

Then there are those upright and pious individuals whose days do come before the Holy One Blessed is He, who conduct themselves in a whole manner with regard to Torah and mitzvos, but do not reach old age, dying while still in their youth. Avraham, on the other hand, enjoyed both blessings. He had length of years and all his days came before the Holy One Blessed is He, resplendent with good deeds. Thus, the verse is to be rendered, "And Avraham was old" — that is, he reached old age — and in addition he was "coming with his days."

Every person should take this to heart and not allow even one of his days to be prevented from coming before the Holy One Blessed is He. For the trap of death will come upon him suddenly, and then he will realize that all the allusions revealed by our Sages are the true essence of the Torah, while the words of the Torah are merely a garment. A demonstration of this can be seen in the book of Yonah. You should know that the entire story of the prophet Yonah being cast into the sea and then swallowed up by a great fish is a metaphor for what occurs to the soul after death, as is explained in the Zohar in Parashas Vayakhel (199a). Here is what the Zohar says in brief:

Yonah himself is a metaphor for the soul, which is likened to a dove (a yonah in Hebrew). His boarding of the ship is a metaphor for the soul's descent into the body, for a human being in this world is compared to a ship traversing the sea. Just as a ship in the ocean faces many perils, so does a person in this world face numerous challenges. Numerous charges are filed against a person every day in the Heavenly court on account of his sins and transgressions and the Omnipresent has no shortage of agents to carry out His judgments. Nevertheless, most people give no thought to the fact that they are heaping up offenses, and delude themselves into believing that they will in any event never be held accountable for them. It is as if they believe, Heaven forbid, that Heaven disregards their corrupt behavior.

But the truth is that the Holy One blessed is He is merely holding His peace until the person exceeds his limit. Meanwhile the case against him continues accumulating until Divine wrath strikes at him all of a sudden, just like the storm that struck Yonah's ship. And just as the tempest grew stronger and stronger until it threatened to destroy the vessel, so do Heaven's judgments shake up a person's entire body until he is so agitated and feverish that he must take to his sick bed, where he lapses into deep sleep. This is parallel to what is written in the book of Yonah, "And Yonah went down to the depths of the ship and fell asleep" (1:5). While the person is still confined to his bed a spirit begins to awaken within him. It is the evil inclination, which on this occasion urges him to repent without delay, for the day of his departure from this world is drawing near. This is alluded to in the verse, "And the captain approached him" (1:6). As the Zohar tells us, "this is the evil inclination," the "captain" of the body. "And he said to him, 'Why are you sleeping? Get up and call upon your God!'" In other words, his evil inclination implores him, "This is no time to sleep! You are about to be judged concerning everything you did in this world! Be sure to confess to your Creator!"

"What is your craft?" (1:8). That is, "Recall how you performed your task in this world. How many lies and deceptions did you perpetrate in the practice of your profession and the pursuit of your livelihood? Make acknowledgment and do not be proud, for you can see that the day of your death is approaching. "And from where do you come?" (1:8). That is, "Cast aside your pride and arrogance and recall that you were formed from a putrid drop!" "Which is your land?" (1:8). That is, "Take note that you were created from the earth and that you will return to the earth." "And of which people are you?" (1:8). That is, "Examine whether you have enough ancestral merit to protect you in your time of trouble." These are the thoughts that the evil inclination awakens in a person's heart as he lies upon his sickbed. (In light of this we can understand a passage in Midrash Rabbah, Bereishis 9:10. Commenting on the verse, "And indeed it was very good," Bereishis 1:31, the Midrash first declares: "This refers to the evil inclination." But afterwards the Midrash says: "This is the Angel of Death." Perhaps what the Midrash is alluding to is that as death approaches even the evil inclination becomes good, arousing a person to repentance and confession.)

Meanwhile on High, the Heavenly court is sitting in judgment. The defending angels find merit for him while the accusers bring up his offences, each side making its case before the Holy One Blessed is He. If the decision is in the person's favor, good and well. But if it is decreed, Heaven forbid, that he must die, then it can be said that the defenders toiled and wearied themselves in vain to save him. This is alluded to in the verse, "And the men rowed hard to return to the dry land but were unable to do so" (1:13). The inability to return to "dry land" signifies the failure of the defenders to enable him to rise from his sickbed in light of the ruling of the Heavenly court. Then three emissaries are dispatched: one that has been recording all his merits and debits; one to make the reckoning of his days in proportion to his years, as discussed earlier; and one that has accompanied him ever since his soul was first instilled in his body in his mother's womb.

The decree of Heaven does not rest and will not be silenced until it has completed its task and taken his soul from his body. This hinted at in the verse, "And they bore Yonah" (1:15). That is, upon his death a person's body is born to the cemetery. As this is taking place heralds go ahead of his casket. If he has lived meritoriously, they proclaim, "Give honor to the image of the King! Let him come in peace!" (Yeshayahu 57:2). This is alluded to in the verse, "And your righteousness will go before you" (ibid. 58:8). That is, it will go ahead of your casket. But if he sullied himself with sin, Heaven forbid, then they proclaim, "Woe to So-and-so! It would have been better had he not been born!" Concerning this was it written, "And they cast him into the sea and the sea stopped its raging" (Yonah 1:15). That is, when they brought him to the cemetery. The fish that swallowed Yonah represents the grave. During the first three days that the body is in the grave the intestines burst open. After three days they cast their filth upon his face, saying, "Take back what you put into me! You ate and drank but did not give to the poor. You spent all your days as if they were holidays and festivals, while the poor went hungry and were not invited to eat with you. So, take back what you put into me." This is the meaning of the verse, "And I will scatter excrement upon your faces, etc." (Malachi 2:3).

Afterwards, appointed angels come and return the soul to the body where it remains until thirty days have passed since his death. During these twenty-seven days the body undergoes terrible and bitter afflictions. His judgment begins with the sins that he committed with his eyes. Afterwards he receives cruel blows for the sins that he committed with his hands and feet and the rest of his body. When the thirty days are over the soul ascends On High to give an accounting and to accept punishment in Gehinnom and other forms of judgment while the body endures the terrible torment of being devoured by worms.

The idea behind this is that a person undergoes seven distinct judgments upon leaving this world:

1. When the soul first leaves the body.
2. When he is carried to the graveyard and the heralds proclaim his evil deeds, to his great shame and disgrace.
3. When he is placed in the grave.
4. His terrible suffering during the first thirty days.
5. When his flesh is devoured by worms.
6. When he is punished in Gehinnom.
7. When the soul is pushed outside the Holy Partition to return to earth, where it finds no rest until it has been cleansed of its sins and transgressions.

Therefore, it behooves a person to recall how many ordeals he will go through, how many afflictions he will be suffer and how much trembling, shuddering, shaking, sweating and shivering he will experience before his soul comes to its place of rest. Concerning this matter the Zohar advises that one pray continually, reciting daily the Psalms that begin, "Let my soul bless Hashem, etc.," Chapters 103 and 104. Afterwards let him recite the following:

May it be Your will, Hashem my God and God of my fathers, to pardon and forgive me for the transgressions and sins that I have committed whether with the sight of my eyes or with the deeds of my hands, feet and body. And since when the time comes for me to leave this world, I will no longer be able to bless you nor to repent, therefore I request now that You should not afflict me after my death but return my soul to Gan Eden without fear or dismay."

Thus, it is written, "Let my soul praise Hashem, Hallelu- yah!"

Chapter 40

"God, create within me a pure heart and renew within me an amended spirit" (Tehillim 51:12). The great luminary Rabbi Moshe Alsheich, z"l, explains that Dovid HaMelech was praying to be spared from reincarnation. Ordinarily whoever fails to acquire perfection while he is here must return in another body to complete the task. Therefore, Dovid HaMelech pleaded that he be spared this fate, asking that Hashem renew his spirit while it was still within him instead of first causing him to die and then returning his soul to earth in another body.

Indeed, you should know that rectification of the soul can be accomplished through two different processes. In the first one a person does not have to die and be reborn in another body to accomplish rectification. Instead, while he is still alive a second soul, in addition to the one he already has, enters his body. This new soul joins with his original one as a fetus is joined with its mother. For this reason, this is known as the "gestation" procedure. And just as a fetus is covered over and concealed within its mother, so is this new soul covered over and concealed within the person's original soul until the damage to his soul has been rectified. When this has been accomplished the new soul then departs for a place of repose that is fitting to it. This form of rectification is not a severe one. But if the damage he caused was great, it can be rectified only by the reincarnation of his soul alone in a new body, where it must remain for many days, (that is, from the moment of conception until the end of his life). Sometimes the loss he suffers through this process is greater than his gain because in his new body he may not only fail to rectify his soul's existing blemishes but may actually bring upon it more serious ones through his sins and transgressions. This is a great misfortune for the soul.

There is one commandment in particular that people consider of minor significance but which carries a very severe penalty. That is the one regarding the returning of lost objects to the owners. If a person sees a lost item belonging to his colleague and fails to retrieve it in order to return it he is compelled to undergo reincarnation in a newly conceived fetus, after which he must endure many years of affliction and suffering. For this offense it is not sufficient for him to undergo the less severe method of rectification, the "gestation" procedure in which a new soul is covered over by and concealed within his original soul. The Ari, z"l, explains in Sefer HaGilgulim that this is because he violated the verse, "And so shall you do to all the lost objects of your brother … you may not conceal your eyes" (Devarim 22:3). For the Holy One Blessed is He always judges a person "measure for measure." Therefore, whoever fears Hashem and trembles before Him should pray to be spared from reincarnation. The masses may consider it a minor punishment but the wise will contemplate the matter and realize that even if he is reincarnated in the body of an upright individual it would have been better had he already reached his resting place. For the Sages tell us that a single moment of the satisfaction one experiences in the next world is better that all the pleasures that this world has to offer (Avos 4:17). Now consider the fact that he may very well be reborn into more oppressive circumstances such as the body of an animal or a bird or even an inanimate object! For example, one who habitually engages in derogatory speech is reincarnated in a rock lying in a field where he remains in darkness with no illumination. Similarly, a person who is careless about consuming food of doubtful permissibility is reborn in the leaves of a tree so that every time the wind blows, he is tossed about, causing him indescribable agony.

A communal official who lords over the populace arrogantly is reincarnated in the body of a bee. There he is punished moment after moment, enduring more sorrow than he would in Gehinnom. This is because he is confined in a very narrow place, wallowing in venom. And this is only for the sin of pride! But if in his arrogance he committed other evils such as humiliating those who came to seek out his services and the like, for these crimes he will have to endure other punishments described in the Kabbalistic works, may Heaven spare us!

One who pursues licentious behavior is reincarnated as a prostitute. Then every time someone engages in immorality with her the soul that is within her is defiled more and more, causing it further and further devastation until its desolation is as great as the sea. The terrible afflictions and sorrows that it endures cannot be expressed in words. More details concerning reincarnation will be related in future chapters, with Heaven's help, but worse than what has been described so far is the experience of reincarnation in an impure animal or bird. There the soul sits in darkness and sorrow, suffering terrible and bitter afflictions surrounded by the stench of its bowels and intestines. Meanwhile, at every moment it is subjected to judgments more terrible than those of Gehinnom. Nevertheless, it is not spared from punishment in Gehinnom once the process of incarnation is completed.

Here is an episode that I found recorded in the name of the Ari, z"l (Shivchei HaArizal): In the town of Tzefas lived a certain young man who was the nephew of Rabbi Yehoshua the physician. He was eighteen years old at the time this incident took place and was studying in yeshiva. One time the Ari happened to see him, whereupon he commented to the boy's father, "Your son is possessed by an evil spirit. See to it that you find a cure for him and do not spare any money!" The boy's father responded, "He is not possessed, Heaven forbid, although for the past two years he has suffered from pains in his heart. Whenever his heart is very weak Rabbi Yehoshua the physician treats him and he recovers for a time. But eventually the pain always returns." The Ari retorted, "You will see that I am correct."

Not long afterwards the spirit revealed itself and began speaking from within the young man. As soon as the Ari was informed of this he came and inquired of the spirit how it happened to enter the young man. The spirit replied, "This is how the matter came about: When I lived in Rome, I shared lodgings with a poor man who was dependent upon charity. In his house he had neither bread nor any other food. One day the poor man asked me for bread but I refused to give him any and he died of hunger before my eyes. On account of this the Heavenly court decreed that I must die just as the poor man had died. And so it happened that not long afterwards thieves came and killed me, after which I came and entered this young man." The Ari decreed that the spirit must not cause the young man any harm, Heaven forbid. But the spirit said to him, "If you wish me to abandon this youth, I will do so on one condition. After I leave him, he must not see the face of a female for three days. If he violates this condition, I will kill him!" Then the spirit left.

The Ari, z"l, issued instructions that a guard be placed over the young man while he sat in the study hall, for he knew that the spirit was lying in wait to see if the condition would be fulfilled. At one point the guard, the leader of the generation, our teacher Rabbi Chayim Vital, z"l, left the study hall to make preparations for his Rosh Chodesh feast, leaving Rabbi Yehoshua the physician in his place. But eventually he too went out to attend to some urgent matter, leaving his nephew alone in the study hall. In the meantime the boy's mother and aunt came to see him. When they found him they went over to him and kissed him. At that very moment the spirit returned to him and strangled him. When the Ari heard what had transpired, he was concerned that the gentile authorities would claim that the Jews had killed the young man, so with the help of two reeds he condensed his journey and arrived instantaneously in the city of Tiberius accompanied by his disciples. It was twilight and the Ari prayed that the mouths of their accusers be silenced. And so it was. Afterwards he returned to Tzefas, may it be rebuilt speedily in our days.

In light of this episode one can imagine the punishment awaiting the man who gazes at strange women. For this youth only looked at his mother and his aunt, yet look at what befell him! How much more so if one stares at women to whom he is not related! Concerning this did the Sages say, "Whoever engages in too much idle talk with a woman causes evil to himself" (Pirkei Avos 1:5).

It is also very praiseworthy for a man to avoid seeing them even from a distance by directing his gaze downward at all times. This was the custom of the pious of earlier generations. Their eyes were always directed downward towards the earth while they prayed for the unification of the Holy One Blessed Is He and His Shechinah. For the four colors of the eye hint at the four letters of the Divine name (Tikkunim 70, 128a) while the earth (eretz) hints at the Shechinah, which is known as the "Holy Land (Eretz HaKadosh)" because it is holier than all the lands (Zohar 3:243b). Thus, it is written, "My eyes are upon the faithful of the earth that they may dwell with me" (Tehillim 101:6). But concerning "the haughty-eyed and avaricious-hearted" the Holy One Blessed is He says, "Him I cannot" (ibid. 101:5). That is, "I cannot join with him" because he separates between those that were joined (i.e., the Holy One Blessed be He and the Shechinah). Whoever allows his gaze to fall upon forbidden sights draws the Sitrah Acharah upon him and does himself great harm. For he causes himself to possess an evil eye, thereby bringing a curse upon himself as well as all those he upon whom he gazes. Thus, the Sages proclaim that ninety-nine out of a hundred die of the Evil Eye (Bava Metzia 107b), by which they mean that they are harmed by the gaze of other people. All this is brought about by gazing at idolatry, for it is forbidden to look even at an idolatrous statue. Instead let a person habituate himself to gazing at holy things, as I have already mentioned in Chapter Two.

Another lesson to be derived from this chapter is that a person should never ignore an appeal for charity. For when the spirit failed to sustain the poor man in the episode related above, allowing him to die before his eyes, it was decreed that he also would be killed. Then on account of this sin he was condemned to suffer the punishment of the "slingshot," resulting in his transformation into a spirit, as related earlier. Therefore, let every person develop a compassionate heart and let him immerse his heart and eyes and the rest of his limbs in holy matters. Then he will merit beholding the Shechinah with his eyes three times a year, Amein.

Chapter 41

It is written in Heichalos (Heichal 9, par. 2): Blessed are you to Hashem! Blessed are you to Me, O Heaven and earth and you who descend upon the Throne. If you wish to relate to My children what I do for Israel when they recite the Kedushah, teach them and tell them as follows: Lift up your eyes On High and see what I do for Israel when they recite the Kedushah. For I have no other pleasure from My world that can compare with that moment when their eyes are raised towards Me and My eyes towards them. Then the breath of their mouths ascends before Me like a pleasant fragrance. At that moment I kiss and hug the image of Yaakov engraved upon the Throne of Glory.

See how great is Israel's love for their Father! How can we not serve our Heavenly Father with trepidation and awe and with all our heart and soul? For He is remote from the wicked and near to the righteous and to all who call upon Him sincerely! Whoever trembles before Him will be sure to fulfill what is written here so that he may achieve the greatest possible love and merit the World to Come through his service of the Creator. And the way to accomplish this is by taking time every day to contemplate the Creator's awesome sanctity. This is expressed in our Yom Kippur prayers: "And Your holiness is in their mouths" (the Shacharis

Amidah); "And You desired the praise of flesh and blood, of withering grass, of passing shadows, of the burden of the womb... Who die through judgment and live through mercy" (the Mussaf Amidah); "And Your holiness is in their mouths." Reflecting on this will cause a person's heart to become enthusiastic in its service of the Holy One Blessed is He. Thus, the Zohar explains in Parashas Vayakhel (198b) that when a person thinks of serving the Creator the thought ascends first to the heart, which is the sustainer and foundation of the entire body. Afterwards it spreads to the other limbs of the body. Then the thoughts of the heart and the limbs unite, drawing upon them the radiance of the Shechinah, causing it to dwell among them. Then the person becomes the portion of the Holy One Blessed is He.

One must also cleave to fear of Hashem, for love and fear go together. This is explained in Reishis Chochmah (Sha'ar HaYirah; Sha'ar HaAhavah; Preface; Ch. 1) and in Seifer Chareidim (Mitzvas HaTeshuvah, Ch. 1) commenting on the verses, "To fear the honorable and awesome name" (Devarim 28:58), "and to love Him" (Devarim 10:12). The basic idea is this: Whenever a person mentions Hashem's name his entire body should be filled with trembling. And every time he recites a blessing, he should enunciate it clearly and feel it with his entire body. He should certainly not spit out the words of the blessing hurriedly, Heaven forbid. I have often witnessed the following scenario among the masses. A person is holding some item of food or drink in his hand. What he would really like to do is just to toss it into his mouth but he realizes that he must recite a blessing. However, since his main goal is to enjoy his food, he rattles off the blessing as quickly as he can without enunciating the words clearly. As I have already mentioned in Chapter Eighteen, the punishment for such conduct is very great. Recall the incident that is cited there from Seifer Chassidim. The same punishment awaits one who recites the Songs of Praise (Pesukei DeZimra) at the beginning of the service hurriedly, swallowing the letters and words. Most people are careless about this.

A special admonition should be given to the chazzanim. In most cases they pay great attention to the melody but give little thought to the actual prayer. Their only goal is to show off their voices. As a result, they swallow up or cut short the most important praises of the Holy One Blessed is He. These chazzanim will be unable to stand in the future. For the word chazzan is an acronym for the final letters of the phrase Yifra ch ke'ere z balevano n — "He will flourish like a cedar in Lebanon" (Tehillim 92:13). This indicates that a chazzan who prays with complete concentration will flourish like the cedars of Lebanon in the future. Know also that the word chazzan contains within it three sacred Divine Names: the ineffable name, the name "L-rd," and the name "A-lmighty." Spelled out in full the word chazzan is written: ches (חי"ת), zayin (זי"ן), nun (נו"ן). The numerical value of the initial letters (חז"ן) is 65, which is equal to the value of the name "Master" (אדנ"י). The value of the middle letters (יי"ו) is 26, which is equal to the value of the Ineffable Name (הוי"ה). And the value of the final letters (תנ"ן) is 500, which is the value of the "filling" of the name "A-lmighty" (שד"י). That is, if one spells out this name in full it is written: shin (שי"ן), dalet (דל"ת), yud (יו"ד). Now omit the initial letters (שד"י) and the value of the letters that remain (ינלתו"ד) is 500.

This should give you some idea of the power that lies within a chazzan, who unites within him these three Names. But if the chazzan is lightheaded and does not pray with the intention to fulfill the congregation's obligation, then he sullies these three holy Names. This is reckoned as if he made blemishes in the sacrifices because in our times prayer takes the place of the sacrifices. I have found it written in the name of the scholars of earlier generations that there is an esoteric allusion hidden within the verse, "Return to your rest, O my soul, for Hashem has dealt bountifully with you" (Tehillim 116:7). Among the letters of this verse are the letters of the Divine name מו"ם (part of the seventy-two-letter name; see Rashi, Sukkah 45a). Therefore, if one recites the word "rest" hurriedly and without enunciating it properly, one blemishes this name and in consequence is denied rest in the World to Come! This same Divine Name (מו"ם) is alluded to in the initial letters of the phrase from the Morning Service, "He fashions servants and His servants, etc." A mnemonic to help one bear in mind not to blemish one's prayers is the sentence, "For there is a blemish in it, it is abominable, it will not find favor as a sacrifice to Hashem" (a composite of Vayikra 21:23, 19:7 and 22:27). And since in our times prayer is in place of the sacrifices whoever swallows letters in his prayers is reckoned as if he made blemishes in the sacrifices. Harsh punishment also awaits those who interrupt their prayers where it is forbidden to do so. Thus, it is related in the Pesikta: A certain pious man once encountered the prophet Eliyahu, may he be remembered for the good, who was leading three hundred camels laden with afflictions. The pious man inquired, "Who are these intended for?" Eliyahu responded, "For anyone who talks between "Blessed is He who spoke" (Baruch She'amar) and "Let Your name be praised" (Yishtabach) or between "Let Your name be praised" and the Shemoneh Esrei." For the person who speaks and interrupts his prayers impairs Israel's effectiveness as they strive to fashion a crown with their prayers. His punishment is especially great if he interrupts his prayer to speak words of mockery, for then he mixes the shell of the Sitrah Acharah into the Sitrah Kadishah. It is evident that there is no fear of Heaven in the heart of such a person, nor is the love of Hashem engraved there. Even when he does fulfill the mitzvos it is only out of compulsion. Woe to his soul!

Similarly, when a person studies Torah he must delve deeply according to his ability, not hurriedly or with intention to show off, Heaven forbid, for someone who studies in this manner is not interested in getting to the heart of the matter, therefore his punishment will be very great.

One must also be willing to receive Torah from any source, even from children. We find several illustrations of this in the Zohar (for example, 1:69b, 186a) but the most outstanding example is a passage in Parashas Vayechi (238b-240a): Rabbi Yehudah and Rabbi Yitzchak were traveling along the road. While they were walking, they met a child who was obviously fatigued. "Give me bread," he pleaded, "for I have not eaten today!" They took out some bread and gave it to him. Then a miracle occurred and they found a spring beneath a tree and drank from it. The child then began speaking, "[It states,] 'And He called to Moshe' (Vayikra 1:1). Why is the alef (at the end of the world Vayikra — "And He called") written small? It is because this 'calling' took place outside of the land [of Israel] in the desert, in a defiled land and not in the Holy Land, for perfection can be found only in the Holy Land."

Rabbi Yehudah then said, "It would have been better for the child if he had not known so much, for I am afraid that he will not be allowed to remain in the world on this account." Rabbi Yitzchak asked, "Why not?" "Because he may glimpse at what is not permitted," he replied. "I am afraid that before he grows up and reaches maturity he will gaze and be punished." The child overheard him and said, "I am not afraid of punishment at all, for when my father departed this world, he prayed for me. And I know that my father's merit will protect me." "Who was your father?" they asked. "I am the son of Rav Hamnuna the Elder," he answered, whereupon they took him and carried him upon their shoulders for three miles.

From this passage you can see what love of Hashem and love of Torah mean. For although these were two great scholars of the Mishnaic period, they were willing to listen to the words of a child and they treated a child scholar with honor. Fortunate are they in this world and it will be well with them in the World to Come.

Chapter 42

It is written, "And when the daughter of a Kohein shall be widowed or divorced, having no offspring, and she returns to her father's house as in her youth…" (Vayikra 22:13) [and in the previous verse it is written,] "…she shall not eat of an offering of the holy things." According to the Zohar (2:95b; 3:7a) this is an allusion to the soul. The soul was created to enter the body in order that it should be rectified and adorned with good deeds. But when a person transgresses, he blemishes his soul, causing it to cry out to Hashem, saying, "Hashem has delivered me into the hands of one against whom I cannot stand" (Eichah 1:14). When the Holy One Blessed is He hears this cry, He says to the soul, "My precious daughter, you were raised in illumination and honor beneath the Throne of Glory and were called, 'precious daughter.' Then I lowered you into a human body, intending to elevate you to the highest levels through that human being's good deeds. But now that he has sinned you have been degraded, plummeting from a lofty rooftop to the deep pit of the human body." At this point the soul becomes known as a "divorcee" because it is banished from its place against its will ("divorced" and "banished" are expressed by the same word in Hebrew). But Hashem hears its cry and takes the soul from the body and purifies it though chastisements, after which it is able to relish the delights of its Heavenly Father.

Thus, the verse can be paraphrased as follows: "And when the daughter of a Kohein" — that is, the soul. "…Shall be widowed or divorced" — that is, at the death of its human host when it is banished from the body. "…Having no offspring" — that is, it performed no mitzvos or good deeds and consequently did not give birth to any of the holy angels that are formed from every good deed that a person does. "…And she returns to her father's house" — that is, after its purification through chastisement. Nevertheless, "she shall not eat of an offering of the holy things," as she had been accustom to do in the past, because she had become like a "stranger," of whom it is written, "And no stranger shall eat of the holy things" (Vayikra 22:10). For only the righteous and pious may eat of them, as it is written, "Eat, dear ones, drink and become drunk, beloved ones" (Shir HaShirim 5:1).

Concerning this matter a call goes out every day proclaiming that one must not cause his soul to be banished. Thus, the Zohar relates (1:62a, Tosefta): A voice from a voice descends from On High, shattering mountains, proclaiming: Who are they who see but do not see? With stopped up ears and closed eyes they neither see nor hear nor understand! These are the ones who cause the holy soul to be banished from its place so that it is not inscribed in the Book of the Living. Thus, is it written, "Let them be erased from the Book of the Living and let them not be inscribed with the righteous" (Tehillim 69:29). Woe to them, for when they leave this world, they are delivered into the hands of the angel Dumah to be burned with fire!

Therefore, let every Israelite who fears and trembles before Hashem contemplate his end every day. Let him realize that he is drawing further away from life and closer to death. Let every person make a reckoning of how long he has to live, for the natural life span of a human being is only seventy years. And even if he is still young, no one has a written guarantee of how long he will live and death may come upon him suddenly. Proof to this can be seen in the passage in Nedarim (3b) in which it is taught that if a person says, "I will not leave this world without having become a nazir," he becomes a nazir instantly because he might die at any moment. For this reason, the Sages warn (Shabbos 153a): "Repent one day before your death! — Hence you must spend all your days in repentance!" It is essential that every man possess a list of the things that obstruct repentance. And if he will review it every day, I am certain that he will not stumble. To this end I will present in a separate chapter a list of the twenty-four things that obstruct repentance. Let whoever is concerned about his soul stay far away from them. Then it will be well with him, selah.

Chapter 43
These are the twenty-four things that obstruct repentance:
1. Speaking derogatorily of others or passing gossip from one to another.
2. Being quick tempered.
3. Thinking evil thoughts.
4. Associating with the wicked.
5. Partaking of meals that are insufficient for the host.
6. Gazing at forbidden women.
7. Sharing in the spoils of a thief.
8. Declaring, "I will sin and then repent."
9. Declaring, "I will sin and Yom Kippur will atone for me."
10. Denigrating Torah scholars.
11. Cursing the multitude.
12. Dissuading the multitude or even an individual from performing a good deed.
13. Influencing one's fellow to abandon a good deed and commit a transgression instead.
14. Using a poor person's deposit.
15. Accepting bribes.
16. Finding a lost object and failing to announce it.

17. Refraining from rebuking one's children when he sees them turning to evil ways.
18. Separating oneself from the community.
19. Attaining honor through a colleague's disgrace.
20. Harboring suspicions about the innocent.
21. Despising rebuke.
22. Ridiculing the words of the Sages.
23. Ridiculing the mitzvos.
24. Ridiculing the customs of the pious.

These are the twenty-four things that a person must avoid. Now let every God-fearing individual copy them down and keep the list in his prayer book so that he can review it twice a day, each morning and evening, so that he will be spared from stumbling in any of them.

These twenty-four categories include many subcategories. I will explain a few of them here, with Hashem's help: Included in the category of tale-bearing is the prohibition upon a judge not to say to a litigant, "What can I do? I wanted to rule in your favor but my colleagues outnumbered me." Similarly, it is forbidden for a third party, upon hearing the court's decision, to say that the judges did not rule correctly. Even if it seems to him that they are mistaken he should say nothing because a court is assumed to act properly. Moreover, the judges must rule according to what they see (Niddah 20b).

Engaging in derogatory speech includes many things, as is explained in all the mussar (exhortative) literature. However, a good rule to adopt is to judge everyone favorably, even one's enemies.

Being quick tempered also includes: being cruel, being deaf to the cries of the needy, failing to judge others favorably, being vengeful or bearing grudges, being quarrelsome, brazen or shameless, cursing habitually, instilling excessive fear into one's household, failing to treat others pleasantly. Thinking evil thoughts includes: giving advice with ulterior motives, conspiring and conniving, maintaining and encouraging factions. Associating with the wicked includes: witnessing injustice and failing to protest and aiding transgressors.

Partaking of meals that are insufficient for the host includes: taking charity when one does not need to do so.

Gazing at forbidden women also includes: gazing at idolatry or watching the frivolous entertainment of gentiles.

Sharing in the spoils of a thief includes: purchasing stolen or plundered goods.

Saying, "I will sin and repent" includes: saying, "I still have time to mend my ways because I am still young." It also includes saying that "heeding admonitions and avoiding sin is only for the deeply spiritual and I am not of that sort," for by saying this he willfully alienates himself from the realm of holiness.

Denigrating scholars includes hearing the denigration of scholars, even not in their presence, and remaining silent. Because this generation is very lax about the denigration of Torah students and scholars, while the punishment for this is very great, we will have to address the matter at length. However, since there is not enough room to do so here, we will leave this for future chapters (54, 65, 66 and 83).

Cursing the multitude includes: casting aspersions upon Israel by speaking ill of the community, interpreting good deeds negatively and uttering imprecations to invoke Divine judgment against the multitude. The punishment for this category is very great. Who is there among us of the stature of the prophets Eliyahu and Yeshayahu? Yet both of them were punished for speaking ill of Israel! Many of the other prophets were also punished for not speaking well of Israel or for failing to pray and intercede on their behalf. Also included in this category is the admonition to those issuing rebuke to the public to exercise forethought and caution. They must be careful to speak in a manner that is pure, clean and respectful so that he does not arouse judgment against the holy people, Heaven forbid, lest it spread to innocent and guilty alike, causing loss and damage, Heaven forbid. Let everyone, including those admonishing the public, take care not to shame the transgressors. And let them be wary of becoming prideful at the moment of their rebuke, for then they mix the shell of defilement into the realm of holiness. For this reason, many have the custom of uttering a short prayer asking that they be saved from becoming conceited or arrogant.

There is one strategy that can save a person from even a trace of conceit when he propounds his Torah insights in public. That is, by recalling that even if he is by far the greatest scholar of his generation, he is still not on the level of Rabbi Shimon ben Yochai, yet Rabbi Shimon was exceedingly humble. Thus it is related in the Zohar on Parashas Shemos (14a): Rabbi Chiyya used to go to the masters of the Mishnah in order to learn from them. When he went to the house of Rabbi Shimon ben Yochai, he saw that it was divided by a partition. Rabbi Chiyya was surprised and said to himself, "I will listen from outside." He heard Rabbi Shimon saying, "[It is written,] 'Flee, my beloved, and resemble a deer, etc.' (Shir HaShirim 8:14). There is no other creature that behaves like the deer. When it flees it goes a short distance and then turns its head to look back at the place from which it fled. Then all along the way it turns its head back constantly. "This is what Israel was saying in this verse, 'Master of the Universe! If we cause you to abandon us, may it be Your will to flee in the manner of the deer by continually looking back towards the place where you left us! This is also the manner of the creature called the 'fawn of the harts.' For this reason, Shlomo said, 'Resemble a deer or a fawn of the harts.' This is what is stated in the verse, 'And yet for all that, when they are in the land of their enemies, I will not revile them nor will I utterly reject them to destroy them, etc.' (Vayikra 26:44)."

When Rabbi Chiyya heard this he said, "Here are these lofty ones engaging in study within the house while I remain outside!" and he began to weep. Rabbi Shimon ben Yochai heard him and said, "Surely the Shechinah is outside! Who will leave? His son Rabbi Elazar said, "Let the Shechinah enter so that the rejoicing will be complete!" Whereupon a voice was heard, saying, "The pillars have not yet received support nor have the gates been prepared to open so that Rabbi Chiyya may enter, for he is among the least of the spices of Gan Eden." So, Rabbi Elazar did not leave.

Meanwhile Rabbi Chiyya sat weeping and sighing. At last he spoke up and said, "Turn, my beloved, resemble a deer or a fawn of the harts." Then the partition opened but Rabbi Chiyya still did not enter, for he was afraid to enter without permission. Rabbi Shimon raised his eyes and said, "Perhaps permission has been granted for the one outside to enter?" So, he stood up and went towards Rabbi

Chiyya. Meanwhile, the fire spread from the place of Rabbi Shimon to the place of Rabbi Chiyya. Rabbi Shimon said, "If the spark of light has spread outside, shall I remain here [that is, shall I not bring Rabbi Chiyya inside]?" Rabbi Chiyya was stricken dumb, and after he entered, he lowered his eyes and refused to raise his head. Rabbi Shimon ben Yochai told his son Rabbi Elazar, "Get up and pass your hand over his mouth, for he is not accustomed to this." So, Rabbi Elazar got up and passed his hand over Rabbi Chiyya's mouth, whereupon Rabbi Chiyya proclaimed, "My eyes have beheld what they have never beheld before!"

While they sat there, they were encompassed all about by fire and sparks and thousands upon thousands of bands of fiery angels surrounded them. Two hundred and sixty worlds shuddered at the words emanating from Rabbi Shimon ben Yochai's mouth. The Heavenly hosts were astonished, declaring, "Is this Rabbi Shimon ben Yochai who is agitating all the worlds? Who can stand before him?" "For when Rabbi Shimon ben Yochai opens his mouth to engage in study, all the thrones of all the firmaments listen to his voice and all the Heavenly hosts singing the praises of the Holy One Blessed is He fall silent. No sound is heard from any angel or saraf or ofan or keruv in all the supernal worlds, so that they may listen to the voice of Rabbi Shimon ben Yochai. "And when he completes his words of Torah, the angels and all the hosts of Heaven break out in songs of praise and joy to the Holy One Blessed is He for having created such a pure and holy soul as that of Rabbi Shimon ben Yochai. Then all the gates and windows of all the chambers of Gan Eden open wide so that the fragrance of the spices may go forth." All this took place in Rabbi Shimon's honor, yet he was not too proud to go out to greet Rabbi Chiyya! How, then, can anyone in our generation be proud? In any event, we have already mentioned that one must pray every day to acquire humility (Ch. 7). And surely, "God will not despise a broken and contrite heart" (Tehillim 51:19).

Dissuading the multitude from repenting or from fulfilling any of the mitzvos refers to the situation in which a group of especially dedicated individuals undertake to engage in some holy endeavor or to give charity. But then one among them, one whose heart is bent on evil and whom pride prevents from caring about his

Maker's honor, tries to dissuade them from carrying out their plan and this act of Satan succeeds. Woe to him and woe to his soul! The authors of the mussar literature liken him to a member of a gang of bandits who heard that a delegation of the citizenry was on its way to the palace with presents for the king. So, they set an ambush and seized all the gifts. When a long time had passed and the delegation did not arrive, the king launched an investigation into the matter. Upon discovering what had transpired he ordered that the bandits be subjected to terrible tortures for depriving him of his honor in their wickedness.

So, too, if someone prevents others from fulfilling any of the mitzvos or from carrying out any holy endeavor the punishment awaiting him is beyond expression. Also included within this category is the one who says, "I will not give and I do not want others to give either." The Sages teach that such a person is called "wicked" (Pirkei Avos 5:13). Therefore, communal leaders must be careful not to hinder private individuals from carrying out worthy projects. Influencing others to transgress includes backing up the words of a cruel hearted man for the sake of the food and drink one enjoys in his house. Concerning this the prophet said, "Woe to those who say of evil that it is good" (Yeshayahu 5:20). In their hearts they know that all his deeds emanate from the shells of impurity and that all his words are meant for evil. They know that his only interest is in vengeance, grudge- bearing, theft, injustice, vanity, falsehood, defilement and abomination. But what they fail to realize is that Hashem will bring all these things to judgment. Therefore, they foolishly glorify and praise him, telling him what a great sage he is and ascribing to him other such distinctions, when in fact they only flatter him in order to satiate their gullets because this cruel fellow sometimes invites them to dine with him. They are unaware that in the final analysis all the sustenance that they received from him was filled with swords and javelins that will cause them plagues, cuts, blisters and wounds. For they will suffer greatly for having partaken of the bread of man with an evil eye, as has already been explained (Ch. 26). Ultimately, they will experience blow after blow and devastation after devastation until they fall helpless.

Therefore, let a man always be on Hashem's side in aid of the mighty ones, giving encouragement and succor to those engaged in good deeds, especially charity. For as the Sages tell us, "Greater is the one who prompts others to do than the one who does himself" (Baba Basra 9a). Then it will be well with him, selah.

Chapter 44

The punishment for using the security of the poor is very great because while the rich man is in a position to protest against the lender, the poor man does not have that option. In most cases he merely witnesses or hears of his loss but has no means of standing up to the lender. Meanwhile the lender is confident that the borrower will not say a word against him. This is a tremendous iniquity. Included within this is the subcategory of behaving haughtily towards the pauper and speaking to him in a harsh tone that one would be afraid to use towards someone of more means. Because of his indigence the speaker treats him callously, with arrogance and contempt, knowing that the pauper will not dare to respond. But the Holy One Blessed is He is listening and watching and in the end, He will take up the poor man's quarrel and do justice on his behalf, bringing to light the righteousness of his cause.

Taking bribes includes accepting verbal bribes. Just as a judge must refrain from sitting in judgment for the sake of financial gain, so must he refrain from doing so for the sake of lesser benefits. Let the judges be scrupulous in this matter lest they blemish their souls. Neglecting to announce lost articles that one has found includes neglecting to use information that he has to save one's fellow from a loss.

Refraining from rebuking one's children when one sees them turning to evil ways includes every type of evil behavior, for instance, gluttony and drunkenness or coveting the wealth of others. Many other examples could be given as well. It is the father's duty to supervise his children and chastise them.

Devouring wealth that was plundered from the poor, the widowed and the orphaned includes the misappropriation of public funds that were collected from the poor and needy. The yoke they bear is very weighty and they are unable even to provide proper clothing for themselves and their wives, therefore the one who devours the communal funds through embezzlement or outright theft is reckoned as if he devoured their flesh and blood. These funds also include the wealth of widows and orphans, but the embezzler does not recall that the Holy One Blessed is He is the Father of orphans and the Champion of widows and the attribute of strict justice will surely be leveled at the thief. The authors of the mussar literature have already elaborated on the punishment awaiting him. This is illustrated by the story of the widow of Rabbeinu Yechiel, z"l, father of the Rosh. After Rabbeinu Yechiel passed away, his wife was left to raise three small children by herself. One Friday night Rabbeinu Yechiel appeared to her in a dream and instructed her to flee the city immediately because Hashem was about to destroy it through some unspecified calamity. She awoke trembling but then returned to sleep. Again, he appeared to her with the same message. This time, as soon as she awoke, she took her children and traveled about a mile beyond the city gates to the house of a certain gentile. When morning came the town was attacked by bandits who slaughtered the populace, plundered their property and then fled. But the Rosh's mother returned home safe and sound. Later on, Rabbeinu Yechiel appeared to her again and informed her that this decree had been issued against the community because they had robbed the poor through taxes and levies that the rich avoided paying.

Separating oneself from the community includes neglecting to pray with the congregation and refusing to help shoulder the common burden through the payment of the communal taxes when one has the means.

Transgressing the words of the Sages includes treating rabbinical prohibitions leniently or violating the Sages' decrees and enactments. It is forbidden to transgress the words of the Sages even for the sake of a mitzvah. This includes, for example, studying or praying by lamplight on the Sabbath under circumstances in which the Sages forbade it lest one tilt the lamp, and all other similar cases. Heaven forbid that one should transgress any decree of the Sages, of blessed memory. Needless to say, the punishment for ridiculing the words of the Sages is very great. In fact, this is one of the things for which one forfeits his portion in the World to Come.

Attaining honor through a colleague's disgrace is a serious offense. As we have already mentioned, it is one of things that obstruct repentance. It is also forbidden to refrain from setting one's colleague straight when he sees that he has erred in some matter. Thus, the Zohar relates (Parashas Shelach 167a) in the name of Rabbi Shimon ben Yochai that the Heavenly court once convened in the presence of the Melech HaMashiach, the Anointed King, to examine the case of a fellow who was waiting at the entrance to Gan Eden. The cherubim had detained him and did not allow him to enter. He cried out in his sorrow at the entrance to Gan Eden and a proclamation went forth that all the members of the Heavenly academy to assemble right then before the Mashiach to examine the fellow's case. "You may not reveal this person's identity," they told Rabbi Shimon ben Yochai, "because it is not in vain that this punishment has come upon him." At last the Mashiach ruled that this man would have to remain standing outside in sorrow for forty days, at the end of which he would be afflicted in Gehinnom for one and a half hours. All this was because it occurred one time that a colleague had been explaining a passage from the Torah and when he came to a certain matter this man knew that his colleague had erred, but he told the other participants, "Be silent and do not say anything to him!" Because they remained silent his coleague stumbled [in a halachic matter and] was humiliated. It was his embarrassment that caused this fellow to be punished so severely. For the Holy One Blessed is He does not overlook even by so much as a hair's breadth any iniquity in matters pertaining to the Torah.

Thus, the Torah is an elixir of life, but only for those who study it for pure motives and do not seek honor through the disgrace of their colleagues. It protects those who study for pure motives from thoughts of sin and it stands by them at the moment of judgment. Thus, it is taught in the Zohar (Parashas Vayakhel 200a): When one studies Torah it is as if one were in the palace of the Holy One Blessed Is He. For when a person engages in study the Holy One Blessed Is He is present, listening to his voice. Thus, the man is saved from three judgments: from judgment in this world, from judgment by the Angel of Death [that is, he dies by a kiss from the Holy One Blessed is He instead], and from judgment in Gehinnom. But this is true only if he studies for pure motives and with love. Then the Holy One Blessed is He glories in him, saying, "I have fashioned this people for Myself, etc." (Yeshayahu 43:21) and calls him, "Israel, you in whom I glory" (ibid. 49:3).

Chapter 45

The Ari, z"l, teaches that it is a great mitzvah to accustom oneself to performing the Kabbalistic "unifications" on behalf of the Shechinah (Sha'ar HaYechudim 3b). In this manner one gives support and aid to the Shechinah and expedites the redemption. However, not everyone is capable of performing these "unifications" while he is praying or fulfilling any of the mitzvos. For one thing, he may simply lack the requisite knowledge. For another, he may not feel confident that he can avoid stray thoughts while praying, in which case he would actually be causing harm rather than good. Moreover, a man cannot remain in a state of purity at all times. And just as it is forbidden for a man to come into contact with the sacrifices when he has become defiled through an emission of seed, so is it forbidden to perform any of the "unifications" if he has not immersed after having had such an emission. Thus, if a person prays and performs the mitzvos with simple but heartfelt intentions, without any admixture of stray thoughts, surely the Merciful One will accept them with mercy and favor. Even so, it is still preferable for him to recite the meditation, "For the sake of the unification of the Holy One Blessed is He and His Shechinah," before he prays. Similarly, when a man studies Torah let him say beforehand, "For the sake of the unification of the Holy One Blessed is He and His Shechinah," so that he does not appear to be foregoing this holy practice willingly. Thus, we find in Eiruvin (28b) that when Rabbi Zeira was too weak to study he would sit near the entrance to the yeshivah of Rabbi Yuda bar Ami so that he would be able to rise before the scholars as they entered and not be entirely devoid of mitzvos. I have also been told by men of great deeds, that when they are unable to perform a mitzvah, they finger their tzitziyos and gaze at them because this is in itself a lofty matter that causes the Shechinah to be elevated in the midst of the exile. Those who understand the Kabbalistic principle of "unification" have in mind as they gaze at their tzitzis a certain great and awesome Divine name, the numerical value of which is equal to the word ayin — "eye." Through this they are able to fulfill the concept behind the blue thread of the tzitzis even today.

I am now going to reveal to you a little bit but conceal twice as much regarding the concept behind the blue thread (techeiles) of the tzitzis: The value of the word ayin — "eye" — is 130, but since a man must gaze at his tzitzis with both eyes this comes to a total of 260. Add to this the numerical value of the word tzitzis, which is 590, and one receives a total of 850. This is exactly equal to the numerical value of the word techeiles. I have received an oral tradition from the illustrious Rabbi Yaakov Temerles of Lublin that a person should have this in mind while gazing at the tzitzis. Through this he helps eliminate the darkness intervening between us and the Shechinah, alluded to by the prophet Yirmiyahu in the verse, "You have led me into darkness and not light!" (Eichah 3:2). The main thing to recall is that the Holy One Blessed is He did not create the human being in this world for the benefit of his body, for the body is destined to disintegrate in the earth. Rather He created him for the benefit of his soul, which was carved out from beneath the Throne of Glory and is a portion of the Divine come down from On High. The soul was only brought here in order to rectify it and adorn it with good deeds that expedite the redemption and cause the Shechinah to rejoice in this bitter exile. Through this the soul refines the body as well, causing it to radiates with a clear light, especially when the body is "warmed up" by the performance of one of the mitzvos.

It was not in vain that the Sages said that when a person responds, Amein, yehei shemeih rabba with all his might, Gehinnom is cooled off on his behalf. This should be take at face value — namely, that one should say the words, Amein, yehei shmeih rabba, with all one's might. However, this does not mean that one should raise one's voice excessively and become an object of ridicule.

Rather, it means that one should say it with the force of all one's limbs. Thus, it is taught in the Zohar (Parashas Pinechas 220a) that a person must arouse all his limbs with great force, so that his heart will be shattered along with the power of the Sitra Achara. Even the wicked find rest when Israel recites these words, as is related in the Zohar in Parashas Noach (62b, Tosefta): When Israel raises its voice to respond aloud, Amein, yehei shemeih rabba, the Holy One Blessed is He becomes filled with mercy, bestowing life to all. Then the Holy One Blessed is He motions to the angel called SAMRYEL, holder of the keys to Gehinnom, and he opens three doors on the side of the desert so that the wicked will be able to enjoy the light of this world. But the smoke comes and blocks the view so that they cannot see it. Then three appointed angels wave fire rakes to push the smoke back for an hour and a half in the merit of the response of, Amein, yehei shemeih rabba, that Israel recite every day. After this the wicked must return to Gehinnom.

Just how precious this praise is to the Holy One Blessed is He can be seen from an incident cited in the Zohar in Parashas Terumah (165b—169b): Rabbi Chiyya and Rabbi Aba were staying at an inn. They arose at midnight to engage in study and the innkeeper's daughter stood holding the lamp for them while they studied. At one-point Rabbi Aba looked back and noticed that she was holding the lamp. He said, "[It is written,] 'For a mitzvah is a lamp but Torah is light' (Mishlei 6:23). A woman is commanded concerning the Shabbos lamp but not a man. This is because a woman corresponds to the Shechinah. "[And it is written,] 'But Torah is light.' This refers to the Torah that her husband studies, for a man is commanded to study Torah. This gives as much illumination as the mitzvah of the Shabbos lamp that the woman kindles. Thus, the two of them are illuminated both by the light of the Torah and the light of the Shabbos. Fortunate is the woman who merits a husband who is a scholar!"

When the young woman heard these words, she began to weep. In the meantime, her father entered and saw her weeping. He asked why she was weeping but in her bitterness of heart she did not respond. Then her father also began to weep. Rabbi Aba observed, "From her weeping I understand that her groom is an ignoramus and not a scholar." The girl's father replied, "That is indeed the case. I took him for my daughter because I once saw him jump from a rooftop to hear Kaddish along with the congregation. Just as soon as he left the synagogue, I offered him my daughter, assuming, based on that leap to hear Kaddish, that he was a great scholar, even though he was still young. For I did not know him previously. "But as it turns out, he does not even know the Grace After Meals and I do not have any means to compel him to study or to recite the Shema or the Grace After Meals." Rabbi Aba said, "So exchange him for another [that is, compel him to divorce her and then betroth her to a scholar]!" Then he thought about the matter again, "Alternatively, perhaps his son will be a scholar." In the meantime, the groom came over and sat down among them. Rabbi Aba looked at him and said, "I see in this youth that great illumination will indeed come out of him."

Then the youth spoke up, "My teachers, allow me to say something. [It is stated,] 'I am young in days and you are elders, therefore I groveled and dared not express my opinion among you' (Iyov 32:6). The pillars of the world have noted that it is written of Elihu that he was 'of the family of Ram.' But it is also written that he was 'the son of Barachel the Buzzite.' He was only called by this name ['the Buzzite'] because he would degrade [mevazeh] himself before those who were older than he was. This is the meaning of his statement, 'I am young in days.' "I too diminish myself before those who are older than I am. Now, I am a young man whereas in this place there are men who have grown old in wisdom. Therefore I resolved that I would not speak until today. But now that you are hear the time has come for me to open my mouth."

Then he began exounding the verse, "For a mitzvah is a lamp but Torah is light" (Mishlei 6:23), revealing to them numerous esoteric insights. Afterwards he commented, "Know that I am from Babylon and that I am the son of Rav Safra, although I did not merit to know my father. I was exiled to this place and was afraid to speak because the inhabitants of this land are lions in Torah. Therefore, I resolved that I would not speak any words of Torah for two months. Today those two months are complete. How fortunate I am that I met you here."

Rabbi Yose raised his voice and wept and all of them arose and kissed him upon the head. Rabbi Yose said, "If we had come here for no reason other than to hear from your mouth these words of the Ancient of Days, the like of which I have never heard before, it would have been enough for us." They all took their seats and the groom said, "My teachers, when I saw the pain of my father-in-law and his daughter, my wife, over the fact that I did not know the Grace or the Shema, I resolved that I would not approach my wife until I had revealed to you some of the wondrous esoteric meanings behind the Grace after Meals." While the young man spoke, Rabbi Yose, Rabbi Aba, Rabbi Chiyya, his father-in-law and his bride all rejoiced and when he had finished, they again arose and kissed him. Rabbi Yose declared, "This is surely a match that the Holy One Blessed is He is pleased with." Then they turned to the bride and showered her with blessings. Afterwards they instructed her father to prepare a place for the wedding, "For we will not leave here," said Rabbi Yose, "until it has been held!" The entire town gathered to participate in that joyous occasion. They called her "bride" and rejoiced with them by reciting words of Torah. During the wedding feast the groom delivered a discourse at the table, explaining the concept of the seven blessings, revealing numerous awesome secrets and insights. Everyone rejoiced and the townspeople unanimously selected him to be their rabbi and halachic guide. When the wedding was over, Rabbi Yose, Rabbi Aba and Rabbi Chiyya arose, blessed them and continued on their way.

When they came to Rabbi Shimon ben Yochai, he looked up at them. "I was observing you today," he said, "and I saw that for two days you have been lodging in the Tabernacle of a youth who is actually the angel Metat and that he taught you many lofty secrets. How fortunate is your portion!" Then they reviewed for him the entire course of events, after which he again observed, "Fortunate are you and fortunate is your portion." Then he added, "And fortunate is my lot! For I recall the day that Rav Safra, the groom's father, accompanied me and I blessed him that he would have son who would be a lion of Torah. But I did not bless him that he would merit raising him or that he would see him reach that stage.

We can learn from the conclusion of this passage that when a rabbi blesses his disciple that he merit scholarly sons, he must also bless him that he merit raising them and witnessing the light of their Torah in his lifetime. We can also learn from this excerpt that one must not seek prominence among the great and that the young should to try to hear words of wisdom from the elderly, for they will undoubtedly hear things that they have never heard before, thereby causing their wisdom to increase. Furthermore, we learn from this incident that one should try to master the Kabbalistic "unifications." For we see that Rav Safra had taught to his son, the groom, the "unifications" behind the Grace After Meals and the Shema as well as those that lie behind the propounding of Torah insights, despite the fact that his son was still very young. And we can learn that one never loses by the performance of the mitzvos. For when the innkeeper saw the groom leaping from the roof to hear Kaddish and respond, Amein, yehei shemeih rabba — that is, when he saw him fulfilling the mitzvos mitzvos — he gave him his daughter to wife. And this was on account of only a single mitzvah! Therefore, a person must be diligent in the fulfillment of the mitzvos and in study. Then Hashem will protect him while he is involved with them and even when he is not, and peace will encompass all that he has.

Chapter 46

It is taught in the writings of the Ari, z"l (Sha'ar HaMitzvos, Parashas Shemini 21a) that one of the things that prevents a person's prayers from being accepted is the lack of bodily cleanliness, for example, the presence on his body of filth, feces or drops of urine. You should know further that bodily cleanliness is in general a positive matter. In the book of Shmuel (I:24:4) it is written that King Dovid stealthily removed the corner of Shaul's cloak. Now if Shaul had been wearing the cloak at the time surely, he would have felt Dovid cutting off the corner. Therefore, it seems clear that he must have removed it completely. Seifer Chassidim (775) relates that this cloak was the garment with which King Shaul would enwrap himself in Hashem's honor whenever he prayed. That is why he removed it before performing his bodily functions. Similarly, it is the custom of men of deeds to leave their outer garments outside when they enter the outhouse on their way into the synagogue. For the synagogue is considered a minor Temple, therefore one must enter it wearing only respectable garments. This is especially important on the Sabbath. Thus, it is taught in the second chapter of Chagigah (20a) in the name of Rabbi Yonason ben Amram: "If his Sabbath clothing became mixed up with his weekday clothing and he wore it [during the week], it becomes defiled." [The Gemara is speaking of someone who eats all his food in a state of purity.] This is because he generally guards his Sabbath clothing more carefully against defilement. For the same reason it is fitting to have a separate pair of shoes to wear in the synagogue and it is a good idea not to wear them when going to the outhouse. Another matter that interferes with the acceptance of a person's prayers even if his garments are clean is the presence of a forbidden mixture of wool and linen (sha'atnez). Even if this presence is unintentional, it still prevents one's prayers from being entirely heard and accepted. This is true even if one prays with the proper devotion. Therefore, tailors must take pains to ensure that they do not cause harm to their customers by causing them to pray in garments containing sha'atnez. Otherwise the tailor himself bears responsibility for the sin of the multitude.

But even if one's garments are free of all filth and of sha'atnez, his prayers will not be accepted if any theft is involved. Suppose, for example, that he makes his livelihood through fraud and deceit and then arrays himself with an elegant garment of which he is very proud. This is what the prophets refer to as a "swindler's garment" — beged bogdim; (Yeshayahu 24:16). Every time he dons this garment in order to pray, he reawakens the memory of his sins and iniquities, causing his prayers to be cast to the demons. Woe to him and woe to his soul! This is the case even if his only sin was the failure to pay the tailor his due, if the latter did not press the issue but allowed him special terms against his will, or if he withheld his employee's wages. For in all these cases he is guilty of theft. Moreover, the employee looks to him for survival. Heaven forbid that a person should withhold a worker's wages or even pay him less than his due! For it is written, "Because the children of Israel are servants to Me, they are My servants!" (Vayikra 25:55). Therefore, his punishment is very severe [as I have already explained at length in Chapter 14]. Just as the employer is commanded to pay his worker on time and in full, so is the worker commanded not to ruin the garment and not to take any of the materials for himself, even the leftovers. Rather he must return to the customer even the smallest quantities.

Nowadays, the iniquitous practice of stealing [the leftovers] has become very widespread among the tailors. Through this they commit two evils: First of all, they spoil the garments they make. Secondly, they violate the commandment against stealing, behaving as if it were permitted. They do not even take the matter seriously enough to feel regretful about it or to make confession over it, having become so accustomed to it. They do not realize the severity of the punishment that awaits them. Therefore, I admonish every tailor who has stumbled in this sin: Let him repent and take it to heart to return to the owners what he has stolen or else to do something on behalf of the public. For it was only on account of theft that the fate of the Generation of the Flood was sealed (Sanhedrin 108a). I know of one tailor in the holy community of Brisk in Lithuania who instructed the Burial Society before his death that they should construct his coffin out of his work-table and place his measuring stick in his hand. When they asked him the reason for this request, he explained that his work-table and yardstick were his two faithful witnesses that in his entire life he had never stole even one piece of his working materials. Fortunate is he for wishing to benefit only from the work of his hands and not from theft.

Another practice that interferes with the acceptability of a person's holy endeavors is the donning of two garments together, namely, donning one of them when the other is already inside it. According to an oral tradition handed down to us from the disciples of the Ari (Pri Eitz Chayim, Sha'ar HaTefillah, Ch. 2) this practice is very injurious to a person, for it allows the Sitrah Acharah a certain degree of access to him. This is especially true regarding the donning of one's Sabbath clothes, which require extra care, as we have already mentioned. For the Sitrah Acharah surrounds a person striving to cling to him, especially when he is dressed in his Shabbos clothing. Therefore, the Ari advised that as a person dons them, he should recite the verse, "No weapon that is fashioned will succeed against you and every tongue that rises up against you in judgment will you condemn. This is the inheritance of the servants of Hashem and the recompense from Me for their righteousness, says Hashem" (Yeshaya 54:17). It is also appropriate to recite this verse as one dons one's outer garment to pray. One should thoroughly examine one's garments at other times, too, and not only when one is about to pray, because sanctity does not devolve upon any place that is repulsive or soiled.

For the same reason every Jew should ensure that the area around his mezuzah is clean. It is related in the Zohar (3:263b) that the function of a mezuzah in a Jewish home is to bring to mind the supernal lovingkindness with which the Holy One Blessed is He watches over our entryways and maintains the remembrance of us before Him at all times. Through this a person is also prevented from forgetting Hashem's commandments forever. See what I have written in Chapter One regarding the protection that a mezuzah provides.

It is also written in Sifra DiShelomo HaMelech (Zohar, ibid.) that a certain demon rests beside the entrance of one's home, waiting to cause harm to whoever enters. But when this demon sees the name "A-lmighty" inscribed upon the mezuzah he is prevented from causing harm. It follows that one should not pour out foul water near the mezuzah for two reasons: First, in order not to show contempt for the holy name of the Master of the Universe. And second, lest the demon that is there be allowed to cause harm, Heaven forbid. But if the environment of the mezuzah is clean and the person shows his affection towards it by kissing it as he goes in and out, the demon is compelled to bless him, saying, "This is the gate of Hashem, let the righteous enter it" (Tehillim 118:20). On the other hand, if a person does not have a mezuzah at the entrance to his home at all, then the demon has permission to cause harm. Woe to the owner of the house for showing concern over the small sum that it would cost to purchase a mezuzah but not for his own welfare! Children, in particular, die of a disease called rablis if there is not a proper mezuzah in every room of the house. For this reason these two verses are adjacent to one another in the Torah: "And you shall write them upon the doorposts [mezuzos] of your house and upon your gates" (Devarim 11:20), and, "In order that your days and the days of your children shall be increased" (ibid.

21). Similarly, in Maseches Shabbos (32b) the Sages of blessed memory proclaim that children die young on account of the neglect of the mitzvos of mezuzah and tzitzis. Supervision of this matter is the duty of the rabbis and the heads of the community. Whoever is meticulous about it will merit the fulfillment of the verse, "Fortunate is the man who listens to Me…to guard the doorposts of My entrances, for whoever finds Me finds life" (Mishlei 8:34-35). And may that life be long, Amein.

Chapter 47
The Gemara tells us in Nedarim (10a) that the pious of former times longed for the opportunity to bring sin-offerings. It seems to me that this is because they were in general very strict with themselves, desiring that no blemish should be found in them even through an unintentional sin. Therefore, if they did commit a sin, they would rectify it immediately in order not to remain under the dominion of the Sitrah Acharah even for a short time. Thus, they would fulfill in themselves the verse, "And do not allow anything of the forbidden things to cling to your hand" (Devarim 13:18). If they were so careful to offer sacrifices for their accidental sins, how much more so must one make amends for intentional transgressions! For Hashem will bring all deeds of judgment. A person might wonder how it is possible for anyone to survive and endure all these judgments and afflictions. But Hashem is merciful and gracious. He does not desire the death of the wicked, only that they turn back from their evil ways and live! This is why repentance preceded the creation of the world (Pesachim 54a) — to teach that were it not for repentance the world could not survive even for a moment. At all four turning points of the year [possibly the solstices and equinoxes] a call to repentance goes forth. Thus, we find in the Zohar (Parashas Vayikra 15b): It was taught: At the four turning points of the year, judgments are aroused but repentance can suspend their effects until one makes amends. Just as soon as these judgments are aroused, a proclamation goes forth from one end of the world to the other and the emissaries ascend

and then descend again. But the herald makes his announcement and no one is stirred! This is what the Sages were alluding to when they warned that one must be wary of "a drop of blood" at the four turning points of the year. For the "drop of blood" hints at the judgments that are aroused to enter into the world. The remedy for the effects of these turning points is the placing of a piece of iron [on top of all food and drink]. One explanation of this that has found favor in the eyes of God and men is that it is an allusion to the verse, "Shatter them with an iron rod [sheivet barzel]" (Tehillim 2:9).

Thus I have seen it written in the name of one great scholar that Dovid Hamelech was asking the Holy One Blessed is He to break and destroy Israel's oppressors in the merit of the twelve tribes [shevatim] who were born to the four Matriarchs. For the acronym of the names of the Matriarchs is the word barzel — "iron": **B**ilhah, **R**ochel, **Z**ilpah and **L**eah. The merit of the Matriarchs stands by us to deliver us from the harsh judgments alluded to by the word "blood" because these derive from the female aspect of the Sitrah Acharah. This is the evil Lilis and her entire camp, who incorporate within them the five shades of impure blood. The Sages rule in Niddah (30b): "the daughters of the Kusim have the status of menstruating women from the crib [arisah]." Arisah is a euphemism for Lilis' camp because of its connection with the word eres (venom) — a reference to the venom of the primordial snake. Similarly, Amos (6:4) speaks of, "Those who lie upon beds of ivory and stretch themselves out upon their couches [arsosam]. The camp of the Shechinah, by contrast, is called a "bed," as in, "Behold, Shlomo's bed [mitah] has sixty warriors surrounding it" (Shir HaShirim 3:7). Since the "blood" mentioned above derives from the five shades of impure blood, which in turn derive from the evil Lilis, the female counterpart of the Samech Mem, the only way to weaken it is by invoking the female aspect of the realm of holiness, that is, the Matriarchs. For it is from them that the twelve tribes derive. In light of the above one must instruct the women to have in mind the merit of the Matriarchs — Bilhah, Rochel, Zilpah and Leah — as they put these metal pieces in place at the turning points of the year. For it is their merit that stands by us to deliver us from all evil decrees and it is a very praiseworthy that one's deeds be accompanied by thought. This act of "unification" is of great significance and preciousness to the Holy One Blessed is He. Therefore, it has the power to deliver a person from all evil and from all mishap, with the help of Hashem, God of Israel.

We can now understand why it is that when sinners increase among Israel, Heaven forbid, the attribute of judgment specifically brings upon them bloodshed. Thus we find in the Zohar (Parashas Shemos 12a): "And Pharaoh's daughter went down to bathe upon the Nile" (Shemos 2:5) — that is, the attribute of judgment went down to bathe in the blood of Israel. "Upon the Nile" — that is, to avenge the disgrace of the Torah [that is likened to water]. However, repentance can avert the entire decree, as Rabbi Yehudah says in the continuation of that passage: Everything in the world depends upon repentance and upon the prayers that human beings offer up to the Holy One Blessed is He, especially if they shed tears while praying, for there is no gate through which tears cannot penetrate. What is meant by the verse, "And she opened it and saw the child" (ibid. 6)? "And she opened" — this refers to the Shechinah, for it opens regularly in the merit of Israel. And once it is open, then, "she saw the child" — this refers to Israel, as is written, "A delightful child" (Yirmeyahu 31:19). "And behold there was a crying youth" — that is, Israel repented and wept before Hashem. "And she had pity upon him." All the judgments and evil decrees were averted from them and Hashem had mercy upon them. "And she said, this is one of the Hebrew children," because he had a pliant heart made of flesh. That is, because they were not too obstinate to repent. You should know that on the four turning points of the year a call to repentance goes forth, as I mentioned earlier. Therefore, it is an appropriate time to arouse oneself to repentance. This true of the turning point of Tammuz [i.e., the summer solstice], which is more severe than any of the other turning points. How can anyone fail to take this matter to heart and to tremble in anticipation of judgment? Let every person regret his sinful deeds and repent with weeping and supplication! Then, as the prophet has promised, "He will go back and heal him" (Yeshayahu 6:10).

Chapter 48

It is a custom of Israel to begin blowing the shofar on the first day of the month of Elul, that is, thirty days before Rosh HaShannah. This can be likened to a debtor whom the court grants thirty days to raise the funds to pay his creditors. In the same way the Heavenly court grants a person thirty days to repent so that he may clear himself in their eyes through acts of penitence, prayer and charity, which together avert the evil decree. The shofar is meant to awaken us it because reminds us of the horn of Israel and the horn of the Binding of Yitzchak, as it is written, "There was a ram behind him entangled in the thicket by its horns" (Bereishis 22:13). According to the Midrash (Yalkut Bereishis 101) this indicates that although Israel are entangled in sin they are destined to be redeemed by the horns of this ram, as it is written, "On that day He will blow upon a great shofar" (Yeshayahu 27:13). Thus, Avraham observed the ram freeing himself only to become entangled once more. He observed its suffering [symbolizing the suffering Israel was to endure in the course of the four exiles]. Hashem said to him, "This ram represents Your children who will become free of the kingdom of Babylon only to become entangled in the kingdom of Media. Then from Media they will pass to Greece and from Greece to Yishmael and Edom. Yet they are destined to be redeemed by the horns of this ram, as it is written, 'And Hashem, God, will blow upon a shofar; Hashem of Hosts will protect them' (Zecharyah 9:14- 15)." Therefore, whoever trembles at the word of Hashem must also tremble when he hears the sound of the shofar. Let him shudder and quake with fear of Hashem and His exalted majesty.

The word shofar hints at the admonition, "Improve [shapru] your deeds and abandon your evil ways!" The tekiyah [a long unbroken blast] is a form of prayer and the one who hears it should say, "Master of the Worlds! Insert teka] Your name Y-ah [the last two letters of the word tekiyah] among Israel like a peg that is firmly imbedded [takua], as it is written, 'His hand was upon the throne of Y-ah' (Shemos 17:16). The shevarim [a blast broken into long segments] is a hint that the Holy One Blessed is He will shatter [yeshabeir], cast down and eradicate the throne of the Sitrah Acharah so that it no longer has any dominion over Israel. This is followed by a teruah [a blast broken into many short segments], indicating that at that time, "they will make a joyful sound [yisro'a'u] and sing together" (Tehillim 65:14). For the letters vav and heh of the word teruah (תרועה) represent the vav and heh [of Hashem's name], which will join together [with the first two letters, i.e. the yud and heh alluded to above], in fear and love in the name of all Israel.

Therefore, let every individual arouse himself at the sound of the shofar, calling, arousing and admonishing us to repentance. Arise and cry out to your God in weeping and supplications. For this is the way of men of deeds; when the shofar is blown on the first of Elul, they turn their faces towards the wall and call upon Hashem in weeping and wailing, pleading, "Have grace upon me! Have grace upon me, O Hashem!" Then they proceed with the invoking of the thirteen attributes of mercy: "God, O King who sits upon the throne of mercy, act with lovingkindness ... And Hashem passed over his face, proclaiming, 'Hashem, Hashem, God who is merciful, etc.'" Afterwards let him arouse his companions to repentance as well, especially if he has seen in one of them some unseemly conduct. Then he is obliged to rebuke him, saying gently, "My brother and beloved friend, the time has come to repair that which has been twisted and to straighten the way. Please hear my words and remove this stumbling block from yourself, for you have committed improper deeds and I am obligated to admonish you. "And if you have seen in me any impropriety, you should also say to me, 'You have done such-and-such.' For we are like brothers; our souls derived from the same source, from beneath the Throne of Glory."

This is illustrated by the conduct of a certain pious man named Rabbi Avraham who was a disciple of the Ari, z"l. He used to pass through the marketplaces and streets calling on people to repent. One day Rabbi Avraham assembled the townspeople in the Ashkenazic synagogue and urged them to follow him in accepting upon themselves the four types of execution [stoning, burning, strangling and the sword]. He then climbed into a sack and instructed that he be dragged the entire length and breadth of the synagogue. This was in order to debase himself and humble his evil inclination. Afterwards he instructed that each of them takes a stone weighing a pound or a pound-and-a-half and throw it upon him. Then he climbed out of the sack. In the synagogue Rabbi Avraham had prepared a bed covered with stinging nettles. He removed his clothing and cast himself upon them naked, rolling in them until his flesh was covered with blisters. Afterwards they administered to him thirty-nine lashes corresponding to execution by the sword. Finally, he immersed himself in the mikveh, corresponding to strangulation. When he had finished, he said to them, "My teachers, whoever wishes to be spared punishment in Gehinnom should do as I have done." Immediately the entire crowd accepted these afflictions upon themselves with love and affection, lifting their voices in weeping and confessing their iniquities. By the time they left they had all become complete penitents and remained so for the rest of their lives.

But there was one man who did not wish to join them and make his penance publicly known. So, what did he do instead? He waited until after midnight and then went with a sack to the entrance of the synagogue and covered himself over from head to toe so that no one would know who he was. Then he turned his face to the wall and remained that way for the rest of the night and all through the day until the following midnight, a full twenty-four hours, pouring out his heart in prayer and supplication and weeping. When midnight of the second night arrived and the people of the town were asleep, he left the synagogue at last and went home and no one was able to determine who it was. The Ari observed, "This is surely the most perfect penance, for repentance and charity belong in the same category. Therefore, just as the best form of charity is given in secret, so is the best form of penitence carried out in secret. For then the Sitrah Acharah has no sway over him to divert him from the ways of repentance." But the most essential point to bear in mind is that one must first fulfill the verse, "Turn away from evil" (Tehillim 34:15). Then he can be certain that, "whoever strives to purify himself, Heaven assists him" (Shabbos 104a).

Chapter 49

Our Sages have said that fasting is the first step in arousing oneself to repentance. Now we will discuss the power of fasting. But first let us preface with a passage that I found in the Zohar in Parashas Shemos (20a): Rabbi Aba was traveling along the road accompanied by Rabbi Yitzchak. While they were walking, they came across some roses. Rabbi Aba took a rose in his hand and continued walking. Rabbi Yose met up with them and said, "Surely the Shechinah is here and I see something in Rabbi Aba's hands that is intended to teach great wisdom. For I know that Rabbi Aba did not take this rose for any reason other than to teach wisdom." Rabbi Aba said, "Sit my son." So, they sat. Rabbi Aba smelled the rose and said, "It is clear that the world is only sustained by smell. For I see that the soul is only sustained by smell. This is why one must take a myrtle branch [to smell] when Shabbos goes out.

To explain the matter in a way that our ears can understand: The soul, which is called a "small world," is sustained only by smell. Thus, the Sages comment, "What is there that the soul benefits from but not the body? It is smell" (Berachos 43b). In the same way, the large worlds, both lower and upper, are also sustained by smell alone. Thus, for as long as the Temple stood, Israel offered up sacrifices there and while reflecting on all the esoteric "unifications" connected with the sacrifice as well on as the holy Divine Names deriving from the verse, "a fire-offering, a sweet smell to Hashem" (Bamidbar 28:8). In this way the sacrifice would awaken Heaven's favor and all the worlds would be united in a single bond. Thus, the word korban — "sacrifice" — derives from the word keiruv — "drawing close." Nowadays the exhalation of a person's breath in prayer takes the place of the sacrifices, as does Torah study. For instance, whoever engages in the study of the burnt sacrifices is credited as if he offered one (Menachos 100a). In the same way, the breath that is exhaled in prayer on a fast day is also comparable to the fragrance of the sacrifices.

The Zohar explains that just as a rose is red but turns white when cooked on a fire, so too a sacrifice is comprised of fat and blood which are red and white, while the smoke arising from them is entirely white. This suggests that sin, symbolized by the color red, is also turned white. Similarly, when a person fasts, he offers up his own fat and blood. Every fast cause the body to become warm, indicating that the redness [of sin] is being transformed into whiteness through the heat of the fast. This is what Rabbi Elazar meant when he said, "Whenever I would fast, I would pray, "Master of the Universe! It is openly revealed to You that I have offered up my fat and blood and that my body has burned with the warming that derives from its weakening. May it be Your will that the fragrance ascending from my mouth at this time be reckoned like the fragrance of the sacrifices on the altar and may I find favor in Your eyes."

Having mentioned some of the merits of fasting let us now discuss the things that detract from the fast:

1. One must be careful to engage in holy activities when fasting and not behave like those who go and engage in frivolity and mockery, for their gain is nullified by their loss.
2. It is inappropriate to publicize one's fast, for it is like giving a present to a friend and then announcing it in public.
3. Becoming angry during a fast is likened to giving someone a gift while in anger.
4. One should try to study a little before breaking the fast.
5. One should strive to break the fast with bread baked by a Jewish baker.
6. Before breaking the fast, one should send a portion of the food he has prepared to a poor person.
7. Most important of all, one must be careful not to eat in a gluttonous manner when breaking the fast. This is utterly forbidden because it is the way of the wicked Esav, who said, "Pour into me now" (Bereishis 25:30). Similarly, it is written in Mishlei, "The belly of the wicked is always lacking" (13:25). Many people are remiss in this area, gobbling down their food in a gluttonous and drunken manner. This greatly detracts from the merit of the fast.
8. One must not drink to the point of intoxication, for then one is liable to fall asleep while still in a confused and drunken state and neglect to deposit one's soul in Hashem's care with full intention and clarity of thought. This is absolutely essential, as is related at length in the Zohar in Parashas Devarim (260a).

9. A fast day is an appropriate time to lay out one's sins before the Holy One Blessed is He. Then the Satan will be unable to detract from one's sacrifice or prayer with his indictments. Thus, the Zohar relates in Parashas Vayikra (20a): Rabbi Chiya and Rabbi Yose were traveling along a road. While they were walking Rabbi Yose said to Rabbi Chiya, "Come let us engage in Torah study." Rabbi Chiya began, "[It is written,] 'I will tell You my sin' (Tehillim 32:5). From here we learn that any man who conceals his sins and does not acknowledge them before the holy King and seek mercy over them is not granted to open the portal of repentance. But if a person does acknowledge them, then the Holy One Blessed is He has mercy upon him and the attribute of mercy overwhelms the attribute of judgment. "This is especially true if he weeps, for all the other gates of Heaven are blocked up, but the gate of tears is open and his prayers will be accepted. Therefore whoever acknowledges his sins honors the King and causes mercy to overwhelm judgment. Concerning this was it written, 'He who offers confession honors Me' (Tehillim 50:23). [And why is the word 'honor' written with two nuns (yechabda n e n i)?] Because there are two aspects to [Hashem's] honor, one On High and one below, one in this world and one in the next."

Rabbi Chiya continued his discourse, "On the day that the earthly Beis HaMikdosh was destroyed and Israel went into exile with a millstone around their necks and hands tied behind them, the Shechinah [Kenesses Yisroel] was also banished from the King's palace to follow behind them. And as the Shechinah descended into exile it said, 'First I will go and weep over My house and My children and the great unification that took place in the Beis HaMikdosh.' "And when it descended from the Heavenly Beis HaMikdosh and saw the earthly Beis HaMikdosh in ruins with the blood of the righteous spilled therein and the sanctuary and portico burned down, it raised its voice in weeping, creating a stir in all the upper and lower worlds. Its voice ascended until it reached the abode of the King, evoking in Him the desire to destroy the world and return it primordial chaos, which prompted a number of camps of angels to descend to try to console the Shechinah, but I would accept no consolation. This is the meaning of the verse, 'A voice is heard in Ramah, Rocheil weeping over her children, etc.' "When

the Shechinah left of the Temple it dwelt in the Land of Israel. Then it left the Holy Land to dwell in the desert, where it remained for three days, crying, 'O how she sat in solitude, etc.' (Eichah 1:1)."
And Rabbi Chiya and Rabbi Yose wept. While they were sitting there a bird flew by and whispered that they should leave that spot. Rabbi Chiya said, "Let us move on, for undoubtedly there are mountain men in the vicinity." So, they got up and left and when they looked back, they saw that bandits were indeed pursuing them. Miraculously they found a cave before them concealed within a boulder, so they entered and remained there for a day and a night. When nightfall came, the cave was illuminated by the moon. Eventually two merchants passed by with donkeys laden with wine and provisions. They said, "Let us stop here, for we have food and drink both for ourselves and our donkeys. And let us take shelter in this cave." Then one of them said to the other, "Do not go in until you have explained to me the meaning of the verse, 'I will thank You forever for what You have done and I will put hope in Your Name, for [You are] good to Your devoted ones' (Tehillim 52:11)? Is His name not good before others [besides pious ones] as well?" When his companion was unable to answer he said to him, "Woe to the merchant who abandoned the Holy One Blessed is He to engage in trade!"
Then Rabbi Chiya and Rabbi Yose, who were sitting in the cave, rejoiced. Rabbi Chiya said to Rabbi Yose, "See how many miracles the Holy One Blessed is He has done for us. First, He saved us from the bandits and concealed us in this cave in peace and tranquility. And now he has even sent Torah scholars to join us!" So, they came out of the cave and wished the merchants "Peace" and joined their company. Then the first merchant asked them, "What is the meaning of the phrase, 'for it is good before Your pious ones'?" Rabbi Chiya answered, "Certainly the Holy One Blessed is He is only good before the pious and not before the wicked, for they despise the Torah and do not study it!" The merchant replied, "That is a good explanation on the plain level. But one day I was in the company of Rabbi Shimon ben Yochai who explained it esoterically," whereupon the merchant revealed to them a number of amazing secrets. Afterwards Rabbi Chiya and Rabbi Yose went over and kissed him. Then each one proceeded on his way.

From this passage you can see how precious those earlier generations were, for they would study even while traveling and would rejoice if they met up with fellow scholars. Whoever associates with scholars expedites the redemption, for the Shechinah has no place in this bitter exile other than the four cubits of halachah (Berachos 8a), as it is written, "The ways [halichos] of the world are His" (Chavakkuk 3:6). Then the Holy One Blessed is He will spread His wings over him to protect him from every evil decree. Moreover, his prayers will be readily accepted and all that he has will be blessed with every sort of blessing, Amein.

Chapter 50

Although we have already discussed the preciousness of a poor man's prayer (Chapter 5 and Chapter 27), I would now like to elaborate further on this topic. For a poor man's sacrifice is always received by Hashem with favor, as it is written, "God will not despise a broken and contrite heart" (Tehillim 51:19).

It is related in the Zohar (Parashas Vayikra 9a): A wealthy man once brought two young pigeons, a poor man's sacrifice, to a Kohein to offer them up. But the Kohein said to him, "This sacrifice is not fitting for you," whereupon the man returned home sullenly. "Why are you so sullen?" his brothers inquired? "Because the Kohein would not offer up my sacrifice of two pigeons," he explained. "He acted properly," they told him, "for that is the sacrifice of a poor man, as it is written, 'And if he is too poor, etc.' (Vayikra 14:21). Instead you must offer up an ox." The man thought to himself, "If the Torah requires a person to sacrifice an ox to atone for the mere thought of sin, how much more is required for an actual sin! I vow that I will never again entertain thoughts of sin!" So how did he conduct himself from then on? All day long he engaged in business, then at night he would sleep a little bit and call over his brothers to study Torah with him. They began to refer to him as "Yehudah the new man."

One day Rabbi Yeisa the Elder found him dividing up his property. He gave away half to the poor and invested the other half in the

Kav HaYashar

wares of seafaring merchants. Meanwhile he sat and engaged in study. One day the rich man delivered a discourse, "If a person offers a sacrifice with all his heart the Holy One Blessed Is He will come to be near him. "Come and see. The sacrifice of a poor man is valued by the Holy One Blessed is He because it is as if he offered up his own fat and blood, for although he does not have anything, he nevertheless brings a sacrifice. Therefore, at the moment that he offers up his sacrifice a proclamation is made in Heaven, 'For He neither despises nor abhors the poor man's afflictions' (Tehillim 22:25). "Clearly the poor man's sacrifice is the most valued of all, for on account of it I became included within the inheritance of the Holy One Blessed is He. On account of it I became included within the inheritance of the Torah. That is why I gave away half of my property to the poor, for they caused me all this.... "The essence of a sacrifice is the desire on the part of the heart and soul. That is more precious to the Holy One Blessed is He than all else.

Nowadays prayer takes the place of the sacrifices, therefore a person must pray with a broken heart and have in mind to prepare adornments for the Shechinah with his supplications. Those who have this in mind when they perform good deeds bring satisfaction to the Shechinah. These individuals are known as "men of deeds" because the word "deed" [ma'aseh] has the connotation of "fixing" [tikkun]. Thus the word "And He did" [vaya'as; Bereishis 1:7] means in context, "And He fixed" [vetiken]. Similarly, the woman of Shunem said to her husband, "Let us fix up [na'aseh] a small walled-in attic room and place for him there a bed, a table, a chair and a lamp" (II Melachim:4:10). This woman also had in mind to honor the Shechinah, for the four items she mentions are the things that the children of Israel must prepare for the Shechinah. Thus, when a person prays the evening Amidah, he should have in mind that this prayer corresponds to the "lamp." And when he recites the evening Shema, he should have in mind that it corresponds to the "bed." The Verses of Praise and the morning Shema correspond to the "table" and the morning Amidah corresponds to the "chair." He should have all these intentions in mind for the honor of the Shechinah, as is discussed in the Zohar at length (2:133a).

A person must realize just how precious his prayers are when they are prayed with intention, for they bring immeasurable joy to the Shechinah. As the Zohar explains (ibid. 132a): When a person recites songs and praises the Shechinah is adorned with the very crown that the Holy One Blessed is He will one day place upon the head of the Moshiach. On that crown are engraved the same names that were engraved on it when Israel crossed the sea. Therefore, let a person direct his will to these things when he recites this song. For whoever merits reciting the Verses of Praise and the Song of the Sea with intention in this world will merit witnessing the Moshiach adorned with this crown and with his weapons of war in the time to come. Moreover, he will merit reciting this song at that time. When one reaches the blessing "Let Your name be praised" [Yishtabach] the Holy One Blessed is He takes the crown and places it in front of Him. [Through this the Shechinah begins to be adorned to come before the King.] Therefore, one must incorporate into it the thirteen lofty attributes through which it is blessed. These are the thirteen lofty spices:

1. stacte,
2. onycha,
3. galbanum,
4. frankincense,
5. myrrh,
6. cassia,
7. spikenard,
8. saffron,
9. costus,
10. aromatic bark,
11. cinnamon,
12. Carshina lye.

[Either "spikenard"- shiboles neird — should be counted as two or else Cyprus wine should be added to complete the thirteen.] And here [in Yishtabach] the thirteen are:

1. song,
2. praise,
3. lauding,
4. hymns,
5. power,

6. dominion,
7. victory,
8. greatness,
9. might,
10. acclaim,
11. glory,
12. holiness,
13. sovereignty.

These correspond to the Thirteen Attributes of Mercy and should be recited in a single breath so that there will be no pause between them. If one does interrupt in the middle of them a flame comes out from beneath the wings of the cherubim and a great voice announces, "So-and-so interrupted in the middle of the praises of his Master!" His merits are also erased so that he may not behold the majesty of the King, as it is written, "And he will not see the King's majesty" (Yeshayahu 26:10).

In light of this one should be very careful to recite the words of Yishtabach from "song and praise" until "sovereignty" in a single breath. Moreover, it is improper to interrupt in the middle of any holy recitation, for example, the response of Amein, yehei shemeih raba mevorach le'olam ulomei olmaya yisborach. One pious man told me that he was also careful to place his feet together as in the Amidah when responding, Amein, yehei shemeih raba. For this practice indicates the great desire of the Holy One Blessed is He for the prayers of Israel. This is evident from the Midrash on Yechezkeil (Yalkut 337). "See how elevated the Holy One Blessed is He is from His world, yet a human being can enter the synagogue, pray behind a pillar, turn his face to the wall [and whisper his prayer and the Holy One Blessed is He listens to him]!" [The Midrash tells us that he "prays behind a pillar" because] a person should always turn his face towards the wall when praying. And if he is on the road let him turn his face towards a tree. The word "wall" — kosel — contains a wondrous allusion that is explained in the Zohar (2:116a). The word kosel is divided into two parts, ko (כו) and sel (תל). The value of ko is 26, which is the value of Hashem's ineffable Name. A tel is a hill and it alludes to the Western Wall of the Beis HaMikdosh, known as talpios — the hill [tel] towards which all mouths [pios] turn (Berachos 30a).

A person should have all this in mind as he turns his face to the wall. Then let him pray with humility and awe, for the walls of the synagogue are very holy and the light of the Shechinah hovers over them continually. For this reason, it is praiseworthy to kiss the walls of the synagogue to show one's love for the sacred. A proof to this can be found in the Yalkut on Yechezkeil (350): "And the glory of Hashem departed from above the threshhold of the House [Beis HaMikdosh]" (Yechezkeil 10:18). This can be likened to a king who departed from his palace and as he went out, he kissed the walls and hugged the pillars, saying, "May you have peace, O my home! May you have peace, O my palace!" So too the Shechinah kissed and hugged the Beis HaMikdosh, saying, "May you have peace, O My home and sanctuary!" Now that we are in exile the synagogue is the "home" of the Shechinah. Therefore, we must treat it with dignity and sanctity and not display there any light-headedness, as I have already mentioned (Chapter 3). Whoever prays with awe and trepidation and with devotion will merit beholding the pleasantness of Hashem and meditating in His Sanctuary, Amein.

Chapter 51

It is written, "And let your camp be holy" (Devarim 23:15). Just as there is a border surrounding the various hosts and camps of the Shechinah, all of whom are called "holy," so too the body and limbs of a human being comprise a "camp," which if sanctified is also called the "camp of the Shechinah." Thus, it is written, "And I will be sanctified in the midst of (or "within") the children of Israel" (Vayikra 22:32), and "I will dwell among (or "within") them" (Shemos 25:8). But if a person heads in a bad direction he brings into himself the camp of the Sitra Achara. Therefore, one should develop the habit of reciting this brief prayer: "Master of the Universe! Cause me to merit becoming a throne for the Shechinah!" For when the body is sanctified it becomes the throne of the Shechinah, which has a tremendous longing to settle upon the bodies of the righteous, whereas if a person perverts his ways the opposite occurs, Heaven forbid. This is concept is mentioned in the Zohar (Parashas Noach 68b) in connection with the verse, "And the [water] bore up the ark and it was raised from upon the earth" (Bereishis 7:17): "That is, when there are sinners in the world the Shechinah abandons the earth." The Shechinah is called an "ark" — teivah — because if one changes the order of the letters of the word teivah (תיבה) it spells out the words Beis H [ashem] (בית 'ה) — the "House of Hashem." The same passage elaborates on some of the ways in one can sanctify the body, the primary one being through studying Torah as much as possible. It is especially important to study at night, just before going to sleep. Thus, it is related in Midrash HaNe'elam (Zohar Chadash 30b) in the name of Rabbi Yehudah: "Every night Metat, the Prince of the Countenance, takes the souls of all who study Torah and displays them before the Holy One Blessed is He. The ministering angels delay singing their song of praise until the souls of the righteous join with them and then they all sing together to God On High."

Another strategy for sanctifying one's body is to be very meticulous in the reciting of Shema, pronouncing it with great concentration, one word at a time. For the Shema contains 248 words corresponding to the 248 limbs of the body and it is taught in Zohar Chadash (59a) that if a person recites the Shema properly each word bestows its influence upon the corresponding limb. But if one recites it hastily and carelessly while thinking about other matters, so that his mind does not realize what his mouth is saying, then every limb draws upon it the Sitrah Acharah. This causes his body to be afflicted with illness and suffering, all because he was not careful to recite the Shema with concentration.

To understand why this is so one must first know what is written in the book K'li Chemdah on Parashas Bereishis (Drush 2). There it is taught that just as a man's 248 limbs and 365 sinews correspond to and are subordinate to the 248 positive and 365 negative commandments, so too the various lands and places in the world correspond to and are subordinate to the positive and negative commandments. [This is true of the beasts and birds as well. They, too, are apportioned among the limbs of the human body and are subordinate to the corresponding commandments.] Thus, the scholars of earlier generations have said that the scorpion is under the dominion of the commandment of circumcision. The proof to this is that if the foreskin of an infant, who has never experienced an emission, is placed upon the wound of a scorpion, the pain abates and the danger passes. Another amazing remedy to be aware of is the placing of an infant's foreskin in the mouth of a newborn to prevent him from ever suffering from epilepsy.

A person should also know that if he accepts his afflictions with love and affection then those very afflictions will refine, purify and sanctify his body to a great extent. It is explained in the Zohar in Parashas Shelach (168a) that the human soul is likened to a lamp. When a lamp does not give off sufficient illumination the usual procedure is to shake it a little until it burns properly. This is effective, however, only if the lamp is of high quality. If it is of low quality, such shaking will cause it to be extinguished altogether. Similarly, when someone sins his soul ceases to illuminate his body as it should. Therefore, the Holy One Blessed is He brings upon him afflictions to shake him up. If he accepts them lovingly, his soul returns to radiating even greater than before. But if he does not accept them with love, then he is not illuminated even as much as before. On the contrary, the afflictions only make him worse, causing indictments to be raised against him until he plummets to the depths of Gehinnom. Let the one who fears the word of Hashem choose life. Then all will be well with him.

Chapter 52

Shlomo HaMelech writes, "Do not be overly righteous nor overly wicked" (Koheles 7:16-17). Similarly, the Sages warn: "Be wary of charlatans feigning piety, behaving like Zimri but seeking reward like Pinchas" (Sotah 22b).

Sometimes one sees a person who appears on the surface to be continually immersed in heartfelt prayer, arrayed in his tefillin the entire day. Naturally one supposes him to be upright and honest, since one always sees him engaged in the work of Heaven, but one never knows what is in his mind.

Come and see what is related in Midrash Pesikta Rabbati: There once was a rich man who in addition to his fabulous wealth was also a great scholar and very pious. In his old age he decided to move to the Holy Land. Along the way he stopped in the holy Jewish community of a certain Yishmaelite town. There he met a man named Rabbi Alexander who spent most of the day in the synagogue praying while donned with his tallis and tefillin. He assumed that a fellow who spent so much time praying must be very upright and honest. So, he waited until Rabbi Alexander finished his prayers and then said to him, "I have a request to make of you. Since I am a foreigner here and the land is filled with marauding bandits, I am afraid to take my money with me. Please take it care of it along with my silver and gold vessels until I return. For my plan is to travel to the Holy Land and select a city to settle there and prepare a home for myself."

Rabbi Alexander replied, "Very well. Give me the money and the chest of valuables and I will keep them in the room in which I store my own precious things. Then you may continue on in peace to the Holy Land." He promised that when the wealthy man returned, he would give him his deposit in full. So, the wealthy man did as they had arranged, leaving with him a chest filled with money and other precious items and proceeded with his wife to the land of Israel. There he decided to settle in the holy community of Chevron and returned in person to retrieve his money and the rest of the deposit he had left. But when he requested his deposit from Rabbi Alexander, the man who was always praying in his tallis and tefillin, the latter denied the story altogether, claiming, "I do not know you and have never laid eyes on you before!" The rich man was utterly taken aback and fell on his face weeping and pleading. But the man brazenly ignored his pleas and even cursed him, denying that he had ever received anything from him.

So, the wealthy man left in despair and went to the synagogue where he raised his heart Heavenward and prayed, "Master of the Universe! You are the ruler over everything; therefore, my complaint is directed to You. I believed that this man Rabbi Alexander was perfectly righteous because I saw him arrayed in tallis and tefillin most of the day, standing and praying before you with great concentration. "But now I see that it is all a deception and that his heart is not completely with You. Therefore, I deliver my case into Heaven's hands and ask that You avenge me of him so that all will know the greatness and might of Your hand. For I have no complaint against any creature but only against You!" Thus, he wept with a broken and embittered heart. No sooner had he finished speaking than the prophet Eliyahu appeared to him. "Do not be afraid!" he told him, "Go to the man's wife and give her this sign, that she and her husband ate leaven bread that Pesach. Then as a second sign say to her as per her husband's instructions, that her husband also ate on Yom Kippur morning before going to the synagogue."

So, when Rabbi Alexander went to the marketplace to engage in some business the wealthy man went to Rabbi Alexander's home and gave his wife these signs. Assuming that her husband had sent him she immediately went and retrieved the deposit and the wealthy man went on his way with a happy heart and in peace.

When Rabbi Alexander came home, his wife related that the rich man had given the signs mentioned above and that she had returned to him his deposit. When Rabbi Alexander realized that it had become public knowledge that he was thoroughly wicked, he and his wife went and apostatized, may their names and memories be blotted out.

We learn from this incident that a person must not rely on appearances lest he put his trust in someone who behaves like Zimri but seeks reward like Pinchas. Rather let him look for the man who is righteous with regard to money and who does not seek the wealth of others. That is the truly righteous man.

The popular expression says, "Be wary of charlatans and guard yourself against those of whom it is said 'And your righteousness' (Tehillim 71:19)." I have heard of another incident involving the only son of an extremely wealthy elderly man. This son was both handsome and wise and when his father saw that his death was approaching, he summoned him to give him his last instructions. "My son," he told him, "I am bequeathing you much money and many other treasures. It should be sufficient for you to enjoy every good thing in the world throughout your entire life. But I warn you that you must be beware of charlatans and those who behave with greater piety than is normal for human beings. For it is the way of the charlatans to appear especially righteous, although they harbor in their hearts seven abominations. "And beware of those of whom it is said, 'And your righteousness.' Then you and your offspring will enjoy all manner of goodness all your days."

And with that the old man died. Afterwards the young man betrothed a poor orphan girl who was very pretty because she seemed good in his eyes, and after they were married, he rejoiced with his bride. The woman seemed modest and pious in her husband's eyes and when four or five years had gone by, he said to her, "Come with me for a trip through the avenues and plazas so that we may enjoy the beauty of the land." But his wife said to him, "I will not go lest I lay my eyes on other men or lest other men lay their eyes upon me and I cause them to stumble." Recalling his father's instructions, he said to himself, "She certainly acts very righteous." But he said nothing and went for the walk by himself.

What did he do then? About half a year later he instructed that a second key be made for every room in the house and gave one key to his wife and kept the other for himself. But he did not tell his wife about the second key.

One day he informed her that he had to go on a journey to purchase some merchandise and asked that she prepare him provisions for the way. The woman complied because she believed that her husband was indeed going away as was his custom. The next day he took his leave of her and she thought that he had gone off to a distance location. But in fact, the husband had merely been acting with cunning. When he had traveled about ten miles out of the city he ordered the driver to turn about. However, instead of returning home he went to an inn. Only when nightfall came did he go home. When he arrived, he opened first one door and then the next, going from room to room until he came to his wife's room. There he found her asleep in bed with a gentile next to her. When his wife realized that her husband was in the room, she told the gentile to take his sword and kill him. Out of fear he was forced to flee from his own house. Then in his great sorrow he went to lie down in the marketplace and fell asleep.

That night a great treasure was stolen from the king of the city. The thief had taken all the king's jewels. This created quite a furor in the palace and the king commanded that all the streets and houses be searched. The king's servants searched the entire town and when they found the man sleeping in the street and they decided that he must be the thief. So, they arrested him and he was sentenced to be tortured and then executed. While he was being lead to the scaffold to be hung he was accompanied by a priest, as is the way of the gentiles. This priest was very distinguished and highly thought of by the king and as they walked, he tried to persuade him to convert. At one point they came across a dump and worms from the dump were crawling about on the ground. The priest asked the executioner to lead the prisoner by a different path so that they would not inadvertently kill any of the worms. "After all," he said, "It was written in Scripture, 'His mercies are upon all His works' (Tehillim 145:9)." When the man heard this, he said to himself, "This priest is also one of those hypocrites of whom it is said, 'And your righteousness.' Then he turned to the king's servants and confessed that in fact he and the priest had committed the theft together! The priest was immediately arrested and the king ordered that the distinguished clergyman's quarters be searched. There the stolen jewels were indeed found.

Afterwards the king asked the man what connection he had with this priest. He then related to the king the entire story, beginning with his father's deathbed instructions. He related what had befallen him regarding his wife the harlot and what had occurred with the priest. He explained that it was only because of the priest's excessive righteousness that he decided to avenge himself upon him.

Having heard his story, the king immediately ordered that the woman be summoned and the man's story was verified. The king instructed that the man be restored to his home. Then he decreed that the woman and her lover were to be decapitated while the priest was to be hung on the scaffold.

From this episode we again learn that one must not rely on appearances, for even if someone appears blameless one never know what is in his mind. The rule to remember is this: If someone refuses to benefit from the property of others — and needless to say from stolen property — and if he deals with others in good faith, then he is undoubtedly upright and honest. But if he kisses his tefillin while he prays but does not deal with others in good faith, then one must stay as far away from him as possible. For the main area in which fear of Heaven and righteousness are put to the test is with regard to money. Whoever stands firm in his righteousness in monetary matters can be considered truly righteous. Concerning him was it written, "When you consume the labor of your own hands" — that is, honestly — "fortunate are you" — in this world — "and it will be well with you" — in the World to Come, Amein.

Chapter 53

The Holy One Blessed is He created everything in the world only for His honor (Pirkei Avos 6:11). This is especially true of the human being, who is called a "minor universe" (Tanchuma Pekudei 3). Man was created only in order that he should serve the Holy One Blessed is He in fear, awe and love and when a person is clothed in the holy raiment of good deeds — that is when he is known as a "servant of Hashem."

These are the practices that binds a person's body and soul to Hashem's service: love of Torah, concentration of the heart when fulfilling the commandments, concentration in prayer, guarding the sanctity of Shabbos and Yom Tov, guarding the sanctity of his limbs, guarding the sanctity of his thoughts, guarding the sanctity of the "camp," guarding sanctity of rabbinical fences, guarding the sanctity of good character traits.

Let us begin with love of Torah. This means studying only for the sake of the Holy One Blessed is He and His Shechinah and not for personal gain such as to be considered a scholar or even to earn reward in the World to Come. Concerning the person who studies for his own benefit and honor it was stated (Yeshayahu 40:6), "And all of his lovingkindness is like the grass of the field" (Tikkunim 30, 73b; Tikkunei Zohar Chadash 117a).

One must study with joy, for the Shechinah settles on a person only when he is in a state of joy, not sadness (Shabbos 30b).

One must attend the yeshivah of the community's Rav. Rabbi Yaakov Bei Rav wrote concerning this that for every day that a man refrained from attending the yeshivah in this world, he will be denied entry into the Heavenly academy in the World to Come.

A Torah scholar must be particularly careful to avoid pride, as we have already discussed (Chapter 4).

A person must study halachah every day with objective of reading carefully and resolving every difficulty to the best of his ability. By studying in this manner, he extricates the Shechinah from the shells of impurity and adorns it. For the letters of the word h a l a ch a h [הלכה] are the same as the letters of the word h a- k a ll a h [הכלה] ("the bride") (Pri Eitz Chayim, Sha'ar Hanhagas HaLimud). Let him not be ashamed to say regarding a matter that he has not heard, "I have not heard this." Let him study until he sweats, for in this way he shatters the shells of impurity.

One must also be careful to avoid becoming angry while engaging in the give-and-take of the study hall, for this causes a person's wisdom to abandon him. One must not become angry even towards students who fail to understand a matter correctly, as I have already discussed in earlier chapters.

One should set aside a special room for study, to be imbued with the sanctity of the study hall. If this is not possible, one should at least set aside a specific corner of the room for his fixed times of study.

One's main purpose in studying should be to fashion a throne for the Shechinah. But if a person is sullied with iniquity and sin the Shechinah will not settle upon him because every transgression is like a thorn pricking at the Shechinah. For this reason, he should confess his sins before studying so that he will be able to unify the Holy One Blessed is He with His Shechinah in fear and love.

If one finds a text with an error in it one must emend it, as it is written, "Do not allow injustice to dwell in your tent" (Iyov 11:14). Nevertheless, one must not make emendations based on judgment alone. The Ramban, z"l, writes (Baba Basra 134a), "The hand that erases texts without clear proofs should be cut off and the curse of the rabbis will be upon that hand so that it will be cut off."

If one invests effort in his studies, he will not soon forget them. If he studies in the synagogue, he will not forget his learning. If his tongue becomes parched while studying but he refrains from interrupting his studies to drink, it is considered atonement for the sin of speaking vanity.

Just as one is obligated to fulfill the commandment [to be fruitful and multiply] in the physical sense, so is one commanded to do so in the spiritual sense by revealing new Torah insights. Through this, one merits the Torah's illumination. The Sages said, "Acquire for yourself a companion" (Pirkei Avos 1:6). This statement is to be taken literally, but it is also a hint that his pen should be one's companion. That is, one should record his insights. There is even a suggestion of this in the Torah: "Write this as a remembrance in a book" (Shemos 17:14). The word "this" alludes to the Torah (Avodah Zarah 2b), as it states, "And this is the Torah" (Devarim 4:44).

It also states, "Write them upon the tablet of your heart" (Mishlei 7:3). A person must be well rounded in his learning. That is, he must be fluent in all four levels of interpretation: p eshat [the plain meaning], r emez [hints such as numerical values], d erush [application of the various rules of interpretation] and s od [the esoteric meaning]. The acronym for these four levels is the word p a rd e s [the "orchard"]. If one fails to study even one of these levels one must return in another incarnation to complete the task.

One should study the 613 mitzvos regularly.

One must set aside fixed times for study every day. These times must be inviolable, so that even if he stands to make a large profit he must not forego his fixed times. [This is indeed the custom in the holy community of Frankfort-am-Main.] This should be done out of love for Hashem and His Torah.

One must be careful to study more on Mondays and Thursdays than on other days, having in mind to mitigate the strict judgment that reigns on those days more than on others.

One must stay far away from the study of philosophy, for it is an alien fire. Concerning this was it written, "Her house inclines towards death…None that go to her return" (Mishlei 2:18-19). One should even avoid natural science, as the illustrious Rabbi Moshe Landau, z"l, has already warned.

One should be careful to study in a room with windows and gaze frequently at the sky, for this aid's comprehension.

Kav HaYashar

It is forbidden to say something in the name of a particular scholar if there is no tradition that he ever said it.

One must be careful not to speak words of Torah in unclean places. Similarly, one must not speak words of Torah in houses of idolatry. One must not be ashamed to accept the truth even from the youngest of the young.

If one knows that a colleague will be unable to answer a question, he must not ask him, so that he will not be embarrassed, Heaven forbid.

See what is written in this regard in the Zohar (Parashas Shelach 171a): The agents of judgment held onto a certain child, denying him entry into the Heavenly yeshiva. Then the child cried out, sending a shudder through all the members of the yeshiva. The Rosh Yeshivah inquired, "Who is preventing this son of the living God from entering?" Immediately they took hold of the child and brought him before Rosh Yeshivah and many members of the yeshivah gathered round. "Open your mouth and recite, O holy son," the Rosh Yeshivah said. But the child replied, "I am afraid to do so because I really belong in a different yeshivah but I came here and the agents of judgment apprehended me." "Do not be afraid, O holy son," said the Rosh Yeshiva, "you may stay here for seven days and bathe every day in the holy dew. Afterwards they will elevate you to the yeshivah for children." So, the child began a discourse, giving seven interpretations to each of the verses that the Rosh Yeshivah had been discussing, disclosing amazing insights.

At that moment they took the boy's father and crowned him with seventy crowns. The Zohar explains that the agents of judgment detained the boy and wished to afflict him because he had shown a lack of concern for his teacher's honor. He used to ask him difficult questions that the teacher was unable to answer, causing him embarrassment and depression. For this reason, the agents of judgment wished to subject him to harsh punishment. Even though the Rosh Yeshivah apparently saved him, allowing him to remain with him for seven days, this was actually a form of punishment. For throughout those seven days the boy's true form was diminished and he was alienated from his proper place, which caused him much suffering. If even a child had to endure such suffering and the agents of judgment wished to subject him to further affliction, imagine how much greater the punishment must be for an adult who intentionally embarrasses his colleague or mentor. Thus, the Sages have said (Pirkci Avos 3:11): One who embarrasses a colleague in public has no portion in the World to Come. Therefore, whoever values his soul will be careful not to embarrass anyone.

Chapter 54
As an expression of love of Torah, one should see to it that volumes of Torah literature are attractively bound. This is included in the commandment, "This is my God and I will beautify Him" (Shemos 15:2) — "Conduct yourself in a beautiful manner with regard to the commandments" (Shabbos 133b). Seifer Chassidim (97 and 911) relates that a certain scholar was exhumed from his grave and his corpse beaten with sticks because his books were found to be ripped and he never gave them to a bookbinder for repair. One should also see to it that books are not set on the shelf upside down. A certain scholar was once studying in his room and had to consult a passage in the Talmud. When he finished examining the passage, he returned the volume to its place among the other volumes. But when he turned away the book fell down with a large crash. So, the scholar went back and stood it up again, not noticing that it was upside down. Again, the moment he turned away the book fell down with a loud noise. This occurrence was repeated a third time. Finally, he noticed that the book was upside down and immediately righted it, after which it did not fall again. This incident also illustrates the fact that Heaven supervises everything that happens. It is a matter of great importance that books be treated with respect. Thus, for example, an open volume in a room that has been fouled with an offensive odor should be closed or covered with a cloth.

Books must not be left in the room of a married couple [when they might have marital relations], Heaven forbid, unless either the books or the bed are separated with a curtain.

One must not sit upon a bench on which there are books unless they are placed on top of some other item, raised up from the level of the bench.

If one finds a book lying upside down one should right it and kiss it.

One should not place a book beneath the one from which one is studying, as the Turei Zahav (Yoreh Deah 282:13) has already admonished. This practice degrades the lower book by using it for a function that could be fulfilled just as well by a piece of wood or stone. If, however, the bottom book was already there it is permissible to place another text on top of it.

A person should rise before a volume of Chumash [i.e., one of the five books of the Torah written on parchment]. And although many are lenient about this it is worthwhile to be strict. It is recorded that when the Maharil would go around the synagogue from congregant to congregant to bless them for their Yom Tov pledges, in accordance with the custom of Ashkenaz, he would carry a volume of Chumash with him. That way when the people rose to receive their blessings they would be doing so in honor of the Chumash (Minhagei Maharil, Hagahos LeSeder HaKriyah BePesach). Similarly, I observed in Poland that a number of Rabbis have the custom of carrying a volume of Chumash with them when they exit the synagogue ahead of the congregation on Shabbos and Yom Tov. That way when the people rise for them, they will in fact be rising in honor of the Chumash.

A person must feel complete love for Torah scholars and above all for his own mentor. In fact, he should love him more than his own father. One should likewise treat his mentor with awe, which means that the student may not sit until the rabbi instructs him to do so, nor may he sit in his place. When accompanying him he should walk to his left and he should attend to his needs. Whoever delivers good tidings to his rabbi for pure motives will be greatly rewarded. The Zohar (Parashas Shelach 167b) relates: There is a certain palace On High set aside for Basyah bas Pharaoh and thousands of other righteous women along with her. Each one has her own special place where she enjoys tremendous pleasure. Three times a day an announcement is made, "Here comes the image of the faithful prophet Moshe!" Then Basyah goes to a place partitioned off with a curtain. Through the partition she sees Moshe's image and says, "How fortunate is my lot that I raised this light!" Then she returns to the women sitting with her in the room mentioned above. There she sits clothed in beautiful garments, just as her garments shone with a great light in this world. These are called the "women of tranquility."

In the second palace sits Serach daughter of Asher and with her thousands of other righteous women. Three times a day it is announced, "Here comes the righteous Yosef!" Then she rejoices and also goes out to the partition to see the light of Yosef's image and says, "How fortunate is my lot and fortunate was the day on which I related the good tidings [that Yosef was alive] to my grandfather Yaakov!" Then she returns to her place.

In the third palace is Yocheved, mother of Moshe, Aharon and Miryam, along with thousands of other righteous women. Every day they stand and praise the Master of the Universe and she and the other women sing the Song of the Sea. Afterwards she alone sings the verse, "And Miryam the prophetess took the tambourine in her hand" (Shemos 15:20), and several bands of angels listen to their pleasant voices.

In the fourth palace is Devorah the prophetess, along with many other women. They sing the song of Devorah and Barak ben Avinoam. Beyond these palaces are the four hidden palaces of Sarah, Rivkah, Rochel and Leah, which are neither revealed nor seen. From their palaces come the souls of converts. Afterwards they enter beneath the wings of the Shechinah, but nothing more may be said about this.

It can be seen from here that Basyah daughter of Pharaoh merited her lofty station because she raised our teacher Moshe while Serach daughter of Asher merited her station because she brought good tidings to the Patriarch Yaakov.

Another way in which one must demonstrate love of Torah is by supporting Torah scholars discretely. Supporting scholars is the equivalent of delighting in the Shabbos because scholars are likened to the Shabbos. For instance, none of the needs of Shabbos may be prepared on the Shabbos day itself because it is forbidden to do any craft. Instead everything must be prepared during the other six days. Similarly, Torah scholars dedicate themselves to their studies to the exclusion of other labor, engaging neither in craft nor in trade like the rest of the populace who can be found making their way through the streets and markets of the city in pursuit of their livelihood. Therefore, the rest of the people must ensure that the scholars are provided with an income. Just as a person is obliged to delight in the Shabbos, so is he obliged to give his gifts to the scholars in a dignified manner and not with contempt. This is the meaning of the verse, "And you shall call the Shabbos 'delight,' to the holy one of Hashem [you shall call] 'honored'" (Yeshayahu 58:13). The "holy one of Hashem" refers to the scholar. Fortunate is the person who honors scholars and fortunate is his lot. Concerning him was it written, "Rejoice Zevulun in your going out and Yissachar in your tents" (Devarim 33:18). But as for those who cause the scholars anguish, woe to them and woe to their souls! Their punishment is described in the Zohar (Raya Meheimna, Parashas Bamidbar 124b-125b) in too great length to cite here.

Therefore, let every person take care lest he detract from the honor of the scholars, as it is written, "Let no hand touch him lest he be stoned" (Shemos 19:13). See the passage from the Zohar. But whoever honors them will be honored by Heaven.

Chapter 55

It is written, "And Hashem said to Moshe, 'Write this as a remembrance in a book and put it into Yehoshua's ears'" (Shemos 17:14). In this verse the Holy One Blessed is He admonishes Moshe, Israel's teacher, concerning the need to write things down because this greatly facilitates memory. If it was necessary for God to tell this to Moshe, how much more so to the rest of us! For we must reflect on our deeds continually, examining them for traces of sin. And if a person realizes that he has indeed committed a sin he should record it so that he will remember to rectify it. Similarly, if he discovers in some text a means of rectifying his transgressions, he should record that as well so that he will be able to make amends without delay. If a person recalls that he has sinned against his fellow by speaking to him harshly, causing him anguish, or if he attributed to him some impropriety or caused him shame, let him weep and feel remorse and resolve immediately to appease him the very next day. Moreover, this should be his first order of business on the following morning. Needless to say, if recalls that he sinned against someone of greater stature than himself he should immediately be filled with anguish and plead with God not to record the matter in his ledger of debits. And again, he should resolve to rectify the matter the following morning.

If another person sinned against him by speaking to him in an oppressive manner let him forgive him instantly, declaring, "May the Master forgive anyone who has caused me anguish." Then let him recite the bedtime Shema with concentration, after which he should be careful to read the Ten Commandments every night. Specifically, he should read them as they appear in Parashas Va'eschanan. For in Parashas Yisro it is written, "Remember [the Shabbos day]" (Shemos 20:8), reflecting the attribute of the day, while in Va'eschanan it is written, "Keep [the Shabbos day]" (Devarim 5:12), reflecting the attribute of the night (Zohar 1:48b and 2:138a). Through this recitation a person attains two crowns [corresponding to "We will do" and "we will hear"]. For this reason, the Ten Commandments have two sets of ta'amim [musical cantillation marks], one written above the letters and one written below them. In the morning, before leaving the house one must first wash his hands. Then let him go to the mezuzah and place his hand upon it, reflecting that the Holy One Blessed is He is the real Master of the house, whereas we are merely his houseguests. And let him reflect on the name Shadd-ai, as was mentioned in the first chapter. Afterwards he should say three times, "May Hashem guard my going out and my coming in, in life and peace from now on." Then he should say, "Know Him with all your ways and He will straighten your paths" (Mishlei 3:6). This verse encompasses the entire Torah. It also contains twenty-six letters corresponding to the numerical value of Hashem's four-letter name, which is the "Holy of Holies." Moreover, the verse begins with the letter beis [the value of which is 2] and ends with a kaf [the value of which is 20], for a total of 22, corresponding to the twenty-two letters of the Hebrew alphabet. Let him recite this verse six times while turning towards the six directions: East, South, West, North, up and down. And let him have in mind that he is delivering his life to the Holy One Blessed is He, Ruler of the six directions of the world. In this way he subjugates his soul and body to Hashem.

One who has time should also recite the following verses, each of which alludes to a different limb: "And as for You, Hashem, you shield me, my soul, and lift up my head (Tehillim 3:4). "I proclaim righteousness among a large congregation, behold I will not refrain my lips; You know this, Hashem" (Tehillim 40:10). I called to Him with my mouth and exaltation was beneath my tongue" (ibid., 66:17). "Hashem's instructions are upright, causing the heart to rejoice; Hashem's commandments are pure, illuminating the eyes" (ibid., 19:9). "Hear the sound of my supplication when I cry out to You, when I lift up my hands towards Your holy sanctuary" (ibid., 28:2). "To do Your will, my God, was my desire, and Your Torah was within my intestines" (ibid., 40:9). "All my bones will declare, Hashem, "Who is like You?"" (ibid., 35:10). "I will bless Hashem who advised me, even at night my kidneys rebuke me" (ibid., 16:7). My foot stood upon a plain, among congregations I will bless Hashem" (ibid., 26:12). Afterwards let him recite this Mishnah encompassing the entire body from top to bottom: One may only stand to pray in a spirit of weighty- head edness [i.e., solemnity]. The pious of earlier times would pause for an hour before praying in order to direct their hearts towards the Omnipresent One. Even if the king asks after his welfare and even if a snake is wrapped around his heel he must not interrupt. Afterwards let him say the verse, "The end of the matter when everything is heard is to fear God and keep His commandments, for that is the entirety of a man" (Koheles 12:13). This verse alludes to the observance of all 613 commandments. Whoever conducts himself in this manner will enjoy good fortune, selah.

Chapter 56

The Gemara tells us that attacks by wild beasts are the result of vain oaths (Shabbos 33a). You should know that in general when the

Talmud speaks of "wild beasts" it is referring to the wicked Lilis, mother of the demons. She is responsible for many of the evil decrees that have befallen Israel, on account of our many sins. She is also a regular visitor to houses in which vain oaths are common, often taking up residence there and causing the deaths of the small children. Poverty is also common in the house or city where such oaths are heard.

Come and see the harm that is caused by swearing in vain. The Zohar (Parashas Yisro 91b) relates that when the Hashem decreed that all the water covering the earth be confined to the depths, He made for them a covering, upon which were engraved certain Divine names to prevent the water from gushing up again and inundating the planet. But when a person swears falsely, the water overpowers this covering and the letters of the names flee. At that moment the water has permission to well up and flood the earth. Then the Holy One Blessed is He motions to an angel named YAZRIEL, custodian over seventy keys, to engrave the holy names on the cover once again. This causes the water of the deep to return to its place and the world is saved. Nevertheless, woe to the person who brought about the removal of those holy letters in the first place, thereby putting the Creator to the trouble, so to speak, of having to re-engrave them!

Mortal man! Mortal man! Born from a putrid drop! How dare he trouble his Maker? Undoubtedly those holy names will curse him and raise accusations against him, which if he could hear them would surely cause him to dash his head against a wall in remorse for the blemish that he brought about. The Sages have said that whoever utters the name of Heaven in vain will be uprooted from the world (Pesikta Zuta, Bereishis 1), because simply mentioning His name is vain is a slight to His honor. How much more so, then, is swearing in vain or falsely, Heaven forbid!

The principle to recall is that every false oath that a person makes takes its toll either from his person or from his wealth, whether at that time or in the future. Eventually his iniquity will catch up with him, whether in the home or in the field, on a mountain or in a forest, on dry land or at sea. Thus, it stares, "For Hashem will not exonerate the one who bears His Name in vain" (Shemos 20:7). When a person has the urge to swear, let him imagine that engraved before him in black fire upon white fire are the words, "For Hashem will not exonerate the one who bears His name in vain." Then awe and trepidation will overcome him and he will refrain from swearing falsely.

One must not be in the habit of swearing by one's person or one's soul, for the soul is an element of Divinity from On High. Nor should one swear by the lives of one's children or anything else, following the impetuous and empty-headed. Such people frequently swear for no good reason, saying things like, "If such-and-such is true let my house burn down" or "let me die." All such oaths place a person in tremendous danger. Who knows what astrological configurations were ascendant when he uttered those words? Perhaps the evil that he wished upon himself will come to pass!

The Ari, z"l, also warned his disciples against referring to the angels by their full name (Sha'ar HaMitzvos, Parashas Shemos 11b). Thus, in place of the name MTTRUN one should say only "Metat" and for SNDLFON one should say "Sandal." The same applies to the names of all the angels other than those that are also the names of people, such as Michael, Gavriel, Refael, etc., in which case there is need for concern. This admonition is based on the fact that the Holy One Blessed is He created everything for the sake of human beings. Thus, when He created the angels, He made them swear that they would appear whenever human beings called upon them for deliverance or the like. Therefore, when someone mentions the name of an angel it is compelled by its oath to appear. If it then discovers that it has been summoned in vain it may be prompted to cause the person harm. From this one can estimate the amount of danger a person places himself in when he swears in vain or falsely.

You should know that a handshake is also like an oath. For the soul is dependent upon the palm of the hand to its benefit as well as its detriment. It is dependent upon it to its benefit when a person raises his hands Heavenward to invoke mercy. Moreover, a high percentage of the mitzvos are performed by the hand, including: performing circumcision, offering a sacrifice, separating off the priestly and Levitical gifts, constructing a Sukkah, taking the four species, giving charity, donning tefillin and many others. These are just some of the ways in which the soul is dependent upon the hand. This is what King Dovid meant when he said, "My soul is in my palm continually and I have not forgotten Your Torah" (Tehillim 119:109). That is, I have chosen to use my hands for good purposes and not the opposite, Heaven forbid.

When a person affirms an agreement by placing his own palm within that of the other party, he is symbolically delivering to him his soul as a security. Yet this form of oath is even more serious than if he actually swore by his soul because if he violates it he blemishes the aspect of the soul known as the supernal nefesh, corresponding to the name Ad-n-y. When this name is written out in full it is comprised of twelve letters (אל"ף דל"ת נו"ן יו"ד). These twelve letters correspond to the twelve words of the first line of the Shema and the declaration "Blessed is the name, etc." Thus, one who violates a handshake also blemishes the words of the Shema. Moreover, the numerical values of the middle letters of this expansion (ללו"ו) come to a total of 72. Thus, he also blemishes Hashem's seventy-two letter name, derived from the three verses, "And he went, etc.," "And he came, etc.," "And he extended, etc.," (Shemos 14:19-21; see Chapter 65). The values of the final letters of the expanded name (פתנ"ד) come to a total of 534, for which the usual acronym is תקל"ד. This acronym can be rearranged to form the words das kal ["trivial law"], indicating that he causes a blemish to the holy Torah, concerning which it is written, "From His right [He gave] them a law of fire [eish das]. In addition, the component kal hints that he blemishes the "light cloud" [av kal] upon which Hashem rides, as is known to the Kabbalists.

In view of all this, whoever cares about his soul will scrupulously avoid swearing in vain and will refrain from taking oaths and shaking hands in general, recalling at all times the blemishes these practices may cause to the holy names mentioned above. For Hashem's sake let this iniquity not seem insignificant in anyone's eyes! For the image of the hand that violates a handshake goes ahead of the offender's coffin, while upon each finger are thousands of damaging angels, Heaven spare us! Then, when he arrives in the other world it testifies to the fact that he violated his handshake.

Therefore, a person must warn his children and the members of his household not to be in the habit of swearing, vowing and shaking hands. Moreover, whoever fears Hashem's word should pray that he be saved even from swearing unnecessarily, not to mention making vain and false oaths and giving handshakes. If a person is careless in this matter he grants an opening to the evil Lilis to take up residence and acquire a share in his home, Heaven forbid. In consequence he may lose his young children and the rest of his family may suffer as well. Afterwards bans and execrations will be proclaimed against him in all the firmaments and he will be mentioned continually for evil. Therefore, whoever cares about his soul will avoid this pitfall. Then he may be certain that Hashem will shower him with blessing, prosperity and salvation, amen.

Chapter 57

The Tur (Chapter 1) writes: "In the morning a man must act strong as a lion to arise to the service of his Creator." He should also try to wash his hands by his bedside — pouring the water specifically over a vessel — to remove the filth and the impure spirit from his hands, as is explained in the mussar literature. In any event he must not walk four cubits without washing hands.

It is implied in the Zohar (Parashas Va'eschanan 260a) that the hosts of Heaven look forward to the moment that a Jew will rise from his bed to engage in study and prayer. The proof to this is that when he does so a proclamation goes forth saying, "Behold, bless Hashem all servants of Hashem who stand in the House of Hashem at night" (Tehillim 134:1). Then, when he has risen and gone to the synagogue to beseech his Master they proclaim, "And I will grant you movement among these standing ones" (Zecharyah 3:7). All this is true, however, only if he prays with devotion, pouring out his supplications like a beggar, just as our teacher Moshe did when he said, "And I pleaded with Hashem, etc." (Devarim 3:23).

When a person prays, his eyes should be closed and directed downwards, while his heart is directed upwards (Yevamos 105b). If he is accustomed to pray from a machzor or prayer book let him focus on the writing and not allow his eyes to stray beyond the book, for the Shechinah stands before him and it is forbidden to gaze at the Shechinah. The Zohar relates further: It is stated in the book of Rav Hamnuna the Elder that one who opens his eyes while praying or who fails to lower his eyes to the ground causes the Angel of Death to come to him prior to his death. Then when his soul expires, he is unable to behold the Shechinah. For although it is written, "No man may see Me and live" (Shemos 33:20), every Jew merits to behold the Shechinah at the moment of his death (Zohar 1:98a, 226a; 3:88a). If he is meritorious, the Shechinah arrives early. This is a good sign, for then he knows that his soul will depart easily and peacefully, without suffering.

But if he lacks merit the Shechinah does not arrive early. Consequently, he endures great suffering as the soul separates from him until at last Hashem has mercy upon him and shines a little of the Shechinah's light upon him so that it can depart. Nevertheless, this only happens after he has already endured terrible suffering. It is as if he were being slaughtered with a blemished knife. Meanwhile his intestines also convulse. Concerning this the Zohar warns in Parashas Va'eschanan that if a person gazes this way and that while praying, rather than directing his eyes downward, the Shechinah will not come to him early in order that he will experience the throes of death. It is written, "Concerning this should every pious man pray to You that it should be found when the time comes" (Tehillim 32:6). According to the Sages the "time" referred to in this verse is the moment of death (Berachos 8a). The thing that the pious man is to pray for is an easy death, free of suffering, and a clear mind so that he can confess his iniquities and issue last instructions to his children regarding how they should conduct themselves after his death. Let him urge them to go in the way of the innocent so that he will not suffer shame in the grave. It is a great privilege to die with a clear head enabling one to converse lucidly before one's death. Not everyone merits this. While a person is still healthy let him pray that the Shechinah will come to him early enough to save him from a sudden or bizarre death or from extraordinary suffering.

One great strategy for achieving this is by clinging to the Torah, for through this one clings to the Shechinah even during one's life. Then all the more so will one merit clinging to it after death. Thus, it is related in the Zohar (Parashas Va'eschanan 268a): Rabbi Acha and Rabbi Elazar were standing together one evening after midnight engaged in study. Rabbi Elazar began a discourse: "It is written, 'For it is your life and the length of your days that you may dwell upon the earth' (Devarim 30:20). Come and see. The Shechinah only settles in a place where Torah is studied and in the merit of study is the world sustained. This is the meaning of the words, 'For it is your life…that you may dwell upon the earth.' "But if people fail to study it is said, 'For what was the land lost? And Hashem said, 'Because they abandoned My Torah" (Yirmeyahu 9:11-12)." Then he added: "This applies to one who is able to study and does not." Rabbi Elazar likens this to the case of a modest and pleasant woman whose husband sets aside his conjugal duties (see Shemos 21:10) and abandons her, causing her to cry out to Heaven concerning her abandonment.

In the same way, if a man fails to study when he is able to do so the Torah cries out concerning its neglect. In consequence he may be stricken unexpectedly by the attribute of judgment, Heaven spare us! While Rabbi Elazar was speaking, another man came along and began interpreting the verse, "The wise will inherit honor while fools elevate disgrace" (Mishlei 3:35). He explained that whoever engages in study merits clinging to the Shechinah, which is called 'honor,' and all the hosts of Heaven seek merit on his behalf. By contrast, those who tread crooked paths create through their wicked deeds numerous malignant spirits [chitzonim] to accuse them. Thus, the verse teaches that "fools," i.e., the wicked, "elevate disgrace." That is, they elevate these malignant spirits, which are called "disgrace" because they accuse a person until judgment befalls him. Therefore, let every man be sure to set aside fixed times for study so that the Shechinah will enter his home and shower him with blessings, Amein.

Chapter 58

If a man has been guilty of wasting seed he must repent without delay and remedy the blemish he imparted to the covenant of circumcision, as I will explain later (in this chapter and in Chapter 68). Even if he transgressed numerous times he should know that the Holy One Blessed is He is a merciful King who accepts the penance of those who return to him wholeheartedly, as it is written, "But he who confesses and desists (from sinning) will receive mercy" (Mishlei 28:13). Moreover, he will be granted an increase in awe and holiness. Thus, by repenting a person accomplishes two things: First of all, he receives atonement for his iniquity, and secondly, he inherits the World to Come. This is only true, however, if he also clings to the Torah, immersing himself in its study with diligence. To this end he must set aside fixed times for study, on his own and with others. If he is incapable of studying on his own, he must at least set aside fixed times to listen to words of Torah. For after a person dies, he is granted a position in the next world commensurate with his merit. In that world there is neither eating nor drinking nor commerce, but only Torah study. Whoever loved listening to words of Torah in this world will merit hearing them from the Ancient of Days in the World to Come. But if he reviled them in this world, he will be unable to relate to them in that world either. Moreover, he will undoubtedly be banished from his partition.

Come see what is written in the Zohar regarding this matter (Parashas Shemini 39a-41a): Rabbi Yehudah and Rabbi Yitzchak were walking through the town of Tzippori while a child followed after them leading a donkey laden with containers of honey. Rabbi Yitzchak said to Rabbi Yehudah, "Let us speak words of Torah as we walk." So, he began his discourse. Rabbi Yitzchak interpreted the verse, "And your palate is like fine wine going straight to my beloved, moving the lips of sleepers" (Shir HaShirim 7:10). He explained that the "palate" alludes to words of Torah, which are also likened to fine wine. In fact, they are better than actual wine because the latter is often injurious to body and soul. For example, excessive drink causes a person's head to hurt and sometimes leads to transgression, Heaven forbid. By contrast, the more a person studies the holy Torah the more removed he is from sin. Moreover, he learns to fear Heaven and inherits both this world and the next. He even merits what is described in the end of the verse, "moving the lips of those who sleep." That is, even when he lies in the grave his lips will continue uttering words of Torah.

The Zohar continues: The child asked, "If this is so, why does it say, 'And your palate is like fine wine,' implying that fine wine is comparable to Torah? Should it not have said, 'And your palate is better than find wine'?" They looked at him [realizing from his question that he knew of a deeper interpretation of the verse]. Then Rabbi Yehudah said, "My son, tell us what you have to say, for you have spoken well." The boy said, "Whoever engages in study and clings to Torah, uttering the words of Torah distinctly and out loud…will merit lifting up his voice even after he leaves this world. Thus, it is written, 'going straight to my beloved.' That is, his soul will go straight to the Holy One Blessed is He, impeded by none of the agents of judgment. He will then be permitted to wander about the chambers of Gan Eden [listening to the Torah of the righteous who are resting there]. This is the meaning of the phrase, 'moving the lips of those who sleep.'"

Rabbi Yehudah and Rabbi Yitzchak went over to the boy and kissed him on the head and rejoiced with him. Then he related to them the order of his studies and revealed other amazing insights. Finally, they asked him, "What is your name?" "Yeisa," he replied. They said, "From now on you shall be called Rabbi Yeisa." "Hand the donkey over to your father and come with us," they instructed him. So the boy went with them and when he arrived at the study hall Rabbi Yehudah rose before him, instructing all the students of the yeshivah to treat him with honor… Rabbi Shimon ben Yochai applied to him the verse, "Before I formed you in the womb I knew you" (Yirmeyahu 1:5).

The perceptive individual will note how earlier generations turned to listen to words of Torah even from the mouths of children. This was because in their great love of Torah they were eager to hear novel insights. For they knew that the Torah is our "length of days" (Devarim 30:20) and that it is a "beloved hind" (Mishlei 5:19), finding grace in the eyes of all who study it. Every Jew must love the Torah and cause it to be loved by his children and household.

He must admonish them continually concerning the fulfillment of the Torah and its commandments. In particular he must admonish the women not to allow their hair to be seen, for through this sin they bring poverty upon their children, causing them to be lowly and despised. Moreover, a house in which immodesty is found is frequented by the evil Lilis, who kills the small children of the household, as has already been explained in earlier chapters (24, 56). Therefore, let whoever has stumbled in the sin of wasting seed devote himself with diligence to Torah study and let him engage in four fasts of three days each. That is, he should fast for three days straight in each of the four seasons. Meanwhile let him engage in study. Then, "He will go back and heal him" (Yeshayahu 6:10), and blessings will descend upon his head and all his limbs will be clean and pure forever.

Chapter 59

The Torah commands us, "Your camp shall be holy" (Devarim 23:15). This means that a person must maintain his body and limbs in a state of holiness, for they are the camp of the Shechinah. This is the meaning of the verse, "And I will be sanctified within the children of Israel" (Vayikra 22:32) and the verse, "And I will dwell within them" (Shemos 25:8). But if he adopts bad ways, Heaven forbid, giving himself over to the pursuit of worldly pleasures, then his body becomes the abode of the Satan and Lilis, Heaven spare us. Therefore, one should be in the habit of praying: "Master of the Universe! Enable me to remain pure and to become a throne for the Shechinah. 'Let my soul bless Hashem and all my innards His holy Name' (Tehillim 103:1)."

When Israel sins, the Shechinah abandons them and it is said, "And the Ark went up from upon the earth" (Bereishis 7:17). The Shechinah is referred to in the Zohar (1:68b) as the "Ark" [teivah] because letters of the word teivah [תיבה] also spell out the words Beis H' [בית ה']. For this reason, there are exactly 248 words in the Shema corresponding to the 248 limbs of the body so that when a person recites the Shema with concentration each word imparts sanctity to one of his limbs (Zohar Chadash 59a). This might cause someone to wonder why it is, then, that numerous individuals recite the Shema with great care and intention yet their limbs remain frail nevertheless. You must know, my son, that this matter is discussed in the Zohar in Parashas Shelach (168a). There it is explained that the human soul resembles a lamp. When a lamp does not burn properly the usual remedy is to shake it a bit, which causes the flame to burn more brightly and to shed light as it should. But this is only true if the lamp is of good quality, for if it is of poor quality, then on the contrary, shaking it will extinguish it!

Similarly, if a person sins, thereby preventing his soul from shedding light as it should, the Holy One Blessed is He sends him afflictions to shake him up and to agitate his body and limbs. If he accepts his afflictions with love, acknowledging that they are not without cause and that Hashem does not chastise unjustly, and if he regrets the past and resolves to make amends and establish fences for the future, then his soul will again illuminate as formerly and even more so. However, if he does not accept them with love, rebelling against them instead, then his afflictions may abate for a time. If he returns to his evil ways and deeds, they will return with greater force until they eliminate him from the world. Thus his "lamp," i.e., his soul, is extinguished and descends with him to the depths of the pit.

When the Beis HaMikdosh was standing, a person would bring a sacrifice and make confession over it, at the same time repenting for his sin. Then the kohanim would slaughter the animal and sprinkle its blood on the altar and burn its fat. All this was in place of the sinner's own body and limbs, which had incurred a sentence of death through his sin. Thus, the sacrifice served as the rectification for his limbs. Nowadays, however, the recitation of the sacrifices must take the place of offering them, as it is written, "And let us pay for [the offerings of] bullocks with [the prayers of] our lips" (Hoshea 14:3). Maharam the Babylonian (Ta'amei HaMitzvos, 64) writes that when a person recites the portion of the sacrifices, he should have in mind that the letters on the page represent the body of the sacrifice, while the vowels animating them represent the soul of the sacrificial animal. In this way it is considered as if he actually offered a sacrifice on the altar. The

Kav HaYashar

importance of reciting the portion of the sacrifices every day should not be underestimated. Every morning a certain malignant spirit called Tola is aroused (Sha'ar HaKavanos, Tefilas HaShachar, 13b; Pri Eitz Chayim, Sha'ar Olam HaAsiyah, Part III) and begins lodging accusations against Israel for the sins they committed at night. As long as the Beis HaMikdosh was standing the kohanim were able to weaken its power through the offering of the morning daily sacrifice. Nowadays one should instead have this in mind when reciting the portion, "A continual burnt offering ordained at Mount Sinai" (Bamidbar 28:6). For the word for "[continual] burnt offering" — olas [tamid] — is the reverse of the name Tola. If a person behaves with arrogance, he gives power to this malignant spirit, whereas by conducting himself with humility, in emulation of the sacrifices, he weakens it. Thus, it is written, "God will not despise a broken and contrite heart" (Tehillim 51:19). Concerning this King Dovid wrote, "And I am a worm [tola'as] and not a man" (Tehillim 22:7).

The main point is that the recitation of the portion of the sacrifices is a matter of great importance. This is especially true of the portion of the incense. Thus, the Zohar relates (Parashas Vayeira 101a): Rabbi Acha went to the village of Tarsha and stopped at inn. The people of the village whispered to one another, "A great scholar had arrived. Let us go to him." So, they went to Rabbi Acha and revealed to him that their town was in a dreadful situation because for the past seven days a plague had been ravaging them, may the Merciful One protect us, and each day was worse that the one before. Whereupon Rabbi Acha announced, "Tomorrow we will go to the synagogue and seek mercy from the Holy One Blessed is He." While they were walking, messengers arrived to inform them that two more people had died, while another two were in critical condition. Rabbi Acha responded, "Now is not the time for us to stand idle. Every moment is crucial. Select from among yourselves forty pious and righteous men and divide them into groups of ten. Then let them stand at the four corners of the city; ten shall stand to the east, ten to the south, ten to the west and ten to the north, myself included. And let them recite with great devotion the portions of the incense and the sacrifices." They did this for three days, even dispatching messengers to the homes of the critically ill instructing them to recite the portion of the incense beginning with the verse, "And Moshe said to Aharon, 'Take the pan and put upon it incense" (Bamidbar 17:11). The people complied and the plague abated, after which Rabbi Acha said, "Now let us return home, for the decree has been annulled." Then a voice was heard, saying, "O Pestilence! O Pestilence! Do not come here any more because they know how to nullify you!" This caused Rabbi Acha to become disheartened [over the fact that the town was spared without repenting]. But then he dozed off and, in his sleep, he heard a voice saying, "Just as you have done here, so shall you do in another city."

Finally, he continued on his way, admonishing the people never to neglect the study of Torah. Later on the people changed the name of their town to Masa Machasyah [City of Pity] because the Holy One Blessed is He had taken pity [chas] upon them. In light of this, let every person recite the portion of the incense as well as the baraisa of the making of the incense [Pitum HaKetores] every day, for this is of great benefit. Whoever prays with concentration is assured that his prayers will be accepted and the Holy One Blessed is He will do his will and fulfill his request for the good, Amein.

Chapter 60

You should know that there are 248 positive commandments and that each of a person's 248 limbs is dependent upon one of those commandments. For example, the mouth is dependent upon Torah study and the eyes upon the sanctification of the new moon and the sight of the tzitzis. The mind is dependent upon the commandments of remembrance, such as: "Remember what Hashem did to Miriam…" (Devarim 24:9) ; "Remember the day that you went out of Egypt" (Shemos 13:3) ; Remember what Amaleik did to you…" (Devarim, ibid.) ; Remember the day that you stood before Hashem your God at Choreiv" (ibid. 4:10). For this reason our teacher Rabbi Yitzchak Luria, z"l, wrote that one must incorporate these remembrances into the regular daily prayers. Only in this way will one not forget them (Sha'ar HaKavanos, Kavanas Yotzeir 19a; Pri

Eitz Chaim, Part III of Sha'ar Keriyas Shema). For instance, in the blessing "With great love" when one reaches the line, "For You are a God who brings about deliverances and You have chosen us from all the peoples and languages," one should have in mind the remembrance of our ancestors standing at Mount Sinai to receive the Torah. That is, one should think, "You have chosen us from all the peoples and languages in order to give us the holy Torah." Then in the continuation of this blessing when one says the words, "And drew us close to Your great name," one should remember what Amaleik did to us. For Hashem's name will not be complete until the name of Amaleik has been blotted out (Tanchuma, Parashas Ki Teitzei 10). Until that time it is only revealed as it appears in the verse, "For a hand is raised in oath to the throne of God (Y-ah — i.e., half of the ineffable Name) that there shall be a war for Hashem with Amaleik from generation to generation" (Shemos 17:16).

The blessing continues, "Selah, in truth to acknowledge You." While reciting these words one should have in mind that one's mouth and tongue were created only to praise the name of the King of the Kings of Kings. One should also recall that Miryam the prophetess was stricken with tzara'as for speaking evil gossip and that one must studiously avoid committing the same sin.

During the Shema itself one should recall the exodus from Egypt. This matter should be taken very seriously, for it is well known that if a person neglected even a single commandment, he will have to return to earth again to fulfill it. Thus, if he omits even one of these remembrances he will be made to return. This is hinted at by the author of the Mesorah, who informs us that the word veyatzah ("and she will go out" or "and she went out") appears twice in Scripture. It appears in the verse, "And she shall go out for free, without money" (Shemos 21:1), and again in the verse, "And she went out of his house and she went and was to another man" (Devarim 24:2). What he is hinting at is this: On the plain level the first verse refers to a Hebrew maidservant, who goes out for free if her master does not fulfill one of three options for either betrothing or releasing her. These are alluded to in the words, "And if these three things are not done to her" (Shemos 21:11). On a deeper level, however, this passage is speaking of the soul. The "three things" that a man must do are all of his threefold obligations: Torah,

Prophets, Writings / justice, truth, peace / holiness, purity, humility / awe, love, zeal / Torah, Divine service, acts of lovingkindness. If he fails to fulfill any of these then his soul "goes out for free" from his body. The words, "without money [ein kasef]," indicate that his soul does not merit entering the "world of desire" [alma dekisufin] where the righteous bask in illumination. This is because he failed to perfect himself while he was in this world. On the plain level the second verse, "And she went out of his house," is speaking of a divorcee. But on the deeper level it indicates that the soul that failed to complete its mission on earth is prevented from entering its Heavenly mansion. Instead, it must go and enter another body. This is indicated in the phrase, "and she went and was to another man." There it must endure once more the agony of birth and death, the afflictions of the grave and all the punishments listed in the book Chessed LeAvraham (Ein Mishpat, Ma'ayan 5).

Therefore, O mortal man, examine your ways! Have the foresight to be kindly towards your soul so that it will not be excluded from the holy partition. Woe to the soul that is thus banished! Woe to it for the disgrace that it suffers when it is prevented from coming before the Throne of Glory from which it was excavated! Moreover, the Heavenly hosts chastise the soul, saying, "Woe to you! How could you have shown such ingratitude to your Creator for the lovingkindness He bestowed upon you? For He granted you food and drink, and fulfilled all your needs, yet you repaid good with evil!"

Come see what is written in the Zohar (Parashas Balak, 200b-202b): Rabbi Pinchas went to visit his daughter, the mother of Rabbi Elazar, who was ill. He was riding upon a donkey, accompanied by his companions. Along the way they came upon two Arabs. He inquired of them, "Has any voice ever been heard coming from this field?" They said, "We do not know about 'ever,' but we do know about our own time. One time some highwaymen passed through this field and spied a group of Jews. They were intent on robbing them when the sound of this donkey was heard coming from the field. It brayed twice and then a flame came and consumed them, saving the lives of those Jews." "O Arabs!" Rabbi Pinchas exclaimed, "In the merit of what you have related to me you shall be saved from other bandits who are lying in wait for you!" Then Rabbi Pinchas wept, exclaiming, "Master of the Universe! You performed this miracle to save those Jews in my merit and I was not even aware of it!" He then recited the verse, "To the One who performs great wonders alone, for His lovingkindness is forever!" (Tehillim 136:2). "How many good things does the Holy One Blessed is He do for people, yet no one knows of them other than Him alone! A person is traveling along the road and bandits are lying in wait to kill him. Then along comes another person who has been sent to serve as 'redemption money' so that he may be spared. Yet he is not even aware of the goodness that the Holy One Blessed is He has performed for him. Only the Holy One Blessed is He alone knows. "This is the meaning of the verse, 'To the One who performs great wonders alone, for His lovingkindness is forever!'"

Rabbi Pinchas said to his companions, "I inquired of those Arabs because they are always in the field..." He only asked them whether they had heard any voices because he was expecting Rabbi Shimon ben Yochai and his son Rabbi Elazar to come out to greet him. After they continued along their way the Arabs returned, shouting, "Old man! Old man! You asked us about 'ever' but you did not ask us about today! This very day we beheld a wondrous sight. Five men were sitting together with an old man and then we saw birds gathering round them, spreading their wings over them. When one group of birds would leave another would come, so that the shade never departed from upon their heads. Moreover, when the old man raised his voice towards them the birds would listen!" Rabbi Pinchas responded, "This is what I was really asking you about," and the Arabs were filled with wonder...

Then Rabbi Pinchas ben Yair's donkey brayed and Rabbi Shimon ben Yochai heard it. He said to his son Rabbi Elazar and his disciples, "Let us arise, for the joyous sound of the old man's donkey has come to us!" So, Rabbi Shimon ben Yochai arose along with all the companions. He then began a discourse [regarding the mouth of Bilaam's donkey that was created on the eve of the Sabbath at twilight (Pirkei Avos, 5:6)].

Meanwhile Rabbi Pinchas ben Yair came and kissed Rabbi Shimon ben Yochai, saying, "I have kissed the mouth of Hashem that has been spiced with the spices of His Gan Eden!" First, they rejoiced together and then they sat down. When they were seated all the birds that had been providing them with shade flew off and dispersed. Rabbi Shimon ben Yochai turned and raised his voice towards them, saying, "Birds of the sky! Have you no concern for the honor of your Master [i.e., the Shechinah] who is standing here?" But the birds remained where they were and would not approach. Rabbi Pinchas said to Rabbi Shimon, "Tell them they may go on their way." So, the birds scattered and went on their way. In the meantime, three trees spread out their branches over them and a brook flowed before them, causing all the companions to rejoice. Rabbi Pinchas said, "Those birds provided an abundance of shade but it caused them great sorrow and it is written, "And His mercies are upon all His works" (Tehillim 145:9). For that reason, I did not wish to sit in their shade." Rabbi Shimon ben Yochai said, "I was not the one who put them to the trouble. It was the Holy One Blessed is He who had mercy upon us. Therefore, we bear no guilt, nor can we send them away." Then they all sat together beneath the tree and drank from the water. Rabbi Shimon began a discourse: "Fortunate is our lot that we engage in study. For it is stated, 'But only in Hashem's Torah is his desire ı he will be like a tree set into the ground near streams of water…' (Tehillim 1:2,3) Come and see what the Holy One Blessed is He did for us — He planted for us those three trees and caused this brook to flow from this place!" To this day those trees stand there with their great boughs spread wide and people refer to them as, "The plantings of Rabbi Shimon ben Yochai and Rabbi Pinchas ben Yair."

This incident teaches us the extent to which the Holy One Blessed is He watches over those engaged in study in innocence. For His eyes are always upon those who fear Him and put their hopes in His lovingkindness, to bestow upon them the spirit of purity and holiness and to fulfill all their desires.

Therefore, one must acknowledge Hashem's benevolence and the tremendous mercies that He does for us at all times and at every moment. Moreover, one must pray that we may be granted refuge in the shadow of His wings so that we may be spared from sin and iniquity. One should also ask the Holy One Blessed is He to fill our hearts with awe and trembling. For of what benefit are our lives if we are alienated from holiness, Heaven forbid? And of what benefit to us is all our toil if we remain under the dominion of the evil inclination? Whoever fears Hashem and trembles at His word will resolve in his heart to choose the good and straight path. He will groan with a broken heart over his past deeds and Hashem will forgive him. Then he will prosper in his end many fold. Amein, selah.

Chapter 61

It states, "Do not eat upon the blood [i.e., before you have prayed on behalf of your blood — Berachos 10b)], do not divine and do not augur" (Vayikra 19:26). The connection between these laws is explained in the Zohar in Parashas Vayakhel (215b), based on the teaching in Berachos (57b) that sleep is one sixtieth of death. When a person sleeps his Divine soul [neshamah] exits his body leaving behind only the animal soul [nefesh], which is sustained by the small measure of blood contained in the heart. Therefore, while a person sleeps the Sitra Achara is able to spread throughout his entire body, particularly at night when the malignant spirits [chitzonim] reign. And even if he rises at night to toil in Torah his soul does not completely settle back into his body until after he has prayed. Only then is the soul completely prepared to return to the body.

It is well known that the soul's dominion derives from the realm of holiness, while the dominion of the body and animal soul derives from the influence of the primordial snake (Zohar, 1:79b). Before a person prays in the morning, he is still under the dominion of the animal soul, which resides in the blood. This soul in turn is under the sway of the primordial snake. Therefore, eating and drinking at that time is essentially the same as offing a sacrifice to the snake! This is the meaning of the verse, "Do not eat upon the blood." That is, do not give dominion to the animal soul dwelling in the blood while the higher soul has still not fully returned to the body. For this reason, the verse continues, "nor shall you divine [tenachashu]." That is, do not grant a place to the primordial snake [nachash]. The Zohar goes on to explain that one who eats and drinks before praying, even if it is already light, is literally considered as if he worshipped idolatry!

I have noticed numerous people in this region who are so enslaved to their appetites that immediately upon awakening, even hours before dawn, believe they will die if they do not have a glass of schnapps. They behave as though it is perfectly permitted to indulge one's appetites and to follow the inclinations of one's corrupted mind. Sometimes they even drink to the point of intoxication. Then when the time for prayer arrives, they are unable to pray properly. Even men of stature have stumbled in this terrible iniquity.

If a person is drawn after bodily pleasure and the passions of his mind, to the neglect of his Creator's service, he allows himself to be caught in an evil trap. For in consequence, he will not merit proper burial in a coffin. See the Zohar (2:214b) which elaborates on the principle exemplified by the righteous Yosef, who guarded his covenant [of circumcision] and merited that it be stated of him, "he was placed in a coffin in Egypt" (Bereishis 50:26). One who follows his appetites and heartstrings, by contrast, will inevitably stumble in the sin of wasting seed. Therefore, let whoever fears and trembles at the word of Hashem heed this worthwhile piece of advice. Let him view eating or even tasting before praying as equivalent to consuming non-kosher food. And let him pray with weeping and supplication that Hashem enable him to be satisfied with a minimal amount of food and drink so that he will not need to engage in profuse eating and drinking.

This is especially important in this orphaned generation when there is no man on earth who does only good and does not sin and when we are so much in need of repentance. For this is the first step towards repentance — that despite the craving and desire for food a person holds himself back and refrains from eating, as is explained in the ethical literature of earlier generations (Ba'alei HaNefesh by the Raavad, Sha'ar HaKedushah; Yesod HaTeshuvah by Rabbeinu Yonah). See especially the holy text of Rabbeinu Yeshayah Segal, z"l (Shelah, Sha'ar HaOsiyos, Kedushah, Shulchan, par. 2). In any event, one must not allow excessive eating and drinking in the evening to interfere with the Creator's service. For when a person goes to sleep at night, he must deliver his spirit and soul to Hashem in a clean state for safekeeping. Therefore, He must examine his deeds at that time to see if he has blemished any of his limbs and if he recalls a particular sin that he committed that day he must make a mental note of the need to make amends. A person can engage in such thoughts, however, only if he has time for reflection before sleep overtakes him. But if he eats and drinks until his stomach is bursting and his mind addled, he will have no time to reflect on words of Torah and awe for once he is intoxicated, he falls upon his bed like a swine! How, then, can his soul possibly ascend before the Throne of Glory to receive its outpouring of blessing along with the other pure souls?

See what is stated in the Zohar in Parashas Lech Lecha (83a) regarding the verse, "With my soul I desired You at night, even with my spirit within me I sought you out" (Yeshayahu 26:9). Rabbi Shimon ben Yochai explains that when a person climbs into bed and his soul departs, it is to the soul's benefit if it is pure and free of blemish and iniquity and if all his ways are holy. For then his soul merits witnessing the pleasantness of Hashem and reflecting in His Temple.

Just as sinful deeds prevent the soul from ascending to the realm of holiness, so do slanderous and vulgar speech cause a person to be placed under a ban pronounced by forty ministering angels, that is not lifted until he regrets his words and repents. See the Zohar (2:249b) where this is discussed at length. The same applies to the person who deceives his colleague by uttering one thing with his lips while thinking something else in his mind, thereby causing his unsuspecting colleague to rely upon him.

Thus, Zohar relates in Parashas Naso (121b): The falsehood that a person speaks ascends and pierces the firmaments, remaining there until nightfall. Then his soul ascends and takes hold of that statement and tries bringing it before the holy King. This is the meaning of the verse, "Guard the portals of your mouth from the one who lies in your embrace" (Michah 7:5). Later, both the statement and the iniquity he committed thereby are recorded. Therefore, fortunate is he who conducts himself without guile.

A person may say to himself, "Are there not those whose words disagree with their thoughts and who defraud people with their speech? And do they not profit thereby?" But you should know that the punishment awaiting them is great and, in the end, they will be eliminated from both this world and the next because their way is heretical. For the Holy One Blessed is He personally supervises all speech, for bad and for good.

The Zohar relates in Parashas Shelach (157a): Rabbi Chizkiyah and Rabbi Yeisa were traveling along a road. Rabbi Yeisa said to Rabbi Chizkiyah, "I see in your face that you are contemplating thoughts of Torah." Rabbi Chizkiyah responded, "That is certainly true. I was contemplating what King Shlomo said, 'For the fate of man is the fate of the beast; one fate befalls them both. As this one dies, so does the other die. There is one spirit to them all and the superiority of man over the beast is nothing, for everything is vanity' (Koheles 3:19)." "If this is the case it provides an opening for the wicked and faithless, Heaven forbid." Rabbi Yeisa said, "This verse certainly needs examination."

In the meantime, they noticed a man coming towards them asking for water…Rabbi Yeisa took out a flagon full of water and gave him to drink. When he had finished, they went up the mountain and found there a stream. The man said, "Now you may ask me about some point of Torah and I will explain it…" So, they asked him the meaning of the verse, "For the fate of man is the fate of the beast; one fate befalls them both…" He said to them, "Do you think that Shlomo was speaking for himself? He was repeating the words of the fools of the world. This statement is connected with what precedes it, where it states, 'I reflected in my heart regarding the words of people [who think that] God has chosen them, seeing that they are beasts, unto themselves. [They say,] 'For the fate of man, etc.' (Koheles 3:18-19)." He explained that what King Shlomo meant was as follows: "I reflected in my heart regarding the haughty who say, 'We are too intelligent to mingle with other people, for God has created us to live apart!' And when I thought about their words, I realized that they are correct; they should indeed remain apart — apart from those who fear Hashem! Rather, they should be united with those who pursue worldly matters, giving no thought to their portion in the World to Come. Such people are truly like animals."

This is the meaning of the words, "Seeing that they are beasts, unto themselves." That is, they should remain by themselves and not be associated with the righteous. And what were the words of these wicked ones that Shlomo was reflecting upon? It was their vain and false hypothesis that the same fate befalls both men and beast. On the basis of this doctrine they concluded that everyone may do as he pleases, since there is in any event no reward for the righteous and no punishment for the wicked, nor, in fact, is their any Judge or justice at all! But may their souls expire, for they are like beasts! They are faithless fools! Woe to them and to their souls! King Shlomo continues, "And who knows if the spirit of man ascends on High and if the spirit of a beast descends below to the earth?" That is to say, "who knows" among these fools who have no knowledge of our holy Torah and the ways of awe! They hold fast to the trait of arrogance "in order to join the quenched [i.e., the unintentional sinner] to the thirsty [i.e., the intentional sinner]" (Devarim 29:18). They should be informed that the "spirit of man" — those who are worthy of being called men, that is, the faithful and innocent servants of Hashem — do indeed ascend On High. They rise to the highest levels where they bask in the supernal light and are bound up in the bond of life. As the traveler explained to Rabbi Chizkiya and Rabbi Yeisa, the word "ascend" [olah] hints that the spirit of the righteous resembles a flawless burnt offering [olah] before the King. On the other hand, the "spirit of a beast" — that is, the souls of the wicked, against which they themselves sin by turning themselves into beasts — descends below to the earth. They descend to the place where their souls will indeed expire. Concerning them it states, "Let them be as chaff before the wind with the angel of Hashem thrusting them away" (Tehillim 35:5).

The Zohar continues: Rabbi Chizkiyah and Rabbi Yeisa came and kissed him, saying, "You possessed so much content and we did not know it! Fortunate was the moment that we met you..." Then they asked, "Would you like to join with us?" He replied, "If I did so the Torah would call me a 'fool.' Moreover, I would be worthy of death!" "But why?" they asked. "Because I am an emissary dispatched on a mission. King Shlomo says, 'One who sends things by the hand of a fool [who will fail to complete his mission] wears out his feet [i.e., he will have to go himself] and drinks in violence [i.e., the wrath of the intended recipient]' (Mishlei 26:6). Come and see that the spies incurred guilt in this world and the next only because they were not faithful emissaries." So, he kissed them and departed.

Rabbi Yeisa and Rabbi Chizkiyah continued walking. After a while they came across some people [who knew the man they had met]. They inquired of them, "What was this fellow's name?" "His name is Chaggai," they replied. "He is one of the scholars of our town but his colleagues sent him with an inquiry for Rabbi Shimon ben Yochai…" Rabbi Yeisa and Rabbi Chizkiyah said, "Fortunate is his mother and fortunate are his colleagues who sent him, for he is a faithful emissary.

From this incident we learn that a man must perceive clearly with his mind's eye that the end of everything is to fear punishment and to recall continually the verse with which Shlomo concludes the book of Koheles. That is: "The end of the matter, when everything is heard, is to fear God and keep His commandments, for that is the entirety of a man" (Koheles 12:13). Shlomo adds: "And know that God will bring everything to judgment" (Koheles 11:9). The Sages tell us that if a person says that the Holy One Blessed is He disregards anything, Heaven will disregard his life (Bava Kama 50a). May these words be bound and sealed upon your heart. Then all will be well with us, selah.

Chapter 62

One of the ways in which one's fear of Heaven must be expressed is in the refusal to show favor towards transgressors. If one sees his fellow violating the Torah, he must reproach him, saying, "My brother, what you are doing is not right. Recall that Hashem's eyes roam over the entire earth, so what will you do on the morning that you are called upon to give a reckoning?" This is a serious obligation incumbent upon everyone who knows how to give rebuke. However, one must be sure to rebuke the sinner in private, not in public. For it is written, hoche'ach tochiach ["you shall surely rebuke"; literally, "rebuking you shall rebuke"]. Note that the verb first appears in an impersonal form and only then in the second person. This is to suggest that one must begin by rebuking the offender in an impersonal manner. Thus, one should not immediately say, "What you are doing is not right!" Rather one should comment, as if merely relaying information: "Come and see the consequences of sin; when one commits an iniquity, one incurs a terrible punishment. I have heard that doing such-and-such brings detriment to the world as well as to the doer himself. For the punishment he incurs is such-and-such." In this way perhaps the sinner will realize on his own that he has done wrong and make amends. But if he ignores these words of rebuke and shows no sign of abandoning his transgression, one must rebuke him in the second person, although still in private to avoid humiliating him publicly. One must say to him, "Why did you rebel against Hashem our God by doing such-and-such?"

If the sinner still pays no heed and one know that humiliating him in public will cause him to desist out of shame, one may do so with impunity until he leaves off sinning. Hashem will not consider the humiliation of the sinner in public to be a sin. The guiding principle is that the wise speak and act appropriately and with forethought so that their reward is not offset by guilt, Heaven forbid. But if one sees that the sinner will not accept rebuke it is better not to rebuke him. Concerning this our Sages have said, "Just as it is a mitzvah to say that which will be heeded, so is it a mitzvah to refrain from saying that which will not be heeded" (Yevamos 65b).

In short, if a person sees that his colleague has fallen into sin and there is something, he can do to influence him, he must make the effort. And if Hashem grants him success, he will be reckoned a public benefactor or at least one who brought merit to a colleague, the reward for which is very great. This can be seen from the following passage from the Zohar (Parashas Tazria, 45b):

Rabbi Chiya and Rabbi Yose were traveling along the road when they encountered a man whose face was filled with sores. Rabbi Chiya asked him, "Who are you?" The man replied, "I am a Jew." They looked at him and saw that his face was red from the sores. Rabbi Yose said, "Surely he is a sinner, otherwise his face would not have been disfigured with these sores. Such afflictions are not called 'afflictions of love.'" Rabbi Chiya said, "This is certainly the case. They would be called afflictions of love only if they were hidden from the view of others. And how do we know that a person must give rebuke in private? This can be learned from the way that the Holy One Blessed is He gives rebuke. Someone who rebukes a colleague out of love must do so in private to spare him public humiliation. Thus, public rebuke is not a sign of love. "Similarly, the Holy One Blessed is He first rebukes a person with mercy by striking him in private. If he repents, good and well. If not, He then strikes him openly on his face so that others will look at him and know that he is a sinner and that he is not beloved of his Master.

The man listened to this entire exchange and afterwards said, "Do you say these things about me with a single mind?" Whereupon he approached them, saying, "Surely you are among those who dwell in the house of Rabbi Shimon ben Yochai who fear no one. But if you say such things behind my back your words will indict you! How can you speak so openly?" They responded, "Thus is it written of the Torah, 'She cries at the head of the busiest places, at the entrances of the gates; in the city she utters her words' (Mishlei 1:21). If we were afraid of you in matters of Torah we would be disgraced before the Holy One Blessed is He." Then the fellow recited, "Who is a God like You, bearing iniquity and passing over transgression, etc." (Michah 7:18), and he raised his voice and wept.

In the meantime, his sons arrived. The youngest one observed, "Heaven has sent my father assistance." He continued, "'There is a righteous man who is lost on account of his righteousness, etc.' (Koheles 7:15). This needs explanation. How can a righteous man be lost on account of his righteousness? "The explanation is this: When sinners are numerous and sin and transgression rampant and there is a single righteous man among them, if he fails to rebuke them, he will be punished on their account, even though he is perfectly righteous, never sinning at all. "So, it is with my father. He has been held accountable for the iniquities of his townsmen. For although they all behaved brazenly towards him, he failed to rebuke them and refrained from speaking harshly to them to avoid shaming them. This is why he was subjected to these afflictions."

The boy's father spoke up, "Clearly this is why Holy One Blessed is He punished me. For it was within my power to protest yet I refrained from doing so, shaming them neither in private nor in public." Then another son spoke up, "[It is stated,] 'I was mute with silence, I did not speak of the good and my pain was stirred up' (Tehillim 39:3). That is, I saw that people were going along reprehensible paths, yet I was 'mute with silence.' I refrained from rebuking them to their faces and did not 'speak of the good.' That is, I did not speak beneficial words to turn them from the path of evil to the path of goodness and integrity. Because of this 'my pain was stirred up' — that is, terrible afflictions came upon me openly." When he finished speaking Rabbi Chiya and Rabbi Yose went and kissed him, etc.

From this incident we learn that whoever refrains from giving rebuke out of fear of human beings will be put to great shame before the Holy One Blessed is He. Moreover, even if he is personally righteous, he will be punished on their account, as I have already mentioned. The refusal to flatter the wicked is a source of life to the one who stands up to them and weakens them. By contrast, if he refrains from doing so he may be certain that afflictions will befall him and he will suffer shame and disgrace when he stands in the great court before the Holy One Blessed is He.

Lift your eyes on High and trust in Hashem, for it is He who breaks the arm of the wicked and tramples their fortifications. Be strong and brave in the face of the wicked and you may be certain that all the host of Heaven will assist you. Muster all your limbs and your three hundred and sixty-five sinews in fury against him to prevent him from bringing his evil plans to fruition. If you do this then on account of the fire that burned within you against the wicked it will be reckoned as if your limbs were offered as a burnt sacrifice upon the altar. Even if there is a risk that one will suffer financial loss on account of a particular evildoer, Heaven forbid, one must do his duty. Hashem has many agents and if a person refrains out of concern about financial loss, he will suffer the loss anyway, many times over. For whoever curries favor with an evildoer eventually falls into his hand (Sotah 41b). If a person sees that it is impossible to argue with the one, he is rebuking because fortune is smiling upon him, nevertheless, he may not do anything to strengthen or encourage him, nor may he assist him in pursuing his transgressions, Heaven forbid. Even if a person is liable to come to physical harm, Heaven forbid, it is still forbidden for him to give aid or encouragement to the wicked, unless his life is at risk. Rather he must try to remove himself from the situation. Under such circumstances removing oneself is permitted but aiding transgressors is not.

The obligation to give rebuke falls in particular upon the rabbis, scholars and judges of every town. If there is no rabbi, Torah authority or permanent judge, then the obligation falls upon each individual Jew to rebuke his neighbor. Through this he causes himself to be beloved both On High and down below, in fulfillment of the verse, "Rebuke the wise and he will love you" (Mishlei 9:8). He also merits entering the Gate of Love, Amein.

Chapter 63

King Dovid wrote in the book of Tehillim, "Answer me when I call out, God of my righteousness…, be gracious to me and hear my prayer" (4:2). I believe this verse can be understood in light of the Sages teaching that if person's prayers are answered immediately, he must not become conceited and suppose it to be on account of his righteousness. On the contrary, he should consider himself a sinner from whose prayers the Holy One Blessed is He derives no pleasure at all. Thus, in Ta'anis (25b) the Sages liken this to a leper who approached the king's table with a request. Because the king did not wish for his palace to be sullied by the leper's presence, he commanded that his request be granted on the spot so that he could be sent away. This is what King Dovid meant when he said, "Answer me when I call out, God of my righteousness." That is, he did not wish to be answered immediately. He wished first to find grace and to have his prayer heard and only afterwards to have his request fulfilled.

By the same token, a person who prays at length and is not answered should not despair of praying again. For the Holy One Blessed is He does indeed desire his prayers but He desires that they be with proper intent. That is, the heart must concentrate and know what the mouth utters. Thus, the Zohar warns in Parashas Beshalach (63b): We have been taught: Whoever prays before the

Holy King must make his request and pray his prayer from the depths of his heart so that he is wholeheartedly with the Holy One Blessed is He. Moreover, he must concentrate his mind and will on what he is uttering. Thus, said King Dovid, "I have sought You with my entire heart, etc." (Tehillim 119:10).

It is fitting for every person to pray this short prayer before entering the synagogue: "'Please accept the gifts of my mouth, Hashem, and teach me Your laws' (Tehillim 119:108). May it be Your will, Hashem my God and God of my fathers, that my prayer should be lucid and pure and free of any hindrance that might interfere with proper intention." It is very precious to the Holy One Blessed is He when a person raises his arms and fingers while praying from the bottom of his heart. Thus, the Zohar relates in Parashas Yisro (67a) that ten angels are appointed over the one who lifts up his arms and fingers during prayer or the washing of the hands. However, it is forbidden to raise one's hands and fingers in vain. To this the Zohar applies the verse, "Let them not appear before Me empty-handed" (Shemos 23:15). Then the ten angels mentioned above curse him with two hundred and forty-eight imprecations, Heaven spare us. A spirit of impurity immediately settles upon his hands and no blessing is to be found in them. Thus, it is written of Avraham, "I raised my hand to Hashem, God the most High" (Bereishis 14:22). The Targum renders, "I raised my hand in prayer." That is, he did not raise them in vain, Heaven forbid.

Similarly, regarding Moshe's prayer for the defeat of Amalek it is written, "And it came to pass that when Moshe raised his hand, Israel prevailed" (Shemos 17:11). However, this obligation to raise one's hands only applies during prayer, the recitation of blessings or the expression of acknowledgement." See the passage from the Zohar at length.

From here one can infer the enormity of the punishment that awaits those who raise their hands while swearing vain oaths. According to an oral tradition that has come down to me, whoever raises his hands and fingers unnecessarily and other than in prayer will surely suffer some penalty for it shortly thereafter. And if this does not come to pass, he should be even more concerned, for it undoubtedly means that the Heavenly court is allowing his guilt to accumulate until his measure is completely filled! Therefore, anyone who has become habituated in this sin should erect a protective fence for himself by uttering this verse before praying or reciting the blessing over the washing of the hands: "Lift up your hands to the Sanctuary and bless Hashem!" (Tehillim 134:2). This will give the Holy One Blessed is He pleasure, on account of which He will undoubtedly bestow upon him blessings and goodly gifts. However, this will only be true if his hands are free of robbery and theft. But if his hands are not free of robbery, theft and infringement, then of what significance is the lifting of his hands and fingers? On the contrary, it simply causes his iniquity to be brought to mind, thereby transforming the attribute of mercy into strict judgment.

For this reason, a person must see to it that he earns his livelihood through permissible means so that his money will not be tainted with even a trace of sin. For he will enjoy no profit from his labors unless his deeds and the toil he engages in under the sun are all fitting and proper. Then if he labors with his hands in a permissible manner, he can be certain that when he spreads them Heavenward in prayer, they will arouse Hashem's holy Name and invoke His mercy and loving- kindness. It is especially correct for a person to raise his hands, palms upward, when he comes to those points in the service at which one must offer up one's life for the sake of Hashem's holy name. This will be accredited to him as if he offered a burnt sacrifice.

The first place where when one must offer up one's soul is in the recitation of the Shema, from the time one says the words, "And you shall love Hashem your God with all your heart and with all your soul," until the end of the paragraph. The next place is towards the end of the service in the prayer, "And a redeemer will come to Tziyon, etc.," as one says the words, "Blessed is our God who created us for His glory and separated us from those who stray," until the end of that prayer. Let him reflect at that juncture that if it had been his fate to be born among idolaters his world would have been very dark. How, then, can he ever repay the Holy One Blessed is He for the goodly gift of not being born into those nations? As he brings all this to mind, his heart will surely well up with joy. Then, while he is brimming with the spirit of joy and exuberant love, let him imagine that he is confronted with a blazing pyre and that idolaters are trying to compel him to abandon his faith, Heaven forbid. In his mind's eye let him cast himself into the midst of that inferno with love and affection in affirmation of the unity of the Holy One Blessed is He and His Shechinah. A third point at which to offer up one's soul is in the Shabbos afternoon service in the blessing, "You are one and Your name is one, etc.," as one says the words, "And for their rest they sanctify Your name."

Offering up one's soul to sanctify the name of Heaven is a great matter in the eyes of the Holy One Blessed is He, especially if one does so while reciting the verse, "Because for Your sake we are killed all day long," (Tehillim 44:23). Thus, it is written in the Zohar (Parashas Vayeira 124b): Rabbi Shalom bar Manyumi said: You will find no righteous man among those engaged in Torah study who does not possess two hundred desirable worlds. This is the meaning of the verse, "And two hundred for those who guard its fruit" (Shir HaShirim 8:12). The same applies to those who give themselves over for the sanctification of the name every day. On account of the verse, "Because for Your sake we are killed all day long," they inherit two hundred desirable worlds. And when the time comes for a person who offered up his soul for the sanctification of the name to die, the angel appointed over buried bodies knows how to honor his body in the grave in accordance with his deeds. The Zohar explains (Parashas Vayeira 123b) that before a body can be reckoned among those that are to be revived, the soul must return from Gan Eden and present to the angel Dumah the signs given to it by the cherubim indicating that his body was indeed holy.

Bind the following words of advice to your heart so that you will not forget them: There is one highly effective strategy for ensuring that one's body is clothed in a holy garment in the next world. That is, if he has in mind as he wraps himself in his tzitzis that the holiness of this commandment should cause his body to be sanctified and that he should be saved from all transgression and sin. In Part I (chapters 2 and 24) I have already discussed the principle alluded to in the verse, "In all your ways, know Him" (Mishlei 3:6). In this vein, when donning his garments, he should reflect on the prohibition against wearing mixtures of wool and linen. Even more so he should have the proper intentions when donning his tefillin. In this way he is protected against straying from the realm of sanctity and into the realm of the Sitra Achara, Heaven forbid. For Israel's garments all derive from the realm of holiness. One should be especially careful that the garments he wears on Shabbos and Yom Tov have been designated for the mitzvah, in particular his tallis.

But having done so, he must avoid wearing the small fringed garment known as a sradkil in an outhouse or any other foul place unless it is covered by another garment. A person must make sure that his special Shabbos and Yom Tom garment is untainted by robbery or theft. For if it is, the stain is referred to as a "plague" and the garment as that of "traitors." Thus, the Sages have said that in the future the righteous are destined to rise from the dead in their garments. By this they are referring specifically to those garments that are proper, i.e., purchased with justly earned money (Kesubos 111b). This is the meaning of the Sages' teaching (Kesubos 104a) that when the righteous pass away a Heavenly voice proclaims, "They will rest in peace upon their beds" (Yeshayahu 57b). The letters comprising the word shalom ["peace"] are the same as the letters of malbush ["garment"] in reverse order. For the righteous fashion garments for themselves out of their justly-earned wealth. And whoever's garments are fashioned from justly earned wealth can be assured that his prayers will be acceptable and desirable to the Holy One Blessed is He.

To summarize what we have learned in this chapter: It is better for a person to pray for a shorter amount of time with concentration than for a longer time without it. And let him raise his hands and fingers whenever he prays, utters blessings, gives thanks or recites the Shema or the prayer "And a redeem will come." Let him distance himself from theft and from all ill-gotten gain. Then I will be his guarantor that Providence will cause him to prosper in this world and that his reward will be double in the next world. As it states, "And two hundred for those guarding its fruit" (Shir HaShirim 8:12).

Chapter 64

The Sages have said that hosting wayfarers is greater than greeting the Shechinah (Shabbos 127a). It is obvious that if they spoke in such terms, as if this mitzvah could actually be of more significance that greeting the Shechinah, they must have been alluding to some hidden meaning. The idea, then, is this: The mitzvah of hosting wayfarers can be understood on two levels. On the plain level it refers to an act that is a reflection of good character, namely that the host's generous heart prompts him to invite wayfarers into his home and to give them food and drink. This is a deed that the intellect identifies as proper and good, for through it one performs lovingkindness with those coming in from the road, weary from the trials of the way, their tongues clinging to their palates out of thirst. Even if the wayfarer has the means to pay for his fare, nevertheless when the host offers him food and drink and a mattress and linen to lie upon to refresh his soul and recuperate from his travels, the lovingkindness that he does is very precious. This assumes, of course, that he does so generously and not grudgingly.

On another level, however, this mitzvah can be understood as an intimation of something deeper. Suppose you see the holy Torah standing on the street with no one to gather it in, no one to say, "I will take it into my home so that the sound of Torah will be heard there day and night and it will be a crown upon my head." Similarly, suppose you notice that a particular commandment is taken lightly and that few fulfill it. You can be certain that that commandment is just waiting for some honest and upright fellow to claim it for himself, to observe it meticulously and to urge others to observe with love for the honor and unification of the Holy One Blessed is He. This, too, is clearly a form of "hosting a wayfarer." Moreover, it brings about the unification of the Holy One Blessed is He and His Shechinah, as can be derived from a passage in the Zohar (Parashas Terumah 155b): Rabbi Yose and Rabbi Chiya were traveling along the road while a merchant was leading his donkey after them.

Rabbi Yose said, "Let us engage in Torah study, for the Holy One Blessed is He accompanies those who engage in study. So, Rabbi Chiya began a discourse, "[It is stated,] 'It is a time to act for

Hashem, for they have made void Your Torah' (Tehillim 119:126)." Rabbi Chiya explained the verse as follows: Suppose that people have become neglectful of Torah study or that they are remiss concerning a certain commandment, thereby causing the Shechinah to be distanced from the abode of the Holy One Blessed is He. Whenever this is the case those who tremble at Hashem's word must summon all their strength to exhort people concerning the matter. Let them say, "Arise and take hold of the holy Torah or the neglected commandment! Raise it up from the degradation it has suffered because human beings have slighted it for so long. Let us now fulfill it for the sake of unifying the Holy One Blessed is He and His Shechinah." Fortunate is the one who does this and fortunate is his soul. This is the meaning of the verse, "It is a time to act for Hashem." That is, it is time to do something for the unification of the Holy One Blessed is He and His Shechinah. When is this time? Whenever people have "made void Your Torah." Whoever proves to be eager and meticulous in this regard will be termed "the zealous one" and he will be rewarded for it.

Then the merchant who was leading his donkey after them spoke up, "With your permission, my teachers — surely you have interpreted this verse very well. However, there is one slight difficulty with this interpretation. According to this the verse should have said, 'There is a need to act for Hashem, etc.,' or, 'Let us act, etc.' What is meant by, 'It is a time to act'?" Rabbi Yose responded, "In so many ways the road has been prepared before us! First, because we were two and now even more so because we are three and the Shechinah will surely join with us. Moreover, I had thought you were nothing but a withered tree but now I see that you are as fresh as an olive tree!" So, they asked the merchant to begin his discourse.

The merchant explained that there are times that are under the influence of the realm of holiness and there are times that are under the influence of the Sitra Achara. A time that is under holy influence is called a "time of favor," as it is written, "And as for me, let my prayer to You, Hashem, be at a time of favor" (Tehillim 69:14). This time is illuminated by the name A-d-n-y ["My Lord"]. A time that is under the influence of the Sitra Achara is called a "time of afflictions." These afflictions emanate from the wicked

Lilis and the primordial snake. For this reason, Israel has been warned to stay far from the entrance to her house and to avoid her and all the workers of evil that are dependent upon her. Instead they must draw as near as possible and cling as closely as possible to the "time of favor," which is associated with the Shechinah. For the Shechinah encompasses all the souls of Israel, for which reason it is called Knesses Yisroel — "the Congregation of Israel," as is known to the Kabbalists. Regarding this the Torah warns (Koheles 3:8), "There is a time to love" — that is, one must love the Shechinah — and a time to hate — that is, one must hate the Sitra Achara, which is connected with Lilis. A proof to this can be drawn from the Torah's warning to the Kohein Gadol regarding his entry into the Holy of Holies to arouse mercy for Israel, "And let him not come at all times into the Holy Precinct" (Vayikra 16:2). In other words, the Torah adjures him to enter only with thoughts of holiness, especially on Yom Kippur, which is a time of favor. For this was the day that Israel received atonement for the sin of the Golden Calf, for which reason it was established as a day of forgiveness and atonement for all generations. Therefore, it is forbidden for the Kohein Gadol to enter the Holy of Holies with alien thoughts emanating from the Sitra Achara, Heaven forbid.

Now, when Israel engages in Torah study and observes the commandments, the rectification of the world is affected through Hashem's right hand and in a complete way, with joy and unity. But this not the case when Israel slacks off in its studies and is remiss in its performance of the commandments and acts of lovingkindness, when they are jealous of one another and all their deeds are vanity and deceit, when the name of Heaven is desecrated through infringement. Then woe to them! For then the "time" of holiness sinks into the abyss, on account of our many sins. Then the Shechinah is no longer revealed in a whole way, nor does it radiate with great illumination. Then afflicting angels wax powerful, strengthening the hand of the other nations until they achieve dominion over Israel. Meanwhile Israel's fortunes plummet, Heaven forbid, leading to numerous evil consequences. At that time it is announced in Heaven: "Who is the man who trembles at the word of Hashem? Let him gird his loins like a warrior to strengthen our holy Torah, to do mitzvos and good deeds and to urge the multitude to fulfill the Torah and the commandments! For the time of singing has arrived! It is time to bedeck the Shechinah to bring her to her beloved!" This is the concept of a "time to act for Hashem." That is, one must work to rectify the "time of favor" to reunite it with the Holy One Blessed is He.

[When the merchant finished his discourse] Rabbi Yose and Rabbi Chiya came and kissed him upon the head, saying, "If we had not come into the world for any reason other than to hear this, it would have been enough for us. Fortunate is the generation of Rabbi Shimon ben Yochai in which wisdom can be found even amidst the mountains!" Then they inquired, "What is your name?" He responded, "Chanan." So, they blessed him with the verse, "May God give you grace [yachnecha], my son" (Bereishis 43:29), adding, "May God hear your voice whenever you need Him."

Rabbi Yose said, "Behold, the sun is going down. Behind this mountain there is a little village called by your name, "the village of Chanan." So, they went there fore the night. They spent that night engaged in study, in the course of which the merchant revealed to them many secrets, as the Zohar relates at length. Among the things that he taught them were a number of practices that one should be careful to observe regarding mealtimes: First, when a person indulges himself at his table let him recall the sanctity of the land of Israel and fret over the destruction of the Holy Temple. Then the Holy One Blessed is He will reckon his anguish as if he himself rebuilt the Holy Temple and restored all the ruins of Jerusalem to their former state of glory. Fortunate is his lot!

Second, let the one reciting the Grace after Meals receive the cup of blessing with both hands, having in mind that they represent the two Patriarchs, Avraham and Yitzchak. Avraham corresponds to the right hand, the side of lovingkindness and Yitzchak to the left hand, the side of restraining might. The cup that is held between them represents Yaakov, who encompasses both of his forebears, as is known to the Kabbalists.

Third, one must fix one's eyes upon the cup and concentrate upon it. For in the same way does the Holy One Blessed is He continually keep watch over Israel, His holy nation. Through this we will merit the fulfillment of the verse, "The eyes of Hashem your God are upon [the land] from the beginning of the year."

Fourth, the bread must remain on the table at the time of the Grace so that the table is not empty, for blessing does not settle upon any place that is empty, especially not an empty table. This is the idea behind the custom described by the Sages in which they used to surround the cup of blessing with other full cups (Berachos 51a). For the same reason Rabbi Shlomo Luria, z"l, was careful not leave any empty vessel on the table at the time of the Grace but only full ones. Since we have already begun speaking about empty vessels, I will mention another point about them concerning which the public should be made aware. It is tried and true and therefore anyone who cares for his soul should observe it.

I refer to the Zohar's warning that if any man or woman wishes to set out on a journey or to call on the authorities to tend to some matter and on the way out of the house, he encounters an empty vessel, he should not go that day. The Zohar (1:88a; 2:87b, 157b) cites as proof a passage from II Melachim (4:2) in which the prophet Eliyahu asked the woman of Shunam if she had anything in the house. She replied that she had only a small jug of oil. This prompted the prophet to comment [according to the Sages], "That is surely something upon which a blessing can take effect, as it is written, 'Like fine oil upon the head…like the dew of Chermon descending upon the mountains of Tziyon. For there Hashem has commanded the blessing, life for eternity' (Tehillim 133:2-3)." Concerning an empty vessel, by contrast, it is said that blessing cannot settle upon it. Therefore, one must remove the empty vessels from the table when the Grace is recited. This should be enough of a warning.

The main lessons to be derived from this chapter are:

1) That receiving wayfarers is greater than receiving the Shechinah.
2) That when one sees a commandment that needs doing one must gird one's loins like a warrior to fulfill it and to urge others to do so as well.
3) That one must be careful, even if one is learned, to treat every man respectfully. The proof to this is the way that Rabbi Yose and Rabbi Chiya treated the merchant, Chanan. In the end they even blessed him and they certainly did not lord over him. Additionally,

one must be careful to observe the four practices that I mentioned in connection with meals, the most important of which being that no empty vessel should remain on the table at the time that Grace After Meals is recited. Then Hashem's blessing will fill the cup of blessing, "For there Hashem has commanded the blessing."

Chapter 65

Our Sages have taught (Pirkei Avos 3:15): "The world is judged for the good but everything is determined according to the abundance [or "the majority"] of deeds." My illustrious father, the great Rabbi Aharon Keidnover, z"l, explained this in his commentary on the Torah Birkas Shmuel (Parashas Noach) in the light of another teaching of the Sages. In Kiddushin (40b) the Sages say: A man should always view himself as if he were half guilty and half meritorious. Thus, if he performs one more good deed he is fortunate, for he inclines himself and the entire world to the side of merit. If he does one more evil deed, woe to him! For he inclines himself and the entire world to the side of guilt. Thus, it is written, "And one sinner causes much good to be lost" (Koheles 9:18). The Mishnah from Pirkei Avos addresses a question that was asked by Moshe himself (see Berachos 7a): We see that there are righteous people who have good fortune and righteous people with bad fortune, evildoers who have good fortune and evildoers with bad fortune. How, then, can the Sages say that, "the world is judged for the good"? In answer to this question Sage goes on to say that, "everything is determined according to the majority of deeds." Therefore, even if a man is completely righteous, if he then commits a single transgression at a time that the world is half meritorious and half guilty — thereby inclining it to the side of guilt — he will become a "righteous person with bad fortune." Conversely, if a wicked person performs a single good deed at a time that the world is half-half — thereby inclining it to the side of merit and benefiting the multitude — he will become an "evildoer with good fortune." Thus, the words of the Mishnah are very precise, "everything is determined according to the majority of deeds." This is clear and it illustrates principle that "the words emanating from the mouth of a wise man are pleasing" (Koheles 10:12).

However, it seems to me that there is another way to understand this Mishnah as well. In this world everything is determined according to the abundance of wealth. Thus, the Sages tell us (Eiruvin 86a) that Rebbi [Rabbi Yehudah HaNasi] used to honor the rich. In other words, he would bestow upon them all the illusory honor that abounds in these times. Fools cite Rebbi's example as a proof that the rich deserve honor. What they do not realize is that Rebbi also used to honor poor Torah scholars, for they are the "men of deeds," and in the World to Come honor will be apportioned according to "the abundance of deeds," i.e., and not according to wealth. Thus, the first statement, that the world is judged "for the good," refers to judgment in this world according to wealth. But the second statement, that "everything is determined according to the abundance of deeds," refers to judgment in the World to Come which is rendered according to the abundance of the deeds of the scholars, the true "men of deeds." This should be a great warning to all whom Heaven has blessed with wealth or with the position of rabbi or head of the community or country — let them not denigrate the honor of scholars on account of their wealth or treat them with disdain, Heaven forbid. Rather let them recall at all times that the profession of the scholar is more exalted than any other profession in the world. If a communal leader derives honor from the disgrace of his fellows by lording over them and he fails to greet all who come before him with a pleasant countenance, he will one day be made to reckon for it and will be crushed beneath their feet. He will long to behold and bask in their radiance, but his vision will be darkened by the sight of their glory. There are numerous sources warning against the disparaging of scholars and the punishment for this iniquity is severe. For example, according to the Mishnah a proclamation goes forth every day, saying, "Woe to mankind for the disgrace of the Torah!" (Pirkei Avos 6:2).

Therefore, a person should be careful to treat scholars with deference since the Holy One Blessed is He desires their honor. Let him strive to increase and elevate the honor and glory of the masters of the Torah. And even if a person's own seat is among the great let him recall that the seat of the scholars is greater than his. Thus, we find that whenever a scholar came before King Chizkiyahu he would rise from his throne and step forward to greet him. Then he would embrace him and kiss him, calling him, "My teacher! My teacher! My father! My father! Chariot of Israel!" (Kesubos 103b; Makkos 24a). Similarly, the Roman Emperor Antoninus used to say to Rebbi, "If only I could be a carpet beneath you in the World to Come!" (Avodah Zarah 10b). By contrast, if a leader behaves haughtily for the sake of receiving more honor, he will one day be consumed by maggots and all his honor will descend into the dust.

But the most important thing is to be as careful in honoring one's mentor as in honoring one's parents. One must also pray for the welfare of one's mentor as well as for the welfare of one's father and mother. One should recite this brief prayer: "Master of the Universe! May it be Your will to grant long life, bountiful sustenance and help from Heaven to my father my teacher, to my mother my teacher. And grant long life to all my mentors and to all the members of my family. May the words of my mouth and the meditations of my heart be acceptable to You, my Rock and my Redeemer."

One must cast aside pride and hold fast to humility. It is true that Rabbi Chiya bar Ashi said in the name of Rav that a scholar must possess "one part in eight of an eighth" measure of pride, which should be a crown for him "like the needles on the top of a stalk of wheat" (Sotah 5a). However, I have heard an explanation of Rabbi Chiya's dictum in the name of the illustrious Rabbi Wolf, head of the court of Posen, z"l, according to which Rabbi Chiya actually meant precisely the reverse of what people think. In fact, what he meant was that a scholar must be especially humble! And they therefore said, "one part in eight of an eighth." He explained as follows: In Parashas Beshalach (52a; 270a) the Zohar discusses the Divine Name, comprised of seventy- two three-letter holy Names, that is engraved upon the supernal throne. The letters that make up these names are derived from the verses of Shemos 14:19-21:

And the angel of God who went before the camp of Israel moved and went behind them and the pillar of cloud moved from before them and stood behind them. And it came between the camp of

Egypt and the camp of Israel so that there was a cloud and darkness, but it illuminated the night; and this one did not come near this one all night. And Moshe stretched out his hand over the sea and Hashem led the sea with a strong east wind all that night and made the sea into dry land and the waters were divided. The letters that make up these verses must be rearranged as in the following table (see Rashi on Sukkah 45a):

וה"ו יל"י סי"ט על"מ מה"ש לל"ה אכ"א כה"ת הז"י אל"ד לא"ו הה"ע יז"ל מב"ה
הר"י הק"מ לא"ו כל"י לו"י פה"ל נל"ך יי"י מל"ה חה"ו נת"ה הא"א יר"ת שא"ה
רי"י או"ם לכ"ב וש"ר יח"ו לה"ח כו"ק מנ"ד אנ"י חע"מ רה"ע יי"ז הה"ה מי"כ
וו"ל יל"ה סא"ל ער"י עש"י מי"ה וה"י דנ"י הח"ש עמ"מ נג"א ני"ת מב"ה פו"י
נמ"ם יי"ל הר"ח מצ"ר ומ"ב יה"ה ענ"ו מח"י דמ"ב מנ"ק אי"ע חב"ו רא"ה יב"מ
הי"י מו"ם

It turns out that one of the eight names in the eighth row is the word *anav* — "humble." Thus, Rabbi's Chiya's dictum should be interpreted that a scholar must have the amount of pride that is reflected in "one of the eight [words] of the eighth [row]," that is, he should be humble! This interpretation is easy to understand, causing one's lips to smack with delight! Nevertheless, in my opinion it is significant that Rabbi Chiya did not say straight out that one must be humble but chose instead to express it through a riddle, saying that one must act with an "eighth of an eighth." I believe this was to hint that a scholar should nevertheless conduct himself with a little bit of preening, which should "crown him like the needles on the top of a sheaf of wheat." It was to this that Rabbi Nachman responded, "I do not want any of it, nor even a part of it!" That is to say, he did not wish to engage in even a little bit of preening lest he possess even the smallest trace of pride. He used the ambiguous phrase "any of it" to allude to the eighth row of the table above while the phrase "even a part of it" refers to the eighth name in the row. Thus, Rabbi Nachman indicated that he would minimize pride to the greatest extent possible, not wanting even the small part of a small part indicated by the expression "any of it or even a part of it." Mar Zutra then concluded, "What is meant by the verse, 'An abomination to Hashem is every haughty heart'? Even the slightest trace [of haughtiness] is implied." The reason for this is expressed in the well known dictum, "Whoever is guilty of pride is as if he worshipped idolatry" (Sotah 4b), for pride is indeed like an offering to an idol, as I will explain in later chapters (84 and 88), with the help of Heaven.

For this reason, I must issue an admonishment regarding the trait of humility itself. It is written, "Mount and ride on behalf of truth and righteous humility" (Tehillim 45:5). As this verse indicates, humility must be righteous and not a deception to make an impression on others. This is a matter that God will examine, for the God of all spirits will bring to judgment anyone who fails to conduct himself with integrity and humility. But concerning the one who does behave with integrity and humility it is written, "And those who love Him will be like the sun going forth in its strength" (Shoftim 5:31). Amein.

Chapter 66

In light of what we have written in the previous chapter we can understand Rabbi Yochanan's dictum: "Wherever you find mention of the greatness of the Holy One Blessed is He, there you find mention of His humility" (Megillah 31a). I believe the explanation is this: When Hashem's four-letter name, is expanded into its constituents using the letter yud as the "filling" [i.e., יו"ד ה"י וי"ו ה"י; Tikkunei Zohar Chadash 122b] it has the numerical value 72, which is the same as the value of the word chessed ["lovingkindness"]. The attribute of chessed is also known as the attribute of "greatness." What Rabbi Yochanan meant by Hashem's "greatness" was the translation of His great name into the chessed [i.e., seventy-two] names listed on the table in the previous chapter. As we saw then, Anav ["humble"] is one of these names. Thus, where one finds Hashem's greatness [i.e., the 72 names], there one finds a hint to His humility in the word anav. This should be easy to grasp.

A human being's humility should find its principle expression in the discretion he exercises before acting and his readiness afterwards to examine whether his deeds detracted in any way from Hashem's honor or that of any of His creatures. Pride, by contrast, is displayed in the hastiness with which a person launches into all

Kav HaYashar

manner of evil and iniquitous deeds. In keeping with the dictum that "one sin leads to another" (Pirkei Avos 4:2), pride leads to avarice. The proud man thinks to himself, "I have so many admirable qualities, surely to me applies the verse, 'Do not touch My anointed ones' (Tehillim 105:15). Therefore no one should lay a finger on me and certainly not my wealth or property. But the only way to see that this is fulfilled is by living in isolation, apart from the company of other people.

Pride causes a person to shame others in public because the conceited person stands on his honor to the last detail and since it is impossible for others to avoid infringing upon it he is frequently enraged, his heart burning with the fires of Gehinnom. This causes him to pour out imprecations and insults, to the mortification of his victims. Yet the Sages have warned that one who embarrasses his fellow in public has no portion in the World to Come (Baba Metzia 59a)! Pride also causes a person's thoughts to become confused during study and prayer.

What else can we say about the damage caused by this trait? The page is not long enough to relate it all! Pride causes a person to give false impressions. For example, the braggart may tell someone that he is only doing a certain act in his honor, while in his heart he knows the truth to be otherwise.

Come see what is written in the Zohar in Parashas Vayeitzi (148a-149a) regarding the exactitude that is expected of a person in matters of honesty and integrity: Rabbi Yitzchak was sitting before a certain cave when a man walked by with his two sons. One son said to his brother, "The sun's intensity comes from the south and the earth is only able to survive it because of the cooling wind, bringing sustenance and perfection on every side... "Come and see that when the holy tribes unified Hashem with the declaration, 'Listen Israel, Hashem is our God, Hashem is one,' their father Yaakov joined in with the reply, 'Blessed is the name of the glory of His kingdom forever and ever.'" [If you are among the initiated you will understand that the attribute of lovingkindness (chessed) incorporates the attribute of restraining might (gevurah), represented by the intensity of the sun. Through this all the judgments (dinnim) contained in the attribute of might are mitigated. And all of this is brought about by Yaakov's attribute of truth (emes).]

Rabbi Yitzchak said, "I will join them and hear what they are saying." So, he walked with them and heard a number of secrets of the Torah, as is related there, after which he wept with joy. Then the man said to him: "Continue along your way, for I must enter this town to celebrate my son's wedding." Rabbi Yitzchak said, "Now the time has come for me to continue on my way alone. For they have told me explicitly that I may not go with them and they did not invite me to the wedding."

Afterwards Rabbi Yitzchak went and told over these things to Rabbi Shimon ben Yochai. Rabbi Shimon ben Yochai said, "Surely they spoke well, for these were the sons of Rabbi Tzaddok the weak. And why is he called "the weak"? Because for forty years he fasted to prevent Jerusalem from being destroyed in his lifetime. He used to reveal esoteric secrets in connection with every statement in the Torah." Not long afterwards Rabbi Yitzchak ran into Rabbi Tzaddok and his younger son. He inquired, "Where is your other son?" "I married him off," he replied, "and he remained with his wife." Then Rabbi Yitzchak asked, "Why did you not invite me to your son's wedding?" "I swear," he said, "that I did not invite you on account of three things: First, since I did not know you, I was afraid that you might be a man of stature and that I might detract from your honor. Second, I thought you might be in a hurry and I did not wish to burden you. And third, so that you would not be embarrassed in the presence of our company, for it is our custom that all who dine at the table of the groom and bride give presents and donations to the groom and I thought that you might be poor." "What is your name?" Rabbi Yitzchak inquired. "Tzaddok the small," the man replied. At that moment Rabbi Yitzchak said, "I learned from this man twelve secrets of the Torah!"

From this incident we learn that earlier generations were careful to speak with their mouths only what was truly in their hearts. How praiseworthy are words spoken with integrity! Thus, the Zohar relates in Parashas Pekudei (264b) that special destroying angels under the authority of "Anger and Wrath," are appointed to listen to all those who ridicule words of Torah or of awe and rebuke. They are also designated to listen to whoever disparages a Torah scholar,

Heaven forbid, or any upright person. For with their words they induce the snakes to shed their skins. This causes them pain on account of which they cry out loudly, awakening the destroying snakes standing in the chambers of Gehinnom that are known as "the pit." These, too, shed their skins and cry out, awakening the snake known as the Samech Mem (SME"L), the officer in charge of them all, whose scaly skin lies before him. Then destroying and damaging angels emanating from his scales fly up to invoke evil decrees. And all of this comes about solely because of an unjust statement, as mentioned above.

Other destroying angels, called "cursers of the day" (Iyov 3:7), are assigned over people who curse themselves in anger with an oath or malediction. These angels then take that curse and bring it to the "Twisted Snake" (Yeshayahu 27:1), which also derives its power from the Samech Mem. This enables it to lodge accusations and to bring on many terrible sorrows (Zohar, Pekudei 266a). Another class of destroying angels is assigned over those who make angry threats, which is also not the way of our holy Torah, or who throw vessels in their rage. Then these angels take those ill-spoken words and bring them before their council. "This is the sacrifice that So-and-so has offered to us," they declare. "Woe to him, for he has strayed after, and worshipped, an alien god! (Zohar, Pekudei 263b). Take note of how many angelic emissaries and officers there are and how many misadventures and consequences a mortal is subject to. This is because man was formed from the dust and is destined to return to it. Let a person take all this to heart and consider his end. For one never knows what the day will bring or what the time will cause to pass or even what the very moment has in store for him, as it is stated, "Set your eyes upon it and it is gone" (Mishlei 23:5). The Omnipresent, blessed is He, has many agents with which to afflict a person and he may find himself caught in the trap without any warning. The proof to this is the story of Iyov. He was a God-fearing man who eschewed wrongdoing, yet on account of a minor transgression he was indicted by the Satan and delivered into his hands along with all his children. Then in the blink of an eye his wealth was gone and his children were dead, after which he was stricken with bodily afflictions, as is related in the book that bears his name (chapters 1-2). In his sorrow, Iyov cursed the day on which he was born and spoke harshly towards Heaven. This caused his companions to come and rebuke him, warning him against repudiating his afflictions. For Hashem's conduct towards a person is always just, in accordance with his own conduct. And when Iyov finally heeded their advice and rebuke it was reckoned a great credit, on account of which his prosperity was renewed and he was blessed with many times more bounty than he enjoyed formerly. All of this was in reward for heeding the call to fear Hashem and improve his ways.

I will cite for you here a passage from the Zohar, Parashas Lech Lecha (Zohar Chadash 31b) that is pertinent to this discussion: [It is stated,] "And the king of Sedom said to Avram, etc." (Bereishis 14:21). The moment the soul leaves the body of a righteous person it passes by the entrance to Gehinnom. There it is filled with the desire to call out to Hashem. For such is the power of the righteous that through their prayers they are able to extricate the wicked from Gehinnom. Then the Prince of Gehinnom, who is also called the "King of Sedom," confronts the soul of the righteous man, called Av Ram ["Exalted Father"], to prevent him from praying for this purpose. For of what use is his assignment if even those who have already been delivered to him can be taken out of his control and authority? So the King of Sedom, the Prince of Gehinnom, says to the righteous man, "You are righteous, so what business do you have extricating the wicked who failed to heed the voices of parents and teachers and who were brazen towards the scholars? It is because of this that they belong to me, for they are wicked and deserve to be lost! "Indeed, those who sinned profusely but eventually heeded the words of their parents and teachers, and accepted the dictates of scholars — even if they did not actually repent at all — they are called the 'property' of the righteous, for they caused them at least to contemplate repentance. Such wicked you may extricate from Gehinnom, for they are fitting to be saved by your prayers."

Therefore, it is stated, "And the King of Sedom" — that is, the Prince of Gehinnom. "Said to Avram" — an allusion to the soul of the righteous person. It is called Av Ram, "Exalted Father," because it is a Divine spark from On High. "Give me the souls" — that is, the souls of the wicked who paid no heed to their parents and teachers, ridiculing the words of the Sages instead. "And the property you may take for yourself" — that is, those wicked who listened joyfully to those rebuking them and did not ridicule them. They are the "property" of the righteous, who may take them for themselves and save them from punishment in Gehinnom. Then the soul of the righteous man swears that he will not take those who are the portion of the Prince of Gehinnom because they failed to heed the voices of the Sages. This is the meaning of the verse, "And Avram said to the king of Sedom, 'I raise my hand in oath to Hashem, God the Most High.'" (Bereishis 14:22). That is, he swore that he would not pray for the sake of those wicked who ridiculed the Torah and shamed the scholars.

This is the meaning of the verse, "And I will not take from all that is yours." That is, those evildoers before whom proclamations of admonition were issued to arouse them and stir them to penitence. But they turned away from the road to Gan Eden and the World to Come and ignored the warnings of punishment in Gehinnom, choosing instead to stiffen their necks and refrain from accepting correction. The verse continues, "[I swear that] I will not take anything from a string to a shoelace." This is an allusion to those who disparage the commandment of tzitzis, going without them entirely or for the duration of the Shema and Amidah prayers donning a four-cornered garment with which they do not fulfill their obligation because it does not cover their heads and the upper half of their bodies. "Until a shoelace" — this alludes to those who are not meticulous regarding the commandment of tefillin. For example, they do not check that the straps are black and free of any connecting knot, for each strap must be made of a single piece and not of two or three pieces tied together. I have seen that many people are lenient with regard to these matters. Yet the punishment for transgressing or denigrating the commandments of tzitzis and tefillin, or for ridiculing words of Torah or denigrating the scholars and their disciples, is that they become the portion of the King of Sedom, the Prince of Gehinnom, falling under his authority.

Rabbi Yehoshua ben Levi related: "Once I found myself near the entryway to Gehinnom and overheard the proclamation regarding those who ridiculed the words of the Sages. They were sentenced to more severe afflictions then any of the other evildoers. I also heard their bitter, sorrowful voices crying, 'Alas, Alas! For we heard words of Torah and awe, but we did not incline our ears well, nor take them to heart. Woe to us! We heard the words of the Sages describing the rewards and punishments for obedience and transgression, but we did not live up to them.' "In the meantime, I heard a voice say, 'Son of Levi! Son of Levi! Be on your way! I have come to remind you not to open your mouth to utter any prayer on behalf of those sentenced to punishment in Gehinnom or to pray on their behalf. For it is written concerning them that they are to be ashes beneath the feet of the righteous.'"

Therefore, let this not be a trivial matter in a person's eyes. Let him recall this scene while he is in this lowly world of vanity and emptiness. Let him not be so caught up in his affairs and in earning his livelihood that he forgets entirely about serving his Creator, Blessed Is He, and does not take pains to set aside regular times for study. And if he is incapable of studying on his own let him set aside time to listen to words of rebuke, for when his ears hear them, he will regret his sins and "He will go back and heal him" (Yeshayahu 6:10). Let him also recall that a person is destined to die and that there is no way to escape Heaven's judgment other than by acquiring Torah and mitzvos to protect him. Let him introspect every day immediately upon arising and let his soul weep in private over the sins of his youth and his transgressions and let him sigh brokenheartedly. In the works of character development [mussar] one finds that as a person sighs over his sins he should recite the following meditation in his heart: O you my heart, O you my heart, as hard as stone and impervious to melting on account of your rebelliousness! When you recall these things — even if sin and iniquity have made you like iron and stone — nevertheless you should open up and melt on account of my copious sighing. For it is sufficient to shatter even mountains of iron and stone! Is it better for you to wait until you are in the confinement and darkness of the pit? For then even a small worm will be able to open the mansion of your heart and examine all the chambers therein. It will seek out its livelihood in all of your entrails, going in and out like a lord in his manner! Indeed, it is better for you to open up now to groaning and lamenting over my sins and transgressions, which have waxed numerous through following the passions of my heart. What will I do on the Day of Judgment when my record is examined? What will I answer I must account for my iniquities?

If a person will reflect on these thoughts, cast aside his pride and heed the admonition of his parents and teachers to set aside time for study every day, then even if he fails to repent, he can still be healed through the prayers of the righteous. And if he rouses himself further to heed those pointing out the ways of the just and thereby comes to repent, how much more so can he hope to be healed, for then he will have indeed attained a lofty level. Not only will be spared all the terrible punishments mentioned above, he will also be rewarded, for it is written, "How abundant is Your goodness that You have hidden away for those who fear You." Amein.

Chapter 67

It is stated, "And you shall teach them sharply to your sons, etc." (Deuteronomy 6:7). This is an admonition to fathers that they must study with their sons personally and sharpen their wits so that they do not approach the Torah in a dull manner. And if the father is not himself a scholar, he is commanded, "And you shall speak of them." That is, let him speak with teachers to persuade them to study with his sons. He must also guide his children in the ways of business and proper conduct and in all these matters he must see to it that they do not to transgress the Torah by so much as a hairsbreadth, Heaven forbid.

"When you sit in your house." — One must conduct himself at home with awe of Heaven and guide his household to be open to the poor. One must also see to it that the members of his household are not in the habit of speaking slander or cursing or swearing.

"And when you walk along the way." — One must engage in study and give charity to the extent of his abilities. Thus, we find that Yaakov prepared to meet his brother with three strategies: tribute, appeasement and battle. In our case, "tribute" means giving to the poor, who the Zohar refers to in a number of places as tribute to the

Holy One Blessed is He (2:129a, 198a). "Appeasement" means prayer. That is, appeasing the Holy One Blessed is He with prayers and supplications. "Battle" refers to the "battle" of Torah study, through which one weakens the power of the wicked Eisav and his guardian angel, the Samech Mem (SME"L). See what is written in this regard in the Zohar in Parashas Va'eschanan (269a).

"And when you lie down." — One must conduct himself with holiness and unify the name of the Holy One Blessed is He by reciting the bedtime Shema. Moreover, one must behave with sanctity during marital relations.

"And when you rise up." — One must rise eagerly to pray and offer songs of praise to the Holy One Blessed is He for having restored his soul. Afterwards he may go and engage in his business, in good faith.

Thus, it is fitting for a person to prepare for himself the three strategies mentioned above: tribute, appeasement and battle. "Tribute" means giving a gift to the poor before praying. Prayer itself is the "appeasement." And afterwards let him set aside a fixed time for study, for this is the "battle."

It is fitting to elaborate on the loftiness of the "battle" of Torah, and it can be gleaned from this passage from the Zohar (Parashas Vayeira 98a): Rabbi Eliezer the Great took ill on the eve of Shabbos. He seated his son Horknus to his right and began revealing to him deep secrets. Then the great sages of the generation entered and he cursed them for failing to come and learn from him. Rabbi Akiva wept and pleaded with him to teach him something before he died. So, Rabbi Eliezer began discussing the mystic speculations of the Divine Chariot and the two of them were surrounded by fire. The sages of the generation said, "Apparently we are not worthy of hearing this." So, they went and stood outside the doorway…. Rabbi Eliezer taught Rabbi Akiva three hundred laws about a stark white plague of the skin. Afterwards he taught him some of the secrets of The Song of Songs [Shir HaShirim]. When he came to the verse, "Support me with goblets; strengthen me with apples, for I am sick with love" (2:5), Rabbi Akiva was unable to withhold himself any longer. He raised his voice and wept, but he did not speak out of fear of the Shechinah that was present.

Afterwards Rabbi Eliezer made Rabbi Akiva swear not to make practical use of any verse from Shir HaShirim lest the world be destroyed, for the world is unworthy of benefiting from the secrets of Shir HaShirim, for it is the Holy of Holies. Afterwards Rabbi Akiva went out, his eyes streaming with tears, and declared, "Woe to the world that is orphaned of you Rabbi Eliezer! Then the sages of the generation entered and spoke with him words of Torah. And when Rabbi Eliezer saw that his soul was near to expiring, he placed his hands upon his heart and said, "The supernal world, the light and the illumination will all be hidden away in you. The two Torahs will be forgotten from this world this day!" At that time Rabbi Akiva was not with him. The sages of the generation asked him, "Is the sandal used in the releasing ceremony from the levirate marriage susceptible to defilement or not?" Rabbi Eliezer said, "It is pure," and his soul expired with the word "pure." After Shabbos Rabbi Akiva came to visit him and discovered that Rabbi Eliezer was dead. He rent his garment and wept...And he cried out, saying, "O Heaven! O Heaven! Tell the sun and the moon that the light that used to shine more brightly than them has been darkened."

Rabbi Yehudah said, "When the soul of a righteous person prepares to exit the body it rejoices because of its faith that it will be rewarded in the World to Come. And when it beholds the Shechinah, the holy angels and the souls of the righteous coming to meet and accompany it, it flies out of the body in which it had been installed and bows to the ground before the Shechinah [see Midrash HaNe'elam, ad loc., and find satisfaction].

Therefore, a person should pray that when his end arrives, the Shechinah will come to him, too, and that he will die the death of a kiss in ripe old age. When the Shechinah does come, it is accompanied by three groups of angels (Kesuvos 104a). One says, "Come in peace!" One says, "Go straight ahead!" (Yeshayahu 57:2). And one says, "Let him come in peace; they shall rest upon their beds" (ibid.)

Chapter 68

It is stated, "A lamp of Hashem is the soul of a man" (Mishlei 20:27). The Zohar (Parashas Mishpatim 99b) explains that ner, "lamp," is an acronym for neshamah, ruach, the two aspects of the soul that shed light together. The neshamah is extremely holy, therefore it enwraps itself in the ruach like a garment. There is also a third aspect of the soul called the nefesh, which is a lower level than the ruach. The seat of the neshamah is in the brain, near where the head tefillin are placed. The seat of the ruach is in the heart, across from the tefillin that are worn on the left arm. The seat of the nefesh is in the liver, which is filled with an abundance of blood. Corresponding to the nefesh the Holy One Blessed is He commanded us in the wearing of tzitzis. Thus, the three commandments mentioned above illuminate all three aspects of the soul: the nefesh, the ruach and the neshamah. According to the well-known teaching of the Sages, the tzitzis contains one techeles-colored thread because this shade of blue resembles the firmament and reminds us of the Throne of Glory. The purpose of this thread is to sanctify the nefesh, located in the liver, the main site of both the body's blood and the trait of anger. The word kaved — "liver" — consists of the same letters as the word kavod — "honor" or "glory," except that it is missing the letter vav. This deficiency is what separates it from the "glory" of Heaven. If a person is protective of his nefesh and does not sin with it, he thereby brings it, too, under the domain of holiness in a complete manner.

Then fortunate is he and fortunate is his lot, for the drops of blood in a person's body are counted and weighed up before the Holy One Blessed is He. This is because every drop of a person's blood, along with every limb and sinew, was intended for the service of the Holy One Blessed is He. Thus, a person has eighteen vertebrae in his spine corresponding to the eighteen blessings of the Amidah instituted by the Men of the Great Assembly. Therefore, for every droplet of seed that goes to waste by way of the eighteen vertebrae there is a punishment. The first of these is that his prayers, comprised of the eighteen blessings, are neither desired nor accepted by the Holy One Blessed is He. For the seed originates in the brain, the dwelling place of the pure neshamah, yet he has willfully delivered this holy substance into a place dominated by the filth of the Sitra Achara. The sin is even greater if he expended his seed in a place of defilement, such as in a menstruating woman, a gentile woman or someone otherwise forbidden to him by Torah law. If a man is not mindful of this sin and entices his evil inclination, especially by engaging in vulgarity, concerning him was it states, "And the wicked are like the surging sea" (Yeshayahu 57:20). For it is stated explicitly, "Er was evil in Hashem's eyes and Hashem killed him" — because he wasted his seed.

I will extract for you here that which is relevant to our topic from the text Nachalas Yehoshua, by Rabbi Yehoshua Heschel HaKohen, son of Rabbi Shlomo of Krakow, head of the court and dean of the yeshiva of the holy community of Boskewitz and later Rabbi of Rechnitz. He writes: It is written in Parashas Mishpatim, "Do not delay bringing melei'ascha and your dim'acha ; give Me the first born of your sons" (Shemos 22:28). Rashi explains that melei'ascha refers to the first fruits while dim'acha refers to the kohein 's portion. Nevertheless, he confesses that he does not know the etymology of the word dim'acha. In the tractate Terumah (4a), however, Rashi writes, "Dim'acha refers to the kohein 's portion. It is called this because it creates a forbidden mixture [medama'as] and is nullified by a hundred and one parts." Tosafos writes: "Rashi explains that dim'acha is the kohein 's portion because it creates a forbidden mixture and is nullified by a hundred and one parts. This does not seem correct, however, because that law is only of rabbinic origin. Rabbi Moshe of Ponto'iza explains that the kohein 's portion is called dim'acha because it applies to liquid produce, by contrast with the first fruits, which come only from dry produce." Perforce, Tosafos derives the word dim'acha from the word dima'os — "tears." [See Nesiv Meir and the Rekanti who also relate dim'acha to dimaa'os; "Do not delay" — just as teardrops fall from the eye.]

The Shach [Sifsei Kohen by Rabbi Mordechai HaKohen] on Parashas Ki Teitzei (55a) writes as follows: It is stated, "When a man has two wives, one beloved and the other hated, etc." (Devarim 21:15). This passage can be explained with reference to a man's wife and the wicked Lilis. These are the two "wives." And since only one man in a thousand is spared the sin of wasting seed the Torah warns that a man should at least guard that first drop. Thus, the verse continues, "And the firstborn should be to the hated one [i.e., his real wife]." This is in order that "on the day that he bequeaths to his sons" — i.e., the day of death — he will be able to overcome all the demons, spirits and liliths born from those droplets of wasted seed, which the Zohar (1:54b) calls, the "plagues among Adam's offspring" (II Shmuel 7:14). For when it is time for him to be buried these spirits will try to attach themselves to him but they will be unable to do so because his firstborn son will overcome them. This is the deeper meaning of the verse, "streams of water ran down from my eyes because they did not keep Your Torah" (Tehillim 119:136). Note that the verse does not say "because I did not keep Your Torah," but "because they did not keep Your Torah." That is, a man's eyes will themselves shed tears because of the harm they caused through gazing. For the eye sees and the heart desires, such that all of a man's deeds are caused by the vision of his eyes. This is what brings him to wasting seed. Tears, by contrast, are the rectification for wasting seed. For just as the seed originates in the brain, so do tears. Therefore, a man must pray specifically with tears. He must also shed tears when he mourns for the destruction of the Holy Temple or for an upright individual who has died.

It is related in the Zohar (2:178b; 3:60b) and in the writings of the Ari, z"l (Eitz Chaim, Sha'ar 49, 113b) that the two prostitutes of Shlomo's day (I Melachim 3:16) were actually the two female demons Machalas and Lilis. Machalas is accompanied by four hundred and seventy-eight camps, the numerical value of her name, while Lilis is accompanied by four hundred and eighty camps, the numerical value of her name. When a person rejoices in the performance of a commandment, he subdues Machalas and her cohorts. And when he mourns at a time that he is commanded to do so he subdues Lilis. I believe that this is the meaning of the verse, "It is better to go to a house of mourning than to a house of feasting" (Koheles 7b), for through mourning a man subdues two more camps than he does through rejoicing.

It is well known that the bringing of the first fruits was accompanied by great rejoicing. Thus, it is related in Bikkurim (3:3-4) that a flute led the procession while the Levites sang.

Therefore, I believe that it was for this reason that Scripture mentions melei'acha — the first fruits, which are brought with joy — and dim'acha — "tears." For by means of these two emotions a person subdues the two women, Machalas and Lilis, depriving them of the authority to lure him into sin. And if one succeeds in withstanding them it said, "Give Me the firstborn of your sons." That is, one's first drop of seed will then be delivered into the realm of holiness. That is why Scripture states shortly thereafter, "And you shall be to Me men of holiness" (Shemos 22:30). For whoever guards his sign of the covenant is called "holy." Therefore, whoever has blemished his sign of the covenant should shed tears while praying. Then he will be able to subdue those "plagues among Adam's offspring." For the Gates of Tears were never locked (Berachos 32b). King David also says, "Every night I cause my bed to float with tears; I cause my couch to melt" (Tehillim 6:7). He says further, "My tears were my bread, etc." (Tehillim 42:4).

The Ari, z"l, (Pri Eitz Chaim, Sha'ar Keriyas Shema ; Sha'ar HaKavanos 56b) warns that women must recite the bedtime Shema as well. For the Shema nullifies the "plagues among Adam's offspring." And just as men are commanded, in connection with the sin of wasting seed, that they must not fantasize in the daytime so that they should not come to defile themselves at night, so women are commanded not to engage in wicked fantasies. For the recitation of the Shema is a rectification for wasting seed. Of this it can be said that, "the words that emanate from a wise man's mouth are pleasing" (Koheles 10:12).

Alternatively, one can explain the verse, "When a man has two wives, one beloved, etc.," in this way: The "beloved wife" refers to Machalas, who appears to men arrayed in finery, continually engaged in dancing and laughter. The "hated wife" refers to the evil Lilis, who is perpetually immersed in wailing and weeping. The passage continues, "He may not give preference to ... the firstborn son who was born from his proper wife" (Devarim 21:16). (That is, if he stumbles with his first drop his son from his proper wife will not have the power to overcome the demons and spirits born from his wasted seed.) That is why one must be very careful to cling to his wife at the very least with his first drop. If a man has already stumbled in this iniquity, Heaven forbid, he should examine what we have written in Chapter Two and later on in Chapters Sixty-nine and Seventy. Then let him be swift to repent and all will be well with him, selah.

Chapter 69

One must know that this demon Machalas and her hosts, mentioned in the previous chapter, sometimes appear to a man even when he is awake. She comes to him in the form of a beautiful woman with a smiling countenance. She laughs with him and bears him children called, "foreign sons" (Hoshea 5:7) or "destructive sons" (Yeshayahu 1:4). And in the end, she kills him along with his offspring and his entire family. We have heard tell of just such an incident that took place in our own time. I will relate to you, my friend, how the matter fell out: It happened during the years 5441 and 5442. On a busy street in the holy community of Posen there was a solitary stone house with a cellar that was always kept locked and no man was allowed to enter. One day a certain young man did go in and about a quarter of an hour later the residents of the house found him lying dead on the threshold. No one could ascertain the reason for his death. About two years after the young man's death malignant spirits [chitzonim] began to frequent the outbuilding where all the domestic chores were done. Whenever anyone prepared food to place on the stove they would later find filled with dirt and ashes, rendering it unfit for consumption.

With time the spirits expanded their range, entering even into the main living quarters where they would take hold of the hangings and lanterns decorating the room and throw them to the ground. Still, they never harmed the residents physically. They merely caused them consternation. Eventually they started wandering freely throughout the house. The human residents were so filled with fear by this point that they had no choice but to move elsewhere. This was a source of great anguish to the holy community of Pozen and the citizenry took council together to decide on a course of action. First, they tried the strategies of the gentile priests, called yez viter. But when that failed to dislodge the spirits from the house, they sent a messenger to the famous Ba'al Shem ["Master of the Name"] of that generation, Rabbi Yoel Ba'al Shem of Zamusht.

As soon as Rabbi Yoel arrived he placed the spirits under oath using Divine names and compelled them to reveal why they had come to that house. For the spirits are not permitted to take up residence in settled areas but only in dilapidated houses or in the wilderness. The spirits replied that this house was rightfully theirs by Torah law, but they agreed to appear before the rabbinical court of Posen to present their case. A day or two later the judges of Posen went with Rabbi Yoel Ba'al Shem and took their seats in the court. Then a voice began addressing them, although they could not see any form. One of the spirits explained that this house formerly belonged to a man named So-and-so who was a smith. He used to cohabit with a certain female demon, who bore him "foreign sons" and "destructive sons." He had a human wife as well, who also bore him sons. But the smith was very much in love with the demon to the point that his soul was bound up with hers. Sometimes he was obliged to interrupt his prayers and leave the synagogue in order to fulfill the wishes of the demon.

One time the smith was leading the Seder on the first night of Passover, in accordance with Jewish custom everywhere, when suddenly he rose from the table to go to the outhouse. His wife said nothing but she immediately went after him to see what business he had there. Through a chink in the wall of the outhouse she saw that inside there was a luxurious room with a table set with vessels of silver and gold and a bed spread with beautiful coverings. In the bed she saw a beautiful naked woman to whom the smith was clinging firmly. Filled with fright the woman went home, her mind in turmoil. About a quarter of an hour later her husband returned to the Seder and she did not say a word to him about what she had seen.

The next day she went to speak to the illustrious Rabbi Sheftel (son of the Shelah) and related to him everything that had transpired. The rabbi sent for the smith who confessed that he had a foreign wife who was not of human stock. Then the rabbi composed an amulet containing holy names by which he compelled the smith to abandon his foreign wife, the malignant spirit. Sometime before the man's demise the demon came back to him weeping. "How could he abandon her and her children?" she asked. Then she smiled at him, kissing and hugging and cajoling him until he agreed to grant her and her offspring a portion in his estate, bequeathing to them the cellar. Years later Poland was immersed in a war, lasting from 5408 until 5418. In the course of the war the smith and all his heirs were killed and there was no one left to inherit the house. "Therefore," concluded the spirit, "we spirit are the true heirs, and we have a lawful portion in our father's estate."

The current owners of the house responded that they purchased the structure for the full price from the smith and his representatives. Moreover, spirits do not have the legal status of offspring. Finally, their mother the demon had compelled the smith to live with her against his will! Having heard the two sides, the court handed down its ruling. Indeed, the spirits had no case, nor did they have any share in the estate because their true dwelling place is in the wilderness, not in areas of human settlement. After the ruling was delivered Rabbi Yoel bound the spirits by oath to vacate the premises, including the cellar, and return to the forest and the wilderness. From this incident you have a clear demonstration that when a man clings to Lilis or to one of the cohorts of Machalas he uproots himself and his entire family from the world until no memory of him remains.

Therefore, a man must distance himself from immorality lest a demon come to him in the form of a woman and cling to him or his offspring, Heaven forbid, so that he will cause himself harm. Fortunate is the one who makes protective barriers for himself and adheres to the wife of his youth, who is likened to a grapevine. And fortunate is his soul, for he does not deliver his strength to foreign powers. In any event, a man must be careful not to waste his seed. And if this sin should overtake him against his will, Heaven forbid, let him immediately rectify the blemish through repentance. Then all will be will with him, selah.

Chapter 70

At the beginning of Parashas Tzav it is stated, "Command Aharon and his sons, saying, 'This is the law of the burnt offering, this is the burnt offering upon the fire'" (Vayikra 6:2). Rashi comments, "The word 'command' signifies nothing other than the urging of zeal, as Rabbi Shimon observed, 'It is especially necessary for Scripture to urge zeal in a place where there is financial loss.'"

This comment needs explanation. Why did Rashi cite this teaching of Rabbi Shimon specifically in connection with this verse? I believe this can be understood in light of the Gemara's teaching that the fixed prayers were established corresponding to the daily sacrifices. Thus, the morning service corresponds to the morning sacrifice, the mussaf service to the additional festival offerings, the afternoon service to the afternoon sacrifice and the evening service to the burning of the limbs and fats that were not consumed during the day, having fallen from the altar. For the Torah admonishes the Kohanim to return these limbs and fats back on top of the altar, for which reason it was necessary for the fire to burn upon the altar all through the night. The concept behind this is explained in the Zohar (Parashas Terumah, 130a). There it is taught that the smoke from the main body of the sacrifices used to ascend in a straight column but that rising from the limbs and fats that had fallen from the altar did not. When these limbs were returned to the altar in the evening the column of smoke would bend towards the north, the dwelling place of the Sitra Achara. It was from this column of smoke that the forces of impurity drew their sustenance, at which time they were unable to lodge accusations against Israel.

When this column of smoke inclined to the north it would enter a certain hole there. All the bands of the Sitra Achara knew about this smoke and would gather round. One of them was appointed over all of them and they were accompanied by sixty-thousand myriad encampments of shells of impurity. All of these would gather together in the north and stand beside a certain portal called, "Happenstance [keri]." It is from that opening that all the accusers of Israel would emanate. Concerning this was it stated, "And if you walk with me by happenstance, then I will also walk with you with the wrath of happenstance" (Vayikra 26:21-28). These are the same shells of impurity that go out to fly and hover about at night, appearing to men and engaging them in levity until they have an emission of seed [keri]. The column of smoke mentioned above provides sustenance for these accusers so that they will stay in their place and not spread about the world. It was corresponding to this that the evening service was instituted. And since these bands of accusers come from an eirev rav [a "mixed multitude"], the corresponding prayer is called tefilas erev [the "Evening Prayer"], to weaken the above-mentioned forces. Extreme concentration is required during the Evening Prayer in order to weaken the power of the Sitra Achara, especially during this bitter exile.

Now I must give you some additional background by way of introduction. In the work Shnei Luchos HaBris (Sha'ar HaOsiyos, Kedushas Achilah, 53a) the illustrious author Rabbi Yeshayah Horwitz, z"l, warns that a person must treat crumbs of bread with great care, by analogy with the limbs that fall from the altar. Just as the Kohanim were admonished to take care that the impure forces did not benefit from these limbs directly but only from the column of smoke inclining toward the north, so must one take care not to throw breadcrumbs on the floor. This is particularly true of the crumbs from the initial slice after the recitation of the blessing, hamotzi lechem min ha'aretz. These crumbs in particular correspond to the limbs of the sacrifices. They are called terumas ma'aser [the kohein's portion of the tithe] and are the holiest of the holy [see what I have written I my extensive work, Ofer HaAyalim, Parashas Tzav, and you will be gratified].

Whoever is not careful with crumbs of bread will be set upon by Lilis. The numerical value of her name is 480, the same as the value of pas ["bread"]. She will come with 480 of her forces and settle upon that person's house, bringing him to a state of poverty. This is what the author of the Mesorah meant by his comment on the verse, "This is the law of the burnt offering, this [היא] is the burnt offering." He observes, "It is written הוא ["this" — masculine] but we read it היא ["this" — feminine]." On the surface this is very surprising. However, in light of what I have written it makes perfect sense and teaches an important insight. היא העולה ["this — feminine — is the burnt sacrifice"] refers to the wicked Lilis, who desires to benefit from the crumbs of bread [pas], since the acronym for the numerical value of her name is taf [תף the reverse of pas פת]. She is the one appointed over poverty and indigence. הוא העולה ["this — masculine — is the burn sacrifice"] refers to the actual limbs of the sacrifice that were offered upon the altar. Now we can understand why Rashi cited Rabbi Shimon's dictum specifically in connection with this verse. Rashi was also puzzled why the word "this" is written in the masculine but pronounced in the feminine. He concluded that it must be for the reason explained above. That is, the masculine הוא העולה, refers to the sacrifice, while the feminine, היא העולה, refers to the crumbs of bread. Therefore, he quoted Rabbi Shimon's teaching, that one must be more careful when there is a risk of financial loss, since Lilis is the one appointed over poverty and indigence.

This is illustrated by an episode in Chullin (105b). There Abaye remarks, "To begin with I thought that people sweep up the crumbs merely for the sake of neatness. But the master [i.e., Rabbah bar Nachmani] told me that it was because leaving them on the floor opens one up to poverty." The Gemara relates that the Prince of Poverty once trailed a certain fellow but he was unable to overcome him because he was extremely careful about his crumbs. One day the man ate bread in the middle of a field and the crumbs fell upon the grass in a way that made it impossible to gather them up. The Prince of Poverty thought to himself, "Now he will surely fall into my hands!" But after the man finished eating he took out a trowel and uprooted the entire clump of grass and threw it into the river. Afterwards he heard a voice saying, "Alas, alas! He has banished me from my home!" I believe that this is why Rashi cited Rabbi Shimon's principle in connection with this passage about the burnt offering where there is this discrepancy between the way it is written, הוא העולה, and the way it is read, היא העולה. Since the way it is read alludes to Lilis, the one appointed over poverty, he notes that it is especially necessary for Scripture to urge zeal in a place where there is a risk of financial loss. For whoever is not careful with regard to his crumbs but merely throws them away is liable to come to poverty and indigence. Therefore, Rashi cited this dictum in no context other than that of this commandment. This explanation should be easy to comprehend and is very apt, and in my humble opinion it is the true one.

Thus, a person should be very careful not to cast away breadcrumbs, especially those from the initial slice after the recitation of the blessing. For these have the sanctity of the limbs of the sacrifices. It also seems to me, based on the above, that Lilis and her 480 camps are appointed over emissions of seed [keri]. Therefore, a man must pray that he be spared from wasting seed. And let him flee from wicked thoughts that cause this to happen to a man.

Come and see a worthy strategy that I offer to whoever fears Hashem and trembles at his word, to be saved from the iniquity of wasting seed: I have already mentioned one strategy in the second chapter. Namely, that before a man goes to sleep he should summon up the image of his father. A second strategy is that he should fashion for himself a ring of pure silver and engrave upon it the following holy names that I have received from the saintly Rabbi Yoel Ba'al Shem of Zamusht. They are: ש-די צ-מרכד א-נקתם פ-סתם פ-ספסים ד-יונסים י-והך א-דני. After he has made the ring and engraved it, let him immerse it in a mikveh of forty seah. Then he can bear it with him and go wherever he wishes, confident that he will be spared from this iniquity. He will dwell and lie down securely upon his bed without any mishap or sin.

Chapter 71

It is stated, "And Calev came to Chevron" (Bamidbar 13:22). Rashi explains that Kaleiv went to pray at the Tomb of the Patriarchs that he should be saved from the sin of the spies. Based on this incident there has spread throughout Israel the worthy custom of visiting the grave of one's forebear on the anniversary of his death. And if one is not in the vicinity of the grave at the time of the yahrzeit one should go to another Jewish cemetery to pray, for this causes all the souls in Gan Eden to be aroused, since the entire earth is a single unit. For the Holy One Blessed is He has decreed for Israel's sake that the nefesh (the lowest aspect of the soul) of a righteous person should remain near the cemetery. This is in order that they will hear the supplications of those who come to pray at the grave site. Thus, whoever has a sorrow of any sort should go to the graves of his forebears or other righteous individuals and reveal his sorrow there. For when the nefesh hears the living pouring out their sorrows it ascends to the ruach (the second aspect of the soul) in Gan Eden (Zohar, Part II, 141b). Then the ruach ascends to the chamber of Gan Eden in which the holy neshamos (the third aspect of the soul) dwell and arouses them to come to the Land of Israel to prostrate themselves before the Throne of Glory and pray on behalf of the living.

However, if the neshamah did not yet merit a place in the upper Gan Eden but remains outside the holy partition, wandering back and forth, the ruach and nefesh are also condemned to wander to and fro. And every time they enter the grave and behold the body covered with worms, its mouth agape, swarming with worms, and the intestines filled with maggots and worms, then the neshamah mourns over it, as it is stated, "And his soul will mourn over him" (Iyov 14:22). But none of this is the case if the body was holy and pure. Then the disintegration of the flesh is affected by the soil alone and it immediately turns to dust and ashes without enduring the agony caused by the worms and maggots. This is the reward of the body. As for the reward of the neshamah, it immediately ascends to the upper Gan Eden while the ruach ascends to the lower Gan Eden.

Every Shabbos and Rosh Chodesh the ruach ascends to the upper Gan Eden where it receives the illumination and pure radiance of the neshamah. With this it descends to its place at the conclusion of the day. Afterwards the nefesh ascends and receives some of that illumination and radiance that the ruach brought with it from the neshamah in the upper Gan Eden. Then the nefesh descends and enters the grave where it takes the image of the body as it was when it was alive in this world and through this it clothes itself in a body, precisely as it was when the person was alive. In this manner the righteous stand upon their graves uttering words of praise and acknowledgement to God, may His name be blessed, for the lofty illumination of the neshamah, their faces radiating with great luminance. At that time, they sing many songs and praises, precisely as they originally appeared, their bones knitted together and fleshed out like an actual body. If the living were allowed to perceive them, they would see them at the conclusion of every Shabbos, Rosh Chodesh and Yom Tov in bodily form, standing upon their graves reciting songs and praises. This is the meaning of the verse, "All my bones will declare, Hashem, 'Who is like You!" (Tehillim 35:10). Note that it is not stated that they "say" but that they "will say." This is an allusion to the reciting of songs and praises by the dead at the conclusion of every Shabbos, Yom Tov and Rosh Chodesh.

It has also been passed down to us through the writings and texts of earlier generations that even while a person is still alive his neshamah arouses his heart regarding the word of Hashem. You should know that whenever a good thought suddenly enters a person's heart — such as joy over or love of words of Torah or a commandment — it is a favorable time for prayer. The prayer that one utters at that time will immediately enter the palace of the King of the kings of kings, the Holy One Blessed is He. And if on occasion a person experiences a moment or period that his soul is filled with melancholy, it is very likely that some evil decree has been issued against him, Heaven forbid, or upon a member of his family or upon the entire world. In most cases when decrees are issued heralds are then dispatched to arouse people's hearts. For a person's heart knows the bitterness of his soul, even if he does not hear anything with his ears. Therefore, if a person is slothful and fails to pray immediately, the decree becomes a reality.

For this reason, let him arouse himself to the best of his ability to pray with tears before the Holy One Blessed is He. This is elaborated upon in the Zohar, Parashas Vayikra (15a): One day Rabbi Shimon ben Yochai was sitting in the gate of Lod. He lifted his eyes and saw the sun shining. Then its light became blocked, after which it again shone and again was blocked and again shone and again was blocked. This recurred three times. Meanwhile the light dimmed and the sun became black and green. Rabbi Shimon ben Yochai said to his son Rabbi Elazar, "Follow me and let us see what this means. Surely an evil decree has been issued and the Holy One Blessed is He desires to inform us of it. For whenever a decree is issued On High it is suspended for three days until the Holy One Blessed is He has informed the righteous, as it is stated, "For

Kav HaYashar

Hashem, God does not do anything without revealing His secret to His servants the prophets" (Amos 3:7).

While they were walking, they entered a certain vineyard. There they saw a snake approaching them with his mouth open, moving eagerly over the ground and through the dust. Rabbi Shimon ben Yochai grabbed the head of the snake with his hands and noticed that it was muttering something with its tongue. [That is, it was signaling that the primordial snake, the samech mem and the wicked Lilis should be awakened to invoke harsh judgment upon the world.] Rabbi Shimon ben Yochai addressed it, "Snake, go and tell the one who is called the Supernal Snake that Rabbi Shimon ben Yochai is in the world." He then inserted the head of the snake into a hole in the ground and said, "I decree by the Divine Name that just as the earthly snake has returned to a hole in the ground, so shall the Supernal Snake return to the hole of the great chasm." Afterwards Rabbi Shimon and his son Rabbi Elazar prayed softly and while they were praying, they heard a voice saying, "O heralds of the decrees, return to your places, for the gang of thugs is not to dwell in the world because Rabbi Shimon ben Yochai has annulled the decree." [That is, they heard a Heavenly voice addressing the agents appointed to bring calamity into the world and ordering them to return to their dwelling place, i.e., the desert, because Rabbi Shimon ben Yochai was still in this world, protecting it from all affliction with his merit.]

Know further that even though we have no one in our generation on a par with Rabbi Shimon ben Yochai, who was able to annul evil decrees, nevertheless Hashem's mercies extend to every generation. Therefore, as soon as a decree is made On High, Heaven spare us, emissaries are immediately dispatched to reveal it through the mouths of little boys and girls, who prophesy without realizing it. The Holy One Blessed is He also arouses the hearts of the upright and God-fearing to pray on behalf of their generation. This arousal comes to them from within. The moment some evil is stirred up angels of judgment go about proclaiming it and arrows of judgment are dispersed, bringing enfeeblement or some other ill effect into the world, may we be spared. At such times a person should try to minimize the time he spends out of doors. For the Zohar warns in Parashas Noach (69a) that when license has been granted to the destroyer, its agents have permission to strike those who are found walking about the streets and markets, Heaven forbid. Therefore, one should pray to be delivered from all evil, as we have mentioned above.

A person should also refrain from mentioning his name when praying because this induces the Heavenly court take notice of him and examine his deeds and accusers may be found to cause him harm, Heaven forbid. The Zohar (ibid. 69b) brings a proof to this from what the prophet Elisha said to the Shunamis: [Elisha asked,] "Do you have need to be spoken of to the king?" (Melachim II: 4:13). This refers to the Holy One Blessed is He, for the day [that Elisha spoke to her] was Rosh HaShanah, when the Holy One Blessed is He is called the "Holy King" and "King of Judgment." "And she said, 'I dwell among my people'" That is, [she said,] "I do not wish for you to should mention my name, lest they examine me in particular. Rather, "I dwell among my people." Come and see [a proof to this,] for all the while that Divine wrath was in the world, Noach's name was not mentioned. But once the judgment was over it is stated, "And God remembered Noach." That is, only then did He bring Noach's name to mind. From here we learn that a person is judged on a balance scale and every good deed creates a defender while every bad deed creates an accuser.

Fortunate is the one who loves his soul more than his body, who treats this world as secondary and the World to Come as principle and who has his eye on his end every day, recalling that the end of a human being is death. He will surely succeed through his Torah and good deeds in entering the World to Come.

Chapter 72

Our Sages have said that the world is sustained by the breath of children in the school of their master (Shabbos 119b). From this one can infer the magnitude of the reward awaiting the teacher. Wherever children are found studying with their master, there the Shechinah is to be found. Thus it is taught in Zohar Chadash (Parashas Lech Lecha, 32a):

"When Rabbi Shimon came to observe the children studying with their master he would say, 'I have come to see the face of the Shechinah.'" The words, "When Rabbi Shimon came to observe..." indicate that it was the custom of men of deeds, whenever they were free of their business, to go to wherever the teachers were sitting in order to greet the Shechinah. For this reason, a person must be circumspect whenever he goes to such a place, for there the "mother" — i.e., the Shechinah — crouches upon her chicks and spreads her wings over the young of the flocks. The breath from the children's mouths pierces the firmaments and the intervening atmospheres. The teacher must also take it to heart that the Shechinah dwells with him, practicing his craft faithfully, without deception, for it is Heaven's work. And let care be taken that the room where they sit with their students is clean and pure and free of all filth, in fulfillment of the verse, "Let your camp be holy" (Devarim 23:15), for it is called the "camp of the Shechinah." The Zohar relates (ibid.): Rabbi Elazar son of Rabbi Shimon ben Yochai once had an encounter with Eliyahu in which the latter appeared to him in the form of an elderly man walking with a child. The man was attempting to cross a large river to reach the other side. Rabbi Elazar said to him, "Old man! Put the child on one of my shoulders and you sit on the other and I will carry both of you across this wide river." The old man replied, "Are you not the leader of the generation? Therefore, you cannot carry us across the river!" [That is, "I see that you are a scholar and have therefore been weakened by your studies." For the Torah is called tushiyah, which means, "weakening," because it weakens a man's strength — (Sanhedrin 26b.) Rabbi Elazar replied, "Old man! Old man! If I were to grab you and this child with my two hands, I could bear you a distance of half a mile beyond the river! As for your observation that the Torah is called tushiyah because it weakens a man's strength, it is also called 'healing.' Thus, is it stated, 'It shall be a healing to your stomach, etc.' (Mishlei 3:8), and it states, 'And to all his flesh a healing' (ibid. 4:20). I have imbibed of the Torah for many days as one who imbibes a tonic and my strength has been fortified thereby!" So, he carried them across on his shoulders, after which he proclaimed, "Old man! Old man! My strength is great both in this world and the next and for the sake of this child I will not abandon you. I will not allow the Prince of Gehinnom to touch you but I will bring you into the World to Come with the great power that I have there." Then the old man said to him, "Rabbi! Rabbi! Your strength is indeed great in this world and in the World to Come. You resemble the sun, etc."

The reward for teaching children is very great and their breath has many beneficial effects, including the ability to avert terrible decree. Thus the Sages comment (Midrash Bereishis Rabbah 65:20) on the verse, "The voice is the voice of Yaakov" (Bereishis 27:22), that when the voices of children are heard chirping in the study halls and synagogues of Yaakov, the "hands of Eisav" cannot bring upon us evil decrees, Heaven forbid.

Therefore, we must pray on behalf of the schoolchildren and babes and ask that the Holy One Blessed is He shelter them beneath His wings and protect them from every evil eye, and from every illness and mishap. And let them also be spared from the strangulating disease called askara that comes upon children when the light of the moon is deficient. Thus me'oros, the word for the "lights" in Bereishis 1:14, is abridged [i.e., missing a vav] so that it can be read me'eiras, "a curse" [indicating that when the moon's light is deficient it brings a curse upon the children].

And when the time comes to deliver the child to the charge of the school so that he may study with his teacher, the father should rise early and awaken the child and then take him personally to the teacher's house. Even if the father is elderly or a man of stature or a communal leader or rabbi, let him not be ashamed to bring his son to the teacher's house for the first time. And let him give praise and thanksgiving to the Holy One Blessed is He for granting him the merit of bringing his son under the wings of the Shechinah. Along the way either the father or the mother should cover the child with his garment so that he will not gaze upon any impure creature. Then after the child has been brought to the teacher's house he should be delivered into the teacher's lap, in keeping with the verse, "As a pedagogue bears a suckling child" (Bamidbar 11:12), and the verse, "And I have accustomed Efraim to take them upon his arms" (Hoshea 11:3).

A chart on which the alphabet has been written should be brought so that the teacher may read from it the names of the letters: alef, beis, gimmel, daled, hei, vav, etc. Then in reverse order: tav, shin, reish, kuf, tzadi, peh, ayin, samech, nun, mem, lamed, kaf, yud, tes, ches, zayin, vav, hei, daled, gimmel, beis, alef. The child should be prompted to say the names of all the letters after the teacher and the teacher should read the verse, "Moshe commanded us the Torah, etc." (Devarim 33:4). Then he should read the first verse of Vayikra while the child repeats each word after him. Finally, a bit of honey should be spread upon the chart so that the child can lick the honey from the letters. Afterwards the father should take the child home and seat him in a place from which he can see no impure creature and it is preferable that no menstruating woman touches the child that entire day. It is also proper for the child's parents to fast that day and to pray to God in Heaven that he should be successful in his Torah studies, that he should acquire awe of Heaven and perform good deeds throughout a long life. Towards evening, when the fast is over, they should make a feast for the poor and give charity in accordance with their means. Then the father can be confident that the child will be God-fearing. Let this warning be sufficient.

How great is the reward of those childless individuals who raise orphans in their homes and watch over them, guiding them in the straight path as if they had born them! If it is possible for a person to house Torah scholars in his home and support them so that his house will be filled with Torah, it goes without saying that he will be successful and fortunate will be his lot. It is related that when Rashi left his home among the exiles of France and went into exile he stayed in the home of a certain wealthy communal leader (Shalsheles HaKabbalah, Rashi, 49a). His host pleaded with him to stay longer and continue his studies there and in recognition of the rich man's pleas and requests Rashi composed a work that he called The Parnas [a term for a communal leader] in his host's honor. His intention in doing was to magnify and honor all who perform such acts of lovingkindness.

Fortunate is the man who chooses and sets aside a suitable place in his home for study, for the Holy One Blessed is He frequents a home in which Torah is studied. Great will be the honor of such a home in the future when the exiles of Israel are gathered in. For at that time all the houses of study and the synagogues will also be gathered to the Land of Israel and they shine with glorious beauty, Amein.

Chapter 73

The Sages have said that, "nighttime was only created for study" (Eruvin 65a), and great is the honor of the home in which the sound of Torah study is heard. The concept is as follows: While a man sleeps his soul departs from him and testifies in the Heavenly court regarding everything that he did that day, after which it is judged for good or bad. For the Heavenly court sits in judgment at night. Thus, it is related in the Zohar (1:92a) that during the first hour of the evening, when the sun has just gone into its place, an appointed angel issues a proclamation that passes through twelve gates. These are the gates that open when the sun goes forth to shine and close when it sets, remaining closed all night. Then all the angels that are appointed to watch over the world gather On High. The Gates of Mercy are sealed and the courts of judgment awaken. The angels that are appointed over the sounding of the trumpets arise and blow their horns at midnight as a signal for all the angels to arise, for this is a time that is designated especially for singing songs of praise. The angels arise immediately and stand in fear and trepidation, in holiness and purity, singing and playing before the Holy One Blessed is He.

At the beginning of the night while people sleep, their souls leave them to testify in Heaven regarding the deeds they performed during the day and to face judgment for them. Then at midnight a fierce wind begins blowing from the north, and an appointed angel arises and strikes it with his staff, causing it to calm down. Then the Holy One Blessed be He arouses Himself to go and delight with the righteous. This is the meaning of the verse, "She [i.e., the Shechinah] who sits in the gardens [as well as the] companions [i.e., the righteous] are listening to your voice [i.e., the sound of your Torah study], let me hear it, etc." (Shir HaShirim 8:13). The Holy One Blessed is He draws a thread of lovingkindness over those who arise at night to serve Him, protecting them from injury and mishap. Concerning them was it stated, "By day Hashem will command His kindness, and in the night His resting place will be with me" (Tehillim 42:9). Undoubtedly a thread of lovingkindness will be drawn over them and they will enjoy great illumination from the saplings in Gan Eden, from the place that is called, "the Ancient River" [Nachal Kedumim]. Their portion will be prepared and waiting for them upon their deaths in a place of repose and joy. Fortunate are they and fortunate is their lot.

Therefore, do not take lightly the matter of studying at night. Our predecessors invoked ingenious strategies to know when it was midnight so that they could rise and engage in study. This was in order to unite with the righteous in Gan Eden who hear Torah at that hour directly from the Holy One Blessed is He. Thus, it is related in the Zohar (ibid. 92b-96b): Rabbi Aba and Rabbi Yaakov were traveling from Tiberius to the village of Tarsha. Along the way they stopped at an inn. When they wished to go to sleep, Rabbi Aba asked the host, "Is there a rooster here?" "Why do you ask?" he inquired. "Because we must rise at midnight," Rabbi Aba replied. "I do not need a rooster," the innkeeper explained. "I have another sign. I fill this balance that is beside my bed with water, which drips out slowly until precisely at midnight all the water is gone and the scale tips over, making a sound that is heard throughout the house. Then I know that it is midnight." [He had an instrument near his bed in the form of a wheel from which water dripped, just like the alarm clocks used in Europe. As long as even a little water remained, the wheel would stay in its place. But as soon as the last drop had gone out it would revolve and fall with a crash that would awaken whoever was sleeping in that room.]

There was a certain old man residing at the inn who used to rise every night at midnight to engage in study. It was for him that the innkeeper had devised this instrument. Rabbi Aba said, "Blessed is the Merciful One who directed us to this place!" And when midnight came, they all arose to study… The innkeeper related to his two sons the idea mention earlier that the Holy One Blessed is He enters Gan Eden at midnight to delight with the righteous. He added, "It was with this in mind that David declared, 'I will arise at midnight to acknowledge You.'" Rabbi Aba said, "Surely you have spoken well. But from where do you know this?" He explained, "So did I learn from another elder." The innkeeper also told them, "At the beginning of the first hour of the night all the accusers of the lower world awaken and go wandering about the world. Then exactly at midnight the Holy One Blessed is He arouses Himself to enter Gan Eden, at which time these accusers are not to be found. "All the proceedings of the Heavenly court are carried out only at midnight, as it is stated [regarding Avraham's battle with the four kings], "And the night was divided against them" (Bereishis 14:15). And it is stated [regarding the striking of the first born in Egypt], "And it was at midnight" (Shemos 12:29). We find this to be the case in a number of other places in the Torah as well. Thus, King David called the Holy One Blessed is He, 'Midnight,' literally…." [The idea, for the initiated, is that Nukba is called "the attribute of night," and it comes out from behind the chest, which is the midpoint. Therefore, David referred to the Holy One Blessed is He as "Midnight." Thus, the Zohar was very careful with its words, because He is literally Midnight. This is a great secret that should not be revealed except to the circumspect and the initiated.] The kingship of the House of David is called "the attribute of night," therefore David used to rise at midnight, as it is stated, "I will arise at midnight to thank You for Your righteous laws." Those who are capable of understanding on their own or who have received a tradition regarding these matters will grasp the meaning of the word's "law" and "righteousness." It is from here that judgments emanate. That is the allusion contained in the Sages' principle that "the law of the kingship is the law" [Dina deMalchusa dina]. After this Rabbi Aba and Rabbi Yaakov came and kissed him….

In the meantime, the innkeeper's young son came and asked, "Why is it written, 'mid night'?" [It should have been sufficient to write the word "night," since the verse is referring to Nukba which is called, "the attribute of night." The addition of the word "mid" makes it sound as if it is not completely the attribute of night but only half way.] Rabbi Aba answered, "We have already learned that the kingship of Heaven is aroused at midnight." [That is, from this it should already be clear why the verse says "midnight," for the intention is to the Holy One Blessed is He who is called "Midnight," as was explained above. This is in order to inform us that at midnight the kingship of Heaven, which is called Ze'eir is revealed.] The child said, "I have heard another explanation." So, the child began his discourse, "Since the influences of lovingkindness are revealed at midnight, while at the same time there is also an influence of judgment and mercy, therefore it is called "midnight." For it is only half judgment since during the second half of the night His face shines from the side of lovingkindness." Rabbi Aba stood up and placed his hands upon the child's head and blessed him. Then Rabbi Aba began his discourse, revealing wonderful secrets regarding circumcision. Among other things he explained that when the father brings his son to have his foreskin removed the Holy One Blessed is He calls to His company, saying, "See, My company, what My beloved children are doing in the world!" At that moment the prophet Eliyahu traverses the entire world in four swoops to attend the circumcision. For this reason, it is taught that one must prepare a chair for Eliyahu. Then he ascends and testifies before the Holy One Blessed is He that Israel continues to fulfill the covenant of Avraham...

In the meantime, it had become light and Rabbi Aba and Rabbi Yaakov arose and prepared to depart. But the innkeeper said to them, "You must complete the matter that you were engaged in at midnight!" "What is that?" they inquired. "Tomorrow you must greet the Master of the Covenant [i.e., Eliyahu], for tomorrow we celebrate the circumcision of my son and my wife requests that you remain." Rabbi Aba said, "This is a mitzvah request and we will also merit beholding the face of the Shechinah! Let us remain." So they waited that entire day. That night the innkeeper gathered all his companions and after the feast they engaged in study and no one slept. The Zohar explains that on the night before the circumcision special guarding is required to prevent the malignant spirits from harming either the mother or the newborn. Therefore, it is customary to read and study all night long. [This is called in Yiddish, vein nacht, or in Poland, vach nacht.] Through this they fulfill what is stated (Esther 8:16): "For the Jews there was light" — this refers to Torah; "and rejoicing" — this refers to circumcision; "and honor" — this refers to tefillin (Megillah 16b).

The Zohar then explains at length how the saintly innkeeper gathered his companions, all of whom were scholars, to spend the night immersed in study. We should do the same on the night before a circumcision, for Torah study protects and saves from all injury and from every type of harm in the world. Afterwards the innkeeper said, "I request that each of you reveal a novel insight." So, each of them revealed a novel insight about circumcision. He made this request because he knew these words of Torah would be of great benefit in the protection of both infant and mother. The Zohar also relates that engaging in study during the night of the vein nacht causes Eliyahu to appear, accompanied by great lights of Divine favor, which in turn cause Israel much benefits and numerous salvations. Afterwards Rabbi Aba said to his host and to that elder, "Since you are such great scholars, why do you remain here?" The host said, "If the birds were to abandon their place they would not know where to go, as it is stated, "Like a bird wandering from its nest, so is a man who wanders from his place" (Mishlei 27:8). Similarly, if we were to abandon this place, which is prepared for us to study in, we do not know where we would find a place to settle where we would be able to study. For this place is suited for us to study in and it has caused us to merit Torah.

"This is our custom. Every midnight we engage in study until the morning. Then when morning comes, the fragrance of the field and the rivers of water illuminate the Torah for us, causing it to settle in our hearts. It is a decree from Heaven that we must live in this place. How many princes of the Torah and mighty warriors [in the battle of Torah] have departed [i.e., they were stricken down by plague] because they failed to engage in study! But since that time, we have toiled in nothing but Torah day and night and this place helps us." And so, they remained sitting there until dawn. When it began to be light, they told the children to go out and see if it was yet daybreak, after which each of them would expound a novel insight. So, the children went out and saw that it was indeed daylight. One of the children said, "Today fire will come down from Heaven." Another said, "It will be in this very house." A third said, "There is an elder here who is destined to be consumed by fire." "May the Merciful One spare us!" Rabbi Aba exclaimed. But then he fell silent, unable to speak. At last he said, "The plans of the Heavenly authorities have been apprehended on earth!" [That is, the children knew that fire was destined to descend upon that house.] And so, did the matter come to be. That very day the companions beheld the face of Shechinah and were surrounded by fire [i.e., the fire of the Shechinah] and Rabbi Aba's face flashed like fire out of rejoicing in the Torah.

It was taught: That entire day none of them went out of the house, to which was attached a pillar of smoke. They rejoiced in the novel insights that were revealed as if they had received the Torah from Mount Sinai that very day. As they were bringing the infant to the synagogue, they heard a voice. It was that of the prophet Eliyahu reciting the verse, "Fortunate is the one whom You choose and draw close that he may dwell in Your courtyards; may we be satiated with the goodness of Your House, the holy place of Your Sanctuary" (Tehillim 65:5). This verse contains deep esoteric allusions, for it contains forty-two letters corresponding to the forty-two letter Name, the meaning of which may only be revealed to the circumspect. It also contains ten words, corresponding to which the Zohar teaches that when it is recited at the time of a circumcision the infant is crowned with ten canopies that will await him in the World to Come.

Afterwards one of the children began a discourse, "It is taught: 'Whoever offers his son as a sacrifice [i.e., through circumcision] is credited as if he offered up all the sacrifices in the world to the Holy One Blessed Is He.' For this reason one must prepare an altar in a vessel filled with dirt in order to perform the circumcision beside it. This is reckoned by the Holy One Blessed is He as if he offered upon it a burnt sacrifice and it gave off a savory smell...

"For this reason, fortunate is the lot of one who makes this offering in joy before the Holy One Blessed is He. Let him rejoice that entire day." Rabbi Aba said, "Fortunate are you in this world and the next. Concerning you was it stated, 'And as for you who cling to Hashem your God, all of you are alive this day' (Devarim 4:4)." So, they rejoiced that entire day a rejoicing of good deeds and Torah.

The Zohar relates that the infant that was circumcised on that occasion was Rav Idi ben Yaakov, one of the Sages in the Talmud. Rabbi Aba blessed him and then departed. When Rabbi Aba returned to Rabbi Shimon ben Yochai he was afraid to relate to him everything that he had heard from these saintly men and children mentioned above, lest he cause them to be punished. [That is, lest he decree that they be forced to leave their village so that their Torah will be more widely disseminated and the multitude will learn from them.] When Rabbi Aba finally revealed to Rabbi Shimon ben Yochai all that had transpired, he chided, "You knew so many worthwhile teachings and did not reveal them to me? I decree that for the next thirty days you will forget everything you learn! For it is stated, "Do not withhold goodness from its owners…" (Mishlei 3:27).

Therefore, a man must be careful to rise at midnight to serve his Creator and to engage in prayer and study, each according to his understanding. And let him make study his regular occupation and business a sideline. And if he merits a son let him conduct himself as I have written above. For it is no small matter to save a Jewish soul and to connect Israel with the Shechinah, as it is stated, "And as for you who cling to Hashem your God, you are all alive this day!" (Devarim 4:4). Then their righteousness will endure forever, Amein.

Chapter 74

It is related in Zohar Chadash, Parashas Noach (26b): Rabbi Elazar and his father-in-law Rabbi Yose were traveling from Usha to Lud. Rabbi Yose said to Rabbi Elazar, "Did you happen to hear from your father, Rabbi Shimon ben Yochai, what is meant by the verse, 'And Yaakov went on his way and angels of God met him' (Bereishis 32:2)? Who were these angels?" "I do not know…," he replied. While they were yet traveling, they noticed a certain cave and heard a voice saying, "There were two fawns of a gazelle that brought Me pleasure. They were the holy camp that met Yaakov and then went before him." Rabbi Elazar became extremely agitated and fearful. "Master of the Universe!" he said, "Is this Your way? It would have been better had we not heard this, for now that we have heard it, we still do not know who they were!"

Then a miracle occurred and they heard a voice saying, "They were Avraham and Yitzchak."

Rabbi Elazar fell upon his face, whereupon he beheld the image of his father. Rabbi Elazar told him, "I asked who the angels were and they answered me that they were Avraham and Yitzchak… In other words, the souls of Avraham and Yitzchak came to lead the way for Yaakov as he fled from Lavan the Aramean. And even though Yitzchak was still alive at the time, nevertheless, at the time that he was bound upon the altar his soul left him and ascended to Heaven where it became attached to the soul of Avraham. Then the two of them together went before Yaakov. This is the meaning of the verse, "The God of my father, the God of Avraham and the fear of Yitzchak, was with me" (Bereishis 31:42). Rabbi Shimon then explained that Yaakov was not the only one to be joined by the souls of the righteous. In fact, they come to every God-fearing person to save him from thoughts of sin and needless to say from actual sin. But if a man entertains wicked thoughts, whether in town, in the field or at home, a malignant spirit called ChNYH comes to him. It is appointed over all those who entertain wicked or foreign thoughts while traveling. This malignant spirit clings to the person and does not separate from him until it has led him into a serious transgression. This imparts a blemish to his soul, on account of our many sins, as a result of which he will be filled with regret until the end of his days. Nevertheless, it is a loss than cannot be made good. Know, therefore, that wherever you go you will be joined by emissaries who will further your thoughts, whether for bad or for good.

Afterwards Rabbi Elazar asked his father Rabbi Shimon, "What is our station in the World to Come?" He replied, "I and you will delight together with David, king of Israel." Then Rabbi Elazar arose and while he was standing their Rabbi Yose noticed that his face was beaming like the sun. "Did you hear a novel insight?" he inquired. "No," Rabbi Elazar replied, "but fortunate are the righteous who unite with the souls of the righteous, as it is stated, "For He will command His angels on your behalf, to guard you in all your ways" (Tehillim 91:11).

Therefore, mortal man, for the sake of Hashem, God of Israel, and for the sake of your pure soul that was carved out from beneath the

Throne of Glory, see to your ways and have the wisdom to mend them. Avert your eyes from beholding evil and accustom yourself to gazing upon holy things, as we have already discussed in Chapter Two. And do not entertain envious thoughts about the possessions of others. Then you will be spared from theft and from ill-gotten gains. Conduct yourself according to the proper priorities even if you possess great wealth. And do not pamper yourself excessively with your means. Do not eat or drink to excess but recall at all times that you will one day be made to give an accounting for every word that comes out of your mouth and needless to say for your good and bad deeds. If you suppose that at that time you will be able to conceal things or deny them, know that there are ready witnesses — that is, the angels that accompany a person at all times. They will come and testify regarding the exact day and location in which the iniquity or good deed was performed. Then they will come and strike him on the face, saying, "Wicked one! How dare you deny and speak falsely before your Creator? Do you not know that everything is revealed before Him? He knows all of a person's thoughts and He examines the heart and probes the kidneys!"

Therefore, one must realize in general that the Holy One Blessed is He holds a person responsible even for his casual comments, not to mention for his deeds. He has many agents and many harsh punishments with which to requite those who do not live in accordance with His will. Therefore, let every good deed seem precious in a person's eyes. If the opportunity to perform a good deed comes before him, let him rejoice as if he discovered a precious jewel. Let him give praise to the Holy One Blessed is He for granting him this merit and enabling him to fulfill a commandment. And if there should come his way a commandment that no one else is concerned over, let him be especially eager and quick to perform it to the best of his ability, with his body, his resources and his soul. For a commandment that no one takes interest in is called a meis mitzvah [the name by which the Talmud refers to a corpse that has no one to bury it and that all are required to attend to]. Take hold of it and earn merit through it. At the same time, you will be restoring and elevating the esteem of that commandment in the same way that the Holy One Blessed is He lifts us the poor and needy from the dung heap. Afterwards that commandment will be your defender and a just champion on your behalf before the Holy One Blessed is He. And if Heaven has decreed that some evil is to befall him, that commandment will stand up and confront the Heavenly court and plead for him until the decree is rescinded. Concerning this it states, "If there shall be for him one defending angel in a thousand to tell of the man's uprightness" (Iyov 33:23).

And how much more does this apply if he toils in Torah for pure motives! For Torah study is the choicest of the commandments. Therefore, his reward will be redoubled many times. And when he passes away the Prince of the Divine Countenance, the angel MTTRON, along with all the hosts of Heaven will accompany him and dress him in all sorts of precious garments and crown him with crowns. Then the Prince of the Countenance will kindle before him lamps fashioned from the majesty and splendor of the Shechinah. Concerning this did King David and our teacher Moshe pray when they said, I will walk before Hashem in the lands of the living" (Tehillim 116:9). Therefore, let a person pray at all times that the Holy One Blessed is He, in His abundant mercy and lovingkindness, save him from every sort of iniquity, transgression and vain deed. And may He guide him along the straight and goodly path. For the Holy One Blessed is He, the Master of Mercy, hears the voice of one who beseeches Him with a broken heart and He will grant him a heart of flesh imbued with purity. Then will "Hashem's desire flourish in his hand" (Yeshayahu 53:10), Amein.

Chapter 75

The Sages have said that if Israel had only kept their first Shabbos properly no nation or language could ever have had dominion over them and if they would only keep two Shabbosos they would immediately be redeemed (Shabbos 118b). This is because the commandment of the Shabbos is equal to the entire Torah (Shemos Rabbah 25:12). The Sages also say that whoever takes delight in the Shabbos is granted an unlimited inheritance (Shabbos 118b).

Yet I have observed an evil circumstance that has become widespread among the exiles of these lands, that is, the detraction from the honor of the holy Shabbos day. To begin with, I have seen people going each and every Shabbos eve to the inns, where they eat and drink until they are as intoxicated as Lot. Only then do they make their way home. But then in their drunken stupor they are unable to make Kiddush properly. The Sages have taught (Tosafos, Chagigah 3b quoting Midrash) that there are three parties that testify on behalf of one another. They are: The Holy One Blessed is He, the Shabbos and Israel. Yet we have learned (Shevuos 30a) that one must give testimony in a standing position, whereas a drunkard cannot even stand upon his legs! Can Hashem be pleased that a drunkard is testifying to His uniqueness and unity and to the fact that the Shabbos that is the equivalent of all the 613 commandments? Therefore, one who cares for his soul will stay far from this pitfall, for the punishment will be very great.

A second pitfall that I have observed is that many villagers who live in open settlements with no wall or fence carry freely from their private domains to the houses of their gentile neighbors and vice versa. They rationalize that this is permitted because they are the only Jews living there on a permanent basis, therefore the presence of gentiles does not render carrying forbidden. But in this they are in error and do not know the law clearly. For we rule that a solitary Jew living in a place may carry throughout the city only if it is surrounded by a proper wall and gates (Shulchan Aruch, Orach Chayim 382). Only then is the entire town treated as if it were his own four cubits so that he may carry throughout it. But if the settlement is unwalled, and certainly if it is an open village, there is no justification for permitting a Jew to carry outside of his doorway at all. It is absolutely forbidden. Therefore, whoever trembles at the word of Hashem must inform the villagers, especially those with an unattached dining hall, that if they carry anything in their villages or unwalled towns it is just as if they ate forbidden food.

A third custom I have noticed is that the residents of one village often travel to another village far away to attend services. They do this in fulfillment of the verse, "in a multitude of subjects is the glory of the king" (Mishlei 14:28), the King of the Universe, the

Holy One Blessed is He. But once they arrive, they spend the entire time engaged in vanity. One of them relates how he bought a horse for a good price from a certain gentile and another how he bought a cow and other animals. Their entire conversation revolves around mundane matters. Yet the Sages have taught, based on the verse, "And honor it by refraining from doing your ways...or speaking of a matter" (Yeshayahu 58:13), that one's conversation on the Shabbos should not be like that on a weekday (Shabbos 113b). Since these villagers do not see one another throughout the week but only on Shabbos, they engage in every manner of conversation, including worldly affairs and business. In such a situation it would be better if they remained at home asleep in bed so that they would not speak of mundane matters on the Shabbos. This stumbling block is very common, on account of our many sins, and is to be found among most villagers.

A related plague that I have seen is that in some cases they walk two or three hours from one town to the next to attend services, claiming that it is within the Shabbos boundary. But I know for myself that it is often a distance of two or three times the Shabbos boundary. Therefore, I admonish them that they may count on the Shabbos boundary only where there is a tradition among the residents that some well-known authority measured the distance himself and permitted it for them. They must not rely on a mere schoolteacher or someone not qualified to rule in matters of prohibitions. For on account of our many sins there are many in this generation who are willing to permit the forbidden to ingratiate themselves with the people or for the sake of bribery. This causes them to permit even Torah prohibitions! Therefore, let every individual remove this stumbling block by refraining from traveling to any place until he has received permission from the Rabbi of the country.

A fourth stumbling block that I have seen among some communities is that holy Jews, in their desire to honor the Shabbos to the greatest extent possible, send meat to the shops of non-Jewish bakers to be roasted, since in this region Jews do not usually own ovens. This act of "honoring" the Shabbos involves two evils: First, they send the meat in the care of an unmarried Jewish girl to the baker's shop, where she violates the prohibition against seclusion with a man. This is forbidden even with a Jew because King David and the Prophet Shmuel made an enactment prohibiting seclusion between any man and woman (Avodah Zarah 36b). Therefore, the guardian of the meat, the unmarried girl, is herself in need of a guardian against seclusion. How then can she guard the meat?

Moreover, since no Jew assists the non-Jewish baker in the work, the cooked dish or roasted meat becomes forbidden forever due to the Torah prohibition against non-Jewish cooking. Not everyone is on the level of Mar bar Rav Ashi [one of the Sages] that he can be expected to know of this law. This is certainly true in the smaller communities. As a result, they are frequently guilty of this iniquity, on account of our many sins, and often end up consuming food that is forbidden by Torah law. For I have never found any authority who permits this in practice. Non-Jewish cooking is completely forbidden even if a Jew stands by and supervises, unless he actually assists in the cooking. On account of our many sins, the majority of Poland and Lithuania stumble in this matter because they employ non- Jewish servant girls who cook for them without any assistance from their Jewish employers. Therefore, I admonish every individual to remove this stumbling block from his house. Let him not send the meat with a solitary girl or woman. And if he does send meat to the baker's shop, let him be sure to at least break up the coals or place the meat upon the fire personally, lest he be guilty of violating a Torah prohibition, Heaven forbid.

Whoever is careful about the four things that I have mentioned will be rewarded many folds and merit an unlimited inheritance, as it is stated, "And I will grant you the inheritance of your father Yaakov" (Yeshayahu 58:14). Amein, so may it be His will.

Chapter 76

The prohibition against consuming yein nessech [literally, wine poured out to idolatry] is well known. Our teacher Moshe along with seventy of the elders of his generation instituted a prohibition against drinking all non-Jewish wine, even though it was not actually used in idolatry. This was in order to prevent Jews from being led into immorality, as occurred in the incident of Zimri in Shittim, which resulted in the deaths of twenty-four thousand Israelites (Bamidbar 25). The Kabbalists speak of this prohibition with the utmost gravity, warning of the severity of the punishment awaiting those who violate it.

In most countries in this region, wherever wine is made, there is a tendency to treat this prohibition lightly. Moreover, Jewish manufacturers even sell it to upright Jews under the guise of kosher wine, thereby bringing evil upon others as well, for which they bear responsibility for the sin of the multitude. Therefore, it is the duty of the rabbis and judges of the land to issue a ban of excommunication against these producers. For if wine is touched by a non-Jew any time after it begins flowing into the vat it becomes totally forbidden. For this reason, careful supervision is necessary to avoid transgression. Thus, rabbis must refuse to issue certifications of kashrus until they have ascertained clearly that the wine was made properly.

The deeper significance of yein nessech is tied up with the three injunctions that the Holy One Blessed is He imposed upon a Jewish king: that he may not multiply wives [nashim, literally, "women"], horses [susim] or money [kesef] (Devarim 17:16-17). The acronym for these three items is the word nessech. These three restrictions apply not only to a king but even more so to an ordinary person.

Many men are guilty of chasing after strange women. You must know that a man who imbibes yein nessech in the taverns of the gentiles will inevitably be drawn after strange women as well, because one sin leads to another (Pirkei Avos 4:6). Thus, he violates the injunction against multiplying women. At the same time, he disperses his seed like a horse, for the horse is the symbol of profligacy, as can be seen from the verse in Yechezkeil, "Their stream is like the stream of horses" (23:20). Such behavior is associated with animals. That is why a straying wife was required to bring an offering of barley flour, for barley is used for animal fodder. It turns out, then, that the word nessech contains the important hint that one who partakes of yein nessech will also be guilty of multiplying women, hence multiplying his seed like that of horses. In consequence he will descend into such poverty and indigence that he will want for a loaf of bread. As Scripture warns, "For the sake of a harlot a man will come to a loaf of bread" (Mishlei 6:26). In this way he fulfills the third injunction, "He shall not multiply money." This is why nessech is an acronym for women [nashim], horses [sussim] and money [kessef]. Therefore, let a man stay far from this iniquity.

I heard from my illustrious father, who heard from the saintly Rabbi Yaakov Temerlis that whoever stumbles in the sin of non-Jewish wine will be reincarnated in the form of a donkey, in fulfillment of a linguistic coincidence. For the Aramaic for "wine" is chamar while the word for donkey is chamor. Therefore, let a man distance himself from the prohibition against non-Jewish wine and also from the liquor made from the lees of such wine, which is included in the prohibition. Whoever avoids this prohibition is called "holy" and it will be said of him that he is holy.

Chapter 77
It is stated in Parashas Vayikra, "And the soul that sins, having heard the voice of an adjuration, etc." (5:1). This verse is discussed in the Zohar (Parashas Vayikra 13a). The Zohar says that it is speaking of the soul before it descends into an earthly body. While it is still in Heaven it is given a tour of eighteen hundred worlds to witness the honor and glory of those who toiled in Torah in this world for pure motives, who conducted all their affairs with pure motives and who behaved with humility. There they sit in honor, their faces shining with the radiance of the firmament, while above their heads are canopies made of precious stones.

After its tour the soul is told, "See how much honor the righteous enjoy in Gan Eden. If you conduct yourself properly, as these righteous individuals did, you will also merit such preciousness and glory." Afterwards the soul is brought before the Holy One Blessed is He where it is dressed in a precious garment in the form of the body and visage that it will don in this world and it is allowed to enjoy the splendor of the Shechinah. It is also crowned with numerous crowns. Then they say to it, "We are bestowing upon you all this honor on condition that you conduct yourself with righteousness and that the fear of Hashem is upon your countenance." Then they cause it to swear by the name of the Holy King that it will not sin and they administer to it several warnings, after which it bows towards the Holy One Blessed Is He and descends into its earthly body. If the person behaves righteously, all is good and well. But if he fails to obey the will of the Omnipresent the Torah expresses its astonishment at that evil person, saying, "And will the soul sin?" [This is an alternate reading of the verse above]. Did it not hear the voice of the adjuration and oath that was administered to it On High before it entered the body? And was it not given numerous warnings?

Even so, the sinner must not despair of entering the World to Come, only he must be sure to repair the damage he has done. Thus, regarding sins that he recalls through sight, perceiving the transgression, or that he remembers or knows about, it is stated in the continuation of the verse, "or he saw or knew." For it is possible to do penance for them all. Just let him confess tearfully each transgression. The verse continues, "and he does not tell." That is, if he fails to confess each sin before the Holy One Blessed is He prior to his death, then "he shall bear his iniquity." In other words, he will endure punishment and affliction in Gehinnom as well as other forms of castigation at the hands of cruel agents, all of which he brought upon himself! But Hashem is a merciful King. In His abundant lovingkindness He has appointed emissaries in Heaven to proclaim daily, "Wake up, O people of the world, before the Holy King! Wake up! Have pity upon yourselves! Have pity on your children!" Consequently, a person often finds his hearts suddenly filled with fear and trembling and the recollection of the day of death, which will, in turn, cause him to regret his evil deeds. If he is one who trembles at the word of Hashem, he will then rededicate himself and resolve to adhere to the path of the righteousness and he will be aroused to repent completely.

But if he has a stout heart and a stiff neck, then immediately after entertaining thoughts of regret he will return to his vomit and filth, transgressing as before. In that case hosts of destructive angels lie in wait for him, ready to cling to him and lure him down the path of the wicked and rebellious, urging him to adopt various evil traits.

Thus, he becomes cruel; he begins mocking the words of the Sages; he conducts himself angrily in all his affairs; and he fails to show any concern for the dignity of others. Eventually the destructive angels exercise such dominion over him that they lead him into various kinds of corruption until he is taken from the world in a horrible manner. Some calamity will befall him in such an unexpected manner that all who witness it will wonder what could have brought it about. But the real reason for it is that through his evil deeds he delivered himself into the hands of the Sitra Achara. For the destroying angels appointed over misfortune always lie waiting for the moment that a person commits some sin or iniquity, even a minor one, causing him to fall into their hands.

Thus it is related [Shivchei HaAri z"l] that one of the disciples of the Ari, z"l, an elder and leader of the generation, none other than Rabbi Chayim Vital, was once in the Ari's study hall when an ailing woman was ushered in. It was clear that something terrible had befallen her but no one could determine the exact cause, whether it was a spirit or a demon or something else. The woman told the Ari that formerly she had been healthy and strong, without any pain. Then suddenly she had taken on the appearance of someone stricken with a terrible malady. The Ari examined her pulse and said that she was possessed by a spirit, Heaven spare us, and sent her home. In the evening he instructed our teacher Rabbi Chayim Vital to go to the woman and exorcise the spirit. The Ari warned, "You must be sure to outwit it, for it is a liar and a great deceiver. When you inquire as to its name, it will lie three times." The Ari also revealed to Rabbi Chayim the correct thoughts he should bear in mind while using the Divine names to banish the spirit.

So, Rabbi Chayim went at dusk to the house where the spirit was. But before he even entered the house the spirit told the people around him, "See here, Rav Chayim Vital is coming to chase me out of this woman, but I am not afraid of him." He spoke these words loudly and brazenly, as is the way of such spirits. All this took place before Rabbi Chayim arrived. But the moment the rabbi actually entered the room the spirit began to tremble. The spirit rose before him and then fell on his face terrified. "Rabbi, I am not worthy of beholding your holy countenance," he exclaimed. "Who are you?" the rabbi inquired. "I am So-and-so son of So-and-so," the spirit lied. The rabbi asked him a second and a third time and he continued to lie. But the fourth time that Rabbi Chayim asked, it at last revealed his true identity. Then our teacher Rabbi Chayim Vital began uttering certain holy names and the spirit began speaking harshly and with great audacity. "I will leave immediately!" he said, intending to exit through the woman's throat, perforating it along the way. He also intended on extinguishing the lamps in the room and harming some of the other observers as well.

But Rabbi Chayim knew his evil intentions and commanded him, "I want you to go out through the small toe of the woman's left foot." The spirit said that it would comply, but Rabbi Chayim could tell that he was lying, for it was bent on killing the woman. So the rabbi ordered it not to leave at all, on pain of excommunication. For he knew that if the spirit left now, as a result of the oaths and curses, it would surely kill the woman. So, he let the matter stand for the time being and went to pray the evening service in the home of the Ari. After the service Rabbi Chayim related to the Ari all that had transpired.

The Ari replied, "This happened because you went to the spirit at night rather than while it was still day as I instructed you. At the night the malignant spirits [chitzonim] and the forces of judgment hold sway." Afterwards he bid him, "Go in peace," and walked him part way to the door, which he never did with any of his other disciples. The next day, after the morning service Rabbi Chayim went to bind the spirit with an oath compelling him to leave through the woman's small toe. The men and women who were present all saw the spirit as it came out. He appeared to them as a thread of fire, burning and shouting and crying over its deeds. When the spirit had exited the woman Rabbi Chayim asked him what he had done to be transformed into a spirit. He answered that he had been a well-known informer and had caused Jewish wealth to be delivered into the hands of the gentiles. He then inquired why it had been permitted to enter and take up residence within her. He replied that his supervisors gave him permission. He explained that formerly it had lain in the dust above the stove and had not been granted permission to enter anyone. But one day this woman came to arrange the fire in order to prepare food for the Shabbos meals and as she worked, she sang to herself vulgar songs. It was then that the forces appointed over the spirit had granted it permission to enter into her and it had remained there for three years straight.

See, then, how exacting the Holy One Blessed is He is with His creatures. This informer only sinned with his mouth, slandering his fellow Jews to the authorities, yet because of this he was transformed into a spirit. Imagine, then, what punishment awaits a person who transgresses in a more tangible manner, committing crimes bearing the penalty of excision or the four types of execution, or desecrating the Shabbos in public. And as for the woman, she had been involved in the mitzvah of preparing the Shabbos meals, yet because she was singing licentious songs, a spirit had been granted permission to enter her. Imagine then what awaits one who commits a more tangible sin. Surely then the spirits will be granted permission to cause him actual harm.

Therefore, let each and every Jew pray to his Maker to save him from all transgression and iniquity, and let him not accustom himself to uttering vulgarity. And if it happens that a person is inspired to repent, then even after the moment passes, he must be sure not to regret the repentance he has already done. Rather let him cling to the service of Hashem, for Heaven helps those who endeavor to purify themselves. Then all will be well with him, selah.

Chapter 78

Shlomo Hamelech, peace be upon him, wrote in Koheles, "I have seen all the deeds that are done beneath the sun and indeed they are all vapor and a shattering of the spirit" (1:14). That is, if the vapor of a deed is blemished it does not ascend beyond the sun to the higher regions but floats about beneath the sun. Everything that is done in the world produces vapor. Just as speech produces vapor so do deeds. The vapor of good deeds ascends On High immediately, where it is crowned and becomes a defender for the doer before the Holy One Blessed Is He. But if a person performs vain deeds the vapor floats about in this world. Then as soon as his soul exits his body the vapor takes hold of his soul and casts it several parsaos, afflicting it greatly. This is what King Shlomo meant when he said, "I have seen all the deeds that are done beneath the sun and indeed they are all vapor and a shattering of the spirit." That is, he saw those deeds the vapor of which does not ascend above the sun to the higher regions but floats about beneath the sun. It is then that a person brings about his own detriment, especially if he misused his faculty of speech, uttering unseemly things about his fellow without cause. The vapor of these utterances then goes and accuses him.

This is particularly true when a person speaks slanderously in a public lecture. Speakers often make the mistake of discussing openly the sin of Adam, Yosef's sale or the incident of David and Batsheva, enlarging on these incidents unjustly. One is not permitted to make public that which the Torah concealed. And even if he hit upon the truth, he will still be made to reckon for it. But the matter is more serious still when the lecturer fabricates details, attributing unworthy behavior to Hashem's handiwork and the first human being — Adam, or to the tribes, who are known as the "Tribes of God" [Shivtei Kah], or to King David or other lofty saints.

I will transcribe for you here a passage from Zohar Chadash (Parashas Bereishis 24a): Our Rabbis have taught: When Rabbi Shimon ben Yochai became ill, Rabbi Pinchas ben Yair, Rabbi Chiya and Rabbi Abahu came to visit him. "How can someone who is the pillar of the world possibly die?" they asked. Rabbi Shimon responded, "It is not the Heavenly court that is examining my case. For I have seen that I will not be delivered into the hands of any angel or to the judgment of the Heavenly court, for I am not like other people. Rather the Holy One Blessed is He will decide my case. This is what King David meant when he wrote, 'Judge me, O God, etc.' (Tehillim 43:1). Similarly, King Shlomo said, 'To render the judgment of His servant and the judgment of His people.' That is, the judgment of His servant is rendered separately from that of other people. "Thus, have we learned: 'When a man dies and the Heavenly court considers his case, some members of the court are inclined to exonerate him while others are inclined to condemn him since they see the guilt of human beings. But if the decision is rendered in the presence of the Holy One Blessed is He it will always be for the good.' Why is this? Because we have learned: 'The attributes of the Supernal King always incline to the side of merit.' For He is entirely merciful and it is in His hands to forgive sins and iniquities. "This is the meaning of the verse, 'For with You is forgiveness' (Tehillim 130:4). That is, with Him and with no one else. For this reason, I have asked Him to judge my case. At that time, I will pass through twelve gates in the World to Come that no one has ever passed through other than the Patriarchs and no one will protest. Moreover, I will not need to request permission."

Then Rabbi Shimon whispered something and suddenly they looked at his sickbed and saw that he was no longer there. They were all astonished and stricken dumb with fear. But while they were yet sitting there the fragrance of many beautiful spices wafted in, strengthening them until they could again perceive Rabbi Shimon, who was now speaking with someone, although they could see no one other than him. After a while Rabbi Shimon asked them, "Did any of you see anything?" Rabbi Pinchas answered, "No. But we were all astounded when we did not see you in your sickbed for a long time. Then when we finally saw you again, we could detect the fragrance of the spices of Gan Eden and we heard you speaking, although we did not know with whom." Rabbi Shimon asked, "Did you not hear any speech other than mine?" "No," they replied. "I am surprised that Rabbi Pinchas did not see anything," said Rabbi Shimon, "for I beheld him just now in the other world seated just below my son Rabbi Elazar. They had sent for me from On High and showed me the places of the righteous in the World to Come. As for me, my heart found no place acceptable other than the one alongside Achiyah HaShiloni.

So, I selected my place and then returned. "Along with me came three hundred souls of the righteous and above them all, the soul of Adam. It was he who was sitting and speaking with me. He requested that I refrain from revealing to the world more about his sin than the Torah had already revealed. He had covered himself with that tree from Gan Eden." "I explained that I had already revealed the matter to the companions, but he said that that was alright and acceptable. It was only to the rest of the world that I was not to reveal it. Why? Because the Holy One Blessed is He had pity on Adam's honor and did not wish to reveal the nature of his iniquity but only the tree from which he ate..." Then Rabbi Shimon's son Rabbi Elazar approached him and said, "Father, what is my station in that world?" "Fortunate is your lot, my son," he replied. "A long time will pass before you are buried beside me but in that world your place is beside me. I have already chosen it for you..."

From this passage you can see that public speakers do not do right when they speak openly in the synagogues and study halls before multitudes that include the ignorant and say things like, "Adam was a heretic" or that he was guilty of idolatry, immorality and bloodshed, and the like. How can one say such things about the handiwork of the Holy One Blessed is He, who was in fact a perfect saint? All the souls of all the generations hung suspended from him and the souls of the wicked were also suspended from his soul or from one of his limbs. These are the sinners who behave rashly and are quick to sin. But the unique soul of Adam himself never sinned at all because it was the holy of holies.

As is made clear in the Zohar Chadash a lecturer places himself in great danger when he speaks disparagingly about Adam. In fact, he risks becoming a fulfillment of the verse, "And many of them will perish" (Shemos 19:21), therefore it is proper to rebuke those who do this. For the Holy One Blessed is He is not pleased with those who criticize His people Israel or the souls of the righteous. The Torah displays concern even for the dignity of the wicked. Thus, the Sages comment on the verse, "And you shall kill the animal" (Vayikra 20:15), that this was in order that no one would be able to say, "So-and-so committed a sin with this animal" (Sanhedrin 54a; Tanchuma, Parashas Balak, 9).

Therefore, one should interpret Adam's sin favorably, as well as the sin of the calf and the sale of Yosef. If one adopts the trait of always speaking in praise one will merit length of days and years, Amein.

Chapter 79

It is stated, "Who may ascend the mountain of Hashem and who may stand in His holy place? One with clean hands ... This is the generation of those who seek Him, those who seek Your Presence, Yaakov, selah" (Tehillim 24:3-6). The meaning of this passage is explained in the Zohar (1:97a, Midrash HaNe'elam). There it is related that when a righteous person passes from this world his soul ascends higher and higher until it approaches the worlds just below the Throne of Glory. Then the Holy One Blessed is He says to our forefather Yaakov, "O My precious son who endured the sorrows of child rearing! Behold, the righteous So-and-so son of So-and-so is arriving in this world adorned and arrayed with numerous ornaments and adornments of Torah, mitzvos and good deeds. It is fitting that you should go out to greet him with joy and gladness and wish him peace. Moreover, I Myself will go with you to receive his countenance, for it is a countenance radiating with Torah and awe."

This is the meaning of the phrase, "those who seek Your Presence, Yaakov, selah." For it does not say, "he who seeks out your countenance," but "those who seek your countenance." In other words, the Holy One Blessed is He will seek you out along with Yaakov. And who can observe these two going out and not go out with them to greet the righteous one? Therefore, numerous bands gather and go out to greet him as well, each band waiting beside one of the gates that the righteous soul must pass through. Then all of them open their mouths and proclaim, "Peace! Peace upon you and upon your Torah! Fortunate is the one who bore you! Continue on to your chamber where beautiful canopies have been prepared for you." Throughout that entire day a proclamation is issued in all the firmaments that no one may involve himself in the study of anything other than the insights revealed by this righteous man in his lifetime. Then they read out his insights before him just as the marriage document is read before the groom and bride under the wedding canopy. I believe that this is what the Sages were alluding to when they said, "The reward of the wedding feast is words" (Berachos 6b), that is, the words of the person's own Torah. All the chief scholars On High take those insights and make them known to other bands and groups of the righteous. Then they announce the righteous man's name and all of them open their mouths and proclaim, "Blessed is your arrival in peace!" Afterwards they bring in his father and mother and crown them with numerous crowns on account of their righteous son.

But even before the man's soul leaves his body, bands of the righteous come to meet him. They enter his room and gather round his bed, bringing with them the spices and fragrances of Gan Eden. He beholds them and wishes them peace and they with him peace in return, saying, "Dear righteous one, holy son of the Holy One Blessed is He, let it not seem evil to you that you must depart from this world. For this is a world of vanity and falsehood in which a man must imperil his very life in order to earn his bread. And sometimes in the course of sustaining his life he blemishes his soul and desecrates the Name of Heaven. "But in the next world, in Gan Eden, it is called 'the day that is entirely good.' There is no need for him to endanger his life, nor does any sin come about through him." They say to him further, "All the affairs of this world are vanity and a shattering of the spirit. Therefore, prepare yourself for a goodly road, illuminated with the shining light of the World to Come. Numerous canopies and chambers filled with every manner of goodness have been prepared in you honor. "Therefore, we have come to inform you that in a short while you will come to the house of your rejoicing where you will go from darkness to light until you stand before the Throne of Glory. There you will be seated among the bands of the righteous and you will merit singing songs of praise before the Master of the Universe. Then you will see that a moment of satisfaction in Gan Eden is better than all the pleasures of this world (Pirkei Avos 4:17)."

When the righteous man hears these things, he rejoices and accepts his death happily. It was in light of this that the rabbis incorporated into the Ma'amados for Monday the petition, "And take me out from peace to peace." This is a prayer that one should merit the death of the righteous described above. For it is stated, "For this, let every man of devotion pray to You, in a time when You may be founds" (Tehillim 32:6). The Sages explain: "This is the day of death" (Berachos 8a). In other words, let him pray that bands and camps of holy and pure saints come to greet him so that he may go with them to be crowned among them in great joy and happiness. The verse continues, "...indeed, when mighty waters threaten, they will not reach him." These are the "waters of the wicked" mentioned in Tehillim 124:5, that is, the bands of destroying and damaging angels, Heaven spare us, that prevent the soul of the evildoer from beholding the light of the Shechinah. But as for the soul of the righteous person, who can relate the honor he will enjoy?

Come and see what is stated in the continuation of the Zohar above: The Holy One Blessed is He fashioned a special throne of glory for Yaakov to sit upon as the righteous man enters the next world. Then, when the soul beholds all this honor it blesses and praises the Holy One Blessed is He and prostrates itself before Him, giving praise and acknowledgement for the great distinction and honor it has received. Then it prays for the body as well, asking that it, too, be allowed to rest securely without suffering the afflictions of the grave. And it recites Tehillim 103, "My soul, bless Hashem, and all that is in me [bless] His holy Name, etc." When the other Patriarchs, Avraham and Yitzchak, hear of this, they also go to greet the righteous soul. Concerning this was it stated, "And Avraham lifted up his eyes" (Bereishis 18:2). This actually refers to the soul of the righteous man, for the Zohar terms the soul of a righteous man with the name Avraham. "And Avraham saw" — this refers to the man's soul. "And behold three men were standing over him" — this refers to the souls of Avraham, Yitzchak and Yaakov, along with the glory of the Shechinah. Then immediately it is said that "and Avraham ran" — referring again to the man's soul — "to greet them from the opening of the tent, and he bowed to the ground" — that is, towards the Shechinah. Afterwards the soul prays, "Hashem, do not depart from Your servant!" That is, it requests that the Shechinah accompany it until the gates of Gan Eden to protect and guard it from all its accusers. See the Zohar there at length.

How precious in the eyes of the Holy One Blessed is He is the individual who is accustomed to make regular mention of the merits of the three Patriarchs as well as those of Moshe, Aharon and Miriam and the other prophets and great saints. For all the souls of the righteous rejoice when they see good deeds in a living person and their merits shine down upon us continually. Thus, it is related in the Zohar, Parashas Bereishis (19a): Our Rabbis have taught: Once Rabbi Yose was traveling along the road when he met up with Rabbi Yirmeyah and the two of them continued on together. Eventually they came upon a certain mountain that appeared frightening. Rabbi Yose said to Rabbi Yirmeyah, "Let us speak words of Torah and then proceed." So, he began a discourse, saying, "[It is stated], 'And as for you, do not be afraid, My servant Yaakov' (Yirmeyahu 30:10) …"

While they were yet walking, they heard the sound of a child on the mountain, walking along and weeping. Rabbi Yose said, "Let us go to him, for I am not afraid. After all, we have learned, 'A demon will appear to a lone individual and harm him whereas to two people it will only appear but not harm them.'"

So they went towards the child. When they reached him Rabbi Yose said, "We are the sons of the Master of the Universe and we are not afraid of you!" When the child heard this, he understood that they only said it because they suspected that he might be a demon. Therefore, he said, "I am a Jew, the grandson of Rabbi Chiya the Great. My father used to teach me verses from Shir HaShirim and Bereishis. But after he died, I was kidnapped by bandits and compelled to labor as their servant. Therefore, I fled to this mountain. And now I am crying because I do not know the way back to my mother's house."

Rabbi Yose wept and said, "Woe! Shall the grandson of Rabbi Chiya go on alone?" So, they took him by the hand and went with him. Rabbi Yose said to him, "Tell me, my son, what were you studying with your father in Parashas Bereishis?" The child replied, "I was studying the verse, 'Let there be lights in the firmament of Heaven' (Bereishis 1:14)." Rabbi Yose inquired, "What did your father tell you about this passage?" The child answered, "This is what my father said: Israel had three righteous shepherds in the desert, Moshe, Aharon and Miriam. In Moshe's merit the manna fell for Israel; in Aharon's merit there were the clouds of glory; and in Miriam's merit there was the well. Even after Aharon and Miriam died their merits stood by Israel, for out of the Holy One's great love for them He engraved the images of Moshe, Aharon and Miriam upon the firmament so that their merits would shine upon

Israel. Concerning them was it stated, 'And God placed them in the firmament of Heaven to shine upon the earth.'" Rabbi Yose and Rabbi Yirmeyah came and kissed him and for the next three miles they carried him upon their shoulders, applying to him the verse, "And all your sons will be learned of Hashem, etc."

One must know that all those holy images that the Holy One Blessed is He engraved to shine their merits upon Israel also gaze upon Israel, examining whether they are upright in their conduct or not. For the Holy One Blessed is He has many witnesses and warnings ready and waiting to arouse people's hearts. Thus it is stated in the Zohar, Parashas Pekudei (220a): How important it is that a person know and reflect on the ways of the Holy One Blessed is He because each and every day a voice goes out, proclaiming, "Guard yourselves, O people of the world, lest you sin any further! Close the gates of iniquity lest you be caught in the net [that has been laid to trap sinners], before your feet become entangled in it!" [In other words, rectify your sins against Hashem at the first possible moment.] "Woe to those who fall there, for they will not be illuminated by the light that has been hidden away for the righteous in the World to Come." Heavenly agents are appointed over every utterance and deed, whether for bad or for good. Fortunate is the one who fills the atmosphere of the world with words of Torah and fear of Hashem!

A person must take all these words to heart and recall at all times that Hashem's "eyes" roam about the entire world continually. Here is a valuable principle to adopt: Do not anything in private that you would be ashamed to do in public! Hashem is a merciful and gracious God. When He sees that your intentions are for the sake of Heaven and that you wish to adhere to the path of virtue and integrity, He will send His angel before you to save you from all sin and from every evil matter. And if you do suffer any harm or mishap, accept it with love, as I have already discussed at length (Chapter 31). If you are successful in your business ventures so that your income is generous, do not say, "My cleverness has stood me in good stead." For one must know that, "Bread is not to the wise" (Koheles 9:1). Rather it is all a "gift from God" (ibid. 5:18). Therefore, give praise and acknowledgement to the Holy One Blessed is He for everything. For the Sages comment on the verse,

"Blessed is Hashem day by day" (Tehillim 68:20), that one must give praise and acknowledgement to God every day for whatever He metes out, whether for good or for evil, Heaven forbid (Berachos 40a). On this account Hashem will bless you from Tziyon and you will succeed and flourish in all your endeavors, Amein.

Chapter 80

It is said concerning the holy Ari, z"l (Emek HeMelech, Intro. III, Chapter 4, 11b) that in his lifetime the wicked lived in terror because whenever he saw them he would reveal to them every detail of the transgressions that each of them had committed over the past fifty years. And even if someone merely contemplated sin in his heart the Ari would reveal it. For this reason, the wicked would flee from him in shame so that he would not gaze at them and reveal their guilt. A person should take this to heart. For if such is the disgrace the sinner feels in the presence of a mere human who uncovers his sins through Divine insight, how much greater will be his shame when he comes before the King of the Universe, the Holy One Blessed is He and His Throne of Glory! For the Holy One Blessed is He will reveal his every utterance and will even summon witnesses. Moreover, the person's own hand will record his deeds. What, then, will he do on the day of his judgment? But who knows whether he will even merit appearing before his blessed Creator? Perhaps his soul will fall into the hands of cruel angels upon expiration and will be brought to a deep, dark place with no illumination, to remain there until a defender is finds some merit in him or in a descendant who studies Torah. For we find that many sinners were only saved from the destroyers, may Heaven spare us, through such merit.

It is related, for example, in Midrash HaNe'elam, Parashas Lech Lecha (Zohar Chadash, 60a): A certain man went to the mountains of Ararat along with two other sages. They saw there openings in the ground from which fire and smoke were pouring forth and they heard the voice of a man crying, "Woe! Woe!" "Surely this place is a part of Gehinnom," they surmised. Then they sat down there and dozed off. In their sleep they heard the groans of a man who was gathering large bundles of thistles, which he carried upon his shoulders. Two officers from Gehinnom followed after him, igniting the bundles with fire and burning him as he went. "Woe! Woe!" the man cried. But the officers responded, "If only you had taken note of the lovingkindness that the Holy One Blessed is He did for you as He does with the rest of the righteous, granting them two angels to guard them, as it states, 'He will command His angels to guard you in all your ways' (Tehillim 91:11). For then you would have been spared this punishment. But you abandoned Hashem your God and did not keep the Torah. Instead you heeded the evil inclination and joined with the company of the wicked known as, 'cut down thistles' (Yeshayahu 33:12). It is these thistles that are now burning you."

The Jewish traveler asked the man, "Who are you?" "I am a Jew," he replied, "and I committed many sins and iniquities. I have forgotten my name and the officers of Gehinnom refuse to reveal it to me. I have forgotten it on account of the terrible, bitter and evil afflictions that I am made to suffer. Five times a day I am condemned to be burned, three times during the day and twice at night. This is because I indulged in five types of intimate relations forbidden by the Torah." Afterwards the traveler asked him from where he came. He replied that he was from the Upper Galilee in the Land of Israel and that he had left behind him a young son. Then he said: "I sinned greatly and the angel in charge of graves said to me at the time of my judgment, 'Woe to the one who swore to keep the Torah but failed to do so! Woe to the hands that manipulated forbidden items! Woe to the legs that went to perform forbidden deeds!' "Then as they cruelly administered my lashes, they recounted in detail each of my sins. I also was compelled to admit that I did indeed do such-and-such. I was unable to tell lies because the angels appointed over my soul were standing there with documents in their hands, upon which were recorded the details of all the transgressions I committed and my own signature was inscribed beneath the writing."

Afterwards the Jew went from place to place in the Upper Galilee inquiring whether anyone had recently died leaving a young son.

Kav HaYashar

Finally, in a certain place he received a positive response and was informed that the child had gone to the slaughterhouse and that he was as evil as his father. So, the man went to the slaughterhouse and contemplated the child, who was playing with the youths who were there. The Jew said to him, "My son, come with me." So, he came with him and the man provided him with clothes and found him a teacher to teach him Torah. The teacher taught him a great deal until he became one of the most promising of the students. Then he taught him to read from the [Book of] Prophets in the Synagogue and to pray with the congregation. The young man grew even more learned until eventually people began to call him "Rabbi." At that point the evildoer appeared to the Jew in a dream and said to him, "Rabbi, may the Holy One Blessed is He console you as you have consoled me. For when my son read from the Prophets in the synagogue, they exempted me from harsh judgment. And when he led the prayers and recited Kaddish they tore up my sentence in Gehinnom altogether. "And when my son grew more learned and they began calling him "Rabbi," I was crowned with the crown of the righteous. It was only because of you that I earned all this merit. Fortunate is your lot, for you have brought me into the World to Come. Fortunate is your lot in this world and fortunate is your lot in the World to Come!"

We find a similar incident in Kallah Rabbasi (Chapter 2) in which Rabbi Akiva encountered an evildoer to whom the destroying angels were administering punishment. Rabbi Akiva asked him if he had a son, to which he replied that he did. He also told him where the boy lived. So, Rabbi Akiva went to that place and taught the boy to recite the Kaddish. Then the boy responded, Amein, yehei shemeih raba mevorach le'olam ulolmei olmayo, and the evildoer was immediately released from his suffering. Afterwards he appeared to Rabbi Akiva and informed him that he had been freed from his afflictions. Rabbi Akiva then recited the verse, "Hashem, Your remembrance endures throughout the generations!" (Tehillim 135:13).

This should awaken a person to watch over his children carefully and to teach them Torah and guide them in awe of Hashem because a son can bring his father merit. By the same token, one whose father or mother has passed away must be scrupulous in reciting the Kaddish and responding, Amein, yehei shemeih raba, with all his might. For through this he elevates his father's soul to the upper Gan Eden. Let him not emulate those who take the Kaddish lightly, treating it as a kind of joke and actually making sport of its recital. They do not realize that Heaven and earth depend on the Kaddish. The response, Amein, yehei shemeih raba, contains twenty-eight letters, corresponding to the twenty-eight letters in the first verse of the Torah, "In the beginning God created the Heaven and the earth" (Bereishis 1:1). This is an allusion to what is stated in Tehillim, "The power of His deeds He has declared to His people" (111:6). For the numerical value of the word "power" — koach — is twenty-eight. The first verse of the Ten Commandments also contains twenty-eight letters: "And God spoke all these things, saying" (Shemos 20:1). Therefore, our teacher Rabbi Yehudah Chassid used to instruct the congregation to recite the first verse of Bereishis, followed by the one from the Ten Commandments and afterwards, Amein, yehei shemeih raba. The esoteric meaning of this custom is explained in Megaleh Amukos (Ofen 212).

In light of this a mourner reciting Kaddish for a parent should be careful to recite it with great concentration. It is important that the one reciting Kaddish also respond, Amein, yehei shemeih raba. Let him not emulate the ignorant who stop at the words, "And say Amein" [ve'imru Amein] and then continue with the words "May the name be blessed and praised" [yisborach veyishtabach]. Rather, he must also say, Amein, yehei shemeih raba because that is the most essential part of the Kaddish. In this way he brings pleasure to the Holy One Blessed is He as well as to his father and mother. If a person has no sons let him take an orphan into his home and raise him in the study of Torah and the service of Hashem. For perhaps the father and mother of the orphan were wicked and now their son will bring them merit. Then the one who raised him will have earned a great reward in this world and the next. On the other hand, if someone raises an orphan in his home only in order that he should serve him, then not only does he receive no reward, he is severely punished. For just as a virtuous son brings merit to his father, so does a wicked son cause his parents to be punished because they failed to rebuke him while they were alive. It is for this reason that the sin of the son is visit upon his parents. But if the deceased left a young son and someone else raised him, then they do not punish the father but the one who raised him. Concerning this was it stated, "Each man for his own sin shall they be killed" (Devarim 24:16).

Therefore, I will now present you with a chapter devoted to the subject of raising children. There it will be noted that a father is commanded to rebuke his son while the son is commanded to fulfill his father's words. This is in order that people will not say of him, "Cursed is the one who bore him; cursed is the one who raised him" (Sanhedrin 52a). Then he will be able to go to the next world without shame, Amein.

Chapter 81

It is related in Midrash Rabbah, Parashas Bereishis (5:9) that when Adam committed the sin of eating from the Tree of Knowledge both the snake and Chavah were personally cursed, whereas for Adam's sin the earth was cursed. As the verse states, "The earth shall be cursed on account of you" (Bereishis 3:17). This is because Adam was created from the earth.

The Midrash compares this to a son who turned to evil ways and the people cursed the breasts from which he had nursed as an infant, saying, "Cursed be the breasts that nursed this one." Regarding this Midrash one can ask as follows: Since Adam was created from the upper world as well as the lower world (Bereishis Rabbah 12:8), why was only the earth cursed on account of Adam's sin but not the heavens? I believe the answer is that the creation of Adam came about also through the contributions of male and female aspects (see the Zohar 1:49a and Zohar Chadash, Bereishis 21a). Thus, the earth derives from the female aspect while the soul that was imbued in the human being derives from the male aspect. The soul does not lure a person into sin. It is only the physical body created from the earth that tempts and urges him to sin. For this reason, the earth, representing the lower world, was cursed, whereas the upper world was not cursed. For only the soul originated in the upper world, and the soul does not sin. This is the reason that people say, "Cursed be the breasts that nursed this one." Notice that they do not curse the father but only the mother. This is because of the Sages' great principle that every woman who is modest in her conduct and her thoughts will merit to be the progenitor of prophets, saints and men of good deeds (Megillah 10b). An example of this is Tamar. Conversely, every woman who is not modest in her conduct or who harbors evil and alien thoughts will have offspring who follow in her ways, for as the Sages say, "one ewe follows another ewe" (Kesuvos 63a).

It seems to me that this is why Scripture says, "As a father has mercy upon his children" (Tehillim 103:13). Why is it not stated, "As a mother has mercy upon her children"? The answer is that it is the nature of a father who loves his children to discipline them, as it is stated, "One who spares the rod hates his son, but the one who loves him disciplines him every morning" (Mishlei 13:24). Every man who disciplines his son demonstrates thereby that he loves him, as is elaborated on in Midrash Rabbah, Parashas Shemos (1:1). A woman, on the other hand, is soft-hearted and does not wish for the father or teacher to strike the child. Moreover, while he is yet small the mother fulfills his every wish, granting him all his heart's desires. Then when he becomes a youth, he seeks out what he is accustomed to and eventually turns to evil ways. And all of this is caused by the woman.

A proof to this is an amazing episode that I heard involving the Ramban. In an essay in one of his books the Ramban writes that if a Jew exchanges his religion for one of the idolatrous faiths, one may be certain that he is not really of Jewish seed. Rather he is of the seed of the other nations or else of intended adulterous relationship [that is, his father believed that he was with another woman when he was actually with his wife]. A short time after he wrote these words one of his own sons apostatized. The ruler summoned the Ramban and said, "Look at what you have recently published, and now your own offspring has been tripped up by your words!" All the way home the Ramban was filled with turmoil and when he arrived, he sat on the floor weeping and scourging himself. He was more disturbed on account of the sermon he had published than on account of his son who had abandoned his religion. He refused to eat or drink for several days until at last his wife came to console him and to assure that there was no need for him to be distraught. She then explained that one night when she was on her way back from the mikveh [ritual bath], which was far from their home, a certain nobleman noticed her beauty and ordered his servants to seize her and bring her to his house. The nobleman then [sexually] abused her and it was from him that she had conceived the boy. She added, "And if you do not believe me, see that I still have the finger that I bit from his hand with my teeth."

When the Ramban heard his wife's story he rose from the ground with great rejoicing. "You have consoled me!" he exclaimed. Right away he set out and went to the ruler to related to him what his wife had revealed. The ruler immediately summoned the nobleman who soon arrived. He was wearing a glove on his hand and the ruler ordered him to remove it. When the nobleman refused the ruler ordered his servants to remove it from his hand by force. Then they saw that he was indeed missing a finger on that hand. "What happened to you finger?" the ruler inquired. The nobleman confessed that one time he had abused a Jewish woman and she had bitten it off with her teeth. The Ramban spoke up, "So you see that our Torah is true as are the words of our Sages and our God!

From this story we learn that everything depends upon the mother. For sometimes an evil man has a modest wife and they produce virtuous and upright children. And sometimes a righteous man is married to a wicked woman and they produce wicked offspring.

Therefore, a mother must be sure to guide her children along the path of virtue, and let her not have pity on them when the teacher or her husband strikes them. Let every woman learn from Batsheva, wife of King David and mother of King Shlomo. Batsheva beat her son King Shlomo personally after he once overslept until the third hour of the day with the keys to the Holy Temple beneath his head (Vayikra Rabbah, 12:5). This is alluded to in the verse, "The words of Lemuel who was chastised by his mother" (Mishlei 31:1). Fortunate are the husband and wife who guide their children along the straight and virtuous path. Then they will merit upright offspring and will have cause to rejoice in this world and the next.

Chapter 82

Our Sages have said that in the merit of four things were our forefathers redeemed from Egypt: in the merit of the righteous women, in the merit of not changing their names, in the merit of not changing their language and in the merit of their exclusive trust in the Holy One Blessed is He (Sotah 11b; Vayikra Rabbah 32:5; Yalkut Hoshea 519). And just as it was in our first redemption, so will it be in our final one. Thus, the final redemption will also take place in the merit of the righteous women. This is why women must be more modest than men and refrain from following their heartstrings in imitating the fashions of the nations. I have observed in recent times, for example, that the ranks of the rebellious pursuing the fashions of the gentiles have swelled until there is no longer any distinction between Jewess and gentile. Through this they bring much evil into the world. One evil is that they cause the multitude to sin through gazing at them and their garments. For we rule that it is forbidden to gaze even at a woman's colored garments (Avodah Zarah 20b).

A second evil is that they provoke the jealousy and hatred of the gentiles. For they fix their eyes upon us, noticing that Jewish women appear even more aristocratic than the noblewomen of the nations. The truth is that we are in the midst of a bitter exile. Therefore, it would be more fitting for us to dress in black to show our grief over the length of the exile and the destruction of the Holy Temple, and over the plight of our Jewish brethren immersed oppression and captivity. However, not only do we fail to mourn, we actually add to our sins, for the women go about with their necks outstretched, bare down to their breasts. Who can relate the terrible punishment awaiting them? For they impede the redemption, on account of our many sins.

A third evil is what they do to their husbands. For if a man cannot afford to clothe his wife in the way her friends dress, she curses him and complains until he is compelled to borrow money or even to commit a financial injustice towards his fellow to gain more funds. In the end he is forced to provide his wife with beautiful and immodest garments like those of her companions. Then when he is unable to pay, either he is arrested or else he endures some other indignity. Therefore, a proper and modest woman of Israel must be sure to conduct herself modestly rather than licentiously, so that from her will come forth prophets and saints.

The second merit on account of which our forefathers were redeemed from Egypt was that they did not change their names. In our generation, on the other hand, I have observed that the rebellious of the nations, the same ones who go about dressed after the fashion of the nations, commit the further evil of shaving off their beards, by which they trespass five prohibitions. For there are five corners to the beard, each one of which is a separate transgression (Makkos 20a; Toras Kohanim 19:74). Moreover, on account of this it is often impossible to discern that he is a Jew. Then, when someone asks him his name, he introduces himself by a gentile name. Sometimes he goes traveling with gentile aristocrats to places where he is not known and while he is there, he allows himself to eat carrion and drink forbidden wine, for one sin leads to another, just as one good deed leads to another (Pirkei Avos 4:2). When a person changes his name, not only does he harm his own body and soul, but he also does an injustice to the entire Jewish people. Therefore, one day he will be made to reckon for it and his punishment will be great.

The third merit is that our ancestors did not change their language. Nowadays, however, on account of our many sins, many people have adopted an improper course. For we rule that when one's children are young one must study all things with them in the holy tongue (Sifri, Eikev 46). That way when they grow up, they will become accustomed to the holy practice of conversing in the holy language. But in recent times people have begun accustoming their young children to conversing in French and other languages. Moreover, when they grow older, instead of sending them to the study hall, their father insists that they attend an academy for the study of French and other languages. This is a terrible stumbling block. Although it is true that the members of the Sanhedrin were able to speak seventy languages (Sanhedrin 17a), they studied them only on the side, not as a main course of study. But now these people make French and other tongues their principle subject and study Torah on the side!

The fourth merit is that our ancestors placed all their trust in the Holy One Blessed is He. But now I see that, on account of our many sins, only one in a thousand places his trust in the Holy One Blessed is He, while most people in the world place their trust in wealth or in mortals who have no power to save. That is why we see that the poor have plummeted to such depths. Meanwhile the wealthy, who have taken all the authority for themselves, consider the poor to be a nuisance. As a result of this situation no one places his trust in the Holy One Blessed is He. Instead, the sycophants, who put their trust in the rich, are on the increase. It goes without saying that they do not recall the destruction of the Holy Temple or the bitterness of the exile or its length, nor does it occur to them to pray regarding these things. Whereas if they placed their trust in the Holy One Blessed Is He, mourning over the destruction of the Holy Temple and the length of the exile would always be in the forefront of their minds.

Therefore, a person must resolve in his mind not to delay the redemption but to place his trust only in the Holy One Blessed is He. Whoever is conscientious regarding the four things mentioned above, on account of which our forefathers were redeemed, will merit hastening our redemption. For the final redemption will resemble the first redemption, in that it will also come about in the merit of these four things. May it occur speedily in our days, Amein.

Chapter 83

It is one of the ways of awe to refrain from disparaging any creature in the world without cause. Thus, the Zohar warns in Parashas Yisro (68b) that all the creatures in the world are the handiwork of the Holy One Blessed is He and all are needed. Therefore, one should never kill any creature without cause. Even those that are dangerous like the snake or the spider should not be killed unless they are chasing after a person to harm him [see what I wrote in Part I, Chapter 18].

Come see what is stated in the Zohar in Parashas Yisro: Rabbi Elazar was traveling along the road accompanied by Rabbi Chizkiyah when they saw a snake. Rabbi Chizkiyah arose intending to kill it but Rabbi Elazar said to him, "Leave it alone and do not kill it." "But it is an evil creature that kills people!" Rabbi Chizkiyah observed. Rabbi Elazar replied, "It is stated, 'A snake does not bite without a whisper and there is no benefit to the master of the tongue' (Koheles 10:11). A snake never bites a person unless it receives a whisper from On High, saying, 'Go kill So-and-so!' "And just as it receives a whisper and kills in accordance with the command of the Holy One Blessed Is He, so too it is sometimes the agent through which a miracle is performed on someone's behalf. It is all in the hands of the Holy One Blessed is He. For all creatures are His handiwork and if they were not all needed, He would not have created them. Therefore, a person should not disparage any of the creatures in the world or any of the handiwork of the Holy One Blessed is He." Therefore, those who shoot arrows and bullets at non-kosher birds and animals for no reason other than to practice their shooting skills, thereby killing living creatures in vain, will one day give reckoning for it. This is not the way of Israel, the holy community. Their way is never to harm any creature in vain. This is true not only of animate creatures but also of trees and herbs and other types of foliage. All were created for a purpose; Therefore, one must not treat any of them disdainfully without cause.

Come and see what is stated in the Zohar in Parashas Yisro (80a): Rabbi Yose said: One time I was walking with my son Rabbi Chiya, when we came across a man gathering herbs in the field. We approached him and I inquired, "Of what use are these bundles of herbs to you?" But the man did not raise his head, nor did he say anything. So, I returned and asked him again, but again he said nothing. Then I said to my son Rabbi Chiya, "This man is either an imbecile or deaf, or else he is wiser than us." We sat down beside him and observed that after he gathered the herbs, he covered them with grape leaves. Then he said to us, "I see that you are Jews. They say that Jews are cleverer than other people. If I did not have mercy upon you now you would have be separated from others like lepers who are avoided by all. For I see that the fumes of a certain herb that you passed by have entered into your bodies and would have caused you to become leprous for three days. But I will tell you a remedy for it. Eat some of the wild garlic growing in this field and you will be healed!" So, we did as he said. We ate the wild garlic that we found there and afterwards my son and I fell asleep. For several hours sweat poured from us until at last we awoke. The man told us, "Your God was been with you and caused you to meet me. Therefore, I invite you to come with me and I will teach you, for your bodies have been healed by me."

So, we went with him and he said to us, "You noticed that I did not raise my eyes or my head, nor did I speak with you. This is because with regard to herbs I am the most knowledgeable person of the generation. I learned the ways of all the herbs from my father and I live all year along among them. As for this plant that you saw me cover with grape leaves ׀ there is one herb that is unique among all others and it was very near to where you were sitting. I wished to take some of it because in a place near my house to the north, there is a spring and a mill. Every day a man with two heads comes out from the mill with a sword in his hand and he harries us. It was on account of this that I gathered the herb. Now follow me." While we were on the road he bent down over a hole in the earth and placed some of the herb into the hole and a snake with a large head emerged.

He took a rope and bound the snake just as one binds a young goat. We were afraid but he said to us, "Follow me." So, we followed him until we came to his house. In the dark we saw there the place of which he had spoken. It was behind a wall. He took a lamp and lit a fire all around the mill, warning us, "Do not be frightened by what you see and do not say anything." In the meantime, he released the snake from its bonds and ground some of the herb in a mortar and put it on the head of the snake. The snake entered an opening in the mill and we heard a sound that caused the entire place to shudder. We wanted to leave but the man held onto our hands and said to us, "Do not be afraid. Keep close to me." In the meantime, the snake came out dripping with blood. Again the man took some of the herb and placed it on the head of the snake. The snake once again entered the opening of the mill and in a short while we saw the man with two heads appear from the opening with the snake wrapped around his neck. The man with two heads called out, "Zekita! Zekita!" [This is the name of a small creature that kills snakes.]

Afterwards he lamented that it was his misfortune to be born in this place, for here he could do nothing since the owner of the house was such an expert in herbs. Then he cried out, "Woe! Woe to my mother who brought me to this place!" In the meantime, the mill was uprooted from its place and both the man with two heads as well as the snake came out and fell dead. The man said to us, "This is the power of the herb that I picked in front of you. That is why I neither spoke with you nor raised my head when you approached." He said further, "If people only knew of all the things that the Holy One Blessed Is He has planted upon the earth and all that is to be found in the world they would appreciate the power of their Master in His great wisdom. But the Holy One Blessed is He concealed this knowledge from people lest they stray from His ways and rely upon their wisdom, forgetting all about Him, Heaven forbid!"

A person whom God has blessed with insight and understanding must learn from all this and take it as a warning not to cause pain to any creature, nor even to take lightly the inanimate herbs and plants. And how much more so must one refrain from disparaging one's fellow Jew, the descendants of Avraham, Yitzchak and Yaakov. And even if God has blessed a person with wealth, property and position let him take great care not to conduct himself haughtily, Heaven forbid, towards the congregation of Hashem, His holy flock. Every arrogant or disdainful word that a person utters towards a Jew is immediately inscribed and recorded in a ledger On High. The iniquity remains engraved and preserved there until the time comes that he will be made to suffer severe afflictions on account of it. How much more so must one refrain from denigrating Torah scholars, the punishment for which is many times greater. It is related in the Zohar in Parashas Pekudei (247b) that the angels called serafim are appointed to punish and afflict a person in this world and the next, especially if he shamed someone from whom he learned even one word of Torah, rather than showing him honor and respect. How much more severely, then, will they punish someone who made personal use of a Torah scholar, unless he knew for certain that the scholar had forgiven his honor!

One must learn from the example of the Holy One Blessed is He. For He is the King of the Kings of Kings, yet He chose us out of all the peoples and tongues and called us "My firstborn son Israel" (Shemos 4:22), "the treasured people" (Devarim 7:6) and "Yeshurun" [a straight and honest people] (Devarim 32:15, Yeshayahu 44:2). However, if the children of Israel ignore the will of the Omnipresent, and follow their heart's desire to engage in commerce and worldly pleasures, what satisfaction can the blessed Creator derive from them? Moreover, even if a person prays and dons tefillin and tzitzis on occasion, he prays hurriedly, giving only lip service to Hashem, while his heart is preoccupied with foreign thoughts. Then immediately after he finishes praying, he runs to eat and drink. Concerning such a one the verse declares, "He labors with iniquity and brings forth falsehood" (Tehillim 7:15). Then, one day death suddenly strikes and the person discovers that he has prepared no provisions for the journey that lies before him.

On the other hand, if a person spends his time involved in acts of lovingkindness and Torah study the Holy One Blessed Is He displays His love for him in this world and the next. Thus, is it stated, "Is Efrayim not a precious son to me; a child of delight! Even while I speak of him, I remember him further!" (Yirmeyahu 31:19). Thus, the Holy One Blessed is He loves the righteous, saying of them, "You are sons to Hashem your God" (Devarim 14:1). How much more so, then, should human beings love the righteous. Then they will be rewarded many fold, Amein.

Chapter 84

It is stated, "If you elevate yourself like an eagle and if you place your nest among the stars, from there I will cast you down, says Hashem" (Ovadyah 1:4). I would like to explain this verse homiletically, but first I must preface with a passage from the Talmud (Berachos 6b): What is meant by the verse, "But you have burnt the vineyard; the theft of the poor is in your houses"

(Yeshayahu 3:14)? If someone is poor, what can one steal from him? After all, he is lacking for everything! Rabbi Chalbo said in the name of Rav Huna, "When a poor man greets someone with 'Peace!' and the latter does not respond likewise, he is called a thief.

I have observed that many people are negligent in this area. When someone of modest means greets a wealthy person, the latter turns away and it goes without saying if the one who greeted him was poor. For he does not wish even to look upon the face of a poor man, therefore he behaves as if he neither saw nor heard him. Consequently, according to the passage above he is called a thief. All this is the result of excessive pride. Because the rich man does not wish to respond to one of modest means, let alone a poor person, he turns his face to the side. This causes shame to the poor person who then turns his own face to the other side. Thus, it seems to me that they can be likened to a two-headed eagle, with one head turned this way and one turned the other way. Perhaps it is concerning such a situation that Scripture warns, "If you elevate yourself like an eagle ... from there I will cast you down, says Hashem." For the Holy One Blessed is He is exalted above all else and knows every hidden matter and He will humble the wealthy who behave in this manner. At the same time, He will elevate the lowly ׀ that is, the poor. Thus, the Holy One Blessed is He fashions a sort of "ladder," by means of which, over time, the poor become rich, while the rich man becomes poor.

Therefore, I admonish anyone with sense to remove this stumbling block from before his feet by responding to every man's greeting. If someone greets him with "Peace!" let him respond likewise. This will cause our hearts to draw closer to one another. By contrast, if the rich man does not take the trouble to respond to the poor man the latter cries out to Hashem bitterly in his heart and Hashem surely hears his voice because He is a gracious God.

But there is something else that I have witnessed that is even more despicable than this. If a rich man becomes arrogant on account of his wealth or the clever man on account of his intelligence, one can rationalize on their behalf to some degree because their pride was brought about by their wealth or wisdom. I am more disturbed, however, by those who have nothing to their credit ׀ neither Torah and wisdom nor even material wealth. What is the basis, then, for their pride?

Therefore, my brother and friend, turn away! Turn away from the path of pride and be sure to speak to every man and draw the poor near to you. Be especially careful to greet the poor and certainly to return their greetings, for then the One who makes peace On High will bestow peace upon us and upon all Israel, Amein.

Chapter 85

One of the acts of mercy that Hashem performs on behalf of people is the returning of their souls to their bodies. A person collapses at night exhausted and weary, resembling a corpse. Then the Holy One Blessed is He in His abundant lovingkindness grants him sleep and repose to soothe him of the weariness of his body, the toil of his limbs and the faltering of his loins, thereby relaxing his limbs and bones and restoring his zeal. Obviously the Holy One Blessed is He does not do this in order that the body will be more zealous in sinning, Heaven forbid, but that it will be more zealous in serving Him. Therefore, a person must also appreciate this and seek to fulfill His will. Thus, immediately upon awakening he must purify and sanctify his hands and face. He must not walk four cubits without washing his hands. And when he dons his clothing, he should take care to draw on his left sleeve without binding the garment or undergarment around his arm by means of strings, laces or hooks. This is in order to show that his left arm is obliged in the mitzvah of tefillin. As I have already mentioned, while one dons his tzitzis it is a favorable time to pray to be saved from jealousy, hatred and anger. Therefore, I have listed here some verses that are effective when recited after the blessing over the tzitzis. I received this list from our teacher and mentor, the illustrious Rabbi Yosef, son of the illustrious Rabbi Yudel, z"l:

"I called with all my heart; answer me Hashem, I will treasure Your statutes" (Tehillim 119:145).

"I beseach You Hashem, be pleased with the offerings of my mouth and teach me Your mandates" (Ibid. 119:108).

Kav HaYashar

"I will dwell in Your tent forever; I will take refuge in the shelter of Your wings, selah" (Ibid. 61:5).

"Save me from bloodshed, God, God of my salvation; my tongue will sing of Your righteousness" (Ibid. 51:16).

"I have placed Hashem before me continually; for He is by my right hand so that I will not falter" (Ibid. 16:8).

"God is known among Judah; His name is great among Israel" (Ibid. 76:2).

"I will ascend upon the wings of the dawn; I will dwell beyond the sea" (Ibid. 139:9).

"Let Your hand come to my aid, for I have chosen Your commands" (Ibid. 119:173).

"You lovingkindness, Hashem, fills the earth; teach me Your statutes" (Ibid. 119:64).

"You are illumination, mightier than the mountains of prey" (Ibid. 76:5).

"Save me from all my transgressions; do not attribute to me the shame of an ingrate" (Ibid. 39:9).

"Grant me life according to Your lovingkindness and I will keep the testimonies of Your mouth" (Ibid. 119:88).

"My eyes are constantly upon Hashem, for He will extricate my feet from the net" (Ibid. 25:15).

"Support me and I will be saved and I will speak of your statutes continually" (Ibid. 119:117).

"May it be Your will, Hashem my God and God of my fathers, that I should neither become angry nor cause You to become angry. Master of the Universe, grant me the attributes of humility and submission. Save me from the way of falsehood and bestow upon me Your Torah. Guide me in the way of Your truth and unify my heart to love and fear Your great, mighty and awesome name with all my heart, soul and resources." This supplication is appropriate to recite immediately upon donning one's tallis katan. It is of benefit in saving a person from anger, jealousy and baseless hatred, the three evil traits that are alluded to in the acronym formed by the initial letters of all the verses listed above.

The significance behind the wearing of tzitzis and tefillin is mentioned in the Zohar, Parashas Shelach Lecha (174b). Every individual can reflect on these intentions in accordance with his intellect and it is correct for him to do so. A man must don his tzitzis and tefillin at home so that he will leave the door of his home completed and crowned with tzitzis and tefillin. One who has the time should stop beside the mezuzah in order to make up for the mention of tzitzis [i.e., the third paragraph of the Shema] that is absent from the text of the mezuzah [a mezuzah only contains the first two paragraphs of the Shema]. Afterwards he should place his hand upon the mezuzah and then pass his hand over his eyes and recite this meditation: "Master of the Universe, save me from evil thoughts and let me be spared this day and every day from sin and transgression in the merit of these three commandments that are now joined together. They are the commandments of mezuzah, tefillin and tzitzis. And let me be saved from the evil eye and from sorcery."

Then he should recite as he stands by the doorway beside the mezuzah in his tallis and tefillin: "Hear, O Israel, Hashem is our God, Hashem is one. O Unique and Unitary One, unify my heart to love and fear Your great, mighty and awesome Name with all my heart and soul." Afterwards he should recite the eight-verse beginning with the letter hei in Tehillim, Chapter 119 (verses 33-40). Then he should recite Mishlei 18:10, "The name of Hashem is a mighty tower, the righteous man runs into it and is protected." And Tehillim 122:4: "The tribes of God, as a testimony for Israel to give thanks the Name of Hashem." You recite eight verses of Tehillim 119 because they begin with the letter hei and end with the letter yud, spelling out the Name Y-h, which is the Name that served as testimony to the purity of the tribes of Israel in Egypt, as it is stated H aReuvein y (Bamidbar 26:7). [That is, when the families of Israel are listed in that passage a hei is appended to the beginning of each name and a yud to the end of each name, indicating that Hashem Himself attested to their purity].

Afterwards he should recite: "Master of the Universe, save me, deliver me and give me succor from all sin, transgression and iniquity in the merit of the three commandments mention above. 'I have placed my trust in You; let me not be ashamed forever; spare me in Your righteousness' (Tehillim 31:2)." While reciting this verse one should have in mind that it begins with a beis and ends with a yud, for a numerical value of twelve, an allusion to the twelve tribes. Then he should say: "Master of the Universe, in the merit of the twelve tribes guard me and save me from every sin and from every form of the evil eye. Let them have no dominion over me or my offspring or their offspring forever. And do not allow the evil eye to have dominion over my belongings or my body. Hashem, guard my going out and my coming in. Let them be towards life and peace from now and forever. "Hashem is my refuge upon my right hand. Let us know and run to know Hashem as clearly as the dawn when it has gone forth (Hoshea 6:3). No man shall stand up before you; Hashem your God will put fear and awe of you over all the land upon which you tread as He has promised you (Devarim 11:25). Do not allow a sorceress to live (Shemos 22:17). No dog will wag its tongue towards any of the children of Israel (Shemos 11:7). You have been shown that you may know that Hashem is God, there is no other beside Him (Devarim 4:35)." Afterwards, when a man goes out to the street, his intention should be to meditate continually upon the mitzvos, as I have written above in Chapter Two. Even if he should happen to see snow, he should reflect that it is one of the four shades of skin plagues. And especially if he should encounter an animal, he should conduct himself according to the way I explained in that chapter.

This prayer is of benefit in saving a person from evil spirits and sorcerers and it can help one succeed in business. His prayer will ascend On High to a place beneath the Throne of Glory. Two holy angels are appointed to accompany the man who goes out of his house wrapped in his tallis and with tefillin upon his head (Zohar, 3:301a). These angels bless him and the accuser who waits by the door is denied permission to speak or to cause him any harm. Afterwards he should say, "This gate is Hashem's, the righteous shall enter it" (Tehillim 118:20). Then he should go to the synagogue and pray to God that He grant him a generous income, not through any prohibited means but only from the hand of the Holy One Blessed is He. And let him pray not to be delivered into the hand of flesh and blood.

Come see what is stated in the Zohar, Parashas Lech Lecha (86b-88a): Rabbi Elazar went to visit his father-in-law, accompanied by Rabbi Chiya, Rabbi Yose and Rabbi Chizkiyah. Rabbi Elazar said, "I see that there is never an arousal from above without an arousal from below." What he meant was that they must begin by engrossing themselves in the commandments with affection and then the Shechinah would come and spread its wings over them. Therefore, they immersed themselves in a discussion of Torah. While they were walking, they encountered Rabbi Yeisa, accompanied by another Jew. The Jew began a discourse, "It is stated, 'Of David, to You, Hashem, I lift up my soul' (Tehillim 25:1). Why is it not stated, 'A song of David'? It is because he was actually referring to the spiritual level known as 'David.' His intention was to elevate his soul to the place of supernal holiness that is its source." Rabbi Elazar said to Rabbi Yeisa, "I see that you have come accompanied by the Shechinah …" Rabbi Elazar asked the Jew, "What is you name?" "Yo'ezer," he replied. "The names 'Yo'ezer' and 'Elazar' have the same meaning," Rabbi Elazar observed. They sat down together beside a boulder and the fellow named Yo'ezer revealed to them a number of Torah insights. Then Rabbi Elazar said, "What is your trade?" "I was a teacher of children in my town, but now Rabbi Yeisa from the village of Chanan has come to my town and they took the youths away from me and seated them with him. The people of my town continued to give me my salary just as in the time that the children were with me but I reflected that it was not fitting for me to recei've this benefit for nothing. So, I hired myself out to accompany this scholar."

Rabbi Elazar said, "The blessings of my father are needed here. So, they all got up and went to Rabbi Shimon ben Yochai, and engaged in study in his presence. One day while they were studying the laws of the washing of the hands Rabbi Shimon said, "Whoever does not wash his hands properly is punished here below in addition to being punished On High. The punishment here below is that he becomes impoverished. One who washes properly, on the other hand, receives blessings from above that settle upon his hands, causing him to be blessed with wealth." Sometime later Rabbi Shimon ben Yochai went and observed that this fellow Yo'ezer indeed washed his hands properly, with a generous amount of water. So, Rabbi Shimon prayed, "Let his hands be filled with Your blessings!" And so, did it come to pass. The man discovered a treasure and from that day on he sat and studied all day long. From the treasure he distributed charity and sustenance to the poor with a pleasant countenance. Rabbi Shimon applied to him the verse, "And you shall rejoice in Hashem; you shall glory in the Holy One of Israel" (Yeshayahu 41:16).

From this incident we learn that a man must be exacting about the wages he takes for his labors to see that they are justified. For the people of the village were willing to pay the pious Yo'ezer of their own accord. Even so he was unwilling to receive the money from them for nothing because he wished to benefit only from the fruits of his labor, that is, from money that was earned honestly. Therefore, let every man ensure that he does not benefit from money that was earned dishonestly. And let him also be meticulous in the washing of the hands, both before and after the meal. Then Rabbi Shimon's words, "Let his hands be filled with Your blessings," will apply to him, as well, and blessing and prosperity settle upon the work of his hands and he will succeed in all that he does.

Chapter 86

It is stated, "When I celebrate the appointed Festival; I will judge [its theme] with fairness" (Tehillim 75:3). King Dovid was prompted to write these words because he recognized that our way is not that of the nations of the world, nor is our custom like theirs. For on their festive days they eat and drink to intoxication and go dancing in their public houses and commit other undesirable acts. But this is not the case with Israel, for although they also eat and drink and rejoice in the performance of the commandments, they are careful to spend half the day in prayer, expanding the service with special liturgies, after which they engage in study. All this is hinted at in the word "uprightly" [meisharim], as King Dovid said, "I will judge uprightly." The mem [the numerical value of which is 40] of meisharim alludes to the forty days during which the Torah was given. And although Israel also rejoices on the Shabbos and Yom Tov, they do not neglect the three prayer services, morning, afternoon and evening. These are hinted at in the shi'en of meisharim [a shi'en is comprised of three vertical lines connected at the bottom]. And sometimes a shi'en is written with four heads [a four-headed shin appears on the side of the head tefillin]. This hints at the four prayers that are said on the festivals: morning, additional [mussaf], afternoon and evening. Moreover, we extend our prayers with additional poems and with the liturgical verses of the Krovetz [interspersed with the blessings of the Amidah on special occasions]. The word Krovetz itself is an acronym for the verse, K ol r inah v iyshuah b e'ohalei tz addikim — "The voice of rejoicing and salvation in the tents of the righteous" (Tehillim 118:15). This is hinted at in the letters reish and yud of the word meisharim, which stand for rinah and yeshuah — "rejoicing and salvation." The final mem of meisharim hints at the future redemption, which is alluded to in the phrase, lemarbei hamisrah — "for the increase of the realm" (Yeshayahu 9:6 ; the mem of le m arbei is uncharacteristically a final mem). This is to tell you that although we are filled with gladness and rejoicing on our festivals, nevertheless we pray for the promised redemption. For our happiness will only be complete when the Holy One Blessed is He rejoices with Tziyon and Yerushalayim.

It is stated in the Zohar (Parashas Emor, 94a) that when Israel first lauds the Holy One Blessed is He with songs of praise in their synagogues and study halls and afterwards come home to arrange their houses and tables in honor of Shabbos and Yom Tov, the angels proclaim, "Fortunate is the people whose lot is thus!" (Tehillim 144:15).

Therefore, let not the recitation of the Krovetz seem unimportant in a person's eyes. Rather let him recite them with joy, with concentration of the heart and with careful diction, because each of these liturgical hymns is filled with awesome esoteric allusions. Let them not seem burdensome to him, for they were composed with the assistance of angels from heaven who appeared to Rabbi Eliezer HaKalir. In fact, he arranged them alphabetically, alef to tav and tav to alef, because that is how the angels sing and utter praise On High. The elders and the pious of the generation have passed on to me an oral tradition that if a person belittles the recitation of the Krovetz and downplays the obligation to say it, he will not live out his years, Heaven forbid. For all the unique individuals who composed these poems were leaders of the generation and men of great deeds, for whom numerous miracles were performed both in their lifetimes and after their deaths.

For example, we find the following incident recorded (Shalsheles HaKabbalah, 89a; Seder HaDoros 4830) regarding one leader of the generation by the name of Rabbi Shlomo Gevirol, z"l. He was a master of the esoteric tradition and also of grammar and composed a great number of liturgical poems. But the enemies of Israel were jealous of his vast wisdom, so one day an Ishmaelite lay in wait and murdered him, burying him in his garden beside a fig tree. From that time on this fig tree would always blossom before its time, producing giant and beautiful figs, which was a source of amazement to the entire town. Eventually word of the matter reached the king, who sent for the Ishmaelite and inquired from where he had learned the secret of causing fruit to ripen before its time. Out of his great fear the Ishmaelite was unable to respond, which was the hand of Providence. The king commanded that the man be tortured with harsh and bitter torments until at last he was compelled to confess that from the day that he murdered the Jew, Rabbi Shlomo Gevirol, the tree had begun producing fruit before its time. Upon hearing this the king ordered that the murderer be hung from that very tree.

The point to remember is that the entire congregation of Hashem is holy and the leaders of the generation were the ones who composed these poems. For this reason, it is a good practice to take note of the name of the author of the liturgical or penitential poem one is reciting, as it is recorded in the acrostic. Pray that his merit should stand by you and that the recitation of his words of praise should be acceptable. For the author's soul receives satisfaction when people recite his liturgical or penitential poems with proper concentration. This is especially the case on Shabbos and Yom Tov when the ascending souls bear Israel's prayers On High and the Holy One Blessed is He hearkens to them. This is the reason that we remember the souls of deceased family members on Shabbos and Yom Tov. These are favorable times for pledging charity in their memory, mentioning their names and praying that they be bound up in the bond of life and it is a fitting custom to mention them and pray for them. It is especially important to mention the merit that the souls of one's ancestors and Torah mentors deserve for having disseminated Torah among Israel and for establishing many disciples. But a person should not say that he is praying "in the merit of the charity that I vow to give for the remembering of their souls," lest he delay in fulfilling his vow, Heaven forbid. For then the soul on whose behalf he pledged the donation will turn against him and become his accuser.

Thus did I find it written in the name of the Maharil, z"l (Minhagei Maharil, glosses on the laws of Yom Kippur). I have also heard a fitting explanation as to why the custom in Poland is to remember the souls of the deceased on the last day of Yom Tov. You must know that one of the ten miracles that occurred regularly in the Holy Temple was that three times a year the entire nation was able to enter it, on the festival of Matzos, the festival of Weeks [Shavuos] and the festival of Sukkos. And although the people were crowded together when they stood upright, when they prostrated themselves on the ground there was ample room for all (Avos 5:5), a situation that flew in the face of natural law. The explanation behind this miracle is as follows: On each festival the souls of Avraham, Yitzchak and Yaakov used to visit the heavenly Temple accompanied by the souls of all the righteous. At that time the earthly Temple would move aside and the heavenly Temple would descend to earth to take its place. And since the heavenly Temple was a spiritual edifice it was capable of holding all of Israel. And now that the Holy Temple has been destroyed, on account of our sins, we recall the souls of our holy ancestors on every festival so that their merits will stand by us and our offspring forever, Amein. — Based on the words of my teacher and mentor, Rabbi Yosef, z"l (Yesod Yosef, Chapter 87).

Chapter 87

It is recorded in Sefer Raziel that the wicked do not repent even at the entrance to Gehinnom but may continue to sin and incur punishment as in the case of Navos the Yizre'eilite. This is why we give charity on behalf of the souls of the dead. Then when the living have fulfilled the vows that they made on behalf of those souls they become powerful advocates for the living and on account of this the Holy One Blessed is He bestows His blessing upon all their endeavors. But all this comes to pass only if they neither procrastinate nor delay in fulfilling their vows. After a person leaves the synagogue it is praiseworthy for him to fulfill the mitzvah of greeting his Torah mentor on the festival, which is reckoned as if he received the countenance of the Divine Presence (Mechilta, Parashas Yisro 18:12). For when he beholds his mentor's countenance at that time, he receives the light from a spark of holiness, akin to an extra soul. Afterwards he should go home to eat and drink and rejoice with his wife and children.

One must also distribute generous portions to the poor. You should be aware of what I have found written in the Zohar (Introduction 10b): Rabbi Shimon said: Whoever rejoices on the festivals and does not give a portion to the Holy One, Blessed is He, is called "evil-eyed," and he is hated by the Satan, who immediately comes to accuse him and remove him from the world. How many troubles upon troubles does he cause him! This is because the poor are the portion of the Holy One Blessed is He, who wishes them to rejoice. During these days the Holy One Blessed is He goes up to look in on His shattered vessels. And if He sees that the poor person has nothing with which to rejoice, then the Holy One Blessed is He weeps and desires to destroy the world. At that time all the Heavenly Hosts come before Him, saying, "Master of the Universe! You are called merciful and gracious, so let Your mercies be poured out upon Your children!" The Holy One Blessed is He responds: "Did I not establish the world upon lovingkindness, as it states, 'A world of lovingkindness You did build' (Tehillim 89:3)? Yet I do not see any lovingkindness being performed in the world!" Then the ministering angels say: "It is true that So- and-so is eating and drinking and while he was capable of doing lovingkindness towards the poor, he did not, in fact, give them anything." Instantly the accuser comes and asks for permission to pursue the man. The accuser comes to observe every meal that the person enjoys. If the man is quick to do loving- kindness towards the poor or if there are poor people in the house, the accuser goes away and does not enter. But if not, then he enters and if he sees a tumult of rejoicing without the poor, he ascends On High and indicts him.

In most cases, even at a mitzvah feast, if no words of Torah are spoken and there are no poor people present, quarreling and strife break out. For what pleasure does the Holy One, Blessed Is He, derive from an affair of eating and drinking that is devoid of the rejoicing of a mitzvah? And how much more so if the rejoicing is mixed with thoughts of sin, for instance, when men and women, and teenage boys and girls sit together! Great pitfalls are thus created. Men and women dance in circles together, not realizing that the Satan, with many demons are dancing in front of them. What is the value of such rejoicing? Yet this iniquity has become very common, on account of our many sins, throughout the lands of Poland and Lithuania. Therefore, let every man who fears the word of Hashem be careful to seat the men and women separately in order to distance himself from transgression and in order that the Satan will not mix up the joy of the mitzvah. For it is stated, "In our rejoicing let no stranger mix in" (Mishlei 14:10). [The "stranger" is the Satan, as it is stated, "Do not bow down to a strange god" — Shemos 34:14 — again referring to the Satan.] And let him be sure to grant a portion of every feast to the poor [as I have discussed at length in Chapter Ten].

And let every person reflect in his heart that in the end, everyone must die. And when the soul leaves the body it shrivels and dries, the skin clings to the flesh and bones and worms dominate it. Then let him ponder what becomes of all the dainties and delights with which he pampered his flesh. It is as if they never were and nothing remains of all the moisture he took in with his eating and drinking. His body becomes as dry as a piece of wood. But the iniquity of all that eating and drinking that was not for the sake of a mitzvah remains engraved and the harm that he caused by following his heart's desire and his desires is indelibly impressed upon his body and his bones. Moreover, because of his excessive consumption his thoughts are muddled and he is unable to recite the Birkas HaMazon with proper concentration. This is a tremendous loss.

Come see what is written about this in the Zohar, Parashas Vayakheil (218b): When a person recites Birkas HaMazon properly, with joy and with concentration, then when he ascends from this world a place is prepared for him in the midst of the supernal secrets in the holy palaces. In a number of places in the Zohar (2:154b, 266b; 3:186b, 191b) it is explained that the Sitra Achara stands beside a person's table and one must grant him his portion from the water of the final hand-washing. Therefore, one must be very careful that the Sitra Achara does not remain there after one begins to recite the Grace. When one declares, "Let us prepare to bless!" that is when the Sitra Achara departs. For this reason, the Sages warned that immediately upon washing, one must bless (Berachos 42a). This means that one must not allow any interruption between the final hand-washing and the recitation of Birkas HaMazon. The Ari, z"l, even warned against studying Torah at that time in order that there should be no interruption at all between the final hand-washing and the Birkas HaMazon (Sha'ar HaMitzvos, Parashas Eikev, 45a).

One time a certain Torah scholar came to visit the holy Ari z"l. He was one of the holy disciples of Rabbi Moshe Cordovero and the Ari received him graciously. During the meal the Ari noticed that the man did not eat like a healthy person and that one of his limbs seemed to be causing him pain. The Ari asked his guest why he was not eating and the man replied that for several days his shoulder had been bothering him. Then the Ari peered at him and said, "Undoubtedly you are in the habit of interrupting between the final hand-washing and the Birkas HaMazon." The man acknowledged that this was indeed the case. He was accustomed to study a chapter of Mishnah between the hand-washing and the Birkas HaMazon. This was because he believed that words of Torah were a necessary part of the meal, in keeping with the Sages' dictum that, "Any meal at which words of Torah are not spoken is reckoned as if they had eaten of the sacrifices of the dead [i.e., idolatry]" (Avos 3:3). The Ari explained to the man that it was because of this custom that he had received a pain specifically in the shoulder. For it was in violation of the rule that, "Immediately after the hand-washing must come the blessing," and the word for "immediately" — tekef [תכף]— is comprised of the same letters as the word for shoulder — katef [כתף]. So, the Ari advised the pious scholar to resolve not to interrupt after washing and then he would be healed of his ailment.

You can see from here how exacting the Holy One Blessed is He is with each and every individual and that all of His actions are calculated, measured and weighed. This incident is in keeping with what we have already mentioned — that whoever fails to recite Birkas HaMazon with devotion lives with the Sitra Achara at his table. One who does recite it with devotion, on the other hand, will merit hearing it recited by King Dovid, peace be upon him, when the Holy One Blessed is He makes a feast for the righteous in the time to come (Pesachim 119b). For the Holy One Blessed is He does not withhold the reward of any creature, even for a pleasant turn of speech (Nazir 23b). Thus we find it written in the Zohar, Parashas Terumah (132a), "Whoever recites the Song of the Sea [Shirat HaYam] with devotion merits to see the face of the Moshiach adorned with the crown that the Holy One Blessed is He placed upon him when Israel traversed the sea and merited reciting that song [for the first time]." May it be the will of the Holy One Blessed is He that in the merit of this holy song, which is recited by Israel on the last two days of Pesach, we will be worthy of seeing the face of our king adorned with the crown mentioned above. And may we merit singing that song in the congregation of the righteous, speedily and in our days, Amein. [— Based on the words of my teacher and mentor, Rabbi Yosef, z"l (Yesod Yosef, Chapter 87).]

Chapter 88

It is stated, "This month shall be for you [the head of the months]" (Shemos 12:2). The word lachem [לכם] — "for you" — is comprised of the same letters as the word melech [מלך] — "king," which is a hint that the month of Nissan is the "king" and "head" of all the months. One reason for this is that the twelve months correspond to the twelve permutations of the letters of the Divine Name, so that each month is illuminated by one permutation, whereas the entire month of Nissan is illuminated by the name according to its usual spelling — י-ה-ו-ה. When the order of the letters is altered to form one of the permutations it indicates a slight withholding of Hashem's total mercy, but when the letters are arranged in their proper order it indicates the sway of total mercy. For this reason, the holy souls of the deceased pray for the living in the month of Nissan so that the Divine Name will shine upon Israel with a disposition of mercy.

The dead pray for the living during the month of Tishrei as well, for although the permutation reigning at that time is not one that evokes total mercy, nevertheless, mercy is aroused by means of the shofar instead. Thus, we recite [in the Mussaf service of Rosh HaShanah], "Blessed are You, Hashem, who hears the sound of the [shofar] blast of His people Israel in mercy." And because the principle of "measure for measure" applies at all times, we must conduct ourselves towards those holy souls as one company towards another company by praying for them just as they pray for us. Thus, in the month of Tishrei when this obligation is upon us, and in particular on the eve of Rosh HaShanah and Yom Kippur, we go to the cemetery to pray and give charity on behalf of the living as well as those lying in the earth.

In Nissan, on the other hand, although the Divine Name shines with total mercy, which is why it is forbidden to fast, it is not customary to go to the cemetery to pray beside the graves and recite supplications. This is in order to lend special sanctity to this entire month. How then can we conduct ourselves towards those holy souls as one company towards another, as mentioned above? To this end it is fitting that one adopts the custom of our holy teacher Rabbi Yeshayahu Segal, author of Shenei Luchos HaBris (Part II, beginning of Pesachim). He recommended that from the first of Nissan one should read every day the verses of the inauguration offerings of the twelve leaders as recorded in Parashas Naso (Bamidbar, Chapter 7-8), one prince each day. Then after one has recited the verses pertaining to that day's offering, he should recite this brief supplication: May it be Your will, Hashem our God and God or our fathers, to shed light this day in Your abundant mercy upon the holy souls that are renewed like the birds, chirping their praises and praying on behalf of Your holy people Israel. Master of the Universe, allow those holy birds to enter the sacred place concerning which it is stated, "No eye has beheld it other than You." May it be Your will, Hashem my God and God of my fathers, that if I, Your servant, am descended from the tribe of Such-and-such, about whose leader I have read this day from the Torah, then please cause to shine upon me all the holy sparks and lights that are intermingled with the sanctity of this tribe. And let me be arrayed in the sanctity of this tribe so that I may have understanding and insight into Your Torah and Your awe to perform Your will all my days, myself and my offspring and their offspring from this time forth forever. One should do this every day, for it is an upright custom that is fitting to adopt.

Charity is a "spice" that embellishes every prayer just as an ordinary spice embellishes a dish, improving its taste. Thus it is proper to give charity before praying for those holy souls as mentioned above, provided that one gives his donation in their merit. Therefore, before a person begins reading the portion of each day's prince from the first of Nissan until the twelfth, let him give or pledge to charity a sum commensurate with his means and with this he will bring merit to that entire tribe.

There is another fitting explanation for what I have told you — that the holy souls of the deceased pray for the living specifically in the month of Nissan. According to a well-known dictum of the Sages one should keep his distance from a black ox in the month of Nissan because at that time the Satan dances between his horns. The idea behind this is as follows: The Ari, z"l, writes (Sha'ar HaGilgulim, Introduction 22, 22b; Sefer HaLikkutim, Parashas Bechukosai) that in the month of Nissan the herbs begin sprouting and budding throughout the land, making it possible for the cattle to beginning consuming them. Now, in our times, on account of our many sins, most people in the world are guilty of numerous transgressions. Some are guilty of speaking slander and mockery, some of harboring sinful thoughts and some of sins of action. All sin can be divided into three general categories: Knowing transgression [avon], transgression with intent to rebel [pesha] and negligence [cheit]. Each day a person accumulates more and more of them until at last his iniquities outweigh his merits. As a result, when his soul departs at the time of death it is barred from entering into the holy partition On High, but is instead sent back to earth to be locked in the ground. Then, when the herbs begin sprouting, the souls of the wicked cling to them in order to be consumed by living creatures. Eventually the flesh of those creatures, or the herbs themselves, are eaten by human beings. If a particular plant or piece of flesh is consumed by a righteous individual, the souls incarnate in it receive their rectification and are elevated to the realm of holiness by means of his blessing. In this way the souls that were formerly rejected are enabled to go from darkness to great light.

Now it is the nature of an ox to consume vast quantities of vegetation, causing a large number of rejected souls to accumulate within him. But while they were locked in the ground they absorbed more and more of the foulness and filth of the Sitra Achara. This subsequently finds expression in the increased boldness and ferocity of the ox, creating in him a predisposition to cause damage. This is especially true of a black ox because his blackness indicates that he had a tendency in this direction to begin with. Therefore, it is fitting to pray for these rejected souls, especially those clinging to species of herbs that do not readily make their way to the kinds of places where they will be able to find the repose that they seek.

The time to do this is during the month of Nissan as one recites the words, "Who sheds light upon the earth and those who dwell upon it" [the blessing Yotzeir Ohr in the morning service]. A person should request in his heart that the Holy One Blessed is He in His mercy should shed light upon the world to elevate us along with the rejected souls. These are alluded to in the word "light," as the Ari has stated (Likkutei Torah, Bereishis 6a; Sefer HaLikkutim, Bereishis 1b) in connection with the verse, "And God said, 'Let there be light'" (Bereishis 1:3). It is not by chance that the Satan "dances" between the horns of the ox, for that is the main place where its pride is displayed, just as a rooster's pride is displayed in its comb. Thus, the Satan takes up residence there because it is a center of pride. This should serve as an open rebuke to those who glory in their wealth, cleverness, lineage, learning or whatever it might be. For even if they also engage in study, as long as they are guilty of pride, they act as thrones for the Sitra Achara. This follows from what we have explained — that the Satan dances between the horns of a black ox because they are the locus of his pride.

In light of the above I believe we can now understand the statement in Perek Shirah (Chapter 5) that the song recited daily by the ox is the refrain, "I will sing to Hashem because He has exalted Himself over the exalted, etc." (Shemos 15:1). In other words, the essence of the ox's acknowledgement and praise of Hashem is that pride and grandeur are fitting only to Him, but not to human beings, as it states, "Hashem has begun His reign, He has clothed Himself with majesty" (Tehillim 93:1). Since the entire month of Nissan is a time of favor, the holy souls make no delay in praying on our behalf. Thus, it states, "Due to the holy ones who are in the earth and the mighty, all my desires are [fulfilled] through them" (Tehillim 16:3). They demonstrate their concern for the woes of human beings at all times. For instance, whenever an evil decree is issued, Heaven forbid, they are quick to pray for its rescission. In general, however, they are not permitted to reveal the matter explicitly to human beings. Only on occasion do they come to someone in a dream and reveal it through hints and the like. Thus we find (Shalsheles HaKabbalah, p. 139) that Rabbeinu Yechiel, father of Rabbeinu Asher, had a pious companion whom he loved very much. Both men were elders of the community and both were renowned for their great deeds and their exceptional learning and piety. They swore to one another that whichever of them died first would come to the survivor in a dream and inform him of the ways of death and the subsequent journeys of the soul.

The day finally came and Rabbeinu Yechiel's companion passed away. While the community was assembled in the cemetery prior to the interment Rabbeinu Yechiel addressed them, "Listen to me, my teachers, this is what we swore to one another, myself and my companion now lying before me dead. Therefore, I wish to remind him in your presence to fulfill his oath." At that moment all those present witnessed the deceased's casket move slightly. They quickly opened it up, supposing that the dead man had come alive. But they beheld only the fluttering of his eyelids, which they took as a sign from him that he could not tell them anything. Thirty days later the pious man appeared to Rabbeinu Yechiel pleading to be released from his oath because it was indeed true that he was not permitted to reveal anything.

Kav HaYashar

The thing to remember is that in the month of Nissan we must arouse ourselves to repentance, just as in the month of Tishrei. For it is stated, "Draw and take for yourselves sheep, etc." (Shemos 12:21), which the Sages interpret (Mechilta, Parashas Bo, 11:74), "Withdraw your hands from idolatry." This applies not only to actual idolatry but to all the evil characteristics that are said to resemble idolatry as well. These include: pride and arrogance, turning a blind eye to charity and speaking falsehood. All these transgressions are all considered akin to idolatry. Therefore, since every person knows his own shortcomings, let each one removes these stumbling blocks before the arrival of the Passover season. For our Sages have declared that a person must purify himself on the festival (Rosh HaShanah 16b). This includes purification of the soul as well as the body. And in this merit may we be granted purification and the coming of our Moshiach and the prophet Eliyahu, Amein. — Based on the words of my teacher and mentor, Rabbi Yosef, z"l (Yesod Yosef, Chapter 83).

Chapter 89

[It is stated,] "You shall guard the matzos" (Shemos 12:17). It is worth considering why the Torah expressed this commandment in the form "guarding," because the term "guarding" is usually employed in connection with an item that must be protected from theft. However, you must know that Hashem took His people Israel out of Egypt with great miracles and wonders, after first casting down the guardian angel of Egypt as well as those of the other nations to prevent them from lodging accusations against Israel. The guardian angels of the nations of the world still stand with their accusations in hand, gnashing their teeth against us. And when the holy Yom Tov of Pesach arrives, they are aroused to lodge their accusations in the hope of causing harm to the holy people. But the Holy One Blessed is He commanded and admonished us concerning the eating of matzah and it is that commandment that tips the scales against the Sitra Achara and all our accusers, preventing them from making their indictments against us. This is similar to the concept of the mezuzah affixed to the house with the name Shadd-ai — "Almighty" — inscribed upon it on the outside. And since this is so, the dough of the matzos must be guarded well against the Sitra Achara lest the malignant spirits [chitzonim] have any hold upon it, Heaven forbid. For wherever the word chametz — "leavened bread" — appears in the Torah it is an allusion to the Sitra Achara, while the word machmetzes — "leaven" — alludes to the wicked female consort of the Sitra Achara, the evil Lilis and the Samech Mem SME"L. Therefore, we must guard the matzos to prevent them from leavening. The "guarding" that is mentioned here — "You shall guard the matzos" — is entirely analogous to the guarding that a person must do to protect himself against bandits and brigands that come to kill him and take his possessions, for leaven is a powerful shell of impurity. This is the esoteric significance of chametz and machmetzes. Regarding this impure shell, we declare [in the Rosh Hashanah prayer service], "And all evil will vanish like smoke, etc." Heaven forbid that these forces should have any hold, even the slightest, in the realm of the highest holiness. Thus, it is stated, "Let no trace of the banned property cling to your hand" (Devarim 13:18). This is also why even the smallest amount of leaven bread is forbidden. It is proper to instruct the women of Israel that while they are purifying their vessels of leaven through boiling or scorching, they should pray that the Holy One Blessed is He should eradicate the evil impulse and the wicked Lilis from the earth. For we are confident that one day the Holy One, blessed is He, will uproot the abomination of idolatry from the world.

The customs of the Jewish people have the status of Torah and it is their custom to scrape the tables, benches and walls to eliminate any trace of leaven. Hashem's eyes take in everything that is done by the children of Israel, His treasured community, holy ones descended from holy ones. He notices all the effort they go to in the eradication of leaven throughout the month of Nissan and in return He scrapes away the plagues brought on by Sitra Achara and the accusers, on account of which we must bear the burden of this bitter exile. And since all the labor of preparing for the holy Yom Tov Pesach must be done with love and joy, Israel must guard themselves against anger and certainly against quarreling, squabbling and faction making. When purchasing goods for one's household he should declare out loud, "I am purchasing this for the holy Yom Tov." Needless to say, one must be careful that the money with which he makes purchases for the Yom Tov is free of theft or even a penny's worth of any prohibition. For otherwise one strengthens the Sitra Achara, granting it a portion in the realm of holiness, whereas the law is that even the smallest amount of "leaven" is forbidden (Pesachim 30a).

When the time comes to draw the water to make the matzah, in particular for the mitzvah (i.e., for the Pesach Seder), even a rabbi, a communal leader or a leader of Israel must not allow concern for honor to prevent him from going himself to perform the mitzvah. Every member of Israel must urge himself on in the joy of the mitzvah and in return the Holy One Blessed is He will grant him added life so that he is able to draw water for the matzah and the mitzvah the following year as well. He will also grant him the privilege of drawing water in exultation from the spring of salvation when we merit witnessing with our own eyes the living waters of the well of Miriam the prophetess. One must select perfectly clean vessels with which to draw the water for the mitzvah. One should take two vessels so that one can draw the water for each of the first two nights in separate vessels. This was the custom of the pious Maharil (Minhagei Maharil, Pesach, Hilchos Mayim DeMitzvah). I have also observed that many great scholars use a small jug to draw the water and then as they pour it [into the larger container] they count — alef, beis, gimmel, daled, heh, vav — until they have counted all the twenty-two letters of the Torah. This is in order to draw the sanctity of the Torah into the water. One should do the same with the second vessel for the mitzvah water of the second night.

A person who is elderly or infirm and unable to go himself to draw the water should wait by the entrance of his home. Then, when he sees them coming with the water for the mitzvah, let him run to greet them and carry the water into the house. Many great scholars conducted themselves in this way. When they saw the people coming with the water for the mitzvah they would run towards the holy water and then carry it into their homes upon their shoulders. They were also careful to place it in a clean spot. It is very desirable that no menstruating woman be allowed to touch the water. The water should also be covered with a clean cloth. Leaving the water exposed is forbidden because of a concern about snakes [or the primordial Snake] and the Sitra Achara. When one goes to draw the water, as well as on the way back, he should speak to no one in any language other than in the holy tongue, because he is bearing a sacred charge. Before one goes to draw the water he should wash one's hands, and afterwards he should recite the blessing for the search for leaven [chametz]. We have an oral tradition that our mentors used to order that leaven bread be left in ten places. This corresponds to the ten plagues that the Holy One Blessed is He brought upon the Egyptians as well as the ten judgments with which He will one day punish those who oppressed Israel. That is, He will 1) eradicate them, 2) shake them out, 3) cut them off, 4) confound them, 5) destroy them, 6) uproot them, 7) shatter them, 8) abandon them, 9) finish them off and 10) uproot their testicles.

Corresponding to this the Holy One Blessed is He will sanctify Israel with ten levels of holiness, as related in the first chapter of Keilim (Mishnah 6). One must conduct the search for leaven with great diligence and not perfunctorily. During the search one should scrape the leaven from the holes and cracks with the help of a wax candle held in his hand. In the same way the Holy One Blessed is He will one day eradicate all the filth of the Sitra Achara. It will try to bury and hide it from the light of the Divine Presence, but the Holy One Blessed is He will search out Yerushalayim with lamps. Then the evil inclination will be nullified and eradicated from the world along with all the Sitra Achara and the entire land will be purified with ten levels of supernal holiness, speedily in our days, Amein. — Based on the words of my teacher and mentor Rabbi Yosef, z"l (Yesod Yosef, Chapter 84).

Chapter 90

On the eve of Pesach, that is, the fourteenth of Nissan, a person should rise early in order that he should not err, Heaven forbid, in the eating of leaven bread after the fourth hour of the day. The day begins at dawn, when the sky begins to lighten, showing a white line stretched along the eastern horizon from north to south [as explained by the Rambam in his commentary on Berachos 1:1 and in Tosafos Yom Tov there; this is the main opinion]. On account of our many sins many people have become very lenient about this matter, consuming leaven even after the fourth hour. Woe to them for committing such a grievous sin and willfully violating the words of the Sages! To them applies the verse, "One who breaches a fence shall be bitten by a snake" (Koheles 10:8). They bring upon themselves a tremendous punishment for no reason! Experience has shown, and my mentors have also passed on to me, that one who is lenient in consuming leaven after the fourth hour will not escape without some major consequence that very year. And if no consequence befalls him, he should be even more concerned, for it is clear that Heaven is allowing his guilt to accumulate in order to remove him from the world suddenly through some terrible misfortune.

Therefore, every person who fears Hashem and trembles at His word should guard himself against violating this prohibition. For all the words of the Sages are like coals of fire. I have observed that many people are so absorbed with satiating their throats that they fill their stomachs with excessive amounts of food on the morning before Pesach and then drink to intoxication. Because of this, when the time comes to bake the matzos for the mitzvah, they arrive in an inebriated state to assist with the baking of the matzah and the mitzvah and their minds are not clear enough to keep in mind the sanctity of the matzos. Besides this they err in the sale of the leaven to the gentiles. And because they fail to transact it properly, their sale ends up being of no value. All of this comes about simply because they are so absorbed with satiating their throats and pursuing their heart's desire.

This is not the way of Israel, the congregation of the holy people. Rather, all their affairs and deeds must be tended to justly, with insight and understanding, with purity, fear and awe, for the sake of purifying the soul and not for the pleasure of the body. This is especially true with regard to the mitzvos of the festival with which they are involved at this time, some of which carry the penalty of excision. An oral tradition has been handed down to me that through all the effort that a person exerts in honoring of the Yom Tov of Pesach and the weariness and exhaustion it causes, he kills the harmful spirits called the "plagues of men." Thus, one who immerses himself in the preparations for the days of the Yom Tov of Pesach repairs the harm caused by the spilling of seed. Every heart knows its own failings and there is almost no one among us who is free of this sin. Therefore, it is incumbent upon every man of Israel to remedy what he is able. Then, Hashem in His abundant mercy and lovingkindness will accept the good intentions of His people Israel and expedite our redemption.

Every person is obligated to purify himself on the Yom Tov (Rosh HaShanah 16b). This clearly does not mean literally on Yom Tov. Rather he must purify himself before the onset of Yom Tov so that he may greet Yom Tov in holiness and purity. The esoteric significance of a festival is that it embodies the sanctity of the two Divine names, הוי"ה and אהי"ה, spelled out in full, like this: יו"ד ה"י אל"ף ה"י יו"ד ה"י and וי"ו ה"י 72=20+15+22+15] 161=111+15+20+15]]. The total [72+161] comes to 233, which is equal to the value of the word regel [רגל] — "festival." Thus when a person purifies himself for Yom Tov he should have in mind that he is drawing upon himself the sanctity of these two names. The Ari, z"l, writes (Sha'ar HaKavanos, 78a) that while one is ritually immersing himself one should have in mind to accept the illumination of the two names, הוי"ה and אהי"ה, since this is the significance of the mitzvah of purifying oneself on the regel. But if he is elderly, weak or infirm he should not endanger himself for the sake of the mitzvah because the Holy One Blessed is He does not wish for people to endanger themselves. Rather, he should purify himself by pouring over his body nine kav of water drawn in a bucket or he should simply bathe his body from the waist down, and this too will be accepted with favor by the Holy One Blessed is He.

Afterwards one should study as much as possible the laws of Pesach appearing in the Torah. Our teacher the illustrious Rabbi Yeshayah Segal writes in the Shelah: Before immersion it is praiseworthy to wash one's body in hot water. Although this is true on the eve of every Yom Tov, it is especially important on the eve of Pesach. The reason for this is clear in light of what is explained

Kav HaYashar

in the Zohar, Parashas Vayikra (95b). There it's taught that on the fourteenth of Nissan while the chametz is being purged by fire, a person should have in mind that at that very moment he is becoming a free man. For he is leaving the bondage of the evil inclination, which is identical with the Satan who rules over us in this bitter exile. The burning of the chametz indicates that the evil inclination will also be eliminated from the world, after which we will all be holy and Hashem will dwell in our midst. At that time all the shells of impurity and all wickedness will disappear from the earth and "Hashem will be one and His Name will be one" (Zecharyah 14:9). This is why the destroying of the chametz takes place specifically on the fourteenth of Nissan, because that is when the moon is full and the shells of impurity have no dominion over the children. For the shells of impurity would like to invoke judgments against them and cause them to be afflicted with epilepsy, Heaven spare us. But they cannot do so when the moon is full. When it is not full, however, they do have the ability to afflict the children with the disease mentioned above. This is alluded to in the verse, "Let there be lights [me'oros] in the firmament" (Bereishis 1:14). The word me'oros is missing the letter vav, so that it can also be read, me'eras which means "a curse." Therefore, before burning one's chametz he should have in mind that the process be carried out thoroughly, in order that the shells of impurity will be purged.

In keeping with this, I have witnessed a worthy custom according to which the lulav branches are placed with the chametz in the fire. Although there is an esoteric reason for this, the one mentioned frequently by the authorities is that since they were used for one mitzvah, let them be used for another mitzvah. The point to remember is that the elimination of the chametz symbolizes liberation from the Sitra Achara. Therefore, it is very important to immerse oneself in hot water at that time, just as it is the way of freed captives to bathe themselves in hot water. Afterwards one should engage in the fashioning and baking of the matzos, through which one immerses himself in an activity of the highest sanctity. The matzos for the two Seder nights should be made with joy and happiness, for this is a unification of the Holy One Blessed is He and His Shechinah, as is mentioned in the Zohar, Parashas Emor

(95b): Because of this, the holy people Israel prepare [a house] for the unification of the Holy One Blessed is He and His Shechinah the entire day of the fourteenth...For on that night there is aroused a holy supernal joining. This is the meaning of the verse, "This is a guarded night for Hashem" (Shemos 12:42). Why is the word "guarded" written in the plural (shimurim)? To indicate a combining... Regarding the covering the table and the custom of decorating and beautifying the cushion for reclining, they are like all the customs of the holy people of Israel. The main intent is to prepare a place of reclining in honor of the Holy One Blessed is He and His Shechinah. For this reason, the cushion should not be prepared, Heaven forbid, by a non- Jewish maidservant but by a Jewish woman. How fitting it would be if it could be done by a woman who is free of menstrual defilement. And if it could be done by a young girl who has never menstruated, obviously this would be the best and most praiseworthy of all.

It states in the Zohar, Parashas Vayikra (ibid.): One must rejoice on that night because there is rejoicing On High as well as down below. Therefore, one must recite the songs and praises of the night in joy and exultation and refrain from any display of anger. The Zohar warns in a number of places (2:40b, 202b): It is incumbent upon a person to recount the Exodus from Egypt. And at the time of the recounting the Holy One Blessed is He gathers all His hosts and says to them, "Come and hear the relating of praise, in which they rejoice in the secret of their Master's redemption." Then they come and give thanks to the Holy One Blessed is He for all those miracles and mighty deeds. Meanwhile all the hosts of Heaven give acknowledgement to the Holy One Blessed is He regarding the holy people that He possesses on earth, who rejoice in the joy of their Creator's redemption. Then the power and might of Heaven are augmented, while Israel, through their recounting, lend power to their Master. And all the worlds are filled with fear of the Holy One Blessed is He.

So, you can see the tremendous significance of the recounting of the story of the Exodus. Therefore, one must take care to recite the Haggadah at an unhurried pace. One must not view it as a burden, Heaven forbid. You must know that there is a positive Scriptural injunction for each and every Jew to recall continuously throughout his life the miracles that the Holy One Blessed is He did for our forefathers and for us. And when this day arrives, he must recount Hashem's kindnesses to his children, as it is stated, "And you shall say to your children on that day, etc." (Shemos 13:8). This is the essence of the mitzvah of recounting the story of the Exodus every year and in every generation on Pesach night. In merit of this the Holy One Blessed is He will spread His wings over us continually to save us in every place and on every road and will continue performing miracles and wonders on our behalf. But if a person views the recitation of the Haggadah as a burden to be fulfilled reluctantly or listlessly, without joy and intention of the heart, he will not merit having miracles performed on his behalf in times of danger.

I have abbreviated the matter. See the full discussion in Shenei Luchos HaBris (Part II, Pesachim). When one comes to the part of the Haggadah that reads, "An incident [ma'aseh] involving Rabbi Eliezer and Rabbi Akiva," one should have in mind what the Ari, z"l, says about it (Pri Eitz Chayim, Sha'ar, Sha'ar Chag HaMatzos, Chapter 7). He explains that there are 370 lights On High, emanating from the two holy names appearing in the verses, "Who is a G-d [E-l] like You, bearing iniquity and passing over transgression, etc." (Michah 7:18), and "Hashem, a merciful and gracious G-d [E-l]" (Shemos 34:6). For when the name E-l is spelled out in full — אל"ף למ"ד — its numerical value is 185. The numerical value of the two names in the verses thus totals 370. These 370 lights receive the souls of the Torah scholars who study with pure motives and are filled with awe of Heaven. Then the 370 lights shine down upon their heads along with another 45. For this is the value of the four-letter Name when it is spelled out like this: יו"ד ה"א וא"ו ה"א. These 45 lights are granted to the scholars in the merit of their awe. Now, since the scholars of the Mishnah and the Talmud were undoubtedly flawless in their Torah and awe of Heaven, they earned the illuminations of these two sets of lights, indicated by the acronyms 370 [ע"ש] and 45 [מ"ה]. When these letters are rearranged, they spell out the word ma'aseh [מעשה] — "an incident," as in the line from the Haggadah, "An incident involving Rabbi Eliezer and Rabbi Akiva, etc." For the letters of the word ma'aseh allude to the 370 and 45 lights and we mention them in order that they will shine upon us in the merit of the scholars of the Mishnah and Talmud.

You should be aware of an important insight taught by the Ari (Siddur Rabbi Asher 370a) regarding the passage beginning with the words, "And this [Ve'hi] is what stood by our forefathers, etc.," and continuing on until the words, "And the Holy One Blessed is He delivers us from their hand." He writes that one should raise one's cup and hold it aloft beginning with the words, "And this is what stood by," because the word "And this" — Ve'hi — alludes to the Shechinah, who remains with us at all times while we are in exile. The nations of the world and the Satan rise up to destroy us with harsh decrees, Heaven forbid, but the Shechinah stands by us, delivering us from the utter destruction that they wish to wreak upon us with their oppressions and decrees.

Another insight to be aware of, and which I believe to be correct, is that when our teacher Moshe killed the Egyptian it seems to have been the beginning of Egypt's downfall and from that time forth their guardian angel seems to have been on the wane. For the Ari writes (Likkutei Torah, 55a; Sha'ar HaPesukim, 26a) that Moshe killed the Egyptian with the Divine Name Y-CH-SH [יכ״ש], which is one of the components of the forty-two part Name. This name derives from the verse, "Who appointed you to be an officer or judge?" — Mi y sam ch a le'i sh sar veshofeit (Shemos 2:14). For this Name had the power to subdue the Egyptians and to wreak vengeance upon them. King Dovid alludes to it in the verse, "Judge me, Hashem, according to my righteousness" — Sh afteini Y -H-V-H k etzidki (Tehillim 7:9), the acronym of which also spells out this Name.

In view of our obligation to relate the story of the Exodus it seems to me that a hint to the Divine Name mentioned above can also be seen in the acronym of the phrase, "a night of guarding" — l eil sh imurim (Shemos 12:42). For the value of the letters ל״ש [330] is equal to that of the Name יכ״ש [330]. This night is called a "night of guarding" because throughout the night we are protected from harmful spirits (Pesachim 109b). In acknowledge of this we refrain from reciting the [bedtime] Shema on this night in order to demonstrate our faith that the Holy One Blessed is He will protect us from all harmful spirits and other agents of misfortune on the two nights of Passover. For the name mentioned above will vanquish all evildoers. Therefore, our duty is to elaborate on the story of the Exodus and whoever does so at greater length is worthy of praise. — Based on the words of my teacher and mentor Rav Yosef (Yesod Yosef, Chaps. 84-85).

Chapter 91

King Dovid said, "Even the bird has found a house, and the swallow, a nest for itself" (Tehillim 84:4). Surely Dovid did not write these words in vain, nor was he referring to an ordinary bird. For what would be novel in the fact that a bird found a home and a swallow, a nest? Rather, the true meaning of this verse is explained in the Zohar, Parashas Balak (196b): The worlds and chambers On High in Gan Eden where the righteous dwell are arranged in three rows. In these rows are numerous chambers and palaces filled with the souls of righteous and concerning them it is stated, "No eye has beheld it, O God, other than You" (Yeshayahu 64:3). The righteous dwell there in honor and distinction, their crowns upon their heads. Between the rows stroll those righteous souls with less merit than the ones who dwell in a fixed place. But strolling among the rows is also a delight from which they derive great satisfaction. Concerning them was it stated, "Even the bird has found a home." That is, although they remain between the rows, even there they are able to find a home and a place of rest in which to enjoy the delight they are experiencing. Dovid refers to them as "birds" because in the month of Nissan the birds begin chirping. Similarly, in the month of Nissan the souls in Gan Eden don the form of birds and each and each morning they chirp like birds. This chirping consists of the praises of the Holy One Blessed is He and prayers for the living, because at this time of year all Israel are engaged in mitzvos and the fulfillment of the instructions of the Master of the Universe. Those righteous souls who dwell within hidden palaces, concerning which it is stated, "No eye has beheld it," are called dror [which means a "swallow" but also "freedom"] because they have attained freedom and liberty from everything. It is also said of them that they have "a nest," that is, a unique dwelling place, resembling a well fashioned and well-prepared nest.

You may ask. In what way were those who dwell within the concealed palaces more deserving than those between the rows? The answer is that it states, "Where she places her fledglings on the ruins of Your altars, Hashem of Hosts" (Tehillim 84:4). That is to say, those dwelling in the concealed palaces merited this because they raised their sons to be Torah scholars, toiling in both the Written and the Oral Torah, corresponding to the two altars in the Beis HaMikdosh. Three times a year the Holy One Blessed is He desires to take delight in these righteous ones. Therefore, He opens for them a certain palace in which crowns are fashioned, and they will be placed upon the head of our righteous Moshiach in the time to come.

We mentioned earlier that in this month all Israel are busy with mitzvos — eliminating leavened products, purifying their vessels through boiling, scorching, rinsing and pouring hot water, inspecting the grain in a sifter, sifting the flour, grinding it, kneading it, arranging the loaves, stoking the oven and baking. Each of these tasks is reckoned as a separate mitzvah. Therefore, it is fitting and proper that none of them should be performed by gentiles but only by Jews. This being so, it is also fitting for a person to actively seek out mitzvos to perform during this month. Let everyone who fears the word of Hashem consider what new mitzvah practice he can adopt, for this, too, is included within the holy words of the passage above that in this month all Israel are busy with mitzvos. Thus, the words, "This month shall be for you" (Shemos 12:2), can be interpreted very beautifully, "to purify your souls." One must also give charity and sustenance to the poor. For the Talmud teaches that Pesach is the time when Heaven renders judgment regarding our crops (Rosh HaShanah 16a) and Zohar Chadash, Parashas Bereishis (18b) elaborates: "On Pesach they are judged regarding their produce." What is this coming to teach us? Rabbi Yitzchak said: It refers to actual produce. For Rabbi Yitzchak said: Last year the Holy One Blessed is He gave them sufficient produce to satisfy the world… But then He saw that they fell short in giving to charity relative to the abundance that He bestowed upon them and that they failed to tithe or to give sufficiently to the poor, the orphaned and the widowed. Therefore, when Pesach comes, He judges them regarding the past years crop. It follows, then, that a person must consider well, throughout the month of Nissan, whether he has fulfilled his obligation of charity relative to the bounty he received from the Holy One Blessed is He during the past year. It is even more important that the leaders of this holy people make a reckoning concerning the past year and especially concerning the year to come, particularly when it comes to such a great and holy festival, for people's needs at this time are many. All Jews are equal with respect to the magnitude of the miracles they experienced. Therefore, poor and rich alike require matzos, bitter herbs, four cups of wine and the rest of the holiday supplies.

Come and see what is stated in the Zohar, Parashas Beshalach (61a) regarding the special concern Providence shows towards the poor and the needy: Rabbi Chiya said, "I am very perplexed by the verse, 'For Hashem hears the needy' (Tehillim 69:34). Does He hear only the needy and not others?" Rabbi Shimon said, "It is because the needy are closer to the king. For it is stated, 'God will not despise a heart that is broken and contrite' (Tehillim 51:19), and there is no one in the world more broken hearted than the poor." Rabbi Shimon ben Yochai said further, "Come and see. All the inhabitants of the world appear before the Holy One Blessed is He in body and soul, whereas the poor man appears before Him in soul alone. And the Holy One Blessed is He is closer to the soul than to the body."

There was a poor man in the neighborhood of Rabbi Yeisa to whom no one gave any thought and who was very bashful. One day the poor man became weak and fell ill. Rabbi Yeisa came to visit him. While he was there, he heard a voice from Heaven declare, "Wheel! Wheel!" [The Gemara in Shabbos 151b likens poverty to a wheel making its rounds among the inhabitants of the world.] This voice emanated from the "potter's wheel" where the souls go immediately after leaving the body. The voice continued: "This soul is ascending to Me before its time has come! Woe! Woe to mankind because there is no one to restore this man's soul to him!" Then Rabbi Yeisa poured into the pauper's mouth some water in which he had cooked some dried figs and medicinal herbs [which cause the patient to sweat and then to be healed]. A sweat broke out on his face and his soul returned to him. Afterwards Rabbi Yeisa asked the man what had happened to him. He answered, "By your life, rabbi, my soul indeed fled from me and ascended all the way to the throne of the King. It wanted to remain there but the King wished to grant you merit. For they proclaimed about you that, 'One day Rabbi Yeisa will elevate his soul, connecting it with a certain holy chamber from which the companions of Rabbi Shimon are destined to cause an awakening on earth.' They then prepared three thrones for you and your companions." From that day forward people cared for the poor man and provided him with his needs.

And further: Another poor man came before Rabbi Yitzchak carrying a half ma'ah coin in his hand. He said to Rabbi Yitzchak, "Make my soul and those of my sons and daughters whole." Rabbi Yitzchak replied, "How can I make your souls whole when I have only a half ma'ah coin on me?" The poor man answered, "I will complete your coin with the half ma'ah coin that I already have." So Rabbi Yitzchak took out his coin out and gave it to him. Then Rabbi Yitzchak was shown a dream in which he was walking along the shore of the ocean and someone was trying to throw him in. He reached for the outstretched hand of Rabbi Shimon ben Yochai but just then the poor man came along and saved him. When he awoke, this is the verse that came into his mouth, "Fortunate is the one who understands [the needs of] the lowly, on a day of evil Hashem will preserve him" (Tehillim 41:2).

Here you have a number of warnings to be mindful of the poor. This is especially important for charity officers. They must be sure to purchase grain and then grind it, so that they may send flour to the poor. For then the poor are able to benefit more readily. The charity officers also receive greater reward by sending flour and meat to the poor. Thus, we find in the third chapter of Ta'anis (23a) that when the world was in need of rain the rabbis sent a delegation to Aba Chilkiyah. He said to his wife [before the rabbis arrived], "Let us go up to the roof and pray for mercy. Perhaps the Holy One Blessed is He will be appeased and rain will come, so that we will not have to take credit for ourselves." So, they went up to the roof. Then Aba Chilkiyah stood in one corner while his wife stood in another corner and they prayed for mercy. A cloud appeared over where his wife stood first. At that moment the rabbis arrived to ask him to pray for rain. When he came down from the roof they said, "We know that the rain came on account of you. But why did the cloud first appear on the side where your wife was standing?" He replied, "Because a woman can be found both in town and at home, thus she enables the poor to benefit more readily." As Rashi explains, a housewife gives the supplicants bread and beans and the like, which they are able to enjoy without any further effort. "Whereas I," said Aba Chilkiyah, "merely give them money."

From here we see that one who gives the poor money does not receive as much merit as one who gives them bread, meat and wine, thereby sparing them the need to go and purchase these things and enabling them to benefit more readily. For this reason, the ideal custom is to distribute flour to the poor. Although this overtaxes the charity officers, they receive more reward as a result. Moreover, our Rabbis have said of the verse, "And those who lead the many to righteousness are like stars forever and ever" (Daniel 12:3), — "This refers to the charity officers" (Baba Basra 8a).

Why are charity officers likened to the stars? In my opinion it is because the stars shed their light at night, rather than in the daytime, in keeping with the dictum, "Of what benefit is a candle at noon?" (Chullin 60b). In the same way, the special task of charity officers is to shed light in dark places of poverty and indigence. It is in such places that the officers must shine their light and exercise their supervision, examining the situation well to determine how and what should be done to accomplish the most good. Fortunate are those charity officers who tend personally to the great mitzvah of purchasing choice fine flour, for the portion of the poor is Heaven's portion. This is the deeper significance of the verse, "And all your choicest vows that you vow to Hashem" (Devarim 11:12). As Rashi explains, "This teaches that one must give the poor their portion from the choicest part." For the portion of the poor is Hashem's portion, as I have mentioned several times in earlier chapters (7, 10). Look there.

I have seen a tremendous stumbling block among the charity officers of the Polish provinces. The system in those lands is that each officer serves for only a single month, to be relieved by another officer the following month. Then when the months of Nissan and Tishrei arrive, at which time the needs of the poor are particularly great, each of the officers excuses himself from the task, telling the supplicants who come before them, "What do you want with me? Here is the officer of the month. It is his responsibility to fulfill his obligation this month!" Such conduct is very unworthy, for in fact it is incumbent upon all the officers to carry out this holy task. Bekasef yisa'u — "Let them bear the burden of the money!" [this is a play on the words of the verse in Bamidbar 7:9, "They (the holy vessels) bear upon the shoulder," which is pronounced the same in Hebrew]. What is the officer of the month supposed to do? Sometimes he lacks the resources to lend the money for the distribution out of his own pocket, but neither is there enough money in the charity fund. This holy task should be treated as of no less importance than the service of a human king, which is incumbent upon his subjects every day, week and month. No one would think of saying to a human king, "I am exempt this month. I am responsible for a different month." Why, then, should one speak this way regarding the service of the King of the kings of kings, the Holy One Blessed is He, Heaven forbid? Therefore, all the charity officers should gather to examine the situation well in order to determine the needs of the poor and needy. On this account Hashem will bless the labor of their hands and they will merit witnessing the rebuilding of Tziyon and Yerushalayim, Amein, so may it be Heaven's will. — Based on the words of my teacher and mentor Rabbi Yosef, z"l (Yesod Yosef, Chapter 86).

Chapter 92

The Holy One Blessed is He in His great love for Israel commanded them to count forty-nine days from the day after Pesach until the Yom Tov of Shavuos, the day of the giving of the Torah, which is the fiftieth day. As is explained in the Zohar (3:97a), when Israel was in exile in Egypt, they sank into the shell's impurity until the forty-ninth gate of defilement. Had they remained there for even one day beyond the fifteenth of Nissan then we, our children and our grandchildren would still be enslaved to Pharaoh. But the Holy One Blessed is He in His abundant mercy and lovingkindness took us out to freedom and gave us the Torah fifty days later. That is, Israel was required to count forty-nine days, excluding the day of the giving of the Torah, and on each day they ascended to the next of the forty-nine Gates of Holiness, also known as the forty-nine "Gates of Understanding." Because of this the Holy One Blessed is He has commanded us to count seven weeks, parallel to the seven clean days that a menstruating woman must count before she becomes purified and permitted to her husband. For in the desert Israel also had the status of a menstruating woman as a result of their contact with the husks of defilement of Egypt. Therefore, they were required to count seven complete weeks.

In Midrash Rabbah (Bereishis 30:8) it is taught that every individual to whom the term tamim — "flawless" or tamimus — "completion" applies, completed a unit of seven "weeks," corresponding to the forty-nine days. Three days prior to the giving of the Torah Israel was commanded in the mitzvah of "separation" [hagballah], at which time they purified themselves like a woman purifying herself for her husband after menstruation. On the fiftieth day Israel merited to enter the last of the fifty Gates of Understanding, which is called the "Tree of Life that is in the midst of the garden" (Bereishis 2:9). Although there is a dispute between Rabbi Eliezer and Rabbi Yehoshua (Rosh HaShanah 11a) regarding whether the world was created in Nissan or Tishrei, both agree that it was not actualized until Nissan. Therefore, it is from the first of this month that we number the months. Thus, Nissan is called the "first [lit. head] of the months."

It follows, then, that Pesach is the first of the Chagim, Shavuos, the second Chag and Sukkos the final Chag. That is why Shavuos is called the "Tree of Life that is in the midst of the garden" (Zohar, 3:96a), because it is the middle Chag [i.e., sandwiched between Pesach and Sukkos]. The Zohar also refers to Shavuos as the "praise of the Torah," which is highest praise of all. That is why the Torah was given on this day, since the Torah is also called the "Tree of Life that is in the midst of the garden." I believe that it was with reference to this that the Zohar states (ibid.): "And on the

Day of the First Fruits when you sacrifice a new offering to Hashem in your weeks, there shall be for you a holy convocation" (Bamidbar 28:26). Rabbi Shimon began his address, "'Then the trees of the forest will exult before Hashem, for He comes to judge the earth' (Divrei HaYamim 16:23) ... On the surface it is not clear why Rabbi Shimon chose to elaborate on this verse from Divrei HaYamim in this context. I believe that it is because all the trees of the forest of Levanon are bound to the "Tree of Life in the midst of the garden," as I have already explained. In order to demonstrate His affection for Israel before all the nations the Holy One Blessed is He sustained us with manna in the desert. Thus, is it stated, "Behold I will rain upon you bread from Heaven" (Shemos 16:4). He also commanded us to bring an offering of barley flour on the Yom Tov of Shavuos. Concerning this the Zohar (ibid.) teaches, "Meritorious is Israel's lot, for the Holy One Blessed is He tests them with a barley offering, like a straying wife who must bring an offering of animal fodder. So, too, the Holy One Blessed is He commanded them to bring an offering of barley flour.

But at that very moment Israel declared, 'We will do' before 'We will hear' (Shemos 24:7) and all of them were shown to be righteous, as it is stated, "You are entirely beautiful, my beloved, and there is no flaw in you" (Shir HaShirim 4:7). And it is also said of them, "Who can find a woman of valor" (Mishlei 31:10) and, "A woman of valor is a crown for her husband" (Mishlei 12:4). Therefore the Zohar (ibid., 96b) refers to the flour offering of Shavuos as a "jealousy offering" (Bamidbar 5:18). It is also called a "new flour offering" (Vayikra 23:16) because Israel was as if created anew the day the Torah was given. Thus, they resembled a straying wife who is discovered to be unsullied, of whom it is stated, "She shall be exonerated and seed shall be sown and she shall be pure" (Bamidbar 5:28). And so, did Israel become pure after they brought the Shavuos offering.

The Yom Tov of Shavuos consists of only one day to symbolize the Oneness of the Holy One Blessed is He is. Similarly, Israel is called "one nation in the land" to symbolize the fact that they are bound to His unity. It is an allusion to the Tree of Life, which unifies all the trees of Gan Eden and binds them in a total unity.

Therefore it is stated in the Zohar (Parashas Emor, 97a): "And you shall count for yourselves from the day after Shabbos, from the day you bring the sheaf [omer] of the wave offering." When Israel was in Egypt they were under another domain, attached to the realm of impurity like a woman sitting out her days of impurity. But when they underwent circumcision in Egypt, they entered into the holy portion called "covenant" and became freed of their impurity like a woman cleansed of her impurity. What is stated after their impurity ended? "And you shall count, etc." This is parallel to what is stated regarding the woman, "And she shall count seven days." Thus, did the Holy One Blessed is He tell Israel that their reckoning begins from now. "You shall count for yourselves" — specifically "for you," that is, for your own sakes in order that these forty-nine days should be flawless in their purity corresponding to the forty-nine gates into which Israel had fallen in the defilement, through their association with the idolatry of Egypt. And on the fiftieth day Israel became cleansed of their filth and entered the last of the fifty gates of understanding, all of which are pure. That fiftieth day was holy and pure and on that very day Israel was granted freedom from the angel of death and the enslavement of the nations.

Therefore it is fitting for everyone who fears Hashem and trembles at His word to study all night long on the Yom Tov of Shavuos, reciting the Tikkun [a text comprised of passages from all the various sections of the Torah] composed by the disciples of the Ari, z"l. And to toil in the Torah, the Prophets, the Writings, the Mishnah and selected passages from the Zohar. Some recite the Tikkun on both nights of Shavuos and fortunate is the one who does so. For through the arousal from below one arouses a unification On High, resulting in a tremendous outpouring of holiness. In this merit may the Holy One Blessed is He pour down upon us a new light and may we all merit its illumination, Amein.

Chapter 93

Rabbi Yochanan said (Berachos 31a): "It is forbidden to fill one's mouth with laughter in this world, as it is stated, 'Then [in the future] our mouth will be fill with laughter' (Tehillim 126:2)." The Rabbis said of Rabbi Shimon ben Lakish that from the moment he heard this from Rabbi Yochanan he never again filled his mouth with laughter.

The idea behind this is that Hashem created the human being with a heart, a liver and a spleen. The heart is in the upper part of the body and towards the middle, the liver is below it and to the right while the spleen is below and to the left. The liver symbolizes Eisav's spiritual source, which is called "Edom" because the liver is entirely saturated with blood [dam]. For this reason, Eisav himself is also referred to as Edom. Moreover, his food was red [adom], his guardian angel is Adom and his character is permeated with the attribute of judgment. The spleen symbolizes the wicked Lilis and the heart symbolizes the holy people Israel who are holy to their God. For this reason, the heart receives only the most refined and pure portion of the blood, distinguishing between one type of blood and another, that is, between menstrual blood and blood that is pure. The liver, by contrast, draws towards it all the impure blood and makes no difference between one type and another. The liver is always in a state of anger. Therefore, the Sages have said (Zohar, 1:27b; Part 3:179a) that whoever becomes angry is deemed as if he worshipped idols. For I have already noted (Chapter 68) that anger derives from the liver and that it represents the influence of the Samech Mem (SME"L) who is referred to as, "other gods." The spleen represents the influence of the Lilis, whose strategy is to appear to a man at night in a dream and in the daytime in the form of a woman until she succeeds in causing him to spill his seed. For this reason, the spleen is also the source of laughter (Berachos 61b).

While the Holy Temple was standing two lights emanating from two supernal worlds shed their illumination upon Israel. Concerning these it is stated, "Let there be light and there was light" (Bereishis 1:3). From the same two supernal worlds derive the souls of the Matriarchs Rochel and Leah, both of whom contributed to the building of the Jewish nation. They also caused the Samech Mem and his consort Lilis to be humbled, depriving them of the power to cause Israel any harm. The numerical value of "light" — אור — is 207. Thus two "lights" equal 414, identical with the numerical value of laughter" — שׂחוק. But after the Holy Temple was destroyed our iniquities caused these supernal lights to depart. Then the two shells of impurity mentioned above gained dominion. From that time forth the evil Lilis laughs at us, on account of our many sins. Therefore, we are not to rejoice or laugh in this world. But when our Moshiach arrives, "then our mouth will be filled with laughter." A person must realize, then, that if he wishes to appease his Creator, he must not display any jocularity at all as long as the Temple lies in ruins, for it is forbidden for us to laugh. Whoever is careless about this lends power to the spleen and causes the two shells of impurity mentioned above to wax in strength. But it is not only filling one's mouth with laughter that is forbidden. All forms of rejoicing other than those connected with a mitzvah are forbidden. And in connection with a mitzvah one should not rejoice excessively, as our Sages have intimated.

See, for example, what is stated in the Zohar, Parashas Tazria (45b): Rabbi Chiya and Rabbi Yose were traveling along a road. They came to a certain field and saw a balsam tree on the right side of the road. Rabbi Yose said, "A covering, a covering of smoke is in our eyes." In other words, a film of smoke from the burning of the Holy Temple covers the eyes of the righteous who constantly reflect on its destruction. Therefore, from that day onward it has been forbidden to look upon at any scene of rejoicing.

See how great is the obligation to mourn over the destruction of the Holy Temple and the spilling of Israel's blood. Therefore, one must recite the Psalm, "By the rivers of Babylon" (Tehillim 137) and pour out tears over the destruction. One must also recite Tehillim 83 over the slaughter of the righteous. For the gates of tears were never sealed (Berachos 32b), nor are tears ever erased. In Heaven there is an angel especially appointed to receive tears. The same angel is also in charge of receiving the prayers of Israel that are accompanied by tears. He holds command over the Ofanim called YRChMYEL [ירחמיא"ל] (Zohar, 2:245b), and has charge over six hundred Chayos. Nevertheless, says the Zohar, there is another category of tears, concerning which it is stated, "Behold, the mighty ones cry outside; emissaries of peace weep bitterly" (Yeshayahu 33:7): When the righteous leave this world all the tears they shed are taken by the supernal chariots who mix them with those shed over the destruction of the Temple. Concerning this was it stated, "And Hashem God will wipe the tear from upon every face" (Yeshayahu 25:8). Whose "face" does this refer to? It is a reference to the holy supernal chariots." Afterwards, "He will remove the disgrace of His people from upon the entire earth, for the mouth of Hashem has spoken" (ibid.).

The conclusion to be reached from all this is that a person must rouse himself to mourn with a bitter heart over the exile of the Shechinah and to moan over the length of this bitter exile. He must reflect in his heart that as long as we were living upon our land and the Shechinah rested between the two angels on the cover of the Ark, we received daily illumination. Israel was called, "A people that is holy to Hashem" (Devarim 26:19), and we were close to the Shechinah and to holiness. Meanwhile the shells of defilement hid themselves and were banished to the nethermost regions of the deep. But now, by contrast, Israel is pushed and pulled and scattered into every corner and to the very ends of the earth. In their exile they debase themselves greatly before every nation and tongue, treating them with every honor. Meanwhile, Lilis smiles and laughs, deriving great joy from seeing the people of Israel humble themselves before the nations. This is a literal fulfillment of the verse, "For our soul bowed down to the dust" (Tehillim 44:26). We are literally trampled beneath their feet. We are their slaves and maidservants. The fruits of Israel's endeavors and labors inevitably attract the notice of one nation or another, who then come and take it from them by force. Meanwhile we are beaten, killed, slaughtered, and burned for the sanctification of the name of Heaven. How, then, can any God-fearing person not summon all his concentration, whenever the redemption is mentioned in our prayers, to beseech the Holy One Blessed is He to redeem us from nations of the world for His name's sake? For an authentic tradition has come down to me that whoever constantly grieves over the exile of the Shechinah will merit the crown of Torah.

Hear what the Ari, z"l, writes (Or Tzaddikim, Amud HaAvodah, Chapter 17) concerning our teacher Rabbi Avraham HaLevi, author of Tikkunei Shabbos, who lived in Safed, may it be built up and strengthened speedily in our days. Every evening Rabbi Avraham would arise at midnight and make the rounds of all the streets of the Jews calling out bitterly, "Our brethren of the House of Israel! You all know that on account of our many sins the Shechinah is in exile, our Holy Temple has been burnt with fire and Israel is immersed in a bitter exile where they are subjected to terrible afflictions and bitter tortures. "Countless pious men and women and boys and girls, the elderly along with the young, have been killed with all four of types of execution. They are hung and sentenced to harsh and unusual deaths. How, then, can you lie upon your beds in tranquility and confidence? Rise and cry out to Hashem our God, who is a merciful and gracious King. Perhaps He will hear the sound of your prayers and have mercy upon His people, the remainder of Israel." Thus, did this saintly man continue his harangue, refusing to give the people the city any rest until all of them arose to go to the study hall and recite Tikkun Chatzos [the midnight prayers over the destruction]. Afterwards they would engage in study, each one according to his understanding. Some would immerse themselves in Kabbalah and the Zohar, others in Talmud and Mishnah and still others in the Torah, the Prophets and the Writings. Then they would recite songs of supplication and prayers until daybreak. In this way they would arouse Heaven's mercy.

The Ari, z"l, used to speak with enthusiasm about Rabbi Avraham's piety, saying that he was reincarnation of the prophet Yirmeyahu. One time the Ari said to him, "You must know that your days are completed and the time has come for you to die unless you perform the rectification procedure that I will teach you. But if you do perform it, then you will live for another twenty-two years. Your rectification is to go to Jerusalem to pray by the Western Wall and pour out your supplications. Then you will merit to behold the Shechinah." So, the pious Rabbi Avraham went home and secluded himself for three days and nights, immersed in fasting and wearing sackcloth and ashes. Afterwards he traveled to Jerusalem and arrived at the Western Wall, where he prayed with supplications and with great weeping. Then he observed on the wall, the figure of a woman all dressed in black. Immediately he fell upon his face out of fear, crying out and weeping loudly, "Woe to me! Woe to me that I have seen You thus! O woe! Alas for my soul!" He continued this weeping and crying out and the tearing of his hair until at last he fainted and fell asleep. Then the Shechinah came to him in a dream dressed in beautiful garments, saying, "Be consoled, Rabbi Avraham my son, for there is hope for your end and the children will return to their borders. For I will return their captivity and have mercy upon them." After he awoke, he returned to Safed and went to see the Ari. The Ari immediately said to him, "I see upon you that you have merited to see the countenance of the Shechinah. Now you may be assured that you will live another twenty-two years." And so did it transpire that the pious man lived for another twenty-two years after this incident.

From the deeds of the pious man mentioned above one learns the importance of rising at midnight or before dawn to mourn over the destruction of the Holy Temple and the slaughter of the righteous. It is immaterial whether a person does a little more or a little less, as long as his intentions are for the sake of Heaven (Berachos 5b). But let him not do this in order to receive acclaim, for then not only does he receive no reward, but he will even be punished. If his intentions are for the sake of Heaven, however, it states concerning him, "One who keeps a commandment will experience no misfortune" (Koheles 8:5). Moreover, he will merit witnessing the rebuilding of Tziyon and Yerushalayim, Amein. — Based on the words of my teacher and mentor Rabbi Yosef, z"l.

Chapter 94

It states, "Thus said Hashem, for your sake I have sent you into Babylon and I have sent them all down in boats" (Yeshayahu 43:14). [The Zohar comments (Parashas Shemos 2b), "'I have sent you into Babylon' — This alludes to the Holy One Blessed is He."] This illustrates the great love of the Holy One Blessed is He for Israel, on account of which He shares in their afflictions and descends with them into exile. Similarly, regarding the descent into Egypt it is stated, "These are the names of the children of Israel who came to Egypt with [es] Yaakov" (Shemos 1:1). Wherever the word את appears it includes something not mentioned in the verse. In this case it includes the Shechinah, which went down with

Yaakov into Egypt, in keeping with the verse, "I will descend with you into Egypt and I will bring you up" (Bereishis 46:4). Regarding the Babylonian exile, however, not only does it state, "For your sake I have sent you into Babylon," but, "In all their afflictions He is afflicted" (Yeshayahu 63:9). The succeeding exiles were more difficult to bear than the Egyptian exile.

In the Zohar (2:2b) it is taught: Rabbi Shimon ben Yochai said: If a person accustoms himself to identify with the suffering of the Shechinah, even if he encounters suffering, he will bear the burden and not worry. But if he does not accustom himself to identify with the suffering of the Shechinah and of Israel, but spends all his days enjoying the pleasures and delights of this world, when some suffering does befall him it will cause him complete distress. Therefore, every individual must weep while Israel suffers in the exile. Indeed, in Babylon the suffering was complete, because Israel had become accustomed to a life of pleasure. Thus, it states, "The precious sons of Tziyon who were comparable to fine gold, etc." (Eichah 4:2). But then they went into exile with a millstone upon their necks and their hands fastened behind them. And as they went into exile the Holy One Blessed Is He called to all His hosts and said to them, "Why are My children in exile while you remain here? Set out and go down, all of you, and I will accompany you." This is the meaning of the verse, "Thus said Hashem, for your sake I have sent you into Babylon and sent them all down in boats." Who are those in the "boats"? They are the Heavenly chariots and encampments. And as they were on their way down the Heavens opened up and the spirit of prophecy settled upon the prophet Yechezkeil, who said to Israel, "Behold, your Master is here along with all the hosts and chariots of Heaven, who have come to sojourn with you!" But Israel did not believe it until Yechezkeil told them everything that he saw in his vision. Thus, is it stated, "And I saw and behold there was a wind, etc." (Yechezkeil 1:4) ....

Rabbi Shimon ben Yochai said: At that moment Israel's joy was total because they saw that the Holy One Blessed is He was with them.

Now, in every generation there are righteous people who accept upon themselves with great love to sacrifice their lives for the sanctification of the Name of Heaven. Thus, Rabbi Yehudah said,

"If only Israel knew the great love that the Holy One Blessed is He has for them they would roar like young lions and pursue Him" (Zohar 2:5b). Hence, every Jew must accept upon himself the yoke of the exile with love and affection. This is particularly relevant in this bitter exile in which it has often happened that a person sat at home oblivious to everything and suddenly was set upon with false accusations. He would then be taken from his wife, his sons and daughters and his father's house to be sent to a dark place where he was thrown among the snakes and scorpions. Meanwhile members of the wicked nation engaged false witnesses to testify against him, and those who sat in judgment ordered that the Jew be punished with harsh and bitter tortures.

When the man's wife and children heard this terrible news, they would weep and cry out to Hashem and also turn to the community in the hope that they would be able to free the accused through private negotiations. Then the children of Israel, Hashem's holy people, the merciful seed, would take even the shirts from their backs to contribute funds for the redemption of that poor soul from a horrible death. But sometimes all the money in the world was of no avail and the entire nation would weep, family by family, at the news of the grim trial and tremendous suffering caused by the sulfur and fire that were ignited upon the chests of the holy martyrs. And before the condemned man was executed, they would torture him with nails forced up under his fingernails, and weigh him down with iron shoes. Who can relate the enormity of the suffering? And sometimes they would cut out the person's tongue from his throat or else they would cut off his male organ while he was yet alive. Then they would cut open the martyr's stomach and tear out his heart and liver and lungs, and then cut his body into quarters. But the martyrs would endure all this and still refuse to exchange their religion. And the Holy One Blessed is He would take the image of these martyrs and impress it upon His cloak in order so that one day He can avenge the blood of His servants that was spilled in vain. For the nations took souls of these holy ones through libelous accusations.

Every feeling person must weep over all this suffering. Nevertheless, every Jew must also be will to accept it with love should the like ever befall him, Heaven forbid. The Shechinah wails over all such tragedy and the supernal worlds are filled with weeping and sighing over the souls of the holy martyrs. For they are like sacrifices and a sweet savory smell to Hashem because they unified their hearts towards their Heavenly Father and gave their lives for the sanctification of His great Name and for the unification of the Holy One Blessed is He, and His Shechinah.

Know that it states in the Zohar in Parashas Bereishis (38b) that in the fourth of the seven Heavenly palaces there sit the mourners of Zion and Jerusalem along with the souls of all the murdered who gave their lives for the sanctification of the Name of Heaven. And in the second palace there is a partition for the Holy One Blessed is He and the Moshiach. In that place there is great weeping over the destruction of the Holy Temple and Jerusalem and the slaughter of the righteous. At a certain point our righteous Moshiach descends to the fourth palace and begins recounting in detail all the holy ones who gave their lives for the sanctification of Hashem's Name. Then he himself begins weeping profusely and all the princes of the house of David gather to embrace and console him, after which he begins to weep for a second time. The sound of this weeping ascends to a very lofty place where it remains until the beginning of the new month, at which time it descends, accompanied by numerous lights which light up all the palaces. Various types of healing remedies also descend along with that sound to heal the murdered, the sick, the infirm and the suffering.

Then Moshiach dons the cloak upon which are engraved and impressed all the names of all the murdered and he goes arrayed in this cloak to judge the murderers and thieves. One day the Holy One Blessed is He will also don that cloak, as it is stated, "He will render judgment upon the nations that are filled with corpses" (Tehillim 110:6). Until, at last, the Moshiach comes to comfort those souls, accompanied by lights and delights and numerous angels and chariots. And one day each and every angel will also don a cloak like this one, impressed with the images of the slaughtered. Following this, the Moshiach will go with Rabbi Akiva and his colleagues to a place that no eye is able to behold other than that of God. There the Holy One Blessed is He will reveal to him the great reward awaiting the holy ones who sacrificed their lives and then the Moshiach will be consoled.

Therefore, it is fitting for every person of the seed of Israel to lament and weep over the magnitude of the destruction and the yoke of the exile. Moreover, how fitting it would be if they would all mourn and cast themselves upon the ground to wallow in the dust and ashes. This is especially appropriate from the seventeenth of Tammuz onward, for that is a period of sadness during which we are obliged to mourn, and all the more so on [the last day of that period,] the Ninth of Av, which is a day for weeping and sorrow. But in many countries, on account of our many sins, I have seen a great breach on the part of those who come to the synagogue. Not only do they neglect to recite the elegies with weeping and bitterness, but they actually engage in jocularity and levity, rejoicing out loud and conducting themselves as if it were [the festival of] Simchas Torah! They have forgotten that their end will be very bitter and their punishment very great. None of those people will merit witnessing the consolation of Israel when our Moshiach arrives. It is the responsibility of the rabbis and leaders of the generation and the judges of Israel to rebuke these sinners who rejoice on a day of suffering and weeping. They must be fined and it is even appropriate to subject them to ostracism. But if a person mourns continually over the destruction of the Holy Temple and the length of the exile and experiences pain over the suffering of Israel, he will merit witnessing their consolation when our Moshiach arrives. He will also witness the vengeance of Hashem of Hosts and will rejoice in the rebuilding of the Temple and the holy city of Jerusalem. For it states, "Rejoice with her in gladness, all who mourned over her" (Yeshayahu 66:10). Amein. — Based upon the words of my teacher and mentor, Rabbi Yosef, z"l.

Chapter 95

"And Yaakov traveled to Sukkos and he built for himself a house and for his livestock he made shelters [sukkos] therefore he called the name of the place Sukkos" (Bereishis 33:17). All of Israel's customs are Torah and it is our custom that as soon as we come home from the synagogue at the conclusion of Yom Kippur, we immediately immerse ourselves in the mitzvah of building the sukkah. I have found a fitting explanation for this among the essays of Rabbi Shelomo Molcho, z"l (Sefer HaMefo'ar, p. 168), where he discusses why it is that Israel engages specifically in this mitzvah at the conclusion of Yom Kippur as opposed to any other. His explanation is as follows: The Holy One Blessed is He commanded that on Yom Kippur one goat be offered up to Hashem while a second be sent to Azazel. The Kohein Gadol would first confess all the iniquities and transgressions of Israel over the one that was to be sent to Azazel, as it is stated, "And the goat shall bear upon it all their iniquities" (Vayikra 16:22). Through this Israel achieved tremendous atonement. This is an example of the principle that everything that befell the Patriarchs was a foreshadowing of what was to befall their descendants, for in the ritual of the scapegoat Israel inherited a mitzvah recalling an incident from the time of their forefathers. As it is stated, "And Eisav returned along his way to (the land of) Se'ir" (Bereishis 33:16). Then it states, "And Yaakov traveled to Sukkos" (ibid. 17). In other words, after Eisav, who was a hairy man [ish se'ir], had gone on his way to Se'ir — i.e., to receive his portion in the form of the goat [se'ir] that was sent to Azazel — Yaakov went on to Sukkos — i.e., to engage in the mitzvah of sukkah. In this passage the Torah intimates that we must emulate our ancestor by engaging specifically in the mitzvah of sukkah, rather than any other, after we have sent off the scapegoat on Yom Kippur. This is Rabbi Shelomo Molcho's explanation and the words of the wise are pleasing.

But I would like to add another fitting explanation of my own. It is well known that the Satan, the Lilis and the nations have dominion in this world and that they continually find fault with the holy people Israel and are always on the lookout for ways to harm and oppress them. Now, the name "Lilis" has a numerical value of 480, indicating that she has four hundred and eighty hosts who are Israel's accusers. And as everyone knows, on Yom Kippur neither the Satan nor Lilis has any power over Israel. Thus, the Sages note that the name HaSatan [השטן] has a numerical value of 364 whereas the year has three hundred and sixty- five days. This is to indicate that the Satan has no dominion on Yom Kippur but only on the other three hundred and sixty-four days.

Correspondingly, the Holy One Blessed is He has commanded us regarding the mitzvah of sukkah, as it is stated, "On the fifteenth day of this seventh month shall be the Yom Tov of Sukkos for seven days to Hashem" (Vayikra 23:34). The word "Sukkos," which is written without a letter vav, [סכת] has a value of 480 to indicate that whoever fulfills this mitzvah fully, nullifies the power and dominion of the wicked Lilis. Therefore it seems to me that on Yom Kippur neither Satan nor Lilis has any power over Israel, but immediately after Yom Kippur they begin accusing them afresh, it is for this reason that the holy people Israel immerse themselves in the mitzvah of sukkah, with a numerical value of 480, immediately after Yom Kippur, to counteract the accusations of the evil Lilis. For every mitzvah that has a value of 480 has the power to nullify the impure shell of Lilis. Rav Galanti writes concerning the verse, "She [i.e., Jerusalem] was filled with justice but now, murderers" (Yeshayahu 1:21), that in Jerusalem there were four hundred and eighty synagogues (Midrash Eichah Rabbah, Pesikta 12; 2:4) and together with the Holy Temple they totaled 481, the value of the word 'filled' [melei'asi]. But then when Jerusalem was destroyed, Lilis and her cohorts grew stronger so that she was then able to kill a multitude of Israel like the sand of the sea. This was in fulfillment of the words, 'but now, murderers,' on account of our many sins."

Therefore one must not take the mitzvah of the sukkah lightly, for the word sukkah alludes to two Divine names (Introduction to Tikkunei Zohar 2b; Tikkun 13, 29a). That is, the letters heh, samech have a value of 65, which is the numerical value of the name אדנ"י, while the letters kaf, vav have a value of 26, which is the value of the name יה"וה. Thus, when a Jew fulfills the mitzvah of the sukkah properly and in accordance with all its laws, he lends power and strength to the Heavenly host. For the value of the word סוכה is 91, which is equal to that of the word מלאך — "angel." For this reason, we pray [during a blessing in the Evening service], "And spread over us Your tabernacle [sukkah] of peace." For in the merit of our observance of the commandment of the sukkah Hashem's Name will be complete and His Throne of Glory will be complete, whereas in this world they are not complete. This is alluded to in the verse, "A hand is upon the Throne of God" (Shemos 17:16). [Note that in this verse the word for "throne" — כסא — is written in the abbreviated form כס, while in place of the four-letter Name יהו"ה, only the two letter Name י"ה is used.] But in the time to come both the Name and the Throne will be complete. This is why when the nations come in the future and say to the Holy One Blessed is He, "Give us Torah as well and we will fulfill it," He will reply to them, "I have an easy mitzvah called 'sukkah.'" [This mitzvah is called easy because it does not require any monetary outlay]." Instantly they will all go and make sukkos for themselves. But then the Holy One Blessed is He will cause the sun to beat down upon them each one of them will kick down his sukkah and run out. Concerning that moment, it is stated, "The One who dwells in Heaven will laugh" (Tehillim 2:4), for the Holy One Blessed is He will laugh on that day as He has laughed on no other occasion. See the Avodah Zarah 3a for the rest of this episode. On the surface it seems puzzling why the Holy One Blessed is He would instruct the nations to fulfill the mitzvah of sukkah specifically, rather than any other mitzvah. However, in light of what I have written above it is very understandable. For although people take the mitzvah of sukkah lightly, in the eyes of the Holy One Blessed is He it is of great significance, because it has a numerical value of 480 and therefore has the power to humble the impure shell of Lilis, whose numerical value is also 480. Now, in the future the Holy One Blessed is He will eradicate from the earth all forms of idolatry, which also derive from Lilis and her cohorts. And He will humble them specifically through the mitzvah of sukkah, after which His name will be complete and His Throne will be complete. This is why we pray, "And spread over us Your tabernacle of peace [sukkas shelomecha]," because at that time there will again be a complete [in the sense of whole] tabernacle [sukkas shaleim]. For once again there will be four hundred and eighty synagogues in Jerusalem and together with the rebuilt Temple there will be a total of four hundred and eighty-one, the value of the word, "filled [melei'asi] with justice." Then, on that day, "Hashem will be one and His Name will be one" (Zecharyah 14:9).

Therefore, one must be very careful regarding the sanctity of the sukkah, for it is comprised of the two names, יהו"ה and אדנ"י. In particular, once the sukkah has been constructed in accordance with all it laws and in purity, one must not degrade it because it is a throne for the Holy One Blessed is He and His Shechinah. Thus the sukkah fulfills the role of a minor "temple," just as the Holy Temple was called the "Completed Tabernacle [Sukkah]." This is in stark contrast with the attitude of those who treat the sukkah lightly and consider this commandment to be a great burden. They enter the sukkah and recite the blessings over the bread and the sukkah hurriedly and impatiently, and then leave. In this respect they resemble the members of the other nations who revile the sukkah and run out. Moreover, their blessing over the sukkah is in vain because the text of the blessing is "to sit [leisheiv] in the sukkah." They believe that this means that they must sit there for a short while, after which they may leave. But they are in error because the expression, "to sit in the sukkah," actually means to tarry there. Thus, Rashi explains that the term "sitting" [yeshivah] means nothing other than "tarrying" (Vayikra 12:4; Devarim 9:9). Therefore, I admonish every understanding person not to fall into this iniquity. Rather, when he enters the sukkah to eat, let him remain there until he has finished eating so that his blessing will not be in vain and so that he will not be reckoned among the revilers of the mitzvah. Then we will all merit to take shelter beneath the sukkah of the Leviasan, as it is stated, "And a sukkah will be for shade by day" (Yeshayahu 4:6). And the Holy One Blessed is He will cover us with the shade of His wings in the Completed Tabernacle [Sukkah] forever. Amein, so may it be His will.

Chapter 96

We are commanded to acknowledge and praise Hashem's holy and magnificent Name for the great miracle that He performed for our ancestors in the days of the wicked Greek king Antiochus. The latter did numerous evils to the Jewish people but Hashem, in His constant mercy and abundant lovingkindness, dressed Himself in

Kav HaYashar

garments of vengeance (see Chapter 94) and caused two Greek officers to be killed through the Chashmona'i and his sons. These officers were Bagris and Nikanor and in that episode all the troops of the Greek king were delivered into Israel's hands. So, may all the enemies of Hashem be lost.

Afterwards the sons of the Chashmona'i entered the Beis HaMikdosh where they found only a single flask of oil stamped with the seal of the Kohein Gadol. This was the flask from which they would anoint the kings of Israel. Every Kohein Gadol who required anointing was also anointed from that same flask. In this flask was sufficient oil to kindle the lamp for only a single day, but the God of Heaven, who caused His Name to dwell in the Beis HaMikdosh, allowed it to burn miraculously for eight days. This enabled the kohanim to purify themselves for seven days and then to prepare new oil in purity on the eighth day. This is why it was necessary for the oil to burn miraculously for eight days — in order that the kohanim would be able to purify themselves.

In commemoration of this miracle the Jews of every generation must observe the festival of Chanukah for eight days during which they must also kindle lamps. These lamps have the status of mitzvah lamps. In many places we find that such lamps are very precious in the eyes of the Holy One Blessed is He. Thus, it states, "Honor Hashem with lights" (Yeshayahu 24:15). Any lamp that is lit for the sake of a mitzvah has wondrous and immeasurable sanctity. If we merited the spirit of prophecy, we would recite the blessings over them and immediately attain understanding and insight into the future by means of the kindling of the lamps. For a mitzvah lamp causes an outpouring of prophecy completely analogous to that of a prophet prophesying by the command of Hashem.

The illustrious Maharshal (Rabbi Shlomo Luria), z"l, writes in the introduction to his work, Yam Shel Shlomo: One time it happened that through a mitzvah lamp I received as if a sign from Heaven granting me authority and encouragement from the firmament and they opened up for me the Gates of Light. I received from my mentor a tradition regarding the incident the Maharshal refers to. When Rabbi Shlomo was researching and composing his work, Yam Shel Shlomo, it once occurred that there was only a small candle burning before him, that was on the verge of expiry. Nevertheless, it burnt for several hours more than three or four complete candles would have done. His disciple and grandson had this to say about the matter, "The owner of the candle recognized through the miracle of his candle that Hashem was with him." Thus, the illustrious scholar mentioned above experienced a miracle that was literally a repeat of the miracle of the holy oil in the holy flask in the Beis HaMikdosh. May his merit stand by us. Fortunate is he and fortunate is she who bore him.

The point to remember is that every mitzvah lamp draws down an aura of sanctity from above and arouses the kindling of the holy lamps On High. Thus, we find in the Zohar (Tikkun 29, p. 73a) that Eliyahu stood behind the walls of the study hall of Rabbi Shimon ben Yochai and declared, "Arise, O holy lamp, and kindle the holy lamps On High." For this reason, it is the custom of the meticulous that if a lamp was kindled for the sake of a mitzvah, whatever remains of it is put away in order that it will not be used for any mundane function but only for another mitzvah. This is especially important in the case of lamps that are lit for the sake of Torah study. Mitzvah lamps bring about many forms of benefit for the soul.

The Chanukah lamps, which are meant to recall the tremendous miracle that occurred, are imbued with the highest sanctity. They represent the Heavenly lamps and the attributes that are aroused and enflamed with might to execute judgment against the wicked. For this reason, Maharil Segal (Minhagim, Hilchos Bedikas Chametz) writes that it is proper to wash one's hands before reciting the blessing over the kindling of the Chanukah lamp. However, lest a person appear ostentatious about his religiosity the later authorities (Teshuvos Maharil 86; Bach, Orach Chayim 432) write that it is preferable that he cause himself to be obligated to wash his hands [by defiling them]. Then at the same time he can wash them in anticipation of the kindling of the lamps.

It is well known, as I have already mentioned in Chapter Fourteen, that from every commandment that one performs holy angels are born and created and that all the angels created from a particular commandment are called the "camp" of that commandment. Needless to say, when one recites the blessing over that

Kav HaYashar

commandment all those angels gather round him to hear his words and respond "Amein." An allusion to this can be seen in the fact that the numerical value of the Hebrew word for angel, מלאך [91] — is identical with of the word, "Amein." Thus, when a Jew responds "Amein" to a blessing or to Kiddush he should have in mind that the angels are responding along with him.

The first blessing over the Chanukah lamp contains thirteen words. Therefore, when reciting it one should have in mind to arouse Hashem's thirteen attributes of mercy. The second blessing also contains thirteen words, which also have the power to arouse the thirteen attributes of mercy. The two blessings together contain twenty-six words corresponding to the value of the name יהו"ה. A person must concentrate well when reciting the blessing over the lamps in order to say them with joy. For a mitzvah that is performed only once a year should seem very precious to him at the moment of its performance. In honor of the holy angels that visit one's house on account of the mitzvah one should kindle the lamps while wearing an outer garment as one does when going to the synagogue. One should light immediately at nightfall in keeping with the dictum, "when a mitzvah comes into your hands, do not let it ferment [i.e., do not delay]!" (Mechilta, Parashas Bo, 12:17). The number of lamps that one kindles over the course of the Chanukah festival is thirty-six. In addition, one lights another eight shamashim [the extra lamps that are lit so that one will not inadvertently make use of the actual Chanukah lamps]. It is the custom of Israel to place the shamash above the other lamps. There is a hint to this in the verse, "And fiery angels [seraphim] were standing above him [lo, the numerical value of which is 36]" (Yeshayahu 6:2; Maharil, Minhagim, Hilchos Chanukah). This shows that there is great sanctity in the shamash lamps as well. In fact, their sanctity is even greater than that of the Chanukah lamps themselves, for the shamash is comparable to the kohein who kindles the lamps in the Beis HaMikdosh and to the fiery angels who kindle the holy lamps illuminating Hashem's Throne of Glory. From this one can understand the great harm that is caused by the practice I have observed among the majority of the populace of taking the shamash away from the other lamps in order to use its light for mundane purposes. An even worse iniquity, for which they will one day be made to reckon, is the custom of playing cards or dice by the light of the shamash. They do not realize that the shamash is of greater sanctity than the Chanukah lights themselves, as the Maharil notes, based on the hint in the verse, "And fiery angels were standing above him," alluding to the shamashim standing above the 36 lamps of Chanukah. Therefore, one who treats this mitzvah lightly will surely be subjected to harsh punishment. By contrast, one who observes it meticulously and does not allow the shamash to be moved from its place will merit seeing the lamps that will be kindled in the Beis HaMikdosh, speedily and in our days, Amein.

Chapter 97

The Fast of Esther was established on the basis of a statement in the Talmud (Megillah 2a) that the 13th of Adar is "a time of gathering for everyone." The commentaries explain (Rosh, ad loc., sec. 1; Ran, 1b) that everyone gathers for the Fast of Esther and village dwellers come to the city to recite prayers of repentance and supplication. This is because on that day the Jews gathered to defend themselves and were in need of mercy. Therefore, this day was established for the reciting of prayers of repentance and supplication. Village dwellers are obliged to come to the city on the Fast of Esther so that they may join with their fellow Jews in the reciting of the penitential prayers, for this is the meaning of the Sages' statement that the 13th is "a time of gathering for everyone." The Holy One Blessed is He loves when people gather in the cities to recite penitential prayers with the congregation. This is because "in a multitude of people is the glory of the king" (Mishlei 14:28). Through these prayers they arouse abundant mercy on the part of the Heavenly host.

Another reason for the Fast of Esther was revealed by the Maggid, the angel that used to teach the Beis Yosef, z"l (Maggid Meisharim, Parashas Vayakhel, V.I). The Holy One Blessed is He watches over Israel continually because they are His inheritance and treasured community and He is desirous of bringing them merit so that He may bestow upon them a goodly reward in the World to Come. Now, when the 14th of Adar arrives and Israel rejoices and celebrates in gladness the great miracle that the Holy One Blessed is He performed for them in destroying Haman and His sons and Israel's other enemies, it is called a "mitzvah celebration." Therefore, the Sages said that a man is obligated to become intoxicated on Purim (Megillah 7b). However, this raises the concern that in consequence of the copious eating and drinking and rejoicing, Israel may come to sin. Therefore, the Holy One Blessed is He preceded this day with a fast, because fasting has the power to protect a person from sin. In this way the Satan and Lilis will not have the power to accuse them nor to cause them to sin through an excess of eating and drinking. In the penitential prayers, when one recites the poem, "Few in number," and one reaches the line, "Hear prayer and remove vanity, etc.," it is praiseworthy to intend that we be saved from sin and iniquity through excessive eating, drinking and rejoicing on Purim, Heaven forbid. By means of the prayers of repentance and supplication that we recite in assembly we invoke the merit of Mordechai and Esther. For regarding Mordechai, it is stated, "And Mordechai knew everything that had transpired and Mordechai rent his garments" (Esther 14:1).

It is explained in the Zohar on Bereishis (Tikkunim 69, 117a) that other people only know what their eyes see, that the enemies of Israel like Haman and his colleagues seek to uproot Israel and that they continually increase in strength and renew their evil decrees daily. But Mordechai knew the essence of the matter and the source of the power of the husks of impurity from which the souls of these evildoers and sinners derive. This is the meaning of the verse, "Mordechai knew everything that had transpired." He reflected that the husks of impurity had waxed in strength on account of the sins of Israel in that generation. This made him aware of the need for great self-mortification and prayerful outcry to weaken the power of the Sitra Achara and arouse mercy on Israel's behalf. Thus, it states, "And Mordechai rent his garments and donned sackcloth, etc." Meanwhile the righteous Esther, who merited the spirit of prophecy, also knew the essence of the matter mentioned above. Therefore, it states concerning her, "And Esther stood in the courtyard of the king, etc." (Esther 5:1). The Zohar (3:109a) explains that the word "standing" refers to nothing other than prayer, as it is stated, "And Pinchas stood and prayed" (Tehillim 106:30). Esther prayed again and again until her prayers ascended On High to a holy and awesome place called, "the houses of the courtyard." This "courtyard" is before the Heavenly Beis HaMikdosh, from where Hashem's four-letter name radiates. This is the meaning of the verse, "And Esther stood in the courtyard of the king." The "king" here refers to the Holy One Blessed is He. For this reason, it does not state, in the courtyard of King Achashveirosh. It is also written concerning Esther, "The king extended the golden scepter to Esther" (Esther 5:2). This means that Holy One Blessed is He caused there to descend upon her a thread of grace. The Zohar (ibid., 44b) adds, "And not only to her did the Holy One Blessed is He extend the golden scepter, but even to all who unite with her."

Therefore we, the community of Israel dwelling in exile and suffering the sorrow of the exile for the honor of the Holy One Blessed is He, must unite and assemble in our synagogues, which are also called the "courtyard of the King," that is, the King of the Universe. And surely through the recitation of prayers of repentance and supplication we will succeed in invoking merits of the righteous Mordechai and Queen Esther. And surely they join with us on the Fast of Esther, on which we recall their merit, saying, "And as in the days of Myrrh [an allusion to Mordechai] and Myrtle [hadas — Esther, who is also called Hadassah] when You saved Your children" [Selichos liturgy of the Fast of Esther]. For this reason, villagers must also join the holy assembly in the synagogue on the Fast of Esther. For this day is very auspicious for our prayers to be heard in the name of Mordechai and Esther. Whoever is in need of mercy regarding any matter requiring prayer should set aside time for it on the day of the Fast of Esther. Let him begin by reciting Tehillim 22, "To the Chief Musician, upon ayeles hashachar." The Sages interpret the words Ayeles HaShachar as a reference to Esther (Yoma 29a; Shocher Tov, Tehillim 22). Afterwards let him pour out his heart before Hashem and make his request. And let him invoke the names of Mordechai and Esther, in whose merit he is beseeching the Holy One Blessed is He. Then

Hashem will open for him the Gates of Mercy and his prayer will be accepted with favor.

The Sages teach (Megillah 16a) that when Haman came to lead Mordechai upon King Achashveirosh's horse and to honor him as the king had commanded, he found Mordechai with the scholars seated before him, demonstrating the laws of kemitzah [the taking of a fistful of flour from a meal offering]. Rashi explains that Mordechai was merely lecturing on the subject matter of the day, because that day was the 16th of Nissan, which is the day that the offering of the new grain [the Omer] was made. Haman lamented, "Your fistful of flour has come and pushed aside my ten thousand talents of silver!" Therefore, it is proper to immerse oneself in the laws of kemitzah on the 16th of Nissan. All of this is in order to invoke the merit of the righteous.

Therefore, beloved ones, community of the holy people gathering for Hashem's sake to hear the Megillah on this special day of Purim, of which it is said that all other festivals will be nullified but not Purim (Midrash Shocher Tov, Mishlei 9), let us recall the merit of Mordechai and Esther. For the Fast of Esther and Purim are days of favor and love. Therefore, it is good to pray on the Fast of Esther, and may the One who hears prayer accept our prayers with mercy and favor, Amein.

Chapter 98

At the outset of creation, the Holy One Blessed is He saw that the world could not survive on the basis of strict judgment. So, what did the Holy One Blessed is He do? He appended the name of mercy [יהו"ה] and created the world (Bereishis Rabbah 12:15; Pesikta Rabbasi, 41). Thus it states, "In the beginning God [Elokim] created" (Bereishis 1:1) — that is, with strict judgment because the name Elokim indicates the attribute of judgment. But afterwards it states, "On the day that Hashem God [יְהֹוָ"ה Elokim] made earth and Heaven" (Bereishis 2:4).

In the writings of the illustrious author of Toras Chayim (Chullin 86a) I have found a worthy explanation for the principle that the righteous suffer for the iniquities of the generation (Shabbos 33b). He writes that the attribute of judgment would really like to destroy the world whenever people fail to fulfill the will of the Master of the Universe, but the Holy One Blessed is He in His abundant mercy takes pity on His handiwork. This is, after all, the reason that He adjoined the attribute of mercy, that is, the name יהו"ה, to the attribute of judgment. However, the attribute of judgment continues to complain and demands that the Holy One Blessed is He should execute judgment upon the world. So what does the Holy One do? He grants the attribute of judgment a single righteous person who is weighed up against the entire rest of the world. In this way Hashem silences the attribute of judgment and saves the world. But just as soon as one righteous individual dies, another is born, in keeping with the verse, "The sun shines and the sun sets" (Koheles 1:5). This is the explanation of our teacher the illustrious Rabbi Chayim Shor in his commentary on the tractate Shabbos; see there.

According to this I believe we can resolve a very difficult problem arising from the verses of Megillas Esther. It is stated, "Haman saw that Mordechai would not kneel and bow to him and Haman was filled with wrath. But it was contemptible in his eyes to set his hand upon Mordechai alone…And Haman sought to destroy all the Jews in the entire kingdom of Achashveirosh, the people of Mordechai" (Esther 3:5-6). On the surface it is difficult to understand why Haman sought to uproot and eradicate all the Jews when Mordechai alone refused to bow to him.

But I believe that the explanation is as follows: We know that the Jews of that generation were deserving of death either because they bowed to the idol erected by Nevuchadnetzar or because they participated in the feast of the wicked Achashveirosh (Megillah 12a). Both Haman and Satan lodged accusations against them in this regard and in accordance with the attribute of judgment Israel should have been destroyed. Haman then became concerned that the Holy One Blessed is He might do exactly as described above, that is, take away a single righteous individual who was equal in weight to the entire rest of Israel. He knew that if this were to happen, another righteous person would be born on the spot and Israel would remain alive and well! Therefore, it states, "And it was contemptible in his eyes to set his hand upon Mordechai alone." For he knew that through the death of a single righteous individual, Israel would achieve atonement and he realized that Mordechai was equal to the rest of Israel put together. Therefore, Haman and the Satan sought to destroy all the Jews in Achashveirosh's kingdom. Now, according to the view that Israel had incurred the penalty of death in that generation because they participated in the feast of Achashveirosh it is impossible to say that they were guilty of consuming forbidden foods. For it states, "And the drinking was according to law, without compulsion" (Esther 1:8). This means that the drinking was in accordance with the laws of each individual. Therefore, since it is forbidden for a Jew to drink wine that had been poured out by idolaters, they were served kosher wine served only by Jewish waiters. Similarly, the food that was served to them was cooked by Jews. Achashveirosh did not compel them to eat or drink anything that was forbidden to them, as it is stated, "without compulsion ... according to the will of each man" (ibid.). Rather, their crime was that Achashveirosh's evil intention in inviting Israel was to divert the flow of bounty descending to them from On High so that instead of pour down through Shechinah it would pour down through the Sitra Achara. This is why he invited Israel — to divert them into his spiritual realm. This is called "injecting filth into them" because the flow pouring down to Israel would then come to them by way of the Sitra Achara. This is how the impure forces inject filth into concepts and conduct in this bitter exile, Because of our many sins, they partake of this flow before us and then we receive it only through them. Thus, it is stated, "Her oppressors became the head" (Eichah 1:5). This is also the meaning of the Sages' teaching that Jews who live abroad "serve idols in purity" (Avodah Zarah 8a). If Israel had not taken part in the feast of that evildoer, he would have been unable to do anything to them because the realm of holiness would not have received any of its bounty from the Sitra Achara. But since Israel did partake of the feast of Achashveirosh it was if they drank from the Sitra Achara itself. Therefore, that feast caused filth to be injected into them, even though they ate only kosher food and drank only permissible wine. Nevertheless, it was as if they partook of the feast of the Sitra Achara.

For this reason, we must be wary when the other nations make feasts not to derive any benefit from them, as mentioned above. The only exception is when the non-Jew sends animals, poultry, fish and the like to the home of the Jew. Then it is permissible. But it is forbidden for a Jew to eat in the home of the non-Jew, even if he consumes only kosher food and drinks only kosher wine. Whoever is lax about this commits a grievous sin and incurs severe punishment. Moreover, the Shechinah cries profusely over such people. The proof is that it was on account of this sin that Israel was considered deserving of death in the days of Haman and Achashveirosh. That is why Mordechai alone refused to benefit from the feast of that evildoer in order that in his merit all of Israel would be saved. But even so, the attribute of judgment wished to strike against all the Jews of that generation. For just as Hashem said to Moshe, "I will consume them in a moment" (Bamidbar 16:21), and "I will make you into a great nation [in their stead]" (Shemos 33:10), so too the attribute of judgment wished to multiply Mordechai's seed like the sand of the sea [in Israel's stead]. But Mordechai nullified the decree with his prayer just as Moshe Rabbeinu had nullified the decree against the Jews of his day with his prayer.

This is the meaning of the verse, "And Mordechai knew" (Esther 4:1). That is, he knew the essence of the matter — that the decree had been issued on account of the great harm they had done to the Shechinah when they benefited from the feast of that evildoer. Therefore, it states, "And Mordechai donned sackcloth and ashes and cried out with a great and bitter cry." "And he donned sackcloth" — This was to atone for the sin and to weaken the power of the "four hundred men" who accompanied Eisav when he came to meet his brother Yaakov. For it is stated concerning this event, "And Yaakov was very afraid" (Bereishis 32:8). That is, he was afraid of the four hundred impure husks and destroyers that accompanied Eisav. This is why Mordechai donned sackcloth, because the numerical value of the word "sackcloth" [שק] is 400. Thus, his intention was to weaken the power of the wicked Eisav. Then Mordechai informed also Esther of the great harm that had been done at the feast of Achashveirosh. Therefore, it states immediately after this, "And Esther donned 'kingship'" (Esther

5:1). That is, she donned the spirit of prophecy (Megillah 14b). Esther then proposed that they fast for three days and three nights in order to counteract the filth that Haman and Achashveirosh had injected into them by means of their feast. In this way the power of the filth that had sullied them through that eating and drinking would be enfeebled, for it was weakened through their fasting, thereby enabling the collective soul of Israel to shine as before.

We now have another explanation for the Fast of Esther that we have been observing for generations. Accordingly every individual should reflect and pray on this day that if anything has clung to us during this bitter exile in which we are sometimes forced to dine with members of the other nations [and we are all guarantors for one another; Sanhedrin 27b] that the merit of Mordechai and Esther should stand by us. For they are the ones who enacted this fast, decreeing that we fast on the 13th of Adar in order to weaken the effects of the Israel's dining with members of other nations. Then the merit of the Fast of Esther will stand by us to shatter, weaken and eliminate the power of the Sitra Achara who desires to cling specifically to the realm of the sacred. But by means of the fast Israel is purified and cleansed of this great blemish. And if a person declines to benefit from others at all, and especially not from the other nations, concerning him was it stated, "When you consume the toil of your hands you are fortunate and it will be well with you" (Tehillim 128b). "You are fortunate" — in this world. "And it will be well with you" — in the World to Come (Berachos 8a).

Chapter 99

The Sages teach in the tractate Megillah (7a) that Megillas Esther was delivered through the spirit of prophecy. For this reason, it contains numerous esoteric secrets. We will discuss just one of these here in a general way: It is stated in the Zohar, Parashas Pekudei (249b) that there is a chamber On High with four entrances directed towards the four cardinal directions. There are ten officers appointed over each of these entrances and one officer, named VHRYEL appointed over all the others. This officer belongs to the class of the Ofanim and it is his task to take action and revenge against Israel's oppressors. This Ofan together with the other forty officers ascends On High to a certain place that is called, "the chamber of the runners" (Melachim I:14:28) and other angels, known as CHSHMLM, ascend with him. They run ahead eagerly to wage war with the guardian angels of the nations to defeat them and wreak vengeance upon them. But when sin interferes, Heaven forbid, there are other runners emanating from the Sitra Achara, who proceed ahead with their accusations in order to rule over Israel and cause them misfortune. This is the meaning of the verse, "The runners went out hurriedly" (Esther 3:15). That is, they went out from the Sitra Achara to provoke decrees against Israel, whereupon it is stated, "And the city of Shushan was thrown into dismay" (ibid.). Afterwards, the prayers of Mordechai and Esther caused Israel to repent completely in order to avert Haman's evil plans. These prayers ascended On High and were accepted by Hashem in His mercy so that a time of favor was revealed. At that point it is stated that, "the runners, riders of the horses, went out hastily" (Esther 8:14). In other words, the holy angels ran to take vengeance upon the wicked Haman, after which it is stated, "And the city of Shushan was exuberant and joyful" (Esther 8:15).

For this reason, one must read the Megillah word for word slowly. For every word and letter possesses sanctity and harbors esoteric secrets. It is also worthwhile mentioning the merits of Mordechai and Esther with intent because they sacrificed themselves on Israel's behalf with their cries and prayers. Esther also sacrificed herself by going in to Achashveirosh, as she herself declared, "And if I am lost, I am lost" (Esther 4:16).

It is related in Yalkut Shimoni (Esther 1056) that Esther prayed with the words of Tehillim 22, "My God, my God, why have You abandoned me?" This was explained by the holy mouth of the Ari, z"l (Pri Eitz Chayim, Sha'ar HaPurim, Chapter 6; Sha'ar HaKavanos, 109b). The idea is that the Holy One Blessed is He in His abundant mercy and lovingkindness supervises and watches over us in order to grant us illumination and to bestow upon us a holy outpouring of the spirit of wisdom and understanding from above, by means of His holy names. Each of these names is an instance of the name "God" — א"ל. The first one comes from the verse, "Who is a God like You?" (Michah 7:18). The second comes from the verse, "Hashem, Hashem, merciful and gracious God" (Shemos 34:6). When this name is spelled out in full [אל"ף למ"ד] it has a numerical value of 185. Thus, twice this name totals 370, corresponding to which there are 370 lights illuminating 370 worlds. These in turn illuminate the souls of the righteous departed who toiled constantly in Torah and were diligent in their studies, clinging uninterruptedly to the Torah, which is called "light," and to the commandments, which are called "lamps." These two names possess the power to arouse an outpouring of lovingkindness from these 370 lights, which is evoked by the responding of "Amein" with concentration. For whoever responds, "Amein" with intention and also rushes to the synagogue in order to respond "Amein," merits these 370 lights through his response of "Amein." On the other hand, if a person despises and takes lightly the response of "Amein," his soul is met by 370 impure husks, Heaven spare us, which lead him to the chambers of darkness and the shadow of death. Concerning them the prophet declared, "The moth will consume them!" (Yeshayahu 50:9).

These 370 lights shone upon the righteous Esther because her soul emanated from the same source as this illumination. In that place these two instances of the name E-l shine forth — one from the verse, "Hashem, Hashem, merciful and gracious God, long suffering, etc.," and the other from the verse, "Who is a God like You." But when Esther went in to Achashveirosh she was compelled to pass between two houses of idolatry (Megillah 15b), which were sites of the husks of impurity. At that moment she was deprived of the spirit of prophecy, along with the illumination of one of those Names — the one from the verse, "Who is a God like You." This left here with only the illumination of the one from the verse, "Hashem, Hashem, merciful and gracious God." Therefore, she cried out, "My God, my God, why have You abandoned me?" Because until that moment she had received the illumination of two instances of the name E-l, but now she received that of only one.

From this you can appreciate the sanctity of these festivals. Each festival is filled with sanctity and with amazing esoteric secrets. You must also know that there is a new world On High that is so holy and awesome that it is revealed here below only once a year.

It begins to be revealed at the start of the Megillah reading. This is the world from which the soul of the righteous Mordechai was derived. Therefore, we must arouse Heaven's mercy so that this world will again be revealed to bestow an outpouring of bounty and illumination upon the heads of those who gather to hear the Megillah reading with pure hearts and full intent. This is the meaning of the blessing, "Blessed are You, Hashem, who has sanctified us with Your commandments and commanded us regarding the reading of the Megillah." That is, Hashem, may He be blessed, has commanded us to awaken in ourselves the intention to bring that great illumination out into the open. This is what is meant by, "regarding the reciting [or "calling"] of the Megillah." For the word mikra ["reciting" or "calling"] is used here in the same sense as in the verse, "For the calling of the congregation and the embarking of the camps" (Bamidbar 10:2). To this the congregation must answer "Amein!" with much concentration. It is very, very important to make it known at the Megillah reading when they recite the blessing and come to the words, "regarding the reciting [or "calling"]," that the one reciting the blessing should be envelope with trembling and fear. And when the congregation hears him recite these words they must also be filled with great trembling, fear and submission. For they allude to the summoning of that great, awesome and terrifying world, from the light of which will come an outpouring of bounty and a holy and pure spark to shine upon Israel.

Every Jew must have in mind to be a receptacle that is prepared to receive the sanctity and purification emanating from that world. He must also intend that through the influence of that merciful light he will merit life and lovingkindness, that Israel will not suffer any mishap and that the Holy One Blessed is He will have mercy upon us speedily and take us out from thick darkness to light. This is why we kindle numerous candles on Purim until the synagogue is filled with them. This is a hint to the great illumination of the 370 lights. Concerning this was it stated, "For the Jews there was light, etc." (Esther 8:16). Surely everyone who fears and trembles at the word of Hashem will rejoice and exult with gladness and trembling when he hears the sound of the blessing, "Regarding the reading [or "calling"] of the Megillah emanating from the mouth of the chazzan. Therefore, it is extremely important that we purify ourselves in a mikveh before going to the synagogue so that we will be able to receive the pure light and outpouring of bounty. I have transcribed all this from a letter of Rabbi Chayim Vital, z"l (Pri Eitz Chayim, Sha'ar HaPurim, Chapter 5).

The receiving of that light can be compared to the receiving of the extra soul [at the onset of Shabbos] for the one who knows how to direct his thoughts to make himself into a receptacle that is prepared to receive this outpouring of supernal holiness. I have observed a worthy custom in the land of Poland, according to which they dress themselves in clean white tunics and white trousers before the reading of the Megillah and then go to the synagogue dressed in their Shabbos and Yom Tov garments. Between one Megillah recital and the next Israel rejoices and gives praise and thanks for the reprieve and salvation that was granted to the Jews. One must also distribute something to the poor and give portions to the needy. And one must speak words of Torah, as the Sages have said (Megillah 16b), "'For the Jews there was light' — This refers to Torah, as it is stated, 'For a mitzvah is a lamp but Torah is light' (Mishlei 6:23)." It is praiseworthy to study a little before the rejoicing of daytime Purim feast. The meticulous are accustomed to pray Minchah on the 14th before the feast. Then, afterwards, they eat a single cooked dish and pray Maariv. They do not postpone Maariv until later in the night lest they become intoxicated and unfit to pray. After one has prayed Maariv he should relate to his household the great miracle that was performed for our ancestors.

I would now like to present to you an insight from the holy mouth of the Ari, z"l (Pri Eitz Chayim, Sha'ar HaPurim, Chapter 6). For we must be aware of the intentions of the wicked Haman, oppressor of the Jews, that led him to give himself over to oppressing Israel specifically in the month of Adar as opposed to any other month of the year. You must know that there are twelve months in the year, which correspond to the twelve permutations of the letters of the name יהו"ה. Each month is governed by one permutation so that the month of Adar is governed by the last one, in which the letters are completely reversed like this: הו"הי. This is a name indicative of judgment. Therefore when Haman mentioned the four-letter Name he specifically mentioned it in reverse, saying, "And all this is not worthwhile to me" — Vekol ze H einen U shove H l Y (Esther 5:13). The final letters of the words of this verse comprise the permutation in which the letters are reversed like this: הוה"י. His intention was to arouse double judgment against Israel. First by mentioning the Name in reverse, and second by mentioning it as an acronym comprised of final letters rather than initial letters. But Hashem in His mercy heard and heeded the prayers of Israel and the righteous Mordechai and Queen Esther, who had been crowned with a royal crown. On her part Esther intended with her words to transform the attribute of judgment into mercy. For this is the way of the righteous — to transform the attribute of judgment into the attribute of mercy. Therefore, she mentioned the name in an acronym comprised of initial letters and in proper sequence, saying, "Let the king and Haman come today to the feast" — Y avo H amelech V ehaman H ayom el hamishteh (Esther 5:4). Her intention in making that feast was to bring about Haman's downfall, in keeping with the verse, "If your enemy is hungry, feed him bread" (Mishlei 25:21), and the Holy One Blessed is He gave His approval.

In fact, Queen Esther would have liked to have evoked pure mercy, for the Divine name in its simple form [i.e., and not as an acronym] and in proper sequence is a Name of mercy. But if Esther had not mentioned this Name in an acronym of initial letters she would have been unable to defeat Haman. In her wisdom she knew that she must incorporate a small amount of judgment as well as mercy in order that this judgement would take revenge upon Haman, oppressor of the Jews. After this it is stated, "For he saw that the evil was concluded against him from the king" — Ki ra'ah k Y chalsa H eila V hara'a H mei'eis hamelech (Esther 7:7), the "king" being an allusion to the King of Universe. Note that the Divine name appears here in proper sequence indicating mercy for Israel. Nevertheless, it appears as an acronym of final letters to hint at the judgment and destruction that was to befall Haman and his sons. From here we can see the extent of the wicked Haman's evil intentions towards Israel. In him was fulfilled the verse, "He excavated a pit and dug it out" (Tehillim 7:16). That is, he was ensnared by the very trap that he laid. Therefore, the Torah has commanded us to wipe out the name of Amaleik and his seed and the seed of his seed. Thus the Sages have taught (Sifri, Devarim 25:19; Mechilta DeRashbi, Shemos 17:14) that one must blot out the name of Amaleik even from upon the trees and stones. This is the source of the custom — and the customs of Israel are Torah — to bang upon hearing Haman's name, in order to wipe out his name and that of Amaleik. All the authorities, both earlier and later, have written that one must not abolish this custom.

I have heard it said regarding our illustrious teacher Rabbi Heshel, z"l, that whenever he wished to test his quill he would write the name of Amaleik or of Haman and Zeresh and then erase them. This was in order to fulfill the positive injunction, "You shall surely wipe out the memory of Amaleik" (Shemos 17:14; Devarim 25:19). For we are obligated to pray for the eradication of Amaleik in order that Hashem's Name will be complete and His Throne will be complete. At that time, we will see the fulfillment of the verse, "And I will be magnified and sanctified among the peoples" (Yechezkeil 3:23), and the verse, "On that day Hashem will be one and His Name will be one" (Zecharyah 14:9). — Based upon the teachings of our teacher Rabbi Yosef, z"l (Yesod Yosef, Chapter 82).

Chapter 100

"Be wholehearted with Hashem your God" (Devarim 18:13). You must know that the trait of wholeheartedness is the loftiest of all the praiseworthy qualities and traits that a person must acquire. Therefore, it states regarding our forefather Yaakov, "And Yaakov was a wholehearted man, dwelling in tents" (Bereishis 25:27). Surely Yaakov possessed numerous holy qualities and traits, such as piety, awe, humility, holiness and purity. Nevertheless, Scripture does not identify him with any of these traits but only with that of wholeheartedness, as it is stated, "And Yaakov was a wholehearted man." Clearly, then, wholeheartedness must encompass all the other praiseworthy and holy characteristics. And indeed, this is so. For if a person is humble but has the flaw of pursuing wealth or if he yearns for a certain sin, he is not whole in his deeds. Such a person is likened to a beautiful vessel with many chips and cracks. But if a person is wholehearted and complete in every praiseworthy trait, and is God- fearing, beloved, charitable, dwelling in the earthly tents of Torah and toiling in Torah by night — then, when his soul expires, he will merit dwelling in the Heavenly "tent."

This idea is expressed in the Zohar in Midrash Ne'elam, Parashas Chayyei Sarah (123b-125b). There Rabbi Pinchas teaches that before a righteous person leaves this world a Heaven voice proclaims throughout Gan Eden, "Prepare a place for the righteous So-and-so who is about to arrive, etc." Then when the soul enters the gates of the Heavenly Jerusalem the great prince Michoel goes to extend to it a greeting of "Peace!" This causes the rest of the ministering angels to wonder and inquire, "Who is this ascending from the desert?" (Shir HaShirim 3:6). By which they mean from the desolate lower world, which is described as a "desert" by comparison with the upper world. The great prince Michael responds, "She is unique, she is my dove, she is my whole one" (Shir HaShirim 6:9). Note that Michoel does not praise the soul for any particular good deed or righteous quality but only for the quality of wholeheartedness, for this includes all praiseworthy qualities and characteristics. And because this soul embraced all fitting and upright characteristics in the wholeheartedness of its conduct, supernal holiness rests upon it continually. When a person toils in Torah or the performance of the mitzvos, for a distance of four cubits all around him he is encompassed by complete sanctity and his reward is very great.

The Zohar (Parashas Chayyei Sarah, 132a) relates in this regard: Rabbi Shimon ben Yochai was on his way to Tiberius accompanied by Rabbi Aba. Rabbi Shimon said to Rabbi Aba, "Let us go, because I see that a certain fellow will soon meet up with us with novel insights in his mouth." Rabbi Aba said, "I know that wherever the master goes the Holy One Blessed is He sends His angels, soaring upon their wings, that he may delight in them." While they were walking Rabbi, Shimon raised his eyes and saw a man hurrying along, so Rabbi Shimon and Rabbi Aba sat down and waited. And when the man reached them Rabbi Shimon inquired, "Who are you?" He replied, "I am a Jew from Cappotcia, and I am on my way to the study hall of Rabbi Shimon ben Yochai. For a certain group of scholars has voted to accept some enactments and they sent me to him [to inquire about the esoteric reasons for them]." Rabbi Shimon said, "Speak, my son." "Are you the son of Yochai?" he asked. "I am," he answered. So, he related to him, "They decreed that a man must not pass within four cubits in front of one who is praying and that a man must not pray while standing behind his teacher. What is the reason for these things?"

Rabbi Shimon explained, "The idea is this…" [Author's note ׀ The following is the substance of the Zohar and not the exact wording] According to a well-known dictum the Holy One Blessed is He possesses nothing in His world other than the four cubits of the law. These are the four letters of the name אדנ"י, which is called the holy Shechinah. This is the final heh of the name יהו"ה, which is known as Kallah — "Bride." Therefore, the Shechinah is also called Ha Kallah [הכלה] — "the Bride," the letters of which can be transposed to form the word halachah [הלכה] — "law" (Pri Eitz Chayim, Sha'ar Hanhagas HaLimud). This is the meaning of the "four cubits of the law." That is, the unification of the name יהו"ה within the letters of the name אדנ"י like this: יאהדונה"י. This is the unification of the Holy One Blessed is He with His Shechinah. Therefore, before we pray, we begin with the words, "My God [אדנ"י], open my lips and my mouth will tell of Your praise." That is, we ask Shechinah to accept our prayers, because the Shechinah receives all the prayers of Israel. If one recites this meditation with full concentration, with clear, pure and upright thoughts and with a humble and pure heart, one causes the Holy One Blessed is He and His Shechinah to become united. Then one stands literally within the four cubits of halachah, which is comprised of the same letters as HaKallah. It should now be clear the tremendous harm that is caused when one goes and stands within four cubits in front of someone who is praying. For this is as if he interposed himself and caused a separation in the unification of the Holy One Blessed is He and His Shechinah, Heaven forbid. One should even avoid passing within four cubits to the side of someone who is praying, even though strictly speaking this is permitted. As for the prohibition against praying behind one's mentor, this can be understood in light of the Sages' well known dictum regarding the verse, "You shall fear [es] Hashem your God." They comment that the word es [את - an untranslatable word indicating that something not mentioned is to be included] in this context means that one must fear Torah scholars as well (Pesachim 22b).

However, when a person prays, he must not have any other "fear" in front of him besides the fear of Heaven. One can see from here the gravity of praying with concentration. But why should I elaborate further on this matter when I have already spoken of it in earlier chapters? From the incident above we can appreciate the profound wholeness of earlier generations. Just consider — even though this Jew was an emissary regarding a point of Torah, when Rabbi Shimon ben Yochai said to him, "Speak, my son," he first inquired, "Are you the son of Yochai?" Then when Rabbi Shimon answered, "I am the son of Yochai," the man understood that if he said that he was the son of Yochai he surely would not lie, so he related to him the matter of his errand. This is precisely what our holy Torah requires — that every emissary perform faithfully the mission of those who sent him. This is the essence of wholeheartedness — that a person be faithful to his word, and not deviate from it, whether in matters of Heaven or in his mundane affairs, and especially not in monetary matters. One may not seek to gain money dishonestly, for the most fundamental expression of a person's piety and wholeheartedness is in his conduct with regard to financial matters, as I have already discussed at length in Chapter 52. For anyone who refuses to benefit from illegitimate wealth is called whole and righteous.

Even if a person knows how to pray with all the Kabbalistic intentions, he must be wary of doing so because it is absolutely forbidden to pray at length when the rest of the congregation is praying only the plain meanings of the prayers. Thus, the Rivash writes in a responsum (157), "But as for me, I pray like a child who is just learning to pray, intending only the plain meaning of the words and not more." A support for this can be seen in the conduct of Rabbi Akiva (Berachos 31a). When he would pray with the congregation he would begin and end with them, praying only the plain meanings of the words. But when he prayed on his own, one would leave him in one corner and find him later on in a different corner. A tradition has been handed down to me that one who prays for longer than the rest of the congregation is undoubtedly guilty of ostentation and his prayers will therefore not be heard. Similarly, I observed that my illustrious father, Rabbi Aharon Shmuel Kaidenover, z"l and my other mentors did not prolong their prayers at all. In fact, they would heap ridicule upon other rabbis who prolonged their prayers excessively. Whoever has fear of Heaven must be wholehearted with Hashem his God and behave innocently in the eyes of God and his fellow Jews. He must not behave in a way that leads people to say, "This is a pious fool who drags out his prayers," for then he would be guilty of causing the multitude to sin. Rather let him fulfill the verse, "Know Him in all your ways and He will straighten your path" (Mishlei 3:6). Then all will be well with you, selah.

Chapter 101

In Parashas Terumah (128b) the Zohar elaborates on the great reward accruing to those who issue admonishment and benefit the public by saving them from sin. For by doing so they accomplish four things: First — It is well known that the world is judged on a balance scale and is considered half meritorious and half guilty (Kiddushin 40b). Therefore, a single sin can incline the entire world to the side of guilt while a single good deed can incline it to the side of merit. Thus, by issuing rebuke and prompting even a single Jew to repent completely a person causes the entire world to be judged favorably and he receives credit for have brought merit to the multitude.

Second — The admonisher fulfills the positive Torah injunction, "You shall surely rebuke your fellow" (Vayikra 19:17). Moreover, his rebuke increases the amount of holiness in the world until the Sitra Achara becomes subjugated to the realm of the holiness.

Third — He causes the honor of the Holy One Blessed is He to be elevated and exalted, in reward for which he will merit children and grandchildren who are God-fearing and whole in their character.

Fourth — Upon his death his soul will be escorted through thirteen gates of the supernal worlds and no one will object. Concerning such a one was it said, "My covenant was with him, of life and peace" (Malachi 2:5). But on top of this he earns an even greater reward. Indeed, an angel named YHODAYS — יהודעי"ת, has been appointed over the souls of those who issue rebuke for the sake of Heaven (Zohar, 2:129a). This angel takes the visage of the one who benefited the public with his rebuke and inclined the world to the side of merit and brings it before the holy King. He then bestows upon it all the blessings that the patriarch Avraham received for having led idolaters to the worship of the Holy One Blessed is He, as it is stated, "And the souls that they made in Charan" (Bereishis 12:5). Afterwards that visage is allowed to enter seventy hidden worlds to which no one is admitted other than those who benefited the public through their rebuke.

Now if the reward of those who issue rebuke is so tremendous, it is difficult to comprehend Rabbi Akiva's statement that he would be "surprised if there is anyone in this generation who knows how to issue rebuke." Was Rabbi Akiva unaware of all the reward mentioned above? Why did he not rebuke the multitude for the sake of becoming a public benefactor? Moreover, as the outstanding personality of his generation was it not his responsibility to instruct the public? I believe the explanation is that Rabbi Akiva also realized the magnitude of the punishment for rebuking the multitude with impure motives and for shaming people in public. Thus, Midrash Vayikra Rabbah (Parashas Behar, 33:5) comments on the verse, "And Yaravam did not regain his strength again in the days of Aviyahu and Hashem struck him" (II Divrei HaYamim 13:20): Rabbi Shmuel bar Nachmani said, "Do you think that Yeravam was stricken? In fact, it was Aviyah who was stricken!" And why was he stricken? Rabbi Yochanan said, "Because he shamed [Israel] in public, as it is stated, 'But you are a great multitude and with you are the two golden calves that Yeravam made for you, etc.' (ibid. 13:8). If Scripture ascribes punishment to a king who only shamed a fellow king, how much more so a commoner who shames his fellow commoner!"

This is why Rabbi Akiva was so reluctant issue rebuke to the multitude — he was afraid of shaming them in public, for he knew that whoever shames his fellow in public loses his portion in the World to Come (Bava Metzia 59a). Therefore, he declared, "I would be surprised if there is anyone in this generation who knows how to issue rebuke." In recent years, by contrast, I have seen a new brand of admonishers who stand up in public and deliver orations, shaming the community as well as individuals, apparently oblivious to the magnitude of their guilt. Hashem has granted me the gift of language with which to compose this book so that people will read it, and I have no desire to shame them in public. For every individual knows the sorrow of his own soul for what he has corrupted. Therefore, let him rebuke himself and amend his transgressions and sins. Let people not say, "The scholars do not know of our deeds nor are they concerned to watch over us." For you must know that in every community there are those who are aware of the flaws of their contemporaries, but because the traits of flattery have become so predominant they say, "Woe to us if we say anything and woe to us if we do not say anything!" For this reason, I have acted as my heart has instructed me and transcribed here a few words in the form of stories and parables that draw on people's hearts. I place my hope in God that through this work I will indeed bring benefit to the public and receive credit for causing them merit. It is my request that everyone who knows how to read this book will place my words as a seal upon his heart and limbs. And, "may the words of my mouth and the meditations of my heart be acceptable before You, Hashem, my rock and my redeemer" (Tehillim 19:15).

Chapter 102

The Sages relate in Bereishis Rabbah (Parashas Bereishis 20:12) regarding the verse, "And God made tunics of leather [ohr, spelled with an ayin (עוֹר)] for Adam and his wife" (Bereishis 3:21): "In the Torah scroll of Rabbi Meir it was stated, 'tunics of light' [or, spelled with an alef (אוֹר)]." This Midrash is very perplexing. Why did the spelling, "tunics of light," appear specifically in Rabbi Meir's Torah rather in any other? [See what my illustrious father

Rabbi Shmuel Kaidenover writes about this matter in Birkas Shmuel, Parashas Bereishis, 6c, in the name of the illustrious Rabbi Leib Zunz, z"l.]

I believe this can be understood in light of an astonishing, beautiful and satisfying insight I heard from the holy mouth of the saintly Rabbi Heshel Zoref, z"l, in the name of a certain Kabbalist. He said as follows: First you must know that Tzefo son of Elifaz son of Eisav, mentioned in the verse, "the chieftain of Tzefo" (Bereishis 36:15), was the first of the husks of impurity of the seventy nations. Corresponding to this on the side of holiness was the "land of Tzuf" (I Shmuel 9:5), for both names are comprised of the same letters. Tzefo was the first king and his realm was the land of Poland [Polin in Yiddish]. This name alludes to the name Ploni [a nickname for the Samech Mem, the guardian angel of Eisav], for these two names also consist of the same letters. Note that the numerical value of Polin is the same as that of Tzefo. For this reason, too, the kingdom of Edom [Eisav's descendants] is also known as the Metropolis [Metro polin in the language of the Sages] of the seventy nations (Megillah 6a). For this nation is under the guardianship of the angel of Edom, who was the first of the husks of impurity. Know also that the impure husk of Tzefo was a product of the sin of Adam and Chava. The "tree" from which Adam ate was actually the wheat stalk (Berachos 40a), because wheat — chitah [(חטה)] — has a numerical value of 22 (Tikkunei Zohar, Tikkun 16, 31a), indicating that by eating of it Adam blemished the twenty-two letters with which the Torah is written. It is well known that Adam's sin affected the attribute of Splendor [Hod], which is the eighth attribute. Eight times twenty-two is 176, the numerical value of Tzefo. This is because the sin came about through Chavah, who was created from the attribute of Splendor, the eighth attribute, and through her came the blemish to the twenty-two letters, as above.

Now, when the letters comprising the name Chavah are spelled out in full they read, ח"ת וא"ו ה"א. Then if one drops the initial letters so that one is left with only the "hidden" letters [i.e., those that are not pronounced when the name is spoken] one receives, tav, alef vav, alef [תאוא], the numerical value of which is 408. This is a hint that in the 408th year of the sixth millenium [1648, the year of the

Chmielnicki massacres] the husk of Tzefo would wax in its strength. For that year was ripe for the redemption, as is alluded to in the verse, "With this [zos, the numerical value of which is 408] shall Aharon enter the holy place" (Vayikra 16:3). But instead, in that year many in the lands of Poland and Lithuania were martyred. For it is well known the terrible decrees and harsh judgments that befell the Jews of those lands in the year zos, in which tens of thousands of Jews were killed in sanctification of the name of Heaven. When the [three] letters of zos [זי"ן אל"ף ת"ו] are spelled out they read, zayin yud nun; alef lamed pei; tav vav. The numerical value of the "hidden" letters — yud nun, lamed pei, vav — is 176, which is equal to the value of the name Tzefo. This is an allusion to the name Ploni, as was mentioned earlier. This is what is meant by the verse, "From the north [tzafon] the evil will begin" (Yirmiyahu 1:14). For the value of the word tzafon [226] is equal to the value of the names Polin and Lita [Lithuania] combined. Therefore, these decrees occurred specifically in these lands and in the year 408. The words of a wise man are pleasing.

I have received additional esoteric insights from the saintly Rabbi Heshel but I am reluctant to reveal them to anyone but the circumspect. You must know that there is an allusion to the word tzafon [north] — which is equal to the combined values of Polin [176=פולין] and Lita 50=ליטא] — in the verse, "They dug [כרו, the value of which is also 226] pits for me" (Tehillim 119:85). This indicates that that our enemies attacked us with false accusations in order to murder the righteous. It is well known from the sources (Shocher Tov 120; Midrash Shmuel 16) that the impure husk of Eisav is called a "boar of the forest" (Tehillim 80:14). In the book of Tehillim the letter ayin [the value of which is 70] of the word ya'ar — "forest" — is written in large to indicate that all the seventy nations are subservient to Eisav. This is the same ayin that appears in the name of Eisav [עשו]. It indicates at the "tunics of leather [ohr with an ayin]" that replaced the "tunics of light [or with an alef]" that Adam and Chavah wore before they sinned, as is known to the Kabbalists (Eitz Chayim, Sha'ar 49, Chapter 4; Sefer HaLikkutim, 6a). Therefore, in the future when the sin is rectified those tunics will go back to being "tunics of light," as they were before Adam's sin.

Now, Rabbi Meir was a descendant of Emperor Nero (Gittin 56a) and it was he who first began rectifying the blemish caused by Eisav, the "boar of the forest" [ya'ar with a large ayin]. When the ayin of ya'ar is replaced with an alef this word [מיאר] will be comprised of the same letters as the root of the name "Meir" [מאיר]. And when the blemish of Eisav is completely rectified the tunics will again be "tunics of light." Therefore, in the Torah of Rabbi Meir [whose name means "illumination"] the phrase "tunics of leather" was written "tunics of light." This should be clear. Similarly, the word "boar" — חזיר — has a value of 225, which is equal to the value of the word כרה ["dug" in the singular]. But when the [numerical value of] alef [which is 1] from the word "forest" [יער or יאר] — after the ayin of this word has been exchanged for an alef — is added to the word karah, [225, כרה] it will read karu, [226, כרו] as in the verse, "They dug [כרו] a pit for me." For when the redemption arrives the nations who dig "pits" beneath us will be nullified, that is, when the sin of Adam has been rectified and the tunics become "tunics of light" with an alef. This should be clear.

Now let us return to our original subject. As we mentioned, it is stated that, "From the north will the evil begin." Therefore, when the redemption arrives it will begin from the north, that is, in Poland and Lithuania. This is also suggested in the verse, "Awaken O North and come O South" (Shir HaShirim 4:16). For the awakening in anticipation of the redemption will begin in the north. Then afterwards will be fulfilled the words, "Come O South." At that time Israel will merit the great bounty that has been hidden away for the righteous.

I mentioned earlier that on account of Adam's sin the letter alef was exchanged for an ayin in the phrase, "tunics of leather," which should have read, "tunics of light," with an alef. Therefore it states, "The complainer [i.e., the serpent] alienates the Leader [aluf]" (Mishlei 16:28), as is explained in a number of Kabbalistic works (Shelah, Part I, Ma'amar Beis David, 16a). The Patriarchs rectified this sin by means of the three prayer services they enacted, Sh acharis שחרית — Morning service], M inchah [מנחה — Afternoon service] and A rvis [ערבית — Evening service], the acronym for which is the word שמע — "Hear" [as in, "Hear, O Israel, etc.]. And it is well known (Zohar, 1:167a; Tikkunei Zohar, Tikkun 10, 147b) that on account of Adam's sin, two husks of impurity waxed in strength — that of the ox and that of the donkey. The donkey is the husk of Yishmael while the ox is the husk of Edom. The numerical value of Edom and Yishmael combined is 502, which is the exact number of years that the Patriarchs were alive in the world. For Avraham lived 175 years, Yitzchak 180 years and Yaakov 147 years, for a total of 502. This is because the Patriarchs corresponded to those husks on the side of holiness. This is the meaning of the verse, "Do not consume flesh [basar] that has been torn in the field" (Shemos 22:30). For the value of basar [בשׂר] is also 502. This should be clear.

It is well known that Amaleik, who is the "first of nations" (Bamidbar 24:20), is a descendant of the wicked Eisav. He has a share in the concept of an "other god," because the value of Amaleik [עמלק] is 240, which is equal to the words אל אחר — "other god." The corresponding principle on the side of holiness is רוח יהו"ה — "the spirit of Hashem" (Shoftim 11:29), which also has a value of 240. Corresponding to the husks of the ox and donkey on the side of holiness are the two Moshiachs. Moshiach son of David overcomes the husk of the donkey, as it is stated, "A humble man riding on a donkey" (Zecharyah 9:9), while Moshiach son of Yosef is called an "ox," as in the verse, "He has the majesty of a firstborn ox" (Devarim 33:17). It is related in the Zohar (3:124b; Zohar Chadash Ruth, 101b) that from the joining of the two husks of the ox and donkey came another husk known as the "viper" [tzefa], as in the verse, "From the root of the serpent comes a viper" (Yeshayahu 14:29). The value of צפע equals that of "Amaleik" — 240. Therefore, the ink with which a Torah scroll is written must contain mei afatz — "gallnut water" (Gittin 19a), because the word עפץ is the reverse of צפע. Thus, by writing the Torah scroll with gallnut water, we subjugate the husk of the viper.

The word nachash [נח"ש] — "serpent" — is an acronym for n achash [serpent], ch amor [donkey], sh or [ox]. For these were the first three husks of the seventy nations. The numerical value of shor and chamor combined [760] equals that of tzara'as — "leprosy." Therefore, the Sages have said that the pebble-like pattern on a snake is a form of leprosy (Bereishis Rabbah 20:4). This is because the serpent spoke slander, therefore it was stricken with leprosy. The impure husk of Tzefo son of Elifaz son of Eisav, whose guardian angels are the Samech Mem and the wicked Lilis, brought about the terrible destruction of the lands of Poland and Lithuania, as I mentioned earlier. At that time, on account of our many sins, the enemy took hold of the Torah scrolls that were written with sanctity upon leather parchment, specifically on the flesh side of the hide and not on the side of the hair. The word for "flesh" is basar, the value of which is 502. The Torah scroll is also written with gallnut water [afatz] in order to overcome the husk of Amaleik. Therefore, the Sages relate that when the Torah scroll was burned by the Romans together with Rabbi Chanina ben Teradyon, the letters flew off and only the parchment was burned (Avodah Zarah 18a). Similarly, in the pogroms of Poland thousands of Torah scrolls were burned, but their letters flew off and only the parchment and gallnut residue were burned. Moreover, the enemy does not realize that on account of this they no longer have any handhold in the realm of holiness, for the Torah has commanded us, "Do not consume flesh [basar] that is torn in the field" (Shemos 22:30). That is, it is forbidden to consume carrion but it is permitted, nevertheless, to write upon parchment made from the skins of carrion. Through this the impure forces had a handhold in the realm of holiness. But once those scrolls were burned the power of the husks was diminished while the power of the ox and donkey on the side of holiness began to flourish. The ultimate result of this will be that the two Moshiachs, Moshiach son of David and Moshiach son of Yosef, will arrive and the Holy Temple will descend from Heaven to earth.

Therefore, in order to conclude with words of consolation I will write a few words concerning the Beis HaMikdosh that is destined to be established in Jerusalem. The Third Beis HaMikdosh is destined to be eighteen mil [1 mil = 1 kilometer] in length by eighteen mil in width, constructed entirely of precious stones. It will be surrounded by three walls — one of silver, one of gold and one of precious stones that will shine with an array of colors. Each wall will be six cubits thick and outside of them will be another wall composed of fire surrounding the entire structure. The walls will have one thousand four hundred and eighty-eight towers made of gems and between every two towers will be a hundred and twenty gates, each of which will be made of precious stones. Two thousand and three pools of spring water will emerge from the mountains upon which the Holy Temple will stand, for it will be erected upon the summits of the four mountains — Mount Sinai, Mount Carmel, Mount Tavor and Mount Chermon. The city of Jerusalem will be four hundred parsah by four hundred parsah [1 parsah = 4 mil]. And when the Beis haMikdosh descends from Heaven to earth, the Holy One Blessed is He will gather in the exiles of Israel and we will sing a new song. Then Israel will rejoice in its Maker and the sons of Tziyon will exult in their King. With the coming of our Moshiach the Satan and the husks of impurity will be eradicated from the world, for everything will then be rectified and the evil inclination will be nullified. At that time, we will all merit "tunics of light" — [אור with an alef]. For it is stated, "Hashem will be for you an eternal light" (Yeshayahu 60:19). Amein, so may it be His will.

Kav   HaYashar

www.ingramcontent.com/pod-product-compliance
Lightning Source LLC
Chambersburg PA
CBHW070124080526
44586CB00015B/1551